CONTEMPORARY MUSICIANS

Explore your options!
Gale databases offered in a variety of formats

DISKETTE/MAGNETIC TAPE

Many Gale databases are available on diskette or magnetic tape, allowing systemwide access to your most-used information sources through existing computer systems. Data can be delivered on a variety of mediums (DOS-formatted diskette, 9-track tape, 8mm data tape) and in industry-standard formats (comma-delimited, tagged, fixed-field). Retrieval software is also available with many of Gale's databases that allows you to search, display, print and download the data.

The information in this Gale publication is also available in some or all of the formats described here.
Your Gale Representative will be happy to fill you in.

ONLINE

For your convenience, many Gale databases are available through popular online services, including DIALOG, NEXIS (Mead Data Central), Data-Star, Orbit, Questel, OCLC, I/Plus Direct, Prodigy, HOOVER and Telebase Systems.

CD-ROM

A variety of Gale titles are available on CD-ROM, offering maximum flexibility and powerful search software.

For information, call

GALE

Gale Research
1-800-877-GALE

ISSN 1044-2197

CONTEMPORARY MUSICIANS

PROFILES OF THE PEOPLE IN MUSIC

SUZANNE M. BOURGOIN,
Editor

VOLUME 15
Includes Cumulative Indexes

 *Gale Research*

An ITP Information/Reference Group Company

I(T)P
Changing the Way the World Learns

NEW YORK • LONDON • BONN • BOSTON • DETROIT
MADRID • MELBOURNE • MEXICO CITY • PARIS
SINGAPORE • TOKYO • TORONTO • WASHINGTON
ALBANY NY • BELMONT CA • CINCINNATI OH

STAFF

Suzanne M. Bourgoin, *Editor*

Frank V. Castronova, Brian Escamilla, *Associate Editors*

Paul E. Anderson, Robin Armstrong, Rich Bowen, Carol Brennan, Susan Windisch Brown, John Cohassey, Ed Decker, Stewart Francke, Alan Glenn, Daniel Hodges, Anne Janette Johnson, Ondine E. Le Blanc, Sarah Messer, John Morrow, Nicholas Patti, Debra Power, Joanna Rubiner, Pamela L. Shelton, Sonya Shelton, Geri J. Speace, B. Kimberly Taylor, Jeffrey Taylor, Jordan Wankoff, Thaddeus Wawro,
Contributing Editors

Neil E. Walker, *Managing Editor*

Marlene S. Hurst, *Permissions Manager*
Margaret A. Chamberlain, *Permissions Specialist*
Susan Brohman, Diane Cooper, Maria Franklin, Arlene Johnson, Michele Lonoconus, Maureen Puhl, Shalice Shah, Kimberly F. Smilay, Barbara A. Wallace, *Permissions Associates*
Sarah Chesney, Edna Hedblad, Margaret McAvoy-Amato, Tyra Y. Phillips, Lori Schoenenberger, Rita Velaquez, *Permissions Assistants*

Mary Beth Trimper, *Production Director*
Shanna Philpott Heilveil, *Production Assistant*
Cynthia Baldwin, *Product Design Manager*
Barbara J. Yarrow, *Graphic Services Supervisor*
Randy Bassett, *Image Database Supervisor*
Pamela A. Hayes, *Photography Coordinator*
Willie Mathis, *Camera Operator*

Cover illustration by John Kleber

⊗™ This book is printed on acid-free paper that meets the minimum requirements of American National Standard for Information Sciences— Permanence Paper for Printed Library Materials, ANSI Z39.48-1984.

♻ This book is printed on recycled paper that meets Environmental Protection Agency Standards.

ISBN 0-8103-9316-6
ISSN 1044-2197

10 9 8 7 6 5 4 3 2 1

361089

I(T)P™ Gale Research Inc., an International Thomson Publishing Company.
ITP logo is a trademark under license.

Contents

Introduction   ix

Cumulative Subject Index   269

Cumulative Musicians Index   289

Introduction

Fills the Information Gap on Today's Musicians

Contemporary Musicians profiles the colorful personalities in the music industry who create or influence the music we hear today. Prior to *Contemporary Musicians,* no quality reference series provided comprehensive information on such a wide range of artists despite keen and ongoing public interest. To find biographical and critical coverage, an information seeker had little choice but to wade through the offerings of the popular press, scan television "infotainment" programs, and search for the occasional published biography or exposé. *Contemporary Musicians* is designed to serve that information seeker, providing in one ongoing source in-depth coverage of the important names on the modern music scene in a format that is both informative and entertaining. Students, researchers, and casual browsers alike can use *Contemporary Musicians* to meet their needs for personal information about music figures; find a selected discography of a musician's recordings; and uncover an insightful essay offering biographical and critical information.

Provides Broad Coverage

Single-volume biographical sources on musicians are limited in scope, often focusing on a handful of performers from a specific musical genre or era. In contrast, *Contemporary Musicians* offers researchers and music devotees a comprehensive, informative, and entertaining alternative. *Contemporary Musicians* is published twice yearly, with each volume providing information on more than 80 musical artists and record-industry luminaries from all the genres that form the broad spectrum of contemporary music—pop, rock, jazz, blues, country, New Age, folk, rhythm and blues, gospel, bluegrass, rap, and reggae, to name a few—as well as selected classical artists who have achieved "crossover" success with the general public. *Contemporary Musicians* will also occasionally include profiles of influential nonperforming members of the music community, including producers, promoters, and record company executives. Additionally, beginning with *Contemporary Musicians 11,* each volume features new profiles of a selection of previous *Contemporary Musicians* listees who remain of interest to today's readers and who have been active enough to require completely revised entries.

Includes Popular Features

In *Contemporary Musicians* you'll find popular features that users value:

- **Easy-to-locate data sections:** Vital personal statistics, chronological career summaries, listings of major awards, and mailing addresses, when available, are prominently displayed in a clearly marked box on the second page of each entry.

- **Biographical/critical essays:** Colorful and informative essays trace each subject's personal and professional life, offer representative examples of critical response to the artist's work, and provide entertaining personal sidelights.

- **Selected discographies:** Each entry provides a comprehensive listing of the artist's major recorded works.

- **Photographs:** Most entries include portraits of the subject profiled.

- **Sources for additional information:** This invaluable feature directs the user to selected books, magazines, and newspapers where more information can be obtained.

Helpful Indexes Make It Easy to Find the Information You Need

Each volume of *Contemporary Musicians* features a cumulative Musicians Index, listing names of individual performers and musical groups, and a cumulative Subject Index, which provides the user with a breakdown by primary musical instruments played and by musical genre.

Available in Electronic Formats

Diskette/Magnetic Tape. *Contemporary Musicians* is available for licensing on magnetic tape or diskette in a fielded format. Either the complete database or a custom selection of entries may be ordered. The database is available for internal data processing and nonpublishing purposes only. For more information, call (800) 877-GALE.

Online. *Contemporary Musicians* is available online through Mead Data Central's NEXIS Service in the NEXIS, PEOPLE and SPORTS Libraries in the GALBIO file.

We Welcome Your Suggestions

The editors welcome your comments and suggestions for enhancing and improving *Contemporary Musicians*. If you would like to suggest subjects for inclusion, please submit these names to the editors. Mail comments or suggestions to:

The Editor
Contemporary Musicians
Gale Research Inc.
835 Penobscot Bldg.
Detroit, MI 48226-4094
Phone: (800) 347-4253
Fax: (313) 961-6599

CONTEMPORARY MUSICIANS

Cannonball Adderly

Saxophonist

Archive Photos/Frank Driggs Collection

From his earliest appearance on the New York jazz scene in 1955, alto saxophonist Julian "Cannonball" Adderly remained at the forefront of the jazz world. His blues-based tone, Charlie Parker-inspired modernist concepts, and African American religious themes helped to define several of the jazz trends of the postwar era. Paired with the tenor saxophone of John Coltrane in Miles Davis's quintet during the late 1950s, Adderly emerged as a major exponent of hard bop, or what became known as soul jazz. As leader of his own group, Adderly landed two top-selling hits in the 1970s. During his 20-year career as a nationally known talent, Adderly maintained a remarkable devotion to his music and made great strides in the education and preservation of jazz as an American art form.

Son of a jazz cornetist, Julian Edwin Adderly was born on September 15, 1928, in Tampa, Florida. He took up the saxophone at age 14 and two years later, while completing his high school studies, fronted his own band at professional engagements. Originally nicknamed "Cannibal" by high school friends for his voracious appetite, Adderly's sobriquet later evolved into Cannonball. Attending Florida A&M University, he became proficient on trumpet and numerous reed instruments. In 1948 he began a stint as a teacher at Dillard High School in Fort Lauderdale, a job he held intermittently until 1956.

The New York Scene

Drafted into the army in 1950, Sergeant Adderly became leader of the 36th Army Dance Band. Among the members of the 36th Army Band were jazz greats like trombonist Curtis Fuller, pianist Junior Mance, and Adderly's younger brother Nat, a cornetist. As Nat Adderly recalled in *Down Beat,* "Cannonball made some arrangement with the General, so basically all we ever played was dance music and we did very little with the marching band. We played with it on some official functions but other than that we worked with the normal big band of jazz groups." Living in Washington, D. C., Adderly studied music at Maryland's U.S. Naval Academy, and from 1952 to 1953 led an army band at Fort Knox, Kentucky.

Prompted by jump blues saxophonist Eddie "Cleanhead" Vinson, Adderly and his brother traveled to New York City in 1955. The unknown Adderly soon sat in with the band of bassist Oscar Pettiford at the popular Greenwich Village club Cafe Bohemia. Allowed to take the stage due to the late arrival of bandmember Jerome Richardson, Adderly underwent a fierce initiation when Pettiford called out a furiously paced version of "I'll Remember April." But Adderly's study of Charlie Park-

For the Record . . .

Born Julian Edwin Adderly, September 15, 1928, in Tampa, FL; died of a stroke, August 8, 1975, in Gary, IN. *Education:* Attended Florida A&M University, until 1948; studied music at U.S. Naval Academy.

Began professional career, c. 1944; taught at Dillard High School, Fort Lauderdale, FL, 1948-56; served as bandleader in U.S. Army, 1951-54; signed with Savoy label, 1955; led group with brother Nat, 1956-57; member of Miles Davis band 1957-59; organized second group as leader 1959. Led jazz workshops throughout this career. Member of Jazz Advisory Board of the National Endowment for the Arts.

er's alto saxophone solos had prepared him for the challenges of such a breakneck tempo. As jazz historian Leonard Feather wrote in the liner notes to *Somethin' Else,* Adderly "met the challenge with a long solo that just about knocked Pettiford off the stand."

Following Adderly's performance at the Cafe Bohemia, he signed a contract with the Savoy label and became a regular member of Pettiford's band. Attending the band's performances at the club, Miles Davis often sat and watched the 262-pound alto saxophonist perform. "Everybody knew right away that [Cannonball] was one of the best players around," Davis said in his autobiography, *Miles.* "Even white critics were raving about his playing. All the record labels were running after him. Man, he was hot that quick."

To the astonishment of many musicians, Adderly returned to his teaching job in the fall of 1955. But rave reviews and an increasing demand for his presence in New York encouraged Adderly to return to the city in 1956 and form his own quintet with his brother Nat, pianist Junior Mance, and bassist Sam Jones. Plagued by financial difficulties, however, the group disbanded in the fall of 1957.

With the Miles Davis Quintet

In October of 1957, Adderly replaced Belgian saxophonist Bobby Jaspar in the Miles Davis Quintet. Davis recalled his early interest in Adderly's musicianship in *Miles,* remarking, "I could almost hear him playing in my group the first time I heard him. He had that blues thing and I love me some blues." Adderly remembered, as quoted in the book *Milestones,* "I had gotten an offer

from [trumpeter] Dizzy [Gillespie] to go with his small band. I was opposite Miles at the Bohemia, told him I was going to join Dizzy, and Miles asked me why I didn't join him. I told him he never asked me." After a few months, Miles hired Adderly and took him on the Jazz for Moderns tour. Soon afterward, Davis expanded his group to a sextet, bringing together the saxophones of Adderly and John Coltrane. As Davis explained in *Miles,* "I felt that Cannonball's blues-rooted alto sax up against Trane's harmonic, chordal way of playing, his more free-form approach, would create a new kind of feeling."

For two years the saxophones of Adderly and Coltrane, backed by the drums of "Philly" Joe Jones and the bass of Paul Chambers, fueled the creative fire of Davis's group, producing a number of brilliant recordings such as *Milestones* in 1958 and *Kind of Blue* in 1959, the latter featuring the jazz classics "So What" and "All Blues." In March of 1958, Davis made a rare guest appearance on Adderly's critically acclaimed solo album *Somethin' Else*—a session that also showcased the talents of pianist Hank Jones, bassist Sam Jones, and drummer Art Blakey. Reflecting on his experience with Davis's group, Adderly was quoted as saying in *Miles: A Biography,* "I learned a lot with him. About spacing for one thing, when playing solos. Also he's the master of understatement. And he taught me a lot about chords, as Coltrane did too."

In September of 1959, Adderly left Davis's group to reform his quintet, reuniting Nat and bassist Sam Jones, with pianist Bobby Timmons and drummer Louis Hayes. The quintet played hard bop, which, unlike the cool jazz sound of the West Coast, wrote Dizzy Gillespie in *To Be or Not to Bop,* "reasserted the primacy of rhythm and the blues in our music and made you get funky with sweat to play it." Hard bop, Gillespie added, "with its more earthy, churchy sound drew a lot of new black fans to our music." David Rosenthal, in his book *Hard Bop,* wrote that "without renouncing Bebop's discoveries, [hard bop] won broad popular appeal, reestablishing jazz as a staple product on ghetto jukeboxes."

With the popularity of the hard bop sound, Adderly's group achieved instant success. His ensemble attracted a number of first-rate musicians, including Austrian-born pianist Joe Zawinul, who joined the band in September of 1961. The presence of Zawinul in turn enticed saxophonist/flutist Yusef Lateef to join Adderly, which expanded the group to a sextet. "We did nothing but work 46-47 weeks a year," recalled Zawinul in *Down Beat,* "often under the best circumstances. A lot of the time we really had fantastic fun."

In the liner notes to the 1963 album *The Cannonball Adderly Sextet in New York,* noted jazz producer Orrin

Keepnews wrote, "The saga of Cannonball Adderly's band ... has unquestionably been one of the most dazzling success stories in modern jazz history." Unlike many jazz groups of the decade, Adderly's ensemble scored radio hits, with Zawinul's compositions "Mercy Mercy Mercy" in 1967 and "Country Preacher" in 1969. During this time, Adderly also collaborated with singers Nancy Wilson, Lou Rawls, and Sergio Mendes.

Slowed down in the Seventies

Though afflicted by diabetes, Adderly continued to perform live and appear at jazz workshops throughout the 1970s. These seminars consisted of demonstrations and lectures pertaining to both the musical and sociological aspects of jazz. In 1970 Zawinul left the group and was replaced by keyboardist George Duke. In tribute to his ten-year stay with Adderly, Zawinul told *Down Beat*, "The parting with Cannon is friendly. I'll love him forever. It's been a beautiful association."

The death of Cannonball Adderly from a stroke on August 8, 1975, ended the career of a brilliant musician who left an indelible mark on the postwar jazz community. On Adderly's death, Dan Morgenstern wrote in *Down Beat* that the alto master was a "man whose horizon extended beyond musical matters. Cannonball was active in civil rights and support for the arts." Adderly's contributions to the Reverend Jesse Jackson's Operation Bread Basket and as a member of the Jazz Advisory Board of the National Endowment for the Arts reflected his commitment to the role of art and artists in social change. "Cannonball was a great artist," commented Zawinul in *Down Beat*. "I never knew a musician who knew so much about different subjects. He always read *Time* and *Newsweek*, and he could discuss everything from heart surgery to politics. Cannon had more worldly wisdom than any musician I ever met." This world vision and a true passion for music made Cannonball Adderly an educator of the human experience and a heralded genius during his lifetime and beyond.

Selected discography

Solo releases

Presenting Cannonball Adderly, Savoy, 1955.
Somethin' Else, Blue Note, 1958.
The Cannonball Adderly Quintet in San Francisco, Riverside, 1959.
Cannonball Adderly in Chicago, Mercury, 1959.

Cannonball's Shooters, Mercury.
Cannonball: Jump for Joy, Mercury.
At the Lighthouse, Riverside, 1960.
Them Dirty Blues, Riverside, 1960.
African Waltz, Riverside, 1961.
Things Are Getting Better—with Milt Jackson, Riverside.
Cannonball Adderly Quintet Plus, Riverside.
Cannonball Adderly The Poll Winners, Riverside.
The Cannonball Adderly Sextet in New York, Riverside, 1963.
Live Session! Cannonball Adderly with the New Exciting Voice of Ernie Andrews, Capitol, 1964.
Mercy, Mercy, Mercy! Live at the "Club," Capitol, 1966.
Country Preacher, Capitol, 1969.
Inside Straight, Fantasy, 1973.
The Best of Cannonball Adderly: The Capitol Years, Capitol, 1990.

With Miles Davis

Milestones, Columbia, 1958.
Miles and Monk at Newport, Columbia, 1958.
Jazz at the Plaza, Columbia, 1958.
Kind of Blue, Columbia, 1959.

Sources

Books

Carr, Ian, *Miles: A Biography*, William & Morrow, 1982.
Chambers, Jack, *Milestones 1: The Music and Times of Miles Davis to 1960*, William & Morrow, 1984.
Gillespie, Dizzy, *To Be or Not to Bop: Memoirs*, Doubleday, 1979.
Davis, Miles, with Quincy Troupe, *Miles: The Autobiography*, Simon & Schuster, 1990.
Hentoff, Nat, *Jazz Is*, Limelight Editions, 1984.
Milestones: The Music and Times of Miles Davis, William & Morrow, 1984.
Rosenthal, David, *Hard Bop: Jazz and Black Music 1955-1965*, Oxford University Press, 1992.

Periodicals

Down Beat, January 8, 1970; September 11, 1970; December 10, 1970; October 28, 1971; October 9, 1975; June 15, 1978.
Jazz Journal International, May 1988.

Additional information for this profile was obtained from liner notes by Leonard Feather to *Somethin' Else*, Blue Note, 1959, and by Orrin Keepnews to *Cannonball Adderly Sextet in New York*, Riverside, 1963.

—John Cohassey

Steve Albini

Producer, guitarist, songwriter

Photograph by Daniel Corrigan, courtesy of Touch and Go Records

Spawning controversy as well as adulation throughout his career as both a record producer and guitarist, Steve Albini has made a major impact on alternative and punk rock and rock and roll. In his recording efforts, he has striven to create a sound that comes as close as possible to that of a live performance. "All I want to do is, I want to make records that sound realistic and that kick my ass," he declared in *Chicago* magazine. "Everything else is secondary to that."

Albini does not like to be referred to as a producer on the albums to which he contributes; instead, according to *Chicago,* he prefers the designation of "recording engineer." Unlike most big-name producers, he accepts no royalties on records he produces, believing that the producer should have only a technical role in the studio and should totally acquiesce to the artist's goals. "You have to respect the fact that the band does what it does for a reason," Albini commented in *Billboard,* "and those reasons can be intensely personal." As Mark Jannot wrote in *Chicago,* "[Albini's] function, as he sees it, is to be a clear window, transferring the band's sound intact to vinyl or disc."

Experimentation with different sounds is typical when Albini is in the recording studio, and he continually tries to take the guitar to new limits of noise and distortion. "I get as much satisfaction out of making the instrument squeak or sound like rattling chains as I imagine some players get from bona fide soloing," he pointed out in *Guitar Player.* Chuck Crisafulli added in the same article, "[Albini's] sound may be brutal, but it's undeniably straightforward and undoctored."

Observers have noted Albini's obsessive attention to detail, which includes microphone placement and sound level adjustments. When recording away from home, he brings up to 30 microphones with him in order to achieve the effects he wants. He prefers using vintage microphones, claiming that they provide a better quality of sound. *Chicago*'s Jannot wrote, "The hallmarks of the Albini sound are a well-balanced interrelation among all the instruments, vocals that assume equal footing with the music instead of floating above the mix, an extraordinarily wide stereo stage (your right ear hears something different from your left), and a pristine, echoey drum."

A self-proclaimed rock philosopher, Albini has also made numerous contributions to rock magazines. His articles often attack bands that he claims have "sold out" to achieve mainstream success. According to Jannot, "For a decade, [Albini] has spewed streams of bile into the pages of various rock-music fanzines—and into the faces of any less pure wannabes stupid enough to ask him for his honest opinion."

For the Record . . .

Born c. 1963 in Missoula, MT; son of Frank (a mathematician and scientist) and Giana Albini. *Education:* Received B.A. from Northwestern University.

Played in garage-style bands while in college; created band Big Black, 1981, and released debut EP, *Lungs,* Ruthless, 1982; formed band Rapeman; produced first full-length album, the Pixies' *Surfer Rosa,* 4AD/Rough Trade, 1988; produced LPs for Jesus Lizard, the Breeders, Tar, Helmet, Superchunk, Nirvana, PJ Harvey, and the Didjits; formed band Shellac and released twin EPs *The Rude Gesture (A Pictorial History)* and *Uranus,* Touch and Go, 1994. Contributor of articles to *Matter* magazine, mid-1980s.

Addresses: *Home*—Chicago, IL. *Record company*—Touch and Go Records, P.O. Box 25526, Chicago, IL 60625. *Fan club*—Shellac, P.O. Box 442, Evanston, IL 60206.

Having found it difficult to locate other musicians who shared his musical taste, he hoped that the album would help him in his "recruiting." Albini explained in *Chicago,* "I thought, well, if I put out this record, that will give people the idea of what kind of music I want to make and then I'll be able to find people who want to be in a band with me. It worked." Soon Jeff Pezzati, who had sung with Naked Raygun, joined the group as bass player, followed by Santiago Durango on guitar. Dave Riley of Savage Beliefs later replaced Pezzati.

Big Black made a splash with its 1986 *Atomizer* album, which showcased Albini's willingness to let the guitar "attack" the listener. Fans of rock noise jumped on the bandwagon. "Albini perfected a pulverizing, unrelenting guitar sound, closer to industrial than to punk, a radical approach perhaps best captured on Big Black's ... *Atomizer,*" according to *The Rolling Stone History of Rock & Roll. Billboard* was prompted to refer to Big Black as "a key influence on today's 'industrial' sound." *Atomizer* succeeded in making Big Black one of the top alternative rock bands in the United States. It also included Albini's antisocial lyrics, which often focused on perverse topics. The song "Kerosene," for example, touts pyromania as a viable way to escape boredom in the type of small town in which Albini grew up.

Growing up in Montana, Albini encountered an unusual array of guests in his childhood home. His mother, Giana Albini, had a charitable bent, and on Christmas and Easter would serve dinner to parollees who worked in forest-clearing crews. When Albini was 16, his mother started inviting Vietnamese and Laotian foster children to live with the family. Albini's father, Frank, was a well-known scientist and an authority on the mathematical modeling of forest fires.

"A borderline emotional basket case" as a teen, as Albini described himself to Jannot, he became withdrawn during his high school years and developed an intense interest in music. He recalled in *Musician,* "I spent my formative years obsessed with punk rock, and the bands that I've been in have all been punk influenced." While a student at Northwestern University in Illinois, he formed two bands—a garage band called Small Irregular Pieces of Aluminum and a locally popular new wave group known as Stations. The other members of Stations dismissed Albini from the band when he attempted to steer the music in a more punk direction.

In 1981 Albini formed Big Black, a group that helped cement his reputation in the punk world. He played all the instruments himself when he recorded the group's first album, *Lungs,* on a four-track tape deck in 1982.

After recording one more album in 1987, Albini became bored with Big Black and disbanded it. He then formed Rapeman, a band featuring David Wm. Sims on bass and Rey Washam on drums. Albini took a lot of criticism for the group's name, which he took from a character in Japanese comics. Perhaps as a result of the controversy surrounding its moniker, the group broke up soon after its formation, during a tour of Europe.

Found Success as a Producer Underground

As a producer, Albini has recorded nearly 1,000 albums for various underground rock bands in the 1980s and 1990s. His most significant affiliation has been with Chicago's Touch and Go Records, for which he has recorded all of the Jesus Lizard LPs. He has also produced albums for the Pixies, the Breeders, Tad, Helmet, the Didjits, Mule, and Superchunk. Explaining Albini's allegiance to independent (indie) label acts, *Chicago's* Jannot wrote, "In Albini's world, nothing marks you as a sellout more starkly than your signature on a major-label contract."

Albini himself was accused of selling out when, in 1993, he agreed to work as producer for rock band Nirvana's follow-up album to their hugely successful Geffen Records debut, *Nevermind.* The group enlisted Albini partly to regain some of their status as an alternative band. After *In Utero* was recorded, neither Geffen nor the members of Nirvana were satisfied with the results. Nirvana felt that the vocals and bass were too soft, and they hired Scott Litt, fellow rock troupe R.E.M.'s producer, to remix some of the songs for radio play. Litt ended up also changing the tonal balance during mastering. Albini rejected the criticism from the group, claiming that Nirvana was obsessed about the record not being "perfect."

In 1993 *Crain's Chicago Business* included Albini in its "40 Under Forty" profile of the top young entrepreneurs on the rise in Chicago. His experience with Nirvana, however, proved damaging to his career, making him an anathema to major record labels and an abhorred "mainstreamer" to formerly loyal, low-profile punk bands. At the time, Albini was hoping to set up a new recording studio in Chicago that could produce records on a low budget, but he had trouble getting necessary financing due to the bad publicity of his experience with Nirvana.

Avoided "Satan-Worshipping Freak" Image

In the early 1990s Albini formed the band Shellac with bassist Todd Trainer and drummer Bob Weston; Albini took the roles of guitarist and vocalist. From the start he stressed that the group was not interested in having any bizarre image, but only in playing solid rock and roll. "In Shellac, we're not trying to be nine-armed, long-haired, Satan-worshipping 3-D freaks," he proclaimed in *Guitar Player.* "We're normal people who happen to play rock music, and our normalcy makes us distinctive."

Rolling Stone called Shellac "Steve Albini's latest power trio from hell" and added that they "make a superb, corrosive Wire-ish thunder on the twin EPs *The Rude Gesture (A Pictorial History)* and *Uranus.*" Marc Weidenbaum observed in *Pulse!* that *At Action Park,* Shellac's first full-length album, "rekindles the terse rage and skittish fervor of Albini's early bands, Big Black and Rapeman," and that it is "taut with rigor, rage and compression."

According to Albini, *At Action Park* represents rock stripped down to its bare essentials. "My preference is for a very straightforward, very unembellished recording," he revealed in *Pulse!* "The Shellac record is that: It's just a three-piece rock band recorded live and presented without much flash. That's the way I like to hear music, so it only makes sense that my band would be presented that way."

In the mid 1990s Albini was working at the Black Box studio near Angers, France, where he had recorded an album for the German band 18th Dye on Matador, as well as part of his Shellac album. His choice of studio reflects his ongoing concern with keeping production costs low. Albini also has a recording studio in his own home, which helps him maintain total control over the production environment.

Believes Producers Lack Know-How

A master of the technical aspects of producing, Albini claims that many producers lack the proper knowledge of studio techniques. "A lot of people making records don't have a grasp of the process," he opined, according to *Billboard.* "They do it thinking that it's some abstract art form that doesn't need to be comprehended on a technical procedural level. [In those cases] you'll end up with a record that isn't formally completed, but that's finished when the bell rings." Albini further lamented in *Musician* what he calls the industry's assembly line mentality: "The sound of contemporary rock records, especially those made with big budgets, is so homogeneous. You hear exactly the same mix balance, the same dynamic, the same production techniques brought to bear on every single band."

Albini has also pointed out that the quality of his own records has improved, largely because he has stifled former tendencies to "fiddle around" with the music. "In the last few years, I've learned to leave things alone," he remarked in *Billboard.* "Now when I set up a microphone and like the way it sounds, I consider the job done." As of early 1995, Albini was beginning to record new albums for the groups Palace Brothers and Silkworm; an LP he produced for the Fleshtones was scheduled to be released on Ichiban Records in the fall of 1995. He was also considering going on tour with Shellac.

Selected discography

With Big Black; also producer

Lungs (EP), Ruthless, 1983.
Racer X (EP), Homestead, 1984.
Atomizer, Homestead, 1986.

With Rapeman; also producer

Two Nuns on a Pack Mule, 1988.

With Shellac; also producer

At Action Park, Touch and Go, 1994.
The Rude Gesture (A Pictorial History) and *Uranus* (twin EPs), Touch and Go, 1994.

As producer

The Pixies, *Surfer Rosa,* 4AD/Rough Trade, 1988.
Jesus Lizard, *Head,* Touch and Go, 1990.
Nirvana, *In Utero,* Geffen, 1993.
PJ Harvey, *Rid of Me,* Island, 1993.

Sources

Books

DeCurtis, Anthony, and James Henke, editors, *The Rolling Stone History of Rock & Roll,* Random House, 1992.
Larkin, Colin, editor, *The Guinness Encyclopedia of Popular Music,* volumes 1 and 3, Guinness Publishing, 1992.

Periodicals

Billboard, January 7, 1995.
Chicago, May 1994.
Guitar Player, March 1994.
Melody Maker, November 21, 1992; September 4, 1993; March 19, 1995.
Musician, June 1995.
Newsweek, May 17, 1993.
Pulse!, April 1995.
Rolling Stone, June 16, 1994.

—Ed Decker

American Music Club

Rock band

The San Francisco, California-based quintet American Music Club offer their own unique brand of dirge rock and have been compared to Joy Division, the Violent Femmes, R.E.M., U2, the Clash, Elvis Costello, Leonard Cohen, and even Hank Williams at his most melancholy. The fact that the band's music is difficult to describe and often defies comparison is a tribute to its originality. They provide a mixed bag of musical offerings: some songs are underscored with a funeral beat, some feature a danceable, up-tempo pace, and still others are marked by a slight country-music twang. Singer, songwriter, and guitarist Mark Eitzel ensures that all singles are seeped in his despair-laden vocals.

American Music Club was formed by Eitzel, guitarist Vudi, and bassist Dan Pearson in 1983 in San Francisco. Playing together during the rise and fall of punk rock, the three musicians never ventured into hardcore punk; instead, they chose to adopt a softer punk sound, lyrically and plaintively accentuating angst, despair, and longing. Studio owner Tom Mallon played an important role in the early formation of the band: for their first

Photograph by Dennis Keeley, © 1994 Reprise Records

For the Record . . .

Members include **Mark Eitzel** (born in 1959), singer, songwriter, and guitarist; **Tim Mooney** (joined band 1991), drums; **Dan Pearson,** bass guitar; and **Vudi,** lead guitar.

Group formed in 1983 in San Francisco, CA; released debut album, *The Restless Stranger,* Grifter, 1985; released major-label debut, *Mercury,* Reprise, 1993; performed at reopening of Fillmore Auditorium, San Francisco, 1994. Eitzel released solo album *Songs of Love Live,* Demon, 1991.

Awards: Cited in *Rolling Stone* critics' poll for *Everclear,* and Eitzel named best songwriter by *Rolling Stone,* both 1991.

Addresses: *Record company*—Reprise Records, 3300 Warner Boulevard, Burbank, CA 91505-4694; or 75 Rockefeller Plaza, New York, NY 10019-6979.

four albums, Mallon served as a mentor, producer, and, when needed, even a band member. Mallon taught Eitzel how to write music and showed the group how to strip a song down to its essence. American Music Club eventually became known for the dark humor and intelligence found in their lyrics, their eccentric musical shifts, their unexpected psychedelic riffs, and their obvious willingness to experiment.

Spent Early Years on Indie Labels

American Music Club's first album, *The Restless Stranger,* was released in 1985 on the independent (indie) label Grifter. Two years later, in 1987, the band released a second album, *Engine,* on Grifter/Frontier, made available on compact disc (CD) through the Alias label. *Engine* featured "Outside This Bar" and "Nightwatchmen," two songs that would become favorites for live performances. *Spin's* Jen Fleissner dubbed *Engine* a "brilliant" album, and wrote, "[It] incredibly, in retrospect, got by on almost [rock musician Bruce] Springsteenian anthems." The band ceased using keyboards for the album and chose to open *Engine* with a dirge-like, brooding cut. This type of opening would become a trademark for the band.

In 1988 American Music Club released *California,* an album that featured the singles "Western Sky," "Firefly,"

and "Blue and Grey Shirt." Around this time, the band was gaining popularity in Great Britain, where in 1990 they released *United Kingdom* on Britain's Demon Records. Eitzel subsequently went to England for solo performances and released *Songs of Love Live* in 1991 on Demon.

Also in 1991 American Music Club signed with Alias Records for their sixth album, *Everclear,* which had a more commercial sound than the band's previous records, as evidenced by the pop single "Rise." *Everclear* was cited in a *Rolling Stone* critics' poll, and Eitzel was named best songwriter by the magazine. In sharp contrast to its previous situation, American Music Club was soon talking to people from major labels and was made a variety of offers. Before the band made a communal decision, Eitzel spent some time recording with the San Francisco band Toiling Midgets and, as a result, ended up recruiting American Music Club's drummer, Tim Mooney. Once Mooney was part of the band, they chose to sign with Reprise Records.

Critical Acclaim for Major-Label Debut

Mercury was released to much critical acclaim in 1993: *Rolling Stone* gave the album a four-star review and "hot band" status. The LP was characterized as introspective, dour, and "atmospheric." American Music Club began to tour the United States and frequently opened for Seattle grunge rock success Pearl Jam. In 1994 American Music Club released *San Francisco,* which *Rolling Stone's* Lorraine Ali found "more seamless" than any of their other albums. *San Francisco's* appeal, perhaps, is that no two songs are similar on the album; each track is meticulously stylized and unique. Ali also wrote of *San Francisco,* "The rhythms are delicate and sad (occasionally evoking Joy Division), then cocky and catchy, riding freely under the effects of winding bagpipes, jangly tambourines and rushing wind."

American Music Club's lamentable sound and Eitzel's flat tone requires, for some, an acquired taste. After the release of *San Francisco,* for example, *Musician* magazine's Rob O'Connor wrote, "Eitzel might as well be the poster boy for [the anti-depression medication] Prozac." The group, however, has garnered a loyal following; in 1994 they were invited to perform—along with the Neville Brothers, Joe Satriani, and Smashing Pumpkins—at the reopening of the legendary Fillmore Auditorium in San Francisco.

American Music Club frontman Eitzel's onstage antics are the stuff of legend and have on occasion inspired madness: He once crawled through the tables of a club, clad only in his underwear, while the band played

"Highway To Hell." During another performance, he angered a woman in the audience, who stormed out of the club. Eitzel then followed the woman outside to beg for her forgiveness. Giving performances reminiscent of punk rock icon Iggy Pop, Eitzel has been known to kick a bottle into the audience, to grovel on the floor, or to push someone against a wall. After once crippling himself for weeks, he decided never again to jump in the air and land on his knees.

Eitzel Interested in Rock at an Early Age

Eitzel, the son of an army man, was born in 1959 in the San Francisco suburb of Walnut Creek. At the age of seven, he moved with his family to Okinawa, Japan, then to Taiwan, then to Southampton, England. Eitzel was a quiet, studious child who took an inordinate interest in pop music. The Monkees and the Beatles were early influences for him, and by the time he was 14, he was writing songs. Punk rock interested him during his teens, and when his family moved to Ohio, the 19-year-old Eitzel wanted to join a punk band there. He eventually became a member of the Naked Skinnies, which migrated to San Francisco in 1981.

No stranger to the pain of losing a loved one, Eitzel faced the early death of both of his parents. After losing a friend to AIDS, Eitzel and American Music Club contributed the single "All Your Jeans Were Too Tight" to the 1993 No Alternative compilation album, whose profits are contributed directly to AIDS research. Eitzel would witness several of his friends die of AIDS, and his experiences are reflected in some of American Music

Club's singles; "Western Sky," "Rise," and "Johnny Mathis' Feet" were all written for dying friends.

As an explanation for American Music Club's style, and as an example of his own dark humor, Eitzel told Request's David Sprague, "Maybe I do have a morbid bent. But it's my job. I was born to be a sad crooner. I was born with no chin."

Selected discography

The Restless Stranger, Grifter, 1985.
Engine, Grifter/Frontier, 1987.
California, Grifter/Frontier, 1988.
United Kingdom, Demon, 1990.
Everclear, Alias, 1991.
Mercury, Reprise, 1993.
San Francisco, Reprise, 1994.

Eitzel released solo album Songs of Love Live, Demon, 1991.

Sources

Entertainment Weekly, October 21, 1994.
Metro Times (Detroit), March 24, 1993; October 26, 1994.
Musician, May 1993; November 1994.
Pulse!, June 1993.
Request, April 1993; October 1993.
Rolling Stone, April 15, 1993; May 13, 1993; June 16, 1994; December 1, 1994.
Spin, June 1993; October 1994.

—B. Kimberly Taylor

Marcia Ball

Pianist, singer, songwriter

Photograph by Brenda Ladd, courtesy of David Hickey

A well-established presence on the Austin, Texas, music scene, pianist-singer Marcia Ball performs a searing, heartfelt brand of Louisiana-Texas rhythm and blues that is a jubilant celebration of life. Part James Booker and part Professor Longhair, with the sultry, bluesy vocal delivery of T-Bone Walker tossed in for good measure, her rollicking style has won the six-foot Ball notice on the thriving New Orleans R&B circuit. She is particularly impressive during live concerts, when the audience can witness her scream, shout, bang on her piano, shake, wring every drop of emotion out of a word, and keep time to the beat with enviable concentration.

Born in Orange, Texas, and raised in Vinton, Louisiana, which was just across the Sabine River and the Texas border, Ball comes from a long line of instrumentalists: her grandmother was a pianist, her father was a composer, and her aunt was a pianist. Ball's family was her first and strongest musical influence, but local Cajun sounds and the soul music she heard on local radio stations also played roles in developing her musical tastes.

Ball began taking piano lessons at the age of five and would continue taking them until she was 14. She was a cheerleader and church choir member in Vinton, enthralled during the rare times when her father would take her to the Mardi Gras parade in New Orleans. At the age of 13, she saw soul crooner Irma Thomas in concert in New Orleans, and the then-pregnant but amazingly energetic Thomas left a lasting impression on Ball and furthered her interest in performing.

Small state-border clubs with names like the Texas Pelican Club, Lou Ann's, and the Showboat Club lined the roads on the outskirts of Vinton, beckoning to the young Ball to try her hand at performing. She took voice lessons at age 18 and, while studying English literature and journalism at Louisiana State University in the late 1960s, was the lead singer of a band called Gum. In 1970 she moved to Austin, Texas.

Since country music was in high demand at the time, the only jobs Ball could find in Austin were country gigs in what she termed "living room bands." She infused her country songs with as much blues and soul sounds as she could while still maintaining the country music veneer. Austin audiences appreciated her eclectic mix of musical sounds and styles, and by 1972 Ball was playing in a popular local progressive country band called Freda and the Firedogs.

Ball was established as a musician in Austin under her alias in the band, Freda. When Freda and the Firedogs broke up in 1974, she founded a her own band the following year: Marcia and the Misery Brothers. She felt more comfortable using her own name and would later change the group's name to the Marcia Ball Band. Marcia and the Misery Brothers were just as popular on the local scene as Ball's previous band had been. The same year the group was formed, Ball released her first recording, a cover of Patsy Montana's "I Want to Be a Cowboy's Sweetheart," which was punctuated with heartfelt yodels.

In 1978 Ball had her first appearance at the New Orleans Jazz and Heritage Festival. She then released *Circuit Queen* on Capital Records, a hybrid album of country music and rhythm and blues. *Circuit Queen* was not well accepted, and Ball would not record again until 1983, when she released *Soulful Dress* on Rounder Records. *Soulful Dress* contains signature tunes such as the title track, which features the legendary Stevie Ray Vaughan, as well as Laverne Baker's ballad "Soul on Fire" and Chuck Berry's Louisiana love song "Eugene." The LP received warm praise and was followed in 1985 by *Hot Tamale Baby.*

Hot Tamale Baby was a mix of traditional blues and rhythm and blues with no discernible country influence. The album's sound is akin to what you might hear at a bawdy Texas-Louisiana house party, complete with accordionist Clifton Chenier favorites. *Gatorhythms* followed in 1989 and features original ballads written by Ball. In 1990 she released *Dreams Come True* on the Antone label, a collaboration with singers Lou Ann Barton and Angela Strehli. *Dreams Come True* was produced by pianist Dr. John, one of Ball's musical mentors in New Orleans. The album was recorded to unite the three women, who had spent years perfecting their music on stage at Antone's, a blues club and landmark in Austin.

After a few years of touring in the United States and Europe with her own band, and touring with Barton and Strehli to promote *Dreams Come True,* Ball released *Blue House* on Rounder Records in 1994. The album underscored a new direction for Ball: she composed most of the songs on the album and utilized the acoustic guitar and mandolin, both played by Rich Brotherton, for the first time in her recordings. *Blue House* features a haunting gospel melody and rousing piano anthem and also highlights Ball's greatest influences. Shades of Irma Thomas, singer Bobby "Blue" Bland, and pianists Professor Longhair, Jelly Roll Morton, and Dr. John may be detected when listening to Ball's surprisingly eclectic *Blue House.*

Ball's plans for the future include writing original and innovative material, traveling overseas more often to play in Europe, and ensuring that her name is synonymous with New Orleans-style piano playing and rhythm and blues. She told *New Country* magazine, "It really boils down to the Gulf Coast for me. So much music has emanated from this area that encompasses everything from the Mexican border up to the other side of Mobile [Alabama]. That's everything I love to play, listen to and eat."

Selected discography

Circuit Queen, Capitol, 1978.
Soulful Dress, Rounder, 1983.
Hot Tamale Baby, Rounder, 1986.
Gatorhythms, Rounder, 1989.
(With Angela Strehli and Lou Ann Barton) *Dreams Come True,* Antone, 1991.
Blue House, Rounder, 1994.

Sources

Austin American Statesman, October 18, 1990; August 18, 1994.
Billboard, December 1, 1990.
Chicago Tribune, November 22, 1990.
Intelligencer Journal, September 9, 1994.
Los Angeles Times, April 7, 1991.
Metro Times (Detroit), September 28, 1994.
New Country, October 1994.

Philadelphia Inquirer, November 11, 1990.
Rolling Stone, February 7, 1991; February 2, 1995.
Washington Post, July 19, 1991.

Additional information for this profile was obtained from an interview with Ball on March 10, 1995.

—*B. Kimberly Taylor*

Jellybean
Benitez

Producer

Despite the fact that they are often the single-most important force behind the success of a hit record, it isn't often that producers come out of the control room to share in the public spotlight with musicians and vocalists. In this respect, Jellybean Benitez joins the ranks of such notable producers as Phil Spector, Alan Parsons, Quincy Jones, George Martin, and a handful of others who have come to symbolize the certain style and feel of a musical genre. In fact, Benitez's name carries such a recognition factor in the pop and dance music realms that it is often displayed as prominently on the record cover as that of the artist. Occasionally his is the *only* name appearing on the product, as in the case of the four "solo" albums he has released since 1984.

Born John Benitez to Puerto Rican immigrants in the Bronx, New York, Jellybean learned early on that he had a gift for both music and self-promotion. He began playing records in his early teens at parties for friends and before long had maneuvered his way via a combination of talent and style into the position of disc jockey at New York's most popular and exclusive nightclubs, including the Funhouse, Xenon, and Studio 54.

With the rise of the punk rock movement in the mid-1970s, however, rockers around the world cheered gleefully what they saw as the death of the much-maligned disco scene. The truth, however, was different. "I would read in magazines that disco was over," Benitez remembered in *New York* magazine in 1993, "but I was still playing to 2,000 people a night. At three o'clock in the morning, I'd think, The reporter didn't come *here*." In fact, dance music was still very much alive. It had simply altered its appearance slightly and taken on the monikers "techno" and "new wave." The ultrahip Benitez figured prominently in the conversion.

Madonna

By this time, Benitez had earned a spectacular reputation as a DJ and was beginning to make his way into recording and producing. He first captured the public eye when he became pop superstar Madonna's producer/boyfriend in the early 1980s, functioning as the behind-the-scenes architect of some of her biggest hits, including "Holiday" and "Crazy for You." Benitez reflected on his first meeting with Madonna in Norman King's *Madonna: The Book:* "She was introduced to me by her record company. I thought she had a lot of style, and she crossed over a lot of boundaries, because everyone in the rock clubs played her—the black clubs, the gay, the straight. And very few records have *that* appeal." Their business relationship quickly developed into something more. "She didn't bowl me over at first," he continued. "We just used to go to the movies and clubs

For the Record . . .

Born John Benitez in the Bronx, NY.

Established reputation as a disc jockey in New York City nightclubs, 1970s; producer for albums by Madonna, mid-1980s; released first album as producer, *Wotupski!?!,* EMI, 1984; served as music producer and supervisor on numerous motion pictures, including *Mi Vida Loca,.*

Addresses: *Home*—New York City.

together. Then we started holding hands and buying each other presents."

Soon Benitez and Madonna were sharing an apartment in a fashionable district of Manhattan. After the release of her first album, however, Madonna decided it was time to move on. She felt that for her second album she needed a more experienced producer—she is quoted in *Madonna: The Book* as referring to Benitez as "a technician rather than a musician"—and she had grown tired of Benitez's club-hopping nightlife. Apparently there were no hard feelings on either side, as evidenced by Benitez's Top 20 recording of the Madonna-penned "Sidewalk Talk" in 1984 and his production of her Number One single "Crazy for You" in 1985.

Benitez's record-producing success with Madonna and his burgeoning public notoriety unfortunately led to something of a falling-out with the top club owners, but he was not about to let that stop him. He quickly became dance music's most sought-after remix master, working with artists as diverse as Barbra Streisand, Whitney Houston, Huey Lewis, Hall & Oates, Paul McCartney, Michael Jackson, Billy Joel, and the Muppets. As for some of his more unusual choices for collaboration, Benitez explained in *New York,* "I figured if I could have a Huey Lewis dance hit and a Billy Joel dance hit, it would be the ultimate accomplishment."

I Don't Write the Songs

Benitez also takes a rather unique approach to making his own records, expanding on a technique pioneered in the 1970s by pop/rock producer Alan Parsons for his Alan Parsons Project. Benitez does not write the songs, sing the words, or—for the most part—play the music, but he has put out albums of performances by other musicians and vocalists that feature his name on the cover. He has defended this tactic against detractors by arguing that as the producer and visionary he supplies the creative backdrop on which his LPs are based. "Jellybean is the *artist*—it's a concept," he explained in *New York* in 1988. "It might be a little abstract for some people."

Whatever the public's response on an intellectual level, there is certainly no confusion on the dance floor. Benitez's first album, 1984's *Wotupski?!?,* contained the aforementioned Number 18 single "Sidewalk Talk," making him the first former DJ to become a Top 40 pop artist. His later releases, *Just Visiting This Planet,* the greatest-hits collection *Rocks The House!,* and *Spillin' the Beans,* yielded 1987's "Who Found Who," which reached Number 16, and other songs that were hits on the dance charts. "In the beginning, I wasn't sure if it was luck or talent," he revealed in *New York.* "But then I kept having hit after hit after hit, and I realized there was a certain art in what I was doing.... I was functioning creatively in an environment that was usually creative because of musical acumen, and I didn't have any of that. All I had was a feel."

Right Places, Right Times

Benitez also has a feel for meeting the right people and being at the right place at the right time—a talent that has figured prominently in his rapid rise to success. He skillfully built upon his star-quality association with Madonna throughout the 1980s. *New York* quoted an anecdote about Benitez told by "professional party-giver" Alan Rish: "On New Year's Eve, [Benitez] said 'Come over,' and it was the most *amazing* party I've ever seen. There were twenty people in the room, but it was, like, [actors] Cher and Vincent Spano ... and Kelly McGillis and Judd Nelson. I was the only non-celebrity star there, and he was just having a few of his friends over at his apartment."

Another source of Benitez's success is the way he always sets his sights just over the next hill. In 1995, for example, *Entertainment Weekly* reported that he had garnered funding for a new bilingual record label he hopes will become the Latino Motown. Betraying a depth not often found in today's pop world, Benitez also admits to fantasies of working with eighteenth-century classical composer Wolfgang Amadeus Mozart. "I mean, he made incredible symphonies then with a little piano," he told *New York.* "If he'd had synthesizers and all these multitracks and could record stuff ... I mean, it's amazing. Do you understand what this guy could be doing? I would love to be producing this guy."

Benitez walks the middle of the road when it comes to assessing the fruits of his achievements. While not letting his rapid success go to his head, he makes no bones about treating himself to a justly deserved reward or two. "When I was younger, I always wanted a big TV," he revealed in *Vogue.* "I always wanted to have a deejay booth in my apartment. I'm not really a materialistic person, but success has been great."

Selected discography

Wotupski!?!, EMI, 1984.
Just Visiting This Planet, Chrysalis, 1987.
Rocks the House!, Chrysalis, 1988.
Spillin' the Beans, Atlantic, 1991.
(Various artists) *Carlito's Way* (soundtrack), 550 Music, 1993.

Also produced motion picture soundtracks and albums and singles by Madonna, Barbra Streisand, Whitney Houston, Huey Lewis, Hall & Oates, Paul McCartney, Michael Jackson, Billy Joel, and others.

Sources

Books

King, Norman, *Madonna: The Book,* Morrow, 1991.

Periodicals

Entertainment Weekly, May 12, 1995.
Musician, August 1989.
New York, March 28, 1988; November 22, 1993.
Rolling Stone, July 14, 1994.
Seventeen, May 1991.
Vogue, May 1988.

—*Alan Glenn*

Mary Black

Singer

Photograph by Mike Bunn, courtesy of Curb Records

Sustained effort and an elegiac voice have enabled singer Mary Black to emerge as one of Ireland's top musical exports. With a silky, controlled vocal style that leaves listeners breathless, her music seamlessly blends traditional Irish folk, conventional pop, country, and rock and roll. She began her career in the late 1970s as a folk singer working with General Humbert and De Dannan, both successful Irish folk acts. Branching out from her folk beginnings, she has capitalized on her interest in music of many styles and resists being confined by the limits of any single genre. Folk-tinged versions of blues artist Billie Holiday and pop composer Burt Bacharach complement her otherwise balled-laden repertoire, and she has been named Ireland's female artist of the year twice, garnering several gold and platinum records along the way. Black's notoriety in the United States has been limited by the lack of a major label record deal, though that barrier was overcome in 1994 when her husband and manager, Joe O'Reilly, negotiated a deal with Curb Records, an Atlantic subsidiary based in Nashville. Black's 1995 Curb release, *Looking Back,* reached the Billboard Top Ten in the world music category in April of 1995 and signaled a high-water mark for her career in the United States.

Through the use of artful arrangements and talented backing musicians, Black has moved beyond Dublin's pubs to London's Royal Albert Hall. She shies away from songwriting, admitting that her talents do not include the necessities for penning emotive melodies, but has taken full advantage of a wealth of Irish songwriters pleased to have Black perform their works. She told a reporter for Glasgow, Scotland's *Herald,* "I can honestly say I'm not a songwriter. Sure, I could write some sort of a song ... but I think it's a talent, an inspiration, and I feel I don't have that gift, I just don't have it." Black noted in the same interview, "Ireland is small enough to get to know people, and all the Irish songwriters I work with are friends. They don't write for me; they're inspired, not commissioned." Quick to point to the quality of her band and the direction she has received from her husband as crucial to her success, it is nevertheless her own voice that has brought her critical acclaim.

Born into a Musical Family

Raised in Dublin, Black was perhaps destined for a career in music. Her father was a fiddle player from Rathlin Island, off the Antrim coast, while her mother, a Dublin native, sang traditional Irish folk songs. The pair nurtured in their five children a healthy bent for music that led to a successful family act, appropriately titled the Black Family. The Blacks enjoyed some success in Dublin's folk music scene and released two albums. Black commented to a reporter from the *St. Louis Post-*

For the Record . . .

Born May 22, 1955, in Dublin, Ireland; daughter of Kevin Black (a plasterer) and Patricia Daly; married Joe O'Reilly (manager of a record label); children: Roison (daughter), Danny, Conor.

Began career with siblings as member of band the Black Family, c. 1965; joined Dublin-based Irish folk group Terrace (name later changed to General Humbert), c. 1977; released self-titled solo album on Dara Records, 1982; member of traditional folk group De Dannan, 1983-86; released U.S. major label debut, *Looking Back,* Curb/Atlantic, 1995; appeared on television special *The Music of Ireland,* TNN, and embarked on North American tour, 1995.

Awards: Named Best Female Irish Artiste, Irish Recorded Music Awards polls, 1987 and 1988; Irish Independent Arts Award for Music, 1982, for *Mary Black*; honored at a Tavern on the Green dinner, 1995.

Addresses: *Home*—Dublin, Ireland. *Publicity*—Shock Ink, 1108 16th Avenue South, Nashville, TN 37212. *Record company*—Curb AG, 47 Music Square East, Nashville, TN 37203.

Dispatch, "[Music] was a very strong, big, big, part of our growing up. My parents had very strong musical sort of leanings, but neither were professional. They both literally did it for the love of it, and that's why I went into it. And I still feel that's why I do it."

In the 1970s Black landed her first professional gig with a folk group known as Terrace, which would later become General Humbert. The band released two albums and toured Europe, enjoying the benefits of a folk revival that also gave rise to Irish talents Christy Moore and Van Morrisson. In 1983 Black joined the well-known folk outfit De Dannan, who were looking to replace their singer. This experience afforded her the opportunity to tour the United States on four separate occasions while also contributing to many successful records. Though the band's fan base was largely European, De Dannan's solid musicianship and energetic renditions of traditional Irish jig-and-reel tunes helped establish a solid following among Irish Americans anxious for native sounds.

Black's star began to rise after appearing on an Irish television program known as *Christy Moore and Friends.* Though she never actually saw the program—her wed-

ding took place the day it was aired—she learned of her newfound appeal. At the insistence of her new husband, an employee of Ireland's Dolphin Records, a solo project was planned. Black's music did not correspond with that of other artists promoted by Dolphin, so O'Reilly established a subsidiary label, Dara Records, to promote her talents. Noted musician and producer Declan Sinnott was brought in to produce and assist with the arrangements for the record, and Black and Sinnott have been working together since. The self-titled release hit Irish record stores in 1982 and went gold, earning Black an Irish Independent Arts Award for Music.

Set Out on Her Own

By 1986 Black's fondness for traditional folk had begun to wane, and she left De Dannan to focus full time on a solo career. Black admitted in the *Irish Times,* "The folk singer images used to drive me crazy. Although folk and traditional have had a huge influence on me and I would never turn my back on that, I didn't want to be confined to one area of music, I wanted to explore." She counts innovative folk/rock artist Sandy Denny among her most important influences and sees similarities in their styles. "I think that folk flavor, from where [Denny] started off, was always there with her, even though she tried different things. And I'd like to think the same thing goes with me," Black told the *St. Louis Post-Dispatch.*

During her stint with De Dannan, Black had released three solo albums: *Mary Black* (1982), *Collected* (1984), and *Without the Fanfare* (1985). No longer committed to the band, she wasted no time in recording a fourth solo album. Her 1987 LP, *By the Time It Gets Dark,* rewarded her efforts in spades, achieving multi-platinum status in Ireland. Each of the singer's ensuing releases, including *No Frontiers* (1989), *Babes in the Wood* (1991), and *The Holy Ground* (1993), has gone platinum, though in Ireland that accounts for 15,000 copies sold, rather than the one million required for platinum certification in the United States.

Critics in Ireland and elsewhere describe Black's eclectic brand of music as a sophisticated blend of folk, country, and pop, but many wonder where her recordings fall in the commercial spectrum. Too Irish to be considered country and too country to be categorized as Irish, Black's records nevertheless draw attention from both camps as well as from adult alternative and public radio listeners. "It's hard to get airplay because I'm not strictly folk and I'm not jazz and I'm not rock and I'm not pop. I'm a mixture of a whole load of things," Black told the Baton Rouge, Louisiana, *Advocate.* She also faces some close competition from her younger sister, Frances, whose own career has shown signs of taking off following the 1994 release of her first album.

Patient Effort Earned Acclaim

Despite being Ireland's biggest-selling female artist, Black struggled initially for notoriety outside of Europe. Hit singles in Japan, Australia, and New Zealand gave rise to tours of those countries, though success in the lucrative U.S. market was slow in coming. The pace of her career was just fine with Black. She told *Billboard,* "[My band and I are] not in any hurry to conquer the world. We're not 18-year-olds looking for the big deal or the big break. We've done it our way, and feel we should wait for what suits us."

In 1994 Atlantic Records rewarded Black's patience by offering her a deal for U.S. distribution through one of its affiliate labels, Curb Records. It was an opportunity a long time in the making and one that the singer could not refuse. She did have a U.S. deal prior to Atlantic, but it was through an independent label, California's Gift Horse Records, that lacked the necessary promotional abilities to secure even wider audiences for her music. For Black's major-label debut, she was joined by Carl Geraghty on saxophone, Garvin Gallagher on bass, Pat Crowley on piano and accordion, Dave Early on drums, and Frank Gallagher on fiddle, synthesizer, and whistle. Declan Sinnott also continued his long-standing association with Black and played guitar.

Black's contribution to *A Woman's Heart,* a compilation album of Irish female artists, helped it become the most successful record in Irish history. Further good fortune came in March of 1995, when Black cohosted a cable TV special on the Nashville Network (TNN) with country legend Emmylou Harris, titled *The Music of Ireland.* This appearance was carefully planned to coincide with both St. Patrick's Day and the release of *Looking Back.* Harris herself has enjoyed success in Ireland, as have other country artists, many of whom regularly include stops in Ireland on their tour itineraries. The admiration is shared on both shores; as Black observed in *USA Today,* "The Irish people are very open to all kinds of music, and very respectful of talent. When I first came [to the United States] I was amazed at the respect musicians had for Irish music and talent."

Black's comfortably organic voice comes at a time in music when listeners are rediscovering the allure of dressed-down harmony and understated delivery, as witnessed by the rise of such artists as Sheryl Crow. Black noted in *Billboard,* "More people are turning to real music and instruments, and melodies and words are becoming more important again." With a major-

label deal in place in the United States, Black is hopeful that her own melodies and words will reverberate strongly among American music listeners. Her 1995 release, *Looking Back,* would no doubt move her in that direction.

Selected discography

Solo albums; released in Ireland on Dara Records

Mary Black, 1982, released in U.S. on Gifthorse, 1992.
Collected, 1984, released in U.S. on Gifthorse, 1992.
Without the Fanfare, 1985, released U.S. on Gifthorse, 1992.
By the Time It Gets Dark, 1987, released in U.S. on Gifthorse, 1994.
No Frontiers, released in U.S. on Gifthorse/Curb, 1990.
Babes in the Wood, released in U.S. on Gifthorse/Curb, 1991.
The Holy Ground, released in U.S. on Gifthorse/Curb, 1993.
Looking Back, Curb/Atlantic, 1995.

With De Dannan

Song for Ireland.
Anthem.

Sources

Books

The Guinness Encyclopedia of Popular Music, edited by Colin Larkin, Square One Books Ltd., 1992.

Periodicals

Advocate (Baton Rouge, LA), March 17, 1995.
Baltimore Sun, March 17, 1995.
Billboard, August 28, 1993; April 15, 1995.
Daily Telegraph (London), October 15, 1991; November 28, 1992.
Daily Yomiuri (Japan), June 15, 1991.
Evening Standard (London), June 11, 1993.
Herald (Glasgow, Scotland), May 9, 1992; December 10, 1993; January 13, 1994.
Irish Times (Dublin), September 10, 1994.
Rolling Stone, January 24, 1991.
St. Louis Post-Dispatch, November 4, 1993; June 12, 1994.
San Francisco Chronicle, April 5, 1991.
Star Tribune (Minneapolis, MN), March 13, 1994.
USA Today, March 31, 1995.
Washington Post, April 20, 1988.

Additional information for this profile was obtained from Shock Ink publicity materials, 1995.

—Rich Bowen

Cindy Blackman

Percussionist, composer

Exploration, experimentation, and improvisation characterize Cindy Blackman's career and the jazz music she writes and performs. Both her mother and her grandmother were classical musicians, and she fell in love with music at an early age. But Blackman's career has never followed any traditions.

Born in Yellow Springs, Ohio, in 1959, Blackman started playing drums as a child. She moved to Hartford, Connecticut, at the age of 11, and in high school she began classical percussion training at the University of Hartford. When she saw drummer Tony Williams perform, she began to define her own ideas about percussion. "The first drummer I ever *saw,* where I got to *feel* the impact up close, was Tony Williams," Blackman told Chip Stern in the liner notes of her 1992 release *Code Red.* "When I was 16, Tony came to my local drum store with a bassist and did a clinic that left a powerful impression on me. And *that's* what I thought drumming should be: drummers should have a lot of impact and a great sound, without being limited to a conventional role in the band—the drums should speak just as freely as anybody."

After she graduated from high school, Blackman moved to Boston to study at the Berklee College of Music. While there, she trained with Lennie Nelson and the late Alan Dawson. But after just three semesters, she felt stifled by the confines of the college classroom. Blackman decided to leave convention behind. She picked up her drums and sticks and moved to New York City in 1982.

From Street to Studio

During the first couple of years in New York, Blackman played everywhere she could. She performed late night jams at the 55 Grand Club, where Jaco Pastorius would often invite her to play with his Word of Mouth group. She played the after-hours jam sessions that trumpet player Ted Curson organized at Manhattan's Blue Note Jazz Club. She also accompanied saxophonist Sam Rivers with his trio and big band and played some shows with pianist John Hicks and trumpet player Hugh Masekela. And for two consecutive summers, Blackman played for contributions on the sidewalk of 42nd Street and 6th Avenue, near the New York Public Library, with a jazz ensemble led by George Braith. "That was cool because we'd start at noon and go till like six or seven," Blackman recalled in *Down Beat.* "You were able to get like a couple of days of straight playing in just one day. It was fun, for me, and a good experience."

In October of 1984, Ted Curson presented Blackman's talent on his "Jazz Stars of the Future" showcase on WKCR-FM in New York. From there, she started promot-

For the Record . . .

Born November 18, 1959, in Yellow Springs, OH. *Education:* Attended University of Hartford, Hartford, CT, in the mid-1970s, and Berklee College of Music, Boston, MA, in the late 1970s.

Began playing New York jazz clubs, 1982; recorded her first compositions on Wallace Roney's *Verses;* signed with Muse Records, 1987; released debut album as a bandleader, 1988; recorded and performed with a variety of musicians, including Jackie McLean, Lenny Kravitz, and Jacky Terrasson.

Addresses: *Record company*—Muse Records, 106 West 71st St., New York, NY 10023.

ing her composing ability. Her first two compositions appeared on Wallace Roney's *Verses* album in 1987; each one reflected Blackman's early influence, Tony Williams. When Joe Fields, an executive at Muse Records, heard the recordings, he offered Blackman a recording contract to lead her own project.

Blackman released *Arcane,* her debut as a bandleader, in 1988 and launched her career as a composer, bandleader, and acclaimed jazz drummer. Her band included Roney on trumpet, Kenny Garrett on alto saxophone, Joe Henderson on tenor saxophone, Buster Williams and Clarence Seay on bass, and Larry Willis on piano. When she'd finished recording *Arcane,* she went on to write for the Jackie McLean Quartet. "He told me to think of his group as my group featuring him," Blackman told Cliff Preiss in the liner notes for *Arcane.* That same year, she played drums for saxophonist Joe Henderson at the Mt. Fuji Festival in Japan, which featured the original jazz giants of the Blue Note record label. "It was a drummer's dream," Blackman told *Musician.* "Art Blakey, Tony Williams, and Max Roach were all there."

Tribute to a Hero

Between her own albums, Blackman worked with Larry Coryell's quartet, bassist Brian Torff, pianist Stanley Cowell, and Don Pullen's trio. Then, in 1990, she went into the studio to work on her second album, *Code Red.* Around the same time, Blackman's friend and mentor, Art Blakey, died. She decided to record Thelonious Monk's "'Round Midnight" in tribute to Blakey. "[That song] was one of Art's favorite tunes to play on,"

Blackman revealed in the liner notes for *Code Red.* "So in my mind, I dedicated this entire session to Art Blakey. That was pretty emotional for me, because Art was like a father to me. Before he even knew my name, I was his 'red-headed friend.' Art always looked out for me, and so I really felt his passing." In addition to recording "'Round Midnight" in tribute to Blakey, Blackman included a drum solo titled "Something for Art" and dedicated the entire album to his memory.

Muse Records released *Code Red* in 1992. This time, Blackman's band consisted of Steve Coleman on alto saxophone, Kenny Barron on piano, Lonnie Plaxico on bass, and Roney on trumpet. Blackman also played drums on Roney's *Obsession* that same year. Later, Blackman formed a quartet to tour the United States and Europe for about six months. After the quartet of Jacky Terrasson (piano), Clarence Seay (bass), Antoine Roney (tenor and soprano saxophone), and Blackman finished the tour, they recorded *What's New* under Terrasson's name for Jazz aux Remparts. In September of 1992, the quartet began working on Blackman's next album.

The Rock and Roll Beat

In 1993, Blackman took another turn away from the career of a conventional jazz drummer. Her friend Antoine Roney introduced her to rock singer Lenny Kravitz, who happened to be looking for a drummer to tour with his band. Kravitz heard her play drums over the telephone and immediately flew her out to audition for the job. She spent most of the next year and a half playing on music videos and tours with Kravitz and established a firm hold on the rock genre. Blackman said in *Pulse!* that playing jazz and rock 'n' roll definitely requires two different mindsets. "[In rock], you're playing parts, not a groove. You're not quite as free to do as you see fit."

Blackman's work with Kravitz spread her name into new arenas of recognition and fame and set the stage for the release of her next album, *Telepathy,* in 1994. Her first recording with a working group, she named the album *Telepathy* because of the tight communication within the band. "I wanted to do a quartet record because of the amount of space you get with fewer players," she told Kevin Whitehead in *Telepathy's* liner notes. "It's intimate, but more dimensional than a piano trio. I'm really into this sound, and it was nice to play with a group that was a *group.* You can't help but have a better feel when the musicians know each other, are headed in the same direction, and have the same goals. You can make most everything work. You get chances to play a lot of colors, and really stretch your ideas."

Always expanding and exploring, Blackman continued to push the limits of her musical career, talent, and composition. She sees the drums as an instrument with a wide spectrum of potential. "The drums can be bombastic, a vehicle to really shake things up," she told Jim Macnie in *Musician*. "That's one of the things that initially attracted me to them. But they can be romantic and pretty and moody, as well. That range, and the exploration necessary to get it, is what I'm about these days."

Selected discography

Arcane, Muse, 1988.
Code Red, Muse, 1992.

(With Santi Debriano and Dave Fiuczynski) *Trio + Two,* Free Lance, 1992.
Telepathy, Muse, 1994.

Sources

Down Beat, December 1989; March 1992; April 1993; November 1994.
Life, November 1994.
Musician, December 1989; July 1994.
Pulse!, June 1994.
Vibe, September 1994; March 1995.

Additional information for this profile was obtained from Muse Records publicity materials, 1995.

—*Sonya Shelton*

Black Sheep

Rap duo

Black Sheep became part of music's hip-hop landscape in 1991 with the release of their debut album, *A Wolf in Sheep's Clothing,* whose single "Flavor of the Month" sealed the duo's popularity. At the time of their debut, Black Sheep were one of many New York City-based hip-hop and rap groups attracting national attention; Cypress Hill, Naughty by Nature, Brand Nubian, and L.O.N.S. had all paved the way for Black Sheep's appearance.

Black Sheep's members, Dres and Lawnge (pronounced "Long")—two friends raised in New York City's boroughs—met in 1983 in Sanford, North Carolina. Dres, who is black and Puerto Rican, was born Andres Titus and grew up in the Astoria housing projects in Queens. By the time he finished high school, he had served time in jail; this early brush with the criminal justice system convinced Dres not to glorify crime in his music.

Lawnge, whose real name is William McLean, was raised a few miles from Dres in Brooklyn. Citing early

Photograph by James Minchin, courtesy of Mercury Records

For the Record . . .

Members include **Dres** (born Andres Titus in Queens, NY) and **Lawnge** (name pronounced "long"; born William McLean in Brooklyn, NY)

Released debut album, *A Wolf in Sheep's Clothing,* Mercury/Polygram, 1991; embarked on U.S. promotional tour with Ill Al Skratch and the Legion, 1994.

Awards: Gold album award for *A Wolf in Sheep's Clothing.*

Addresses: *Record company*—Mercury Records, 825 Eighth Avenue, New York, NY 10019. *Management*—Shakim Compere, Flavor Unit Management, 155 Morgan St., Jersey City, NJ 07302.

musical influences, Lawnge told *The Source,* "When we were teenagers, like teenagers are now about rap, that's how we used to be.... We worshipped Slick Rick, Doug E. Fresh, [L.L. Cool J.], Run-DMC." Dres added, "Those [rap artists] were Gods."

Dres and Lawnge are both members of the black separatist movements Nation of Islam and Five Percent Nation of Islam, although Dres is also affiliated with the religious sect of Jehovah's Witnesses. "My father is a Jehovah's Witness," Dres revealed in *The Source,* "I listen to my father." Both also claim that seeing miserable living conditions for black people throughout the United States made them want to reach out to the black community and provide inspiration through their music. *Details* magazine described Black Sheep as having "their own mythology: street without gansta pretensions."

When Black Sheep's *Wolf in Sheep's Clothing* was released in 1991, it sold close to 900,000 copies and went gold. Lawnge played the role of the producer, and Dres performed as the rapper and primary lyricist. The album boasts two hit singles, "The Choice Is Yours" and "Flavor of the Month," and is marked by "broadsides," or skits, which are humorous parodies of songs and contain witty, thought-provoking lyrics.

A Wolf in Sheep's Clothing established Black Sheep as part of the unofficial Native Tongue Posse—honest hip-hop groups that are known for following their own beat without concern for public opinion or current trends; a concern for social issues; and the ability to shun commercialism for originality. Other Native Tongue groups include A Tribe Called Quest, De La Soul, the Jungle Brothers, Queen Latifah, and the Beatnuts.

According to *Billboard* magazine's Havelock Nelson, Black Sheep singles from the duo's first album remained popular as "recurrents" on rhythm and blues and Top 40 radio stations for three years after they were released and were not likely to fade from the minds of original listeners. "The Choice Is Yours" spent 16 weeks on the Billboard Hot R&B Singles chart and generated excitement and demand for a second album, which would take more than two and a half years to make.

Black Sheep's second album, *Non-Fiction,* was created and designed as a counterpart to *A Wolf in Sheep's Clothing.* Lawnge told Nelson that Black Sheep is showing new dimensions in its music and that the group's second album was built conceptually on the first. The titles *Non-Fiction* and *A Wolf in Sheep's Clothing* are metaphors for each album's lyrical content. Lawnge commented to Nelson, "*A Wolf in Sheep's Clothing* is not what it appears to be, and nonfiction [literature] exists because there's more for you to know."

By 1995 hip-hop and rap's popularity had extended far beyond New York City-based musicians and encompassed Los Angeles rappers as well as musicians from the South and Midwest. Black Sheep remarked in *The Source* that with their second album they wanted to avoid being branded as "just another one of those New York acts with the same ol' beats." In the single "North, South, East, West," for example, Black Sheep call for an end to regional competition in rap and hip-hop. *The Source* described 1994's *Non-Fiction* as "seventeen testosterone-filled odes to the crew they grew up with, set to jazzy hooks and classic New York beats. This time there is more freestyling, Lawnge on the [microphone], less ho rhymes [usually degrading lyrics about women] and, most surprising for this crew, no skits."

Non-Fiction reveals that Black Sheep has a deepening awareness of social issues pertaining to black Americans. "Freak Y'all" calls for courage and action with such lines as, "I wish my people had the heart to start a revolution." Another song, "Peace to the Niggas," warns against being impressed with or seduced by violent videos. Dres told *The Source* that Black Sheep's philosophy is "Elevation. We don't try to knock people over the heads. But we want them to open up their eyes."

Rolling Stone's Touré described Black Sheep's *Non-Fiction* as the album that "shows that Lawnge has matured as he laces tracks with interesting musical ideas like combining sharp percussion and high-note piano on 'Let's Get Cozy' or letting an antique-sounding piano dominate 'Summa the Time.'" *New York Newsday*'s Jon Young declared, "The easy-rolling groove of 'Without a Doubt' is guaranteed to jump-start the dullest party," while *Billboard*'s Nelson pointed out that Black Sheep "did not fall prey to the trend of making a record that intentionally sounds East Coast or West Coast."

The tone of Black Sheep's second album is grittier than their first and the lyrics are far more serious. Utilizing a technique different from their first album, Dres and Lawnge alternated roles when creating *Non-Fiction;* both artists rap on the album's tracks and both master the production duties.

Because it was considered credible to listeners on the street as well as palatable to radio audiences, "Without a Doubt" was chosen as *Non-Fiction*'s first single. A commercial promoting the album ran on music television stations and featured a bull walking the streets of Manhattan. The ad also depicts black sheep running noiselessly through a public library. To further spread the word about *Non-Fiction,* in October of 1994 the duo embarked on a U.S. promotional tour with fellow rap act Ill Al Skratch and the Legion and also performed in Toronto, Canada, and London, England.

The Source's Clarence Mohammed pointed out the importance of the message contained in Black Sheep's *Non-Fiction:* "In an age of modern day Negro Gangstas being praised for killing half their own people, *Non-Fiction* is definitely a missing component in the hip-hop world. [Black Sheep] present a perfect picture of black men coexisting in peace."

Selected discography

A Wolf in Sheep's Clothing (includes "Flavor of the Month" and "The Choice Is Yours"), Mercury/Polygram, 1991.
Non-Fiction (includes "Without a Doubt"), Mercury/Polygram, 1994.

Sources

Billboard, September 24, 1994.
Details, January 1995.
New York Newsday, January 8, 1995.
Rolling Stone, February 9, 1995.
The Source, January 1995; February 1995.
Vibe, March 1994; December 1994.

—B. Kimberly Taylor

Mary J. Blige

Singer, songwriter

In a 1993 article in *Stereo Review*, Ron Givens wrote, "Mary J. Blige has been called the inventor of New Jill Swing." When the vocalist came to the public's attention the previous year, she became a magnet for the kind of superlatives music critics love to create. In an interview for the *Source,* Adario Strange described his subject as a "delicate ghetto-princess songstress," "the flower of the ghetto," and "the real momma of hip-hop R&B." In his *Washington Post* review of Blige's second album, Geoffrey Himes called her "the premier soul diva of the hip-hop generation." But more than anything else, the music media has crowned her the Queen of Hip Hop Soul.

Part of the fuel for Blige's rocket to hip-hop stardom was her "street cred." Her youth in one of New York's poorer neighborhoods—the Slowbam Projects in Yonkers, where she was born on November 1 in the early 1970s—provided her with the "credentials" demanded by audiences who also grew up on city streets. Blige described the setting for *Essence's* Deborah Gregory, recalling that there "was always some shit going on. Every day I would be getting into fights over whatever. You always had to prove yourself to keep from getting robbed or jumped. Growing up in the projects is like living in a barrel of crabs. If you try to get out, one of the other crabs tries to pull you down." The family, including Blige's older sister and two younger brothers, subsisted on her mother Cora's earnings as a nurse after her father left the family in the mid-1970s. "My mother made me strong," Blige told Strange. "Watching my mother struggle to raise us and feed us made me want to be a stronger woman."

Early Musical Influences

Blige's environment also provided the sound and encouragement that first shaped her musical identity. A professional jazz musician, her father left his mark on Blige's ability to harmonize during the brief time he was present. Block parties in the Bronx taught her the rhythms and sampling styles created by the early hip-hop deejays. At home, her mother played a steady stream of R&B, soul, and funk, including Sam Cooke, Aretha Franklin, Stevie Wonder, Chaka Khan, and Gladys Knight. Blige sang regularly with her mother and sisters in the choir at the House of Prayer Pentecostal Church, honing vocal skills and imbibing gospel. "We used to go to church all night. Everybody would be real good to us," Blige told Emil Wilbekin in a *Vibe* interview. She expanded on the experience for *Essence's* Gregory, remembering that she "felt so much better going to church every Sunday, just being there, testifying and just being kids. It was *a lot* of fun." By the time Blige was a teenager, she had solo spots in the choir and she

For the Record . . .

Born Mary Jane Blige, November 1, c. 1971, in Yonkers, NY; daughter of Cora (a nurse) and a jazz musician.

Sang with mother and sister in House of Prayer Pentecostal Church choir; appeared in local and school talent shows; worked various part-time jobs in late teens. Signed by Uptown Records and released debut album, *What's the 411?,* 1992.

Awards: Soul Train Music Award, 1993; New York Music Award; National Association for the Advancement of Colored People (NAACP) Image Award; double-platinum album award for *What's the 411?*

Addresses: *Record company*—Uptown Records, 729 Seventh Avenue, 12th Floor, New York, NY 10019.

made the rounds of local talent shows. Before she dropped out of school in the eleventh grade, around 1987, she also participated in shows there.

While she enjoyed singing, Blige didn't expect to make her living at it and, like most teenagers in her position, helped bring in money with several part-time jobs. Her first "demo" tape was, in fact, just a karaoke style recording made one night at a mall to entertain friends when she was 17. Before too long, however, the cover of Anita Baker's "Rapture" found its way to Andre Harrell, an executive with Uptown Records: Blige's mother gave it to her boyfriend, who gave it to a friend, who gave it to R&B vocalist Jeff Redd. Redd passed it on, enthusiastically, to Harrell. On Harrell's initiative, Blige was brought onto Uptown's growing roster of young R&B talents. Sean "Puffy" Combs became the young singer's mentor when the company began preparing her album.

In 1992 *What's the 411?* introduced Blige's voice to audiences with a growing interest in the New Jack Swing take on R&B. The album not only fit neatly into that R&B revival, but also began to define it. Driven primarily by the single "Real Love," *411* reached double-platinum status after it sold over two million copies in a short time. Its appeal crossed over from the R&B charts and entered the Top Ten on *Billboard's* pop chart. When Havelock Nelson gave the album an "A" in his *Entertainment Weekly* review in August of 1992, he began with the news everyone would soon know—that Blige was "the first diva to deliver frisky, fly-girl funk" and that she "conquers everything she tackles." He concluded that the album was "one of the most accomplished fusions of soul values and hip-hop to date."

Nelson described, in particular, how Blige took the then male-defined domain of New Jack Swing and remade it in her own image, kicking off the rage for New Jill. She became known as the initiator of a new female incarnation of hip-hop. "Mary has become an icon of today's young Black nation," wrote the *Source's* Strange, "representing the feminine yet strong-willed woman that many young girls hope to be, and the sexy yet not too cute for a ruffneck girlfriend that many brothers from the hood long for." In April of 1993, *Rolling Stone* reviewer Steve Hochman noted that Blige had "become the role model for the new breed of strong hip-hop women." Strange dubbed her the "first true feminine hero of R&B lovin' ghetto residents." The singer commented on the phenomenon herself, telling Hochman, "I think I'm creating a style for women—a more feminine version of the way a lot of hip-hop guys dress now." As Strange noted, the impact of *411* showed up soon on other performers, as "baseball caps and boots suddenly became in vogue for female singers" and "divas everywhere demanded hip-hop tracks to back up their cubic zirconian efforts."

Hip-hop Role Model Stumbled

The applause was marred, however, by some bad publicity. It seemed to begin at the 1993 Soul Train Music Awards, where Blige accepted her award not in the expected glittering evening gown, but in standard street gear: jeans and a shirt. The public expressed its disapproval instantly: as the *Source's* Strange reported, "radio stations everywhere were flooded with phone calls from disgruntled fans." That incident occurred in the midst of other, less public, reports of bad behavior. Wilbekin recounted the history for *Vibe,* recalling that the "stories of tardiness, cancellations, and general lack of professionalism are endless. Mary was eight hours late to one magazine photo shoot, and threw a fit and walked out of at least one more. She conducted interviews where she did as much drinking as talking and acted like a zombie on national television. Then there was the concert in London where she was so out of it the crowd booed her off the stage."

It was only after the release of her second album that Blige was able to reflect on what might have fed her behavior at the time. She speculated that the attention had disconcerted her—that she hadn't been prepared, socially or professionally, for the kind of intense spotlight music celebrity creates. Harrell suggested to Wilbekin in *Vibe* that "the whole experience was overwhelming for her. She wasn't ready to be put under the microscope in that fashion." Friend and manager Steve Lucas told Gregory that "Mary got an undeserved bad rap because of what was going on around her—the confusion, the lack of organization. When you communicate honestly with Mary, there aren't *any* problems. She's willing to cooperate and do whatever it takes to be successful. She's basically a very sweet, humble person." The difficulty of the situation was exacerbated, Blige admitted to *Rolling Stone's* Hochman, by her basic shyness. "I'm just not a very open person," she told him. "The most open I am is when I sing. I've always been kind of shy." On a more concrete note, she also felt there were problems with her management, which she changed before recording the second album. Combs moved out of Uptown and in 1993 started his own company, Bad Boy Entertainment, where Blige took her management business while still recording with Uptown.

Blige also pursued practical measures to prepare herself for the fresh onslaught of publicity that would accompany the second album: she enrolled with a public relations firm, Double XXposure, that trained artists to deal with the demands of public reputation. She worked extensively with the company's president, Angelo Ellerbee, whom she later credited with not just polishing her interview style, but changing her life more broadly. She told Wilbekin in *Vibe* that Ellerbee "gave me a totally new kind of life. There was a time when I wouldn't read nothin'," but Ellerbee sparked her interest in books her for the first time, introducing her, for example, to a novel by Zora Neale Hurston called *Their Eyes Were Watching God.*

Redefined with *My Life*

When Uptown released *My Life* in 1994, it marked many changes for Blige, including the personal refining that turned around her public image. The vocalist also contributed lyrics for most of the songs; she had been writing before the debut album, but had little confidence in her skill as a lyricist. The sound of the music shifted also, due in part to the use of live horns and strings in place of the standard sampling, moving Blige deeper into the fusion of hip-hop and soul. Ultimately, all of the changes added up successfully for Blige and her producers: *My Life* debuted in December in the top position on *Billboard's* R&B album chart.

Geoffrey Himes, among others, paid particular tribute to Blige's new take on R&B; "Blige may be a gospel-trained siren like older soul divas," he remarked in the *Washington Times,* "but these arrangements sound like no record ever made by Aretha Franklin, Diana Ross or Patti LaBelle. All the gooey orchestrations that have sugarcoated romantic crooners from Dinah Washington to Anita Baker are gone, leaving a skeletal rhythm track and a spectacular voice freed from all superfluous sentiment and ornamentation." J.D. Considine, writing for Baltimore's *Evening Sun,* greeted the album by noting that "Blige has more than surpassed expectations" and argued that as "good as the grooves are, it's her vocal work that ultimately drives these songs." Similarly, Himes declared her a "major voice of her generation."

One note sounded very consistently from the first album to the second, and that was Blige's renown for being "real." As Combs explained to Strange in the *Source,* Blige "represents all the honeys in the urban communities in Detroit, Harlem, Chicago and Los Angeles that's growing up and going through regular every day things that are a part of hip-hop culture. This album shows the real of just how strong Black women have become."

Selected discography

What's the 411? (includes "Real Love"), Uptown/MCA, 1992.
What's the 411? Remix, Uptown/MCA, 1993.
My Life, Uptown/MCA, 1994.

Sources

Atlanta Journal, November 29, 1994.
Billboard, January 16, 1993.
Boston Globe, December 15, 1994.
Entertainment Weekly, August 7, 1992; November 20, 1992; December 3, 1993; November 25, 1994.
Essence, March 1995.
Evening Sun (Baltimore, MD), December 2, 1994.
People, December 5, 1994.
Rolling Stone, April 15, 1993.
Source, January 1995.
Stereo Review, April 1993.
Vibe, February 1995.
Washington Post, November 27, 1994.

Additional information for this profile was obtained from Uptown Records publicity materials.

—*Ondine E. Le Blanc*

Blues Traveler

Rock band

Following in the footsteps of the legendary cult band Grateful Dead's dedicated touring schedule, Blues Traveler has lived up to its name. More than its recorded music, touring stints that last months at a time have earned the rock band notoriety. The group started out by playing high school parties, and its members insist they perform better onstage than in the recording studio. Blues Traveler, in fact, was able to maintain a loyal fan base throughout the late 1980s and early 1990s, despite their virtual nonexistence on the music charts. All of that changed in 1995 when the LP *four* produced a Top 40 single and catapulted the band into mainstream success.

Blues Traveler's lead singer, John Popper, spent most of his youth in Stamford, Connecticut, before moving to Princeton, New Jersey, when he was 15 years old. While attending high school, Popper discovered the harmonica and developed a reputation around Princeton High School as "that harmonica guy." He decided to play the instrument in the Princeton High studio band where he met London-born drummer Brendan Hill.

Courtesy of A&M Records

For the Record . . .

Members include **Brendan Hill,** drums; **Chan Kinchla,** guitar; **John Popper,** vocals and harmonica; and **Bobby Sheehan,** bass.

Group formed by Popper and Hill as the Blues Band, 1983; moved to New York and changed name to Blues Traveler, 1987; signed contract with A&M Records, 1989, and released self-titled debut album, 1990; founded H.O.R.D.E. (Horizons of Rock Developing Everywhere) music festival, 1992.

Awards: Platinum album award for *four.*

Addresses: *Record company*—A&M Records, 1416 N. La Brea Ave., Hollywood, CA 90028.

In 1983 Popper and Hill put together the Blues Band. They played high school parties for money, sparking the attention of many of their schoolmates. Two years later, a Princeton High football, lacrosse, and guitar player named Chan Kinchla decided to jam with his classmates in the Blues Band. It turned into a marathon three-hour collaboration that became known as the "black cat jam." The reference to the animal came about because a black cat wandered up after the band finished; Popper explained in *Rolling Stone* that the cat seemed "like it was going 'whoa' with us. Whenever we have trouble, a big event, a crisis of faith, or some milestone, there is a black cat there. This is the truth."

In 1987, two years after the black cat jam, the trio met up with another Princeton High schoolmate, bassist Bobby Sheehan, who finalized the line-up of the Blues Band. When the band members graduated from high school, they moved to New York City to gain more exposure. Popper, Hill, and Sheehan enrolled in New York's New School to study jazz. The band was soon performing in area clubs under the name Blues Traveler.

Shortly after they started playing clubs, Blues Traveler grabbed the attention of late concert promoter Bill Graham, who immediately decided to become the band's manager. (Graham's son David would eventually take over.) With Bill Graham's contacts and support, Blues Traveler signed a contract with A&M Records in 1989. By that time, they had performed live throughout the region and played 16 to 20 shows per month.

Blues Traveler had brought their own style of blues and 1960s rock-influenced music to the stage for several years, and in 1990 the band released their self-titled debut album. Describing Blues Traveler's original brand of rock to *Rolling Stone's* Elysa Gardner, Popper said, "If [blues musician] Muddy Waters was a white guy living in the suburbs in the late '80s, he'd sound a lot like us."

The following year, Jim Gaines produced the band's second album, *Travelers & Thieves.* Their continuous live shows had resulted in many comparisons to both the Grateful Dead and the Allman Brothers Band. After the release of *Travelers & Thieves,* the comparisons increased with the guest appearance of Gregg Allman on keyboards and backing vocals on the song "Mountain Cry."

Blues Traveler had accomplished moderate record sales with very little promotion, mostly due to their relentless touring. But the band insisted that their style of music just worked better on the stage. "The best term for [the Blues Traveler sound] I've heard is 'neo-retro,'" commented guitarist Kinchla in *Guitar Player.* "A lot of music has moved away from that feel of live interaction, so we're getting back to music the audience can feel it's part of." Popper concurred, pointing out in *Billboard,* "We've always been predominantly a live band. Our studio albums are nice tries, but the live shows just totally blow them away."

Commitment to live performance led Popper to organize the first annual H.O.R.D.E. (Horizons of Rock Developing Everywhere) festival. The inaugural line-up included Blues Traveler's high school friends the Spin Doctors, along with Phish, Widespread Panic, and Col. Bruce Hampton and the Aquarium Rescue Unit.

Blues Traveler's whirlwind of recording and touring came to a temporary halt in 1992 after an unfortunate accident. While driving his motorcycle in Bogalusa, Louisiana, Popper was hit by a car. He had several broken limbs and was briefly confined to a wheelchair. At the time of the accident, the rest of the band was in the Studio in the Country laying down tracks for the instrumental song "Manhattan Bridge." Blues Traveler used the period after the accident to spend more time recording the LP *Save His Soul,* produced by Steve Thompson and Mike Barbiero. Released in 1993, the album included some experimentation for the band, including a song called "Trina Magna," which featured a New Orleans gospel trio layered with a New York gospel choir.

During the summer of 1993, Blues Traveler organized another H.O.R.D.E. festival. This time, the bill included Big Head Todd and the Monsters and the Samples, along with the returning Widespread Panic and Col. Bruce Hampton and the Aquarium Rescue Unit. By this time, Blues Traveler had added another item to their list of Grateful Dead comparisons. The Grateful Dead have long been known to have fans, or "Dead Heads," follow them from show to show. Blues Traveler also found van loads of fans hot on their trail; the group's touring cavalcade came to be referred to as "Fellow Travelers."

Blues Traveler continued to release their "souvenir" albums; their fourth LP, released in 1994, was aptly titled *four*. Once again produced by Steve Thompson and Mike Barbiero, *four* arrived in stores with a choice of two covers: one depicted the right side of the band's logo— a cat smoking a cigarette—while the other showed the left side of the cat with no cigarette.

Unlike with Blues Traveler's previous albums, sold solely from the promotion of the band's tours, A&M Records decided to add to their marketing efforts to the release of *four*. The company released the singles "Hook" and "Run-around" to get the attention of radio stations and expand recognition for the band. Top 40 radio airplay earned Blues Traveler increased popularity and spurred sales of *four*. "Run-around" even broke into the Top 40 of the *Billboard* Hot 100 Singles chart in May of 1995. Jim Glass, senior vice president of marketing at A&M, was quoted in *Billboard* as saying, "We have always believed that this band would someday have tremendous success. It was just a matter of patience and timing."

The members of Blues Travelers, however, continued to follow the nomadic lifestyle of the road, playing show after show to their "Fellow Travelers." In the face of their newfound mainstream stardom, the band was excited and felt optimistic that they would not alienate their longtime cult fan base. Guitarist Chan Kinchla ex-

pressed the band's views on fame in *Billboard,* "If it had happened sooner, I'm afraid that it would have changed us too drastically as people or shifted our musical focus. We are more grown-up now and can handle the pressures and demands that come with it."

Selected discography

On A&M Records

Blues Traveler, 1990.
Travelers & Thieves, 1991.
Save His Soul, 1993.
four (includes "Hook" and "Run-around"), 1994.

Sources

Billboard, June 30, 1990; January 25, 1992; August 1, 1992; April 10, 1993; May 8, 1993; August 20, 1994; October 1, 1994; May 20, 1995.
Entertainment Weekly, April 16, 1993; September 30, 1994; December 9, 1994.
Guitar Player, March 1992; August 1993.
Musician, March 1993.
New York Times, July 14, 1992.
Rolling Stone, January 23, 1992; April 16, 1992; May 28, 1992; June 24, 1993.
Stereo Review, July 1993; January 1995.

Additional information for this profile was obtained from the on-line *All-Music Guide,* Matrix Software, 1994.

—*Thaddeus Wawro*

Boyz II Men

Rhythm and blues group

Courtesy of Motown Records

Boyz II Men, a Philadelphia-based rhythm and blues quartet, have literally gone from singing together in a bathroom to performing sold-out concerts in the United States' largest venues. The group's four members—Nate Morris, Michael McCary, Shawn Stockman, and Wanya Morris—experienced an almost overnight success as their debut album went triple platinum in sales and critics of all ages and races heaped praises upon their work. Since the release of the album *Cooleyhighharmony* in 1991 and its follow-up, *II,* in 1994, Boyz II Men have established themselves as innovators who combine the standard elements of R&B with new, hip-hop stylings, all the while relishing old-fashioned romantic love as a theme.

From complete unknowns at the beginning of the 1990s, the members of Boyz II Men have leaped into the limelight to become fashion and music trendsetters. The term "doo-hop" has been coined to describe their sound, the "Alex Vanderpoolera" tag to describe their upscale attire. More importantly, the group has been credited with resuscitating the flagging fortunes of Motown Records, long considered the premier label for black pop artists. Asked about the group's secret for success, Stockman told Knight-Ridder: "Our music makes you feel good. We know life isn't all peaches-and-cream, but sometimes you just want to relax and forget about all that."

"The success of Boyz II Men is no fluke," wrote Patricia Smith of the *Akron Beacon Journal.* "It's odd, it's crazy, it's hard to believe, it's a one-in-a-million shot, but it's no fluke. Four determined young men just happened to be in the right place at the right time—in front of the right person." Good luck certainly played a part in the Boyz II Men saga, but no one leaps to national prominence these days without careful preparation. In the case of Boyz II Men, that preparation included training in classical music, a thorough knowledge of modern black American music, and long hours dedicated to perfecting vocal talents.

Four Nerds from Philly

The members of Boyz II Men have little to say about their childhoods, except to emphasize that their clean-cut image reflects their true attitudes about life. "People call us nerds and stuff," Nate Morris admitted in *Entertainment Weekly.* "[But] the good thing about that is, they're knocking us for what we *are,* not for a facade." All four of the singers were born and raised in Philadelphia, but each one comes from a distinct neighborhood. Nate Morris grew up in South Philadelphia. He is not related to Wanya (pronounced wan-YAY) Morris, who grew up in North Philadelphia. McCary lived in the

Logan section of the city, and Stockman grew up in Southwest Philadelphia. The four did not know each other as children.

Just about the only formative experience the singers will talk about is their musical influences. The two most important were the so-called "Motown Sound" and the street-corner harmonizing that is a staple of Philadelphia neighborhoods. "All we used to grow up on was Motown—Stevie Wonder, Diana Ross, the Temptations," Stockman pointed out in the *Charlotte Observer.* "Just to be on a label with artists like that is definitely an honor."

In the *Philadelphia Daily News,* Stockman gave his home town credit for fostering his and his friends' ambitions. "One of the things we want is to bring back that Philly sound," he said. "In the past, there was a time when Philadelphia was nonexistent as far as the music industry was concerned. Nothing was happening. We saw that Philly has all this talent. We were around it and we had a little something going on, so we said, 'Let's bring back that Philly sound and try to put Philly back on the music industry map.'"

Boyz II Men began experimenting with the "Philly sound"—a cappella R&B harmonies—as students at Philadelphia's prestigious High School for the Performing Arts. The four members, along with a fifth friend, Marc Nelson, would meet between classes and after school in the building's bathrooms to sing together. The bathroom was chosen because it had the best acoustics. Once they had worked out a song, the Boyz might try it on an audience at a favorite teen hangout in Philadelphia, the Gallery in Center City. The group name Boyz II Men was taken from a New Edition song title and was first coined in 1985 by Nate Morris. All of the members admitted a great respect for New Edition and the Christian group Take 6, prominent R&B vocal acts that had achieved success in the late 1980s.

Classy Dress Matched Vocal Stylings

At the Philadelphia High School for the Performing Arts, the members of Boyz II Men studied classical music and vocal arts. They performed in the school's various chorus groups as well as in their private quartet. Although deeply committed to music, the four students pursued their high school diplomas with little time spent looking toward the future. "We just did talent shows in the Philly area, sometimes in Delaware and New Jersey," Stockman told the *Akron Beacon Journal.* "But we really didn't take it seriously. We had our dreams, but we didn't make our minds up about music as a career until we met Michael Bivins."

Bivins was a singer with both New Edition and its spin-off group, Bell Biv DeVoe. He came to Philadelphia in 1989 for a concert at the Civic Center. Mustering their courage, the members of Boyz II Men found their way backstage after the concert to ask Bivins how to pursue a recording contract. Bivins, who was just beginning to manage other performers, asked to hear them sing, and they auditioned on the spot. Impressed, the star gave the boys his phone number and promised to keep in touch. Some weeks later he invited the group to New York City and signed on as their manager. "I was curious where they stood as far as stage presence," Bivins told *Rolling Stone.* "I wasn't seeing the complete package. But I could see that they had the most important piece, which a lot of groups were missing at the time—the vocals."

Bivins's own contributions to the evolution of Boyz II Men was substantial. He matched their street-corner vocal dynamics with jeep beats and hip-hop swing, and he chose their matching super-preppy sweater-and-tie look, basing it on the character Alex Vanderpool from his favorite soap opera, *All My Children.* The members of Boyz II Men were perplexed at the fashion statement, but they soon came to accept and enjoy wearing the upscale clothing. "We weren't really into it at first,"

Stockman told *Spin* magazine. "But once we started wearing the stuff and learning how to put it together, it started to feel good."

After two and a half months of work with Bivins, Boyz II Men went into the recording studio. "Songs just came into our heads, pop, pop, pop," Stockman told the *Akron Beacon Journal*. "We had material from way back, and it felt good to us, so we did it. We wrote seven out of eight songs on the album. When we needed up-tempo, they handed us cassettes with the beats and we wrote the words.... We were ready." Tracks from the budding *Cooleyhighharmony* attracted the attention of Motown Records executives, who signed a contract with the group.

> "We said, 'Let's bring back that Philly sound and try to put Philly back on the music industry map.'"
> —Shawn Stockman

The first Boyz II Men single, "Motownphilly," was released in 1991. According to *Rolling Stone* contributor Alan Light, the song held appeal for "rap fans," but was also "smooth enough for R&B radio and MTV." The song made it into the Billboard Top 20, as did the follow-up single "It's So Hard to Say Goodbye to Yesterday." The song that made the group famous, though, was the smash hit "End of the Road," which was featured in the Eddie Murphy movie *Boomerang*. "End of the Road" spent 13 weeks in the top position on the Billboard Hot 100 chart, breaking a record set by Elvis Presley 30 years ago. In the meantime, *Cooleyhighharmony* was on its way to selling more than 7 million copies. Needless to say, Motown Records top executives were thrilled with their new stars.

Thrilled, too, were music critics who liked Boyz II Men's sound *and* substance. "The vocal quartet Boyz II Men is living, singing proof that the love song—like love itself—will never really disappear," wrote Christopher John Farley in *Time*. "Other performers may grab the headlines and spark debates on the op-ed pages, but by going against the critical tide and recording harmonious ballads, Boyz II Men has won an enormous following.... [They send] a message to the rest of the record industry that nice guys can finish first." *Vibe* music critic James Hunter called the group's work "the strongest pure black pop—not way hip hop, but not rote or old-fashioned, either—anyone's heard in years. Here is *truly contemporary* black music—not Detroit reminiscence, not the new black folk, not new jack city, but something that completely belongs to itself."

As sales of *Cooleyhighharmony* passed everyone's expectations—and Boyz II Men turned to a follow-up album—Motown extended the young group a new contract, estimated to be worth $30 million. The group joined a 1992 tour as the opening act for rap singer M.C. Hammer, and their vast popularity more or less forced them to leave their Philadelphia neighborhoods in favor of homes in the suburbs. Even in the midst of all this happy success, however, tragedy struck. In May of 1992, the group's road manager, Khalil Roundtree, was shot and killed at the Guest Quarters Suite Hotel in Chicago, apparently by robbers. Roundtree's assistant, Qadree El-Amin, was also wounded in the attack. Stunned by the loss of their friend, Boyz II Men quit touring for two weeks and went home to Philadelphia.

"Khalil was more than just a road manager to us," Stockman told Knight-Ridder. "He was a mother figure, father figure, technician, mechanic, scout. He was everything to us. He was like our dad. He did so much, we didn't have to think. All we did was sing, and dance. Which is one of the reasons why we think that he was taken away from us. It was like the Lord's way of saying that we had to learn a lot of things on our own. We wish he was still here, but we realize why—or we think we know why—he was taken away. Because Khalil's death changed us as people. We had to be more responsible for our actions. And we're better people now. We're a lot wiser, and a lot smarter, and a lot more aware of our surroundings."

Aspired to Achieve Long-Lasting Fame

Teenagers when they began their swift rise to fame, the members of Boyz II Men have indeed grown older and wiser after their years at the top of the music charts. "People have some misconceptions about this business," Stockman told Knight-Ridder. "It is a business. It's hard work. And when you get some success, people want more of your time." That time is worth money, however. With the Motown Records contract, product endorsements, a possible clothing line, and major concert appearances, each one of the Boyz II Men quartet can realistically expect to earn several million dollars per year. Stockman told *Vibe* that, with a second album in the Billboard Top Ten and a tour in preparation, Boyz II Men are only beginning to realize their ambitions. "We have a long way to go as far as achieving the kind of success we want," he said. "You know, like the Beatles—that kind of longevity. That's what we're trying to establish."

In the midst of a surge in popularity of the hard sounds of some alternative rock music songs and of gangsta rap, Boyz II Men have indeed established their longevity with time-tested mainstream pop offerings. Songs like "I'll Make Love to You" from their second LP, *II,* ensured that the group would hold a place in pop music's memory. Along with Whitney Houston's "I Will Always Love You," it became the longest-running Number One single of all time.

Fast friends who have maintained their ties to the Philadelphia area, the four Boyz II Men members describe themselves as clean-living Christians who pray together, respect women, and attribute their success to their parents and their high school. Nate Morris told the *Philadelphia Daily News* that he and the other group members are too busy even to revel in their success. Winners of multiple Grammy awards, Image awards from the National Association for the Advancement of Colored People (NAACP), and American Music awards, they are simply working hard, almost numb to the impact they've made on pop music. "When it hits us, trust me, it will hit us," Morris said. "It probably will come at a weird time. You'll be sitting around, eating a sandwich in your home or something, and you'll look on your mantlepiece and see a Grammy up there and say, 'Wow!' You actually get the time to sit down and think for a while."

Stockman told the *Philadelphia Daily News:* "Everything is like a blur. We don't really have enough time to appreciate the fruits of our labor. But we don't want to slouch because the moment you relax, there's another group coming right behind you who is just as good. We have to keep on our toes. There's always room for improvement. That's why we're always singing."

Selected discography

Cooleyhighharmony, Motown, 1991.
Christmas Interpretations, Motown, 1993.
II, Motown, 1994.

Sources

Akron Beacon Journal, January 31, 1992.
Charlotte Observer, October 21, 1991.
Entertainment Weekly, August 20, 1993; September 16, 1994.
Knight-Ridder wire reports, January 6, 1992; August 29, 1994.
Philadelphia Daily News, February 26, 1992; April 1, 1992;
    August 26, 1994; September 13, 1994.
Philadelphia Inquirer, September 6, 1992.
Pulse!, December 1993.
Rolling Stone, March 5, 1992; July 9-23, 1992.
Spin, July 1992.
Time, September 5, 1994.
Vibe, November 1993; October 1994; March 1995.

Additional information for this profile was provided by Motown Records publicity materials, 1995.

—*Anne Janette Johnson*

Benjamin Britten

Composer, conductor, pianist

AP/Wide World Photos

Composer, conductor, and pianist Benjamin Britten was a giant of mid-twentieth-century British music. The creator of *War Requiem,* one of the most performed pieces of classical music, he wrote an important body of songs for amateurs and, perhaps most importantly, revived modern British opera. Britten's operas dealt with themes of compassion, individualism, and threatened innocence. He composed music "in a style noted for its melodic thrust, leanness, and characteristic sound," according to the *Christian Science Monitor.* Although casual listeners might identify his dissonant passages as modern, the *New York Times* observed that he "never embraced the more controversial musical fashions of his time."

The slim, curly-haired Britten was, according to *Publishers Weekly,* "at once gentle and cruel, shy and ruthless, sexually timid and fiercely loving, a good friend and a severe enemy." Born Edward Benjamin Britten on November 22, 1913, in Lowestoft, England, he learned piano early and composed prolifically beginning at the age of five. When his parents brought him to England's Norwich Festival in 1924, he impressed composer Frank Bridge, who took him on as a pupil and encouraged him to look beyond Great Britain's borders to such continental composers as Béla Bartok and Arnold Schoenberg.

In the early 1930s Britten studied at the Royal College of Music. In 1935 he was hired by the British General Post Office to provide music for a series of documentary films. According to *The New Grove Dictionary of Opera,* he had to satisfy the "highly particularized yet diverse demands" of film and in doing so he cultivated "the expressive immediacy and technical aptitude that were to distinguish his operatic work."

On the film set, Britten also met poet W. H. Auden, who was writing scripts. Britten and Auden became friends and decided to collaborate outside the studio. They launched into social and political commentary with the 1936 song cycle *Our Hunting Fathers,* and in 1939 they collaborated on the choral work *Ballad of Heroes.*

With the advent of World War II, Britten and a companion, tenor Peter Pears, traveled to Brooklyn, New York. Outside his native country, Britten freed himself from his musical inhibitions. He used text by the French poet Rimbaud to create the song cycle *Les Illuminations,* which the *Washington Post* called "one of his finest." He also set the sonnets of sixteenth-century Italian artist Michelangelo to music and in 1941 collaborated with librettist Auden on the opera *Paul Bunyan.*

After two years in the United States Britten began to miss his native country and in 1941 decided to go home. "I had become without roots," he recalled in his acceptance speech for his 1964 Aspen Award, as quoted in the *Washington Post,* "and when I got back to England ... I was ready to put them down." During the remainder of the war, Britten wrote music for British Broadcasting Corporation (BBC) broadcasts, gave concerts, and refined his command of setting British verse to music.

With the end of the war, Britten's career took off. On June 7, 1945, his opera *Peter Grimes* debuted at the Sadler's Wells Theater. *Grimes* was an immediate success, and it established Britten as a well-received music dramatist. Many critics were impressed by Britten but some pointed out his "dazzling technical facility [and dismissed] him as a clever but superficial artist," noted the *New York Times.*

Britten produced many compositions through the late 1940s. He set poet John Donne's sonnets to music and wrote a *Young Person's Guide to the Orchestra,* which the *Washington Post* called "witty," "ingenious," and "one of the most popular orchestral compositions of the 20th century." Britten also penned the *St. Nicholas* contata and produced his *Spring Symphony.*

Britten's operatic output, however, was limited by Great Britain's lack of support for that art form. His 1946 *Rape of Lucretia* and 1947 comedy *Albert Herring* had to be performed in concert with a small ensemble of singers.

To remedy this situation and to promote modern British opera, Britten helped form the English Opera Group. In 1948 he and Pears moved from London back to his native region of East Anglia, where they founded the Aldeburgh Festival. The English Opera Group in effect became the house opera company at Aldeburgh, and Britten devoted much of the remainder of his life to writing music for Aldeburgh.

Throughout the 1950s Britten "was inspired by the art and voice of the remarkable English tenor, Peter Pears," according to the *Washington Post.* Concentrating on opera in 1951, Britten wrote *Billy Budd* for the Festival of Britain. When Elizabeth II was crowned in 1953, he presented *Gloriana,* a largely unsuccessful study of Queen Elizabeth I. In 1954 he offered the chamber opera *The Turn of the Screw* at the Venice Biennale and in 1960 created an operatic score for William Shakespeare's *A Midsummer Night's Dream.*

On May 30, 1962, Britten debuted his *War Requiem* at the consecration of the new Coventry Cathedral. The church had been bombed out during World War II and Britten conceived the *Requiem* as a great prayer for peace. For his text, he chose a mixture of the Latin Mass for the Dead and the poems of Wilfred Owen, a young English soldier who had been killed in World War I. The *Requiem* was an instant success with the British public and its appearance marked a second peak in Britten's public esteem.

Also in the early 1960s, Britten established a fruitful partnership with Russian cellist Mistislav Rostropovich. The two produced a cello symphony in 1963 and in 1965 completed a song cycle, *The Poet's Echo,* inspired by a group of poems by Russian writer Aleksandr Pushkin. Turning in another direction toward the end of the decade, Britten wrote the quasi-operatic parables *Curlew River, The Burning Fiery Furnace,* and *The Prodigal Son,* which grew out of his "dual fascination with Japanese classic drama and the rituals of medieval Christianity," according to the *New York Times.*

With the opening of a new larger concert hall at Aldeburgh in 1967, Britten's prowess as a conductor was further recognized. Despite his lack of enthusiasm about conducting, he "consistently touched an intangible" when leading orchestras, as noted in the *Christian Science Monitor.* Britten's extensive library of recordings, of both his own works and works by composers Elgar, Bach, Schubert, and Schumann, was called "one of the great treasuries of contemporary music" by *the Washington Post.*

Britten remained active into the early 1970s, producing *Owen Wingrave,* an opera for television, and *Death in*

Venice, the only opera he wrote expressly for Aldeburgh. In 1973 he underwent extensive open heart surgery and never fully recovered. He died at his home in Aldeburgh on December 4, 1976.

Selected compositions

Simple Symphony for Strings, 1934.

(With W. H. Auden) *Our Hunting Fathers,* 1936.

Variations on a Theme by Frank Bridge (string orchestra), 1937.

Love from a Stranger (film score), 1937.

Concerto in D for Piano and Orchestra, 1938.

Les Illuminations (songs for soprano and strings), 1939.

(With W. H. Auden) *Ballad of Heroes,* 1939.

Sinfonia da Requiem for Orchestra, 1941.

Hymn to St. Cecilia (choral work; text by W. H. Auden), 1942.

Prelude and Fugue for 18 Strings, 1943.

Rejoice in the Lamb (cantata), 1943.

Serenade for Tenor, Horn and Strings, 1943.

The Holy Sonnets of John Donne (song cycle for tenor and piano), 1945.

Peter Grimes (opera), 1945.

Young Person's Guide to the Orchestra, 1946.

The Rape of Lucretia (opera), 1946.

Albert Herring (opera), 1947.

Missa Brevis in D, 1950.

Metamorphoses (oboe), 1951.

Gloriana (opera), 1953.

The Turn of the Screw (opera), 1954.

War Requiem (choirs, orchestra, chamber orchestra, and organ), 1962.

Symphony for Cello and Orchestra, 1963.

Songs and Proverbs of William Blake (songs for baritone and piano), 1965.

Tit for Tat (songs based on the poems of Walter de la Mare), 1968.

Owen Wingrave (television opera), 1970.

Death in Venice (opera), 1973.

Lachrymae (viola and piano), 1976.

Sources

Books

Carpenter, Humphrey, *Benjamin Britten: A Biography,* Scribners, 1993.

Sadie, Stanley, editor, *The New Grove Dictionary of Opera,* Macmillan, 1980.

Periodicals

Christian Science Monitor, December 6, 1976.

High Fidelity, September 1977.

New York Times, December 5, 1976.

Publishers Weekly, May 10, 1993.

Village Voice, December 20, 1976.

Washington Post, December 5, 1976.

—*Jordan Wankoff*

Junior Brown

Guitarist, singer, songwriter, producer, educator

Multitalented Junior Brown is a guitarist, singer, songwriter, producer, and instructor who has made his mark on country music. When he told *Down Beat*'s Bill Milkowski, "A lot of people tell me that they don't like country music but they like what I'm doing," he effectively summed up his appeal and his particular brand of music: country with twists of humor, Jimi Hendrix-style guitar rock, Memphis blues, Texas Swing, rockabilly, and bluegrass. *Request* magazine, in fact, dubbed Brown "the missing link between [legendary country] Ernest Tubb and ... Hendrix." Though he has made forays into other realms, Brown has perhaps best displayed his strengths and talents in the country genre.

Brown became adept at sounding like two, and sometimes three, guitar players at once, due in part to his own musical invention: the guit steel. The guit steel is a dual-necked guitar with a six-stringed top and an eight-stringed lap-steel bottom. The invention came to Brown in a dream in which he imagined himself playing and melding two guitars at once; when he awoke, he called guitar maker Mike Stevens, who was able to make

Courtesy of Curb Records

For the Record...

Born Jameson Brown in 1953 in Arizona; father was a piano player; married Tanya Rae (a guitarist and singer), c. 1979.

Guitarist, singer, songwriter, producer, and guitar instructor; invented guit steel guitar. Played roadhouse circuit, 1960s and 1970s; played with Rank and File, Asleep at the Wheel, and Alvin Crow, Austin, TX; released debut album, *12 Shades of Brown*, Demon, 1990; appeared as a guest on television shows *Saturday Night Live* and *Entertainment Tonight*, 1994.

Addresses: *Record company*—Curb Records, 310 East 46th Street, Suite 9V, New York, NY 10017; or 2132 Sharondale Drive, Nashville, TN 37215.

Brown's dream a reality. The guit steel enables Brown to make swift mid-song transactions.

According to *Rolling Stone's* John Swenson, Brown is a veritable institution among "guitar-playing aficionados" in his hometown of Austin, Texas, with his popularity steadily burgeoning out to the far reaches of the United States. The southwest has left its stamp on Brown's music, particularly when he croons songs like "Broke Down South of Dallas" in an unmistakable rural twang. His vocal delivery as well as his songwriting talent sets him apart from other lauded musicians noted solely for their instrumental prowess. Delightfully quirky, his songs celebrate human foibles and eccentricities.

Stubborn Vision

Brown was born in Arizona in 1953 and moved frequently with his family before settling in rural Kirksville, Indiana, where the youngster discovered he had an affection for country music. His father was a piano player, and there was always music being played or listened to in Junior's childhood home. Brown used to hear country music on the radio and cites Ernest Tubb, whom he would later watch on television, as an early influence.

Brown's parents considered country music to be backward and his classmates found it stodgy, but Brown nevertheless unfailingly embraced country. When he reached his teen years, he relocated with his family to Albuquerque, New Mexico. Though his classmates there also did not like country music, there were plenty of honky tonk bars in town for Brown to visit and hone his

skills. Brown recalled his teen years to Will Van Overbeek in *Request*: "As a kid who dropped out of high school and didn't have any skills at all, I got this job playing six nights in honky tonks when I was seventeen years old. I made $140 a week and I thought I was rich."

Brown played the roadhouse circuit throughout the 1960s and 1970s, devoting a full quarter century to music. He moved to California, Colorado, and Oklahoma before settling down in Austin. There he played with a diverse collection of bands, including the country/punk group Rank and File, the country/pop troupe Asleep at the Wheel, and Alvin Crow, a traditional party band musician.

Brown developed his own signature style, which was a hybrid of music fused into country, and stuck with it throughout various musical trends over the years. He told *Down Beat's* Milkowski, "I've lived through all the movements in Austin—the Outlaw movement, the urban-cowboy movement, the Kenny Rogers country-pop movement. But I didn't change to go along with the trends. I stuck with what I liked."

Influential Fans

Brown is a musician's musician, thrilling a diverse group of accomplished artists in their own right. Ernest Tubb, Carlene Carter, Nick Lowe, Ry Cooder, Chris Isaak, the Butthole Surfers, former Led Zeppelin bassist John Paul Jones, Neil Young, and Jimmie Vaughan have been, at various times, part of Brown's sated audience. Vaughan, in fact, made a guest appearance on *Guit with It's* "My Wife Thinks You're Dead" single and once took steel guitar lessons from Brown. And Lowe is the fan responsible for taking Brown's *12 Shades of Brown* cassette to Great Britain's Demon label; the LP would be released in 1990. Lowe also introduced Brown to Cooder, who was so enrapt with Brown's music that he flew him to Los Angeles to feature him on the original motion picture score of *Trespass*.

It was difficult for Brown to start his own band while keeping up a hectic pace of constant traveling and playing the live music circuit. He had attempted to meet with success in Nashville in the late 1980s, only to discover that his version of country music was a little too offbeat for the Nashville formula. Brown returned to Austin and was able to support himself by performing live, all the while working on a recording to again pitch in Nashville.

Brown's debut album appeared in 1990 as an independent cassette that he sold at his shows, titled *12 Shades of Brown* and subsequently released on Britain's Demon label. The album featured the Brown standard "My Baby Don't Dance to Nothing But Ernest Tubb," along with "So Close Yet So Far Away" and "Party Lights." *12 Shades Of Brown* was reissued in 1993 by Curb Records, due to an upsurge in his popularity upon the release of *Guit with It*. The singles "Guit-Steel Blues" and "Sugarfoot Rag" are examples of Brown's eclectic country hybrid form; both feature a mix of country, blues, and rock.

Wife Is "Backbone" of His Sound

In addition to sometime members Steve Layne and Roddy Collona, Brown's band includes rhythm guitarist and backup vocalist Tanya Rae Brown, who is also his wife. The two met when she was one of his guitar pupils at Oklahoma's Hank Thompson School of Country Music. Brown told *Guitar Player*'s Chris Gill, "She's the backbone of my sound." They have been known to glare at each other during a performance, primarily because Brown can be meticulous about how the music is played, and because Tanya Rae wants to sing with him more often than she is asked. They have also been known to coo at each other and have performed the single "So Close Yet So Far Away" as a duet; the rendition has been favorably compared to that of George Jones and Tammy Wynette.

Commenting on his original-sounding brand of country, Brown told *Request*'s Overbeek, "I've got a foothold on what my style is ... how far I can go without going too far,

how simple I can be without being too simple, and keeping that balance ... finding a place to grow with it without losing it.... That's the thing: Having a tiger is great, if he's trained." After the release of *Guit with It*, the musician made guest appearances on the television shows *Saturday Night Live* and *Entertainment Tonight*. To keep his bearings in the swirl of increased popularity and publicity, Brown follows the advice of Ernest Tubb, who, according to *Down Beat*, once told him, "Keep it country, boy."

Selected discography

12 Shades of Brown, Demon, 1990, reissued, Curb, 1993.
Guit with It, Curb, 1993.
(Contributor) *Trespass* (film score), Sire, 1993.

Sources

Billboard, March 26, 1994.
Country Music, March 1994.
Down Beat, May 1994.
Guitar Player, December 1993.
Musician, January 1994.
Request, November 1993.
Rolling Stone, December 1, 1994.
Spin, March 1994.

—B. Kimberly Taylor

Burning Spear

Reggae artist

Photograph by Tony Ramsay, courtesy of Heartbeat Records

Burning Spear—born Winston Rodney in 1945 in St. Ann's, Jamaica—easily shares the title "The Father of Reggae" with his musical contemporary Bob Marley. Since 1968, Spear's music has defined the genre of "roots reggae," which emphasizes Jamaica's historical links to Africa, the self-determination teachings of black nationalist Marcus Garvey, and black consciousness themes. Spear's resonant voice and hard driving drumbeat and bass lines create a hypnotic sound that lulls the listener and enhances the message of his lyrics. On his 1991 album, *Jah Kingdom,* he sings the praises of black leaders Garvey, Malcolm X, Martin Luther King, Jr., and Nelson Mandela, often delving into historical analyses of Western revisionist history; his acclaimed *Hail H.I.M.* features the song "Columbus," which clearly dismisses the notion that Columbus "discovered" Jamaica, ending with the emotional declaration: "Christopher Columbus was a damned blasted liar."

Yet despite his strident politics, "Rodney views the world and its people as a whole," wrote Ed Paladino in *The Beat.* "Through his everlasting belief in the ideals of Garvey and his preeminent concern for all of Africa's descendants, he has captured an even greater ideal for all of the human race. When he sings on 'World Power': 'Yes we suffer/Let's not talk about race/let's not talk about color,' he surpasses labels and politics." Taking the name of controversial Kenyan freedom-fighter and president Jomo Kenyatta—"The Burning Spear"—Rodney metaphorically unites his political beliefs with his Rastafarian faith, preaching an end to suffering and slavery for all people. Over the course of his career, Spear has released over 20 albums and has been nominated for five Grammy awards. In a 1991 interview with *Mean Street,* he stated that he "would like the people to know when they hear the name Burning Spear that it is a constructive name, a strong name.... The music is for all of the people and the people are for the music."

Garvey's Ghost

Considering his heavy emphasis on the importance of "roots," it is no coincidence that Spear's greatest influences—Marcus Garvey and Bob Marley—also hailed from St. Ann's, Jamaica. Born in 1887, Marcus Garvey moved to the United States in 1916 and started the "Back to Africa" movement based on the belief that blacks would never receive justice in white-dominated or colonized countries. Throughout his musical history, Spear has blended the teachings of Garvey into his lyrics as a way of spreading the leader's message to the people.

There was a time, however, when Spear was neither spiritually nor politically inspired. According to an interview in *Melody Maker,* the moment of his conversion to Rastafarianism—a mystical West Indian religious movement that centers on the end of black oppression and the promise of an African homeland—occurred early one morning when he had returned from a swim and was combing his hair. According to the story, the comb stuck in his hair and snapped, both ends shooting to opposite sides of the room. Spear said that at that moment, he saw Rasta in the mirror; since that time he has been wearing his hair in dreadlocks and following the Rastafarian way of life. Of his musical inclinations at the time, Spear told *High Times* magazine: "I'm not a man with a musical background. I was a flexible man who was there until Jah call I."

The call was answered in 1968 in the form of a trio Spear created with harmony singer Rupert Hines and Delroy Wilmington of the Hep Tones. In 1969, he recorded his first single, "Door Peep Shall Enter," for Studio One after Bob Marley introduced him to the label's owner, Coxsone Dodd. "I just run into Bob one day and as a St. Ann's man like myself, he told me that I should check out [Studio One] as a musical college," Spear mentioned in a 1991 press release. Spear stayed with Coxsone for two years, recording *Burning Spear* and *Rocking Time,* two albums that are now considered collector's items.

Spear took a few years off from recording and moved to Island Records in 1974 to work with producer Jack Ruby on three albums, *Marcus Garvey, Man in the Hills,* and *Garvey's Ghost,* which firmly established him as one of the world's preeminent reggae masters. *Marcus Garvey,* released in 1975, most clearly defines Spear's career and is still considered one of his best recordings, containing the hit singles "The Ghost," and "I and I Survive (Slavery Days)". Spear stayed on with Island Records to self-produce two more albums, *Dry and Heavy* and *Live.* Then, in the early 1980s, he returned to Jamaica to make several recordings on Marley's Tuff Gong label, giving back his talents to the community that helped establish him as an international star.

At this point in his career, however, Spear was more of a hit with white communities in Europe than with African Americans and other people of color throughout the world—a fact that disturbed the singer somewhat. In an interview with *Melody Maker,* Spear told Roz Reines that he found "the white population getting into reggae music much more deeply than the black population.... We're trying to do our best, but our people just sit down like lead." Yet even with a predominantly white audience, Spear continued to make a connection with the people. As Reines went on to observe: "Watching him on stage I've never seen such a large number of people so completely united; I've never witnessed such a direct communication between an artist and his audience."

Life after Marley

Nineteen eighty-one was an important year for Burning Spear; with his new "Burning Band" (Anthony and Devon Bradshaw on bass, rhythm and lead guitars; Nelson Miller on drums; Alvin Haughton, percussion), Spear toured Italy and England. In America, he went on the road with the Clash and Talking Heads. Around the same time, the world learned of the declining health of Spear's idol, Bob Marley. In the *Melody Maker* interview, Spear's response to Marley's lung cancer may have seemed flip: "I say Bob can get better. Why else did Jah create physician?" But Marley didn't recover, and upon his death in May of 1981, Spear was one of the first singers to release a tribute album.

Farover received mixed reviews in the press. Georgia Christgau, writing for the *Village Voice,* described Spear's break from five years of non-U.S. recording as "not hard to like," but "also not hard to dismiss." *Melody Maker's* Steve Sutherland began his review by calling *Farover* Spear's "first vinyl holiday," stating that the singer was "almost irreverent in his strident self-confidence." Yet Sutherland concluded that the album was "an inspired wake" for Marley. Christgau described Spear as having "at least two gifts, his throat and his pen," stating that since his first recording in 1969, "his voice carries [on] with no sign of weakening." She did take issue, however, with the song "Education," describing it as "incoherent" and "insidious" and a "pure sexist put-down." Yet as a whole, the album seemed to reinforce Spear's earlier themes of uniting black consciousness; on the track "Greetings," Spear sings: "One thing I don't understand how so many black people in America/Have no intention, have no respect for their culture."

"Watching him on stage I've never seen such a large number of people so completely united; I've never witnessed such a direct communication between an artist and his audience."
—Roz Reines

Some music critics contend that reggae suffered a serious slump after Marley's death, as watered-down versions of the reggae style mixed with synthesized dancehall music and rap. Spear attempted to stay in control of his career by moving permanently to Queens, New York, in the 1980s and switching to the Slash label, where he recorded *People of the World* and *Mistress Music.* Randall Grass described these two albums in *Musician* as a "stretch toward accessibility, without sacrificing his considerable substance."

Back in 1985, Spear decided to expand his Burning Band to include a brass section made up of musicians Pamela Fleming, Jennifer Hill, and Linda Richards. His 1989 double album *Live in Paris Zenith '88* was a huge critical success. *Village Voice* contributor Ben Mapp wrote that "Spear's output could either deconstruct your worldview, cause a revolution in your mind, or both," adding that the brass section's "punchy attacks" stung "like killer bees."

However, when Spear took his act on the road the next spring, troubles began to brew between the Burning Band and its burning leader. According to the *Village Voice,* Spear became dissatisfied with the growing melodic rhythms of bassist Devon Bradshaw, which he felt too closely mimicked popular reggae. As a result, Devon and his brother Anthony (on rhythm guitar) were kicked out of the band in Hamburg, Germany, halfway through their tour of Europe and Africa. Later in the tour, the brass section—Fleming, Hill, and Richards—left in support of their former bandmates. Spear apparently felt that the members of the brass section were also "part of the bad weed."

Giving Thanks and Growing

"People have gone through a lot of changes since the 70's and 80's, but people think what they're hearing today is original. It's not; it's a copy of the original," Spear told the Jim Beal, Jr., of the *San Antonio Express News* in 1991. In the 1990s, Spear continued to promote his music as unspoiled by dancehall trends. Of his individual tenacity, Spear added: "Some of us have dropped out and couldn't maintain the resistance and have gone the other way. I give thanks and praise to the original most high God Jah Rastafari for keeping I on the original path from that time until this time."

The path, however, was often rocky: in 1990, after three somewhat unevenly produced albums with Slash, Spear returned to Mango/Island Records and released *Mek We Dweet* ("Let's Do It"), earning his fourth Grammy nomination for reggae album of the year. With romantic songs like "Woman I Love You" and "Say You Are in Love," *Mek We Dweet* finished high on Billboard's Top Ten List of World Music Records. Spear received the prestigious Jamaican Federation of Musicians Merit Award after he returned from headlining the 1990 Reggae Sunsplash Tour.

Of his original Burning Band, Spear kept in close contact with drummer Nelson Miller, who helped produce many of the reggae master's later efforts. *Jah Kingdom,* released in 1991, offers a return to Spear's original themes of spiritual devotion. Containing such tracks as "Call on Jah," "Praise Him," and "When Jah Call," the album was described by *Reggae Report* as promoting "incantations of faith and immaculate covenants of love." On the song "Tumble Down," Spear reaffirms his religious roots, singing: "Jah is my light, strength and energy." *Jah Kingdom* also contains Spear's cover of the Grateful Dead song "Estimated Prophet," which he originally recorded for *Dedicated,* a Grateful Dead tribute album that included artists Elvis Costello, Lyle Lovett, and Jane's Addiction.

Throughout his career, Spear has struggled to maintain artistic integrity. In the early 1990s, he sought more control over his own promotion and business dealings with record labels. "Any time you are working with a company, you are sacrificing something," he told the *Daily Californian* in 1991. "You just can't lean back and say O.K., you are with this company, they are going to be taking care of everything.... They ain't going to be doing that." Consequently, Spear hired a publicist, left Island, and returned to Heartbeat/Rounder, which had released *Farover* and *Resistance* in the early 1980s.

Heartbeat re-released *Hail H.I.M.,* two new CDs, and three live albums from 1993 to 1995. *The World Should Know* (1993) won yet another Grammy Award nomination, and in May of 1995, just after his fiftieth birthday, Spear won four International Reggae Music Awards (IRMAs).

In August of 1995, Spear headed off his "50th Birthday Tour" of the United States in promotion of his June release of *Rasta Business.* Interviewing Spear about his career, his birthday, and his prospective tour, Dave Shiffman of *Forward* asked: "And [your] reggae will keep growing stronger and reaching farther?" Spear responded: "Just springing, growing, putting out leaves, branches.... Roots and culture, history and livity. You gonna always hear that, always want that, there's no changes."

Selected discography

"Door Peep Shall Enter" (single), Studio One, 1969.
Burning Spear, Studio One, 1969.
Rocking Time, Studio One, 1972.
Hail H.I.M. (contains "Columbus"), EMI, 1980, reissued, Heartbeat/Rounder, 1994.
People of the World, Slash, 1987.
Mistress Music, Slash, 1988.
Live in Paris Zenith '88, Slash, 1989.
(Contributor) *Dedicated* (appears on "Estimated Prophet"), Artista, 1991.

On Mango/Island

Marcus Garvey (contains "The Ghost," and "I and I Survive [Slavery Days]"), 1975.

Garvey's Ghost, 1975.
Man in the Hills, 1976.
Heavy and Dry.
Live.
Reggae Greats: Burning Spear, 1985.
Harder Than the Best, 1985.
Mek We Dweet, 1990.
Jah Kingdom, 1991.

On Heartbeat/Rounder

Farover, 1982.
Resistance, 1984.
The World Should Know, 1993.
Living Dub, Volume One, 1993.
Living Dub, Volume Two, 1994.
Love and Peace: Burning Spear Live!, 1995.
Rasta Business, 1995.
Fittest of the Fittest.

Sources

Books

Mulveney, Rebekah, *Rastafari and Reggae Dictionary and Sourcebook,* Greenwood Press, 1990.

Periodicals

Anchorage Daily News, December 2, 1991.
The Beat, August 1991.
Daily Californian, August 30, 1991.
Down Beat, July 1985.
Forward (cover story), February 1995.
High Times, December 1991.
Mean Street, September 1991.
Melody Maker, February 7, 1981; May 9, 1989.
Musician, March 1987; August 1990.
Reggae Report, August 1991.
San Antonio Express News, August 15, 1991.
Village Voice, September 21, 1982; May 9, 1989.

Additional information for this profile was obtained from publicity materials prepared by Night Nurse Productions, 1991-92, and Heartbeat Records, 1995.

—*Sarah Messer*

Stephen Curtis Chapman

Singer, songwriter

The fast-growing popularity of contemporary Christian music has been helped along by the songs and albums of Steven Curtis Chapman. The winner of three Grammy awards and numerous Gospel Music Association Dove awards, Chapman has gathered a large following of listeners, sometimes attracting more than 360,000 people to a concert. Although he has become a popular singer and performer, his songwriting skills have greatly contributed to his success; he has either written or cowritten every song on his seven albums. In addition, other well-known Christian and country singers, including Billy Dean, Charlie Daniels, Sandi Patti, and Glen Campbell, have recorded his songs.

A musician from an early age, Chapman began playing the guitar when he was six years old. In his first-grade singing debut, he took the stage with his brother Fred in a school show that featured the boys' versions of Glen Campbell's "Try a Little Kindness" and Mac Davis's "I Believe in Music." The performance established a singing partnership that would last until Fred left for college. Chapman did not concentrate solely on singing, however; he took advantage of being the son of a music store owner by learning to play most of the instruments available to him.

When Chapman graduated from high school he planned on a career in medicine, not because he passionately wanted to be a doctor but because he felt he should pursue something practical. Before embarking on this conventional course, though, he spent the summer performing at the Opryland theater in Nashville, Tennessee. He enjoyed the experience, and during his first semester at Georgetown College in Kentucky, he decided to abandon his premed studies for a musical education. He transferred to Anderson College in Indiana to major in music, tempering the risky move by concentrating on songwriting. Chapman performed each summer at Opryland during his college years, but he continued to feel his best chance at a career in music was as a songwriter. He stuck with that decision after transferring to Belmont College in Nashville.

Gradually, Chapman was persuaded to attempt a performance career. During his college years, several publishing company and record label representatives suggested he could succeed as a recording artist and songwriter. Sparrow Records then confirmed those suggestions by signing the contract that led to Chapman's debut album, *First Hand*. Released in 1987, the LP was the first in a steady string of popular contemporary Christian albums for Chapman. A combination of country, rock, pop, and folk music, *First Hand* contains three songs that made it into the Top Three of the contemporary Christian music (CCM), or inspirational, charts.

For the Record...

Born in Paducah, KY; married; wife's name, Mary Beth; children: Emily, Caleb, Will Franklin. *Education:* Attended Georgetown College, Kentucky, and Anderson College, Indiana; received B.A. from Belmont College, Nashville, TN.

Signed contract with Sparrow Records, mid-1980s, and released debut album, *First Hand,* 1987.

Awards: Grammy awards for best pop gospel album for *For the Sake of the Call,* 1992, *The Great Adventure,* 1993, and *The Live Adventure,* 1994; Dove awards for songwriter of the year, 1989-95; for contemporary recorded song of the year for "His Eyes," 1989, "Go There with You," 1994, and "Heaven in the Real World," 1995; for artist of the year, 1990, 1991, 1993, and 1995; for inspirational recorded song of the year for "His Strength Is Perfect," 1990; for southern gospel recorded song of the year for "I Can See the Hand," 1990; for male vocalist of the year, 1990, 1991, and 1995; for contemporary album of the year for *For the Sake of the Call,* 1992, *The Great Adventure,* 1993, and *Heaven in the Real World,* 1995; and for song of the year for "The Great Adventure," 1993; numerous awards from *American Songwriter Magazine, Campus Life* readers' choice poll, and *CCM Reader,* all 1993; named number one artist of the year in a *Cash Box* year end poll, 1994.

Addresses: *Home*—Nashville, TN. *Record company*—Sparrow Records, Box 5010, Brentwood, TN 37024-5010. *Management*—Creative Trust, 1910 Acklen Avenue, Nashville, TN 37212.

The following year, Sparrow released Chapman's second album, *Real Life Conversations,* which carried the sudden success of the first even further. Several songs rose to the Top Five of the CCM charts, with two songs, "His Eyes" and "My Turn Now," reaching Number One. "His Eyes" won the Dove Award for contemporary recorded song of the year. In addition, the album earned him another Dove Award, for songwriter of the year, and a Grammy nomination for best gospel performance—male.

From the beginning of his recording career, Chapman has upheld a serious commitment to ministering to people through his music. "Since the fall of certain religious leaders," Chapman commented in *Billboard,* "a lot of people are viewing Christianity with a certain amount of skepticism. How I personally respond to that, how I handle that is important. 'For Who He Really Is' [from the album *Real Life Conversations*] is my heart's cry."

Billboard said of Chapman's 1990 release, *For the Sake of the Call:* "Like previous releases, [it] contains plain-spoken spiritual insights, set to pleasant, hummable AC/pop music. Chapman is an affable and appealing artist, but his lyrics are never lightweight." The musician has explained that his lyrics are developed only after serious research and preparation; for the 1990 album, for example, he acknowledges the influence of Dietrich Bonhoeffer's book *The Cost of Discipleship.*

Although some reviews accused *For the Sake of the Call* of following a Christian-radio formula, listeners made it Chapman's most popular release yet. Five songs rose to Number One on the CCM chart, and the LP itself hit the very top of the CCM Top 50 albums chart. The album led once again to his recognition at the Grammys—this time for best pop gospel album—and at the Dove awards ceremony for songwriter of the year. In addition, *For the Sake of the Call* became Chapman's first LP to win the Dove Award for contemporary album of the year.

The sweep of awards continued for Chapman's next two albums, *The Great Adventure* and *Heaven in the Real World.* Not only did new Grammy awards and Dove awards attest to his popularity, but he received numerous *American Songwriter Magazine* Awards, CCM Reader Awards, and recognition in the *Campus Life* Readers' Choice Poll. His *Great Adventure* tour covered 70 cities, and in some places, he played before crowds of more than 360,000. His mid-1990s *Heaven in the Real World* tour was scheduled to cover 70 cities in the United States and to take him to 30 cities around the world, including ones in South Africa, South America, Europe, and Asia.

The *Heaven in the Real World* album marked a transition for Chapman into a new level of musical and marketing sophistication. The artist recorded the LP in Los Angeles rather than in Nashville and was joined by veteran studio musicians. Ed Cherney, who has worked with pop stars Bonnie Raitt and Don Was, handled the recording and mixing. With *Heaven in the Real World,* Chapman became one of the first contemporary Christian musicians to benefit from industry-wide SoundScan retail tracking and wider viewing of contemporary Christian videos. Such factors prompted *Billboard's* Bob Darden to declare that "Chapman is poised to do what [country superstar] Garth Brooks did a few years ago, only in a different genre of music."

Despite the increased sophistication in his production and marketing methods and some speculation over whether he will attempt to "cross over" to the mainstream pop market, Chapman continues to dedicate his musical talent to sharing his religious ideas. His immense popularity in the contemporary Christian music realm was further cemented in 1995, when he won six Dove awards. "My goal isn't just to share what I believe," Chapman proclaimed in a Sparrow Records press biography, "it is to show that belief is important, that it can make a difference, that there can be meaning to all of this we're going through."

Selected discography

On Sparrow Records

First Hand, 1987.
Real Life Conversations, 1988.

More to This Life, 1989.
For the Sake of the Call, 1990.
The Great Adventure, 1992.
The Live Adventure, 1993.
Heaven in the Real World, 1994.

Sources

Billboard, December 10, 1988; December 17, 1988; March 23, 1991; October 31, 1992; April 17, 1993; July 30, 1994; August 6, 1994; February 25, 1995; May 6, 1995.
Cash Box, August 1994.
Detroit Free Press, November 11, 1994.

Additional information for this profile was obtained from Sparrow Records publicity materials.

—Susan Windisch Brown

C. J. Chenier

Accordionist, saxophonist, singer, songwriter

Photograph by Sandro Miller, courtesy of Alligator Records

Before being called out to the Sparkle Paradise Club to take over as saxophonist in his father Clifton Chenier's Red Hot Louisiana Band in 1978, Clayton Joseph Chenier, better known as C. J. Chenier, was working in an oil refinery. He had had little exposure to zydeco, a form of music popular in Louisiana that combines Caribbean and blues sounds and often features lyrics in French. Nevertheless, this son of the undisputed King of zydeco was well suited for the task, having worked as a professional musician in Top 40 bands since the age of 16. Starting with Carl Wayne and the Magnificent Seven doing gigs around his Port Arthur, Texas, birthplace, according to the *Oxford Scene,* Chenier picked up all sorts of instruments, most notably the saxophone and Fender Rhodes piano. Under his father's tutelage, he was soon well versed in the Red Hot Louisiana Band's tradition, becoming its leader in just four years.

Always a quick study, Chenier explained in Concerted Effort publicity materials that he "started playing accordion in 1985, when my daddy was getting sick ... so I started opening shows for him. I learned to play accordion on stage. I had about four months of piano lessons when I was younger, so at least I knew the keyboard, but the other stuff I really had to learn as I went along. It got better. When I joined the band I didn't even know any zydeco songs."

Chenier's playing improved, and by 1989 he was receiving high praise from *Living Blues* writer Jim Trageses, who described his phrasing on the accordion in up-tempo shuffles like "She's My Woman" as harmonica-like, "short riffs and staccato notes, repeating phrases over and over with small but important changes each time, building to a climax that brings the song to a logical, satisfying conclusion." On straight blues numbers his accordion can sound more like a Hammond organ, "with lots of trills followed by short runs." Trageses claimed Chenier's debut as sole leader of the Red Hot Louisiana Band "makes a strong case for crowning [him] as the best living zydeco singer and accordionist. Rockin' Sidney and Rockin' Dopsie have played longer, and Buckwheat Zydeco is more famous, but 'Let Me in Your Heart' stands on a plane surpassed only by Clifton."

Of course, such hyperbole has been the norm since the elder Chenier's death in 1987, as critics and promoters have sought to fix the public's imagination on a never-ending, some would say never-existing, Bayou battle for the zydeco crown. It should also be noted that in addition to inheriting Clifton's name and accordion, C. J. also acquired his band, who have done much to keep him rooted in tradition even as they nurture him in his exploration of new sounds.

For the Record . . .

Born in 1951 in Port Arthur, TX; son of Clifton Chenier (a singer and accordionist) and Mildred Belle.

Accordionist, saxophonist, singer, and songwriter. Began playing saxophone with Carl Wayne and the Magnificent Seven throughout southeast Texas; worked in an oil refinery, until 1978; played saxophone in father's group, Clifton Chenier's Red Hot Louisiana Band, beginning in 1978; became bandleader, 1982; began playing accordion, 1985; released debut album as leader of Red Hot Louisiana Band, *Hot Rod,* Slash, 1990.

Awards: Grammy Award, with Clifton Chenier's Red Hot Louisiana Band, for album *I'm Here,* 1984.

Addresses: *Record company*—Warner Bros., 3300 Warner Blvd., Burbank, CA 91510. *Publicity*—Concerted Efforts Inc., P.O. Box 99, Newtonville, MA 02160.

As Jon Pareles reported in the *New York Times,* the Cheniers' music has inevitably changed between generations. "C. J. Chenier plays accordion less flamboyantly than his father did, and his voice is a smooth soul baritone without the weather-beaten tone and melancholy depths of his father's vocals." Another difference, one that marks the increasing assimilation of French-speaking people in Louisiana, is that C. J. does not speak Cajun French, though he does sing a few French lyrics. While this may offend some zydeco purists, it has served to make the music more accessible to fans.

In fact, in many ways C. J.'s legacy has kept him more traditional than both the generation before him and his more iconoclastic zydeco contemporaries, such as Terrance Simien. Chenier's father's music served as the starting point for most of the musicians who followed him, and the Red Hot Louisiana Band's music often seemed to hearken back to the 1950s and 1960s. As late as 1992, however, C. J. Chenier's publicist was attempting to position the musician as an innovator, noting that he had "gone to great lengths to include songs on [the album] *I Ain't No Playboy* that, while embracing zydeco roots, also turn the genre inside out." Chenier's publicity materials also asserted that the album "takes the music beyond purist zydeco rhythms and traditions to new depths and spaces."

In the same press release, Chenier commented, "In the past, whenever I'd record I'd put the songs like the ones on [*I Ain't No Playboy*] on the back burner. They didn't seem zydeco enough, and just didn't seem right for what I was doing, so I put them to the side. This time though, I thought it was time for me to stretch out a little, I wanted to put a little more variety on the album."

Chenier began playing covers of rock hits like ZZ Top's "Sharp Dressed Man" as well as modern zydeco standards like "Toot Toot." He has also worked with producer Joe Hardy and collaborated with Austin, Texas, songwriter Jeff Hughes. In doing so, he has avoided the danger of his music becoming a cultural curiosity and has instead helped it evolve into a dynamic reflection of the ever-changing, eclectic styles of the region.

Just as his father had created what came to be called zydeco by working the blues and African-Cuban rhythms into traditional Cajun music, itself a mix of French folk songs and New World influences, Chenier has begun to look around and ahead, rather than behind. At the same time, he has not totally abandoned the past. His albums often contain covers of his father's vast repertoire, and 1990's *Hot Rod* included a moving tribute to his father, titled "You're Still the King to Me": "There was a lot of folks/ Always hanging 'round/ Telling a bunch of jokes/ Like 'hey, I got the crown.'/ But like he used to say/ You can have this crown you see/ But if you want to wear this crown/ You got to take it away from me."

It is sometimes difficult to capture the intensity of zydeco music on recordings. Its origins are in hot, crowed dancehalls, where fire marshals often have trouble keeping people out of the aisles. The studio environment presents a problem for some zydeco performers who are great improvisers and whose live sets build as musicians play off each other and the crowd. According to publicity materials, Chenier likes to work fast and catch the immediate feeling that is pervasive in Louisiana clubs. *Hot Rod,* for example, was recorded in a ten-hour session, while *I Ain't No Playboy* was recorded in less than a week. "Originally we were going to have seven days to record [*I Ain't No Playboy*], but I couldn't figure out what we were going to do with all that time," Chenier explained.

Experienced musicians help move things along, and Chenier has added a second guitarist and a saxophone player to the Red Hot Louisiana Band, so the work is more spread out. Another reason for such short recording sessions is that the band rarely comes off the road, playing an average of 200 dates a year at fairs, festivals, and clubs throughout the Americas and Europe. After many of those nights, decked out in costumes befitting royalty, Chenier must truly identify with the words he sings to his father's old waltz, "I'm Coming

Home": "I'm coming home 'cause I feel so all alone./ I'm coming home 'cause that's where I belong."

Selected discography

With the Red Hot Louisiana Band

Let Me in Your Heart, Arhoolie, 1989.
Hot Rod, Slash, 1990.
I Ain't No Playboy, Slash, 1992.
My Baby Don't Wear No Shoes, Arhoolie, 1992.

Sources

Books

Lichtenstein, Grace, and Laura Dankner, *Musical Gumbo: The Music of New Orleans,* Norton, 1993.

Periodicals

BBS Newsletter, October 1992.
Boston Globe, May 16, 1991.
CMJ (*College Music Journal*), November 23, 1990; July 24, 1992.
Living Blues, July/August 1989.
Music City Bluesletter, September 1992.
New York Times, February 9, 1989.
Oxford Scene, April 5, 1990.
USA Today, April 24, 1991.

Additional information for this profile was taken from Concerted Efforts publicity materials, 1992.

—*John Morrow*

Mark Collie

Singer, songwriter, guitarist

Courtesy of MCA Nashville

Even though he has drawn upon musical influences as diverse as Johnny Cash, Leon Russell, and John Cougar Mellencamp, country music performer Mark Collie has blazed his own trail through Nashville. Although he has made his way well outfitted—with competent guitar playing, strong songwriting, a magnetic stage personality, and a captivatingly twangy drawl—Collie's efforts to link up with the Music City mainstream didn't happen overnight. But perseverance has always been Collie's strongest suit. By 1994, with four albums under his belt and several hit singles topping the country charts, it was clear that Collie had found himself a seat on the fast-moving train toward success in the country music industry.

Collie was born January 18, 1956, in Waynesboro, Tennessee, just miles from the Alabama border. Growing up in a large musical family, he was quick to pick up on a broad mix of musical styles—from hard-core honky-tonk to rock to gospel. "My Uncle Joe bought my brother Steve an acoustic guitar one year when I was nine or ten years old," recalled Collie in a *Country Music City News* interview with Shawn Williams. "That guitar changed my life. That's when I started to learn how to write songs." Citing the legendary Johnny Cash as his major influence during his early years as an aspiring musician, Collie focused his bulldog determination on developing the musicianship and the songwriting and performance skills necessary to make a mark for himself in the music business.

During his high school years in Waynesboro, Collie was a DJ on local radio station WAAM and played guitar with local club bands. After graduation, he continued to play and traveled around the country and the world for a while—as far away as Europe and the Far East—to experience life. He then stopped in Nashville to audition for a spot at Opryland; when that didn't pan out, Collie moved to Memphis and formed another band. Several years later, a vacation to Hawaii led to an 18-month stint as the house entertainer for a beach club, where he wowed guests with his country/rock and roll mix.

Made It with MCA

In 1982 Collie found himself in the mainland States once again; he boarded a bus for Nashville, where his songwriting skill quickly landed him a job as a writer with a large music publishing company. Although he made few strides as an entertainer, for five years his songs were recorded by such top artists as Martina McBride, Collin Raye, Marty Stuart, Aaron Tippin, and Randy Travis. In 1987 he chose to get out from behind the scenery and build a more public profile. That decision proved to be a major turning point in his career: perform-

For the Record . . .

Born George Mark Collie, January 18, 1956, in Waynesboro, TN; married; wife's name, Anne; children: Nathan.

Began performing on the road with various bands, c. 1974; moved to Nashville, TN, and worked as a songwriter, 1982; began performing at Douglas Corner nightclub, Nashville, 1987; signed with MCA and released debut EP, *Hardin County Line,* 1989; released *Mark Collie,* 1993; co-sponsored first annual Mark Collie Celebrity Race for Diabetes Cure, Nashville, 1994; signed with Giant Records and released *Tennessee Plates,* 1995.

Addresses: *Record company*—Giant Records, 45 Music Square West, Nashville, TN 37203.

ing in musical showcases at Douglas Corner—a Nashville nightclub notable as a songwriter's hangout—Collie was spotted by MCA's Tony Brown, who liked the performer's twangy style and offered him a record contract.

Collie's first EP, 1989's *Hardin County Line,* showcased the musician's mastery of modern country and rockabilly influences. The album's Collie/Aaron Tippin-coauthored single "Something with a Ring to It" hit the charts in 1990, but Collie's debut effort didn't get the airplay many thought it deserved. A year later, *Born and Raised in Black and White*—while again commended by critics for its insightful lyrics—didn't have what radio programmers were looking for to crack the top of the country charts.

Baring His Soul in a Song

The indifferent response to his first two albums was hard on Collie. "I don't think you ever accept the fact that your records aren't hits," Collie admitted to Michael McCall in *Country Music.* "When you put so much of your heart and soul into something, and everybody seems real positive ... and then it doesn't happen, that can be devastating." "It's a total rejection at the highest level," Collie continued, "at the most fundamental level. They're rejecting the honest expression of your emotion. Nobody wants that."

Collie worked hard at developing his songwriting technique; the critical praise he received for composing the material on his first two albums meant a lot to the singer, who writes several dozen songs a year. "Songwritin' is a very personal thing, it's something you do very privately," Collie explained to *Country Song Roundup*'s Celeste Gomes. "Even in a collaboration, it has to be with somebody that you feel real comfortable with as a friend. And then suddenly, you go from that very private, inner-self approach, to recordin' the songs and you're up on a stage in front of thousands of people you don't know, and you're sharin' all that with them."

Perseverance Paid Off in Spades

Finally, in 1993, Collie's dogged persistence reaped some rewards. With his self-titled third album, he drew on the influences of 1950s rockabilly artists like the Everly Brothers, once again breaking with the "Young Country" fold who seemed to be opting for the Garth Brooks sound. "I always wanted to record some songs like Carl Perkins and Elvis [Presley] and Fats [Domino] and those guys," Collie told Gomes, "but I could never bring myself to record any of the Elvis standards or the classics because they were so good. So I thought, 'Well, I'll write some things that are in that direction.'" However, some critics felt that Collie had compromised his uniqueness for mainstream acceptance. While praising *Mark Collie* for the lean, up-tempo arrangements that have become the characteristic Collie sound, reviewer Geoffrey Himes noted in *Country Music* his "disappointment with the play-it-safe lyrics. Collie's first two albums were marked by some boldly ambitious songwriting.... There's nothing that original on *Mark Collie.*"

Compromise or not, it was the top single on that third album that gave Collie the break to country radio that he had been courting for so long. "Even the Man in the Moon Is Crying" made it to Number Five in 1992, and the following year "Born to Love You" fell on its heels at Number Six on the country charts, giving Collie the name recognition crucial to every successful performer. It also marked the start of a fruitful collaboration between Collie and his cowriter, songwriter/producer Don Cook, who produced Collie's 1994 album, *Unleashed.*

While considered even more mainstream than his previous effort, *Unleashed* provided an excellent showcase for Collie's expressive vocals and continued to demonstrate some sturdy songwriting. Notable on the EP, Collie's cover of the Johnny Cash classic "Ring of Fire" highlights his ability to transcend the norm and imbue material with originality. The track had long been a favorite during Collie's live performances, and the studio version had the benefit of background vocals by

Carlene Carter, daughter of "Ring of Fire" coauthor June Carter Cash.

Giving Something Back

Collie's career has demonstrated the value of not giving up on a goal, a trait the singer has exhibited in other areas of his life as well. As his stature in Nashville has grown, Collie has taken advantage of it to aid a cause that has been close to his heart for many years. Having been diagnosed with diabetes in 1977, he wanted to do what he could to help find a cure for the disease, which affects almost 13 million people in the United States. In the fall of 1994, he helped sponsor the first Mark Collie Celebrity Race for Diabetes Cure. With the participation of many celebrities from both the country music industry and the world of NASCAR racing, this event raised much-needed money to aid in diabetes research.

Continuing to progress in his country music career, in 1995 Collie switched from the MCA Nashville record label to Giant "in search of new momentum—and that elusive big hit," according to *Billboard*'s Jim Bessman. His July 18 release, *Tennessee Plates,* was backed by an aggressive marketing program by Collie's new label. The singer commented to Bessman, "Giant's made a firm commitment to try and get the music heard, and radio's been very supportive in not giving up on me." Indeed, before *Tennessee Plates* was even released, its first single, "Three Words, Two Hearts, One Night," became the most requested song at the WYNY, a country radio station in New York.

Even with raw talent and a desire to make it as a performer, determination has been the real key to success for Collie. As he told Williams in *Country Music City News:* "The one thing that kept me going ... through the dark times in this short little career is ... the real fans of country music who would write me letters or come to the shows.... They made sure I knew that my music was worth making and it gave me the inspiration to sit down and pick up the guitar and write another song for them." For Collie, writing that next song has made all the difference. And Collie put it plainly in an interview with McCall. "There's one thing I know: If you don't stay in the game, you lose. I have stayed in the game."

Selected discography

Hardin County Line (includes "Something with a Ring to It"), MCA, 1989.
Born and Raised in Black and White, MCA, 1991.
Mark Collie (includes "Born to Love You" and "Even the Man in the Moon Is Crying"), MCA, 1993.
Unleashed, MCA, 1994.
Tennessee Plates, Giant, 1995.

Sources

Books

Cackett, Alan, *Harmony Illustrated Encyclopedia of Country Music,* Crown, 1994.
Comprehensive Country Music Encyclopedia, Random House, 1994.

Periodicals

Billboard, July 1, 1995.
Country Music, March/April 1993; January/February 1994; September/October 1994.
Country Music City News, December 1993.
Country Song Roundup, July 1993; April 1994.
Entertainment Weekly, March 20, 1992.
Pulse!, July 1993.

Additional information for this profile was obtained from MCA Records publicity materials, 1994.

—Pamela L. Shelton

Skeeter Davis

Singer, songwriter

AP/Wide World Photos

When the single "The End of the World" burst onto the *Billboard* charts in 1962, it signalled a turning point in the career of country vocalist Skeeter Davis. As one half of the talented vocal duo the Davis Sisters, Skeeter had been poised on the brink of major stardom a decade before, until that group's tragic demise. Her first gold record since going solo, Skeeter's hit was also one of the most notable of the early "crossovers," topping the pop and country charts simultaneously. "The End of the World" set the stage for the beginning of Davis's rise as one of the most popular—as well as one of the most outspoken—female voices in country music in the decades that followed.

Davis was born Mary Frances Penick, in Glencoe, Kentucky, on December 30, 1931. She was the first of seven children born to William and Sarah Penick, and the strong moral values she developed while helping to raise her younger siblings in rural Dry Ridge, Kentucky, would strongly influence her musical career. When her family moved to Covington, Ohio, during her junior year of high school, young Mary Frances made the acquaintance of fellow home economics classmate Betty Jack Davis at Covington's Dixie Heights High.

Thus began Davis's country music career, on the traditional path of a country "sister" act. Although unrelated by blood, Skeeter and Betty Jack—B. J. to her friends—shared a common love of music; they soon sang together every day at lunch and spent so much time in each other's company that they became almost as close as real sisters. Skeeter quickly joined her friend as a singer at the famed "Renfro Valley Barn Dance" broadcast from nearby Renfro Valley; the two also got a steady lunchtime job at a local television variety show while still in high school. The TV show emcee would always be in a rush to announce the girls, who would run over from school to perform on their lunch break. One day he fumbled the name Penick and dubbed the pair the "Davis sisters."

From Radio to Recording

The name suited Skeeter and B. J.; after graduation in 1949, they went to Lexington radio station WLAX and performed regularly as the Davis Sisters. The two spent 1952 on Casey Clark's "Big Barn Dance Frolic" on Detroit's WJR. From there it was off to WKRC-Cincinnati and Wheeling, West Virginia's WWVA. After recording several demo tapes with Detroit's Fortune Records—including a cover of Hank Williams's "Kaw Liga"—the Davis Sisters travelled to New York City in 1952 to meet Steve Sholes of RCA Victor. The trip netted them a record contract with the major label.

For the Record . . .

Born Mary Frances Penick, December 30, 1931, in Dry Ridge, KY; daughter of William (a farmer and electrician) and Sarah Penick; married second husband, Ralph Emery (a disc jockey), 1960 (divorced, 1964); married Joey Spampinato (a singer), 1987.

With friend Betty Jack Davis, formed duo the Davis Sisters, c. 1948; performed regularly on WLEX, Lexington, KY; signed with RCA Records, 1952; released debut LP, *I Forgot More than You'll Ever Know,* 1953; seriously injured in an automobile accident that killed Betty Jack, 1953; performed with Georgia Davis as the Davis Sisters; began solo career, 1958; joined Grand Ole Opry, Nashville, TN, 1959; toured with the Rolling Stones, c. 1965; has toured extensively in the U.S., as well as England, Germany, Jamaica, Japan, Malaysia, Singapore, and Sweden.

Awards: Named most promising female country vocalist by *Cash Box* magazine, 1959; gold record, 1963, for *End of the World;* Peter DeRose Memorial Award, 1965, for "Somebody Loves You"; numerous awards for songwriting from performance rights societies BMI and ASCAP.

Addresses: *Home*—Brentwood, TN. *Office*—Grand Ole Opry, 2804 Opryland Drive, Nashville, TN 37229.

"Our singing style was never something we practiced or sat down and figured out," Skeeter told Bob Allen in the *Journal of the American Academy for the Preservation of Old-Time Country Music.* "The vocal arrangements that we came up with were always completely spontaneous; it just came out when Betty Jack and I sang together." The 1953 release of the Davis Sisters' first album on RCA showcased a vocal duo poised on the edge of country superstardom. The Sisters' harmonies would strongly influence future duos like the Everly Brothers. The album's title cut, "I Forgot More than You'll Ever Know," quickly made the climb to Number One; it would stay on the *Billboard* country charts a record 26 weeks.

But 1953 proved to be a fateful year—not just for the Davis Sisters, but for country music as well. On January 1, while on his way to a concert date in Canton, Ohio, 29-year-old country superstar Hank Williams succumbed to a decades-long addiction, quietly dying of a drug and alcohol overdose in the back seat of his Cadillac. Almost exactly eight months later, on August 2, Skeeter and B. J. would also be involved in tragedy while on the road; a car whose driver had fallen asleep at the wheel struck the duo as they were driving home to Cincinnati from a performance on WWVA. The head-on collision left Skeeter with a concussion and serious internal injuries. It left her best friend dead. Months would pass before Skeeter would recover sufficiently from the shock to resume her musical career.

Moving through Tragedy

Stricken by grief, Betty Jack's family clung to Skeeter. She was paired with B. J.'s sister, Georgia Davis, in an attempt to get a new version of the Davis Sisters out before paying audiences. The two recorded several albums and toured with country talents Hank Snow, Maybelle Carter, and Elvis Presley before Georgie left the music business in 1957 to raise a family. A year later, Skeeter finally broke away from the control of the Davis family and went solo, becoming one of the first RCA artists to work under the guidance of guitarist/producer Chet Atkins. 1959's *Set Him Free* was a success: Davis received her first Grammy nomination for the record, which established her on the country charts and gained her entry into the Grand Ole Opry, the venerable "mother church" of country music then lorded over by the legendary Roy Acuff.

In 1960 Davis married popular WSM radio personality Ralph Emery. But the stress of music-industry demands—as well as Emery's battle with pills and alcohol—would destroy their marriage in four years. Despite the turmoil in her private life, Davis—who had enjoyed several career boosts during the 1950s—achieved star status in the early years of the 1960s. Combining her traditional country roots with pop influences, she co-wrote and recorded "My Last Date With You," her first crossover success. In addition to writing many other songs, Davis began pairing with Connie Francis, Bobbie Vinton, Duke Ellington, and other pop celebrities on vocal collaborations.

When television host Dick Clark welcomed Davis to his rock and roll-oriented *American Bandstand,* it was clear that the road she was travelling circled a mighty long way around the local honky tonk, a fact that dismayed many of her country fans; the increasing notice Davis was receiving outside traditional country music circles didn't seem fitting or proper for an Opry regular. Her continuing flirtation with the works of pop and rock artists—such as the late Buddy Holly and the Rolling Stones, not to mention jazz great Ellington—diminished her appeal to hard-core country fans further. But Davis continued to proclaim her deep country roots, despite her personal satisfaction in broadening her musical scope. As she has often said, "I've been with the Opry since joining in 1959—which proves that my heart's in country."

Hard to Pigeonhole

Davis's continued experimentation with musical genres over the years has made her somewhat difficult for critics to pigeonhole. During the 1970s, she became well known for her renditions of sacred music; her work with televangelist Oral Roberts brought her vocal talents into the living rooms of Americans unfamiliar with her work as a pop/country artist. But, in 1965 she had toured with the Rolling Stones, and in 1985 she was hard at work in the studio recording an album with the rhythm and blues band NRBQ. Davis would marry Joey Spampinato, a member of NRBQ, in 1987.

In addition to recording and her work on television, Davis toured extensively throughout North America and beyond—she claims that she has performed in every major U.S. city at least once during her career. In booking her live performances, however, she has demanded an unusual restriction: that performances not be scheduled where liquor is served. It was not that she personally objected to drinking; rather, she didn't want to put temptation in the path of loyal fans who did not already have a taste for alcoholic beverages. A devout Christian since she was 18, Davis has demonstrated the tenets of her faith by remaining active in community projects for the less privileged residents of the greater Nashville area and performing for church-related events. In fact, her ethical standards once caused her temporary dismissal from the stage of the Grand Ole Opry; in 1973, she spoke out during an Opry broadcast on WSM to criticize the Nashville Police Department's handling of a local altercation. Opry head Acuff, a staunch traditionalist, had no choice but to temporarily censure the popular star.

Despite her somewhat controversial profile, Davis has enjoyed numerous successes throughout her long career. Recording over 60 singles and 30 popular albums for RCA, she has been nominated for five Grammy awards. Her hits have included 1960's "I'm Falling Too," "Where I Ought to Be" in 1962, "He Says the Same Things to Me" in 1964, and "One Tin Soldier," the Top Ten theme to the 1972 movie *Billy Jack*. Her duets with country singers like Bobby Bare, Porter Wagoner, and George Hamilton IV, as well as her strong and continued support of young talent and of the Grand Ole Opry, have more than reaffirmed Davis's roots in country music.

Selected discography

With the Davis Sisters

Hits with The Davis Sisters, Fortune, 1952.
I Forgot More than You'll Ever Know, RCA, 1953.

Solo releases

Set Him Free, RCA, 1958.
End of the World, RCA, 1963.
Cloudy, RCA, 1963.
Let Me Get Close, RCA, 1964.
(With Bobby Bare) *Tunes for Two* (includes "A Dear John Letter"), RCA, 1965.
My Heart's in Country, RCA, 1967.
Skeeter Davis Sings Buddy Holly, RCA, 1967.
Hand in Hand, RCA, 1969.
Bring it on Home, RCA, 1972.
(With NRBQ) *She Sings They Play*, Rounder, 1985.
The Essential Skeeter Davis, RCA, 1995.

Sources

Books

Davis, Skeeter, *Bus Fare to Kentucky: The Autobiography of Skeeter Davis*, Birch Lane Press, 1993.
Malone, Bill C., and Judith McCulloh, *Stars of Country Music*, University of Illinois Press, 1975.
Encyclopedia of Folk, Country and Western Music, St. Martin's, 1983.
Strobel, Jerry, *The Official Opry Picture-History Book*, Opryland USA, 1994.

Periodicals

Country Music, July/August 1995.
Journal of the American Academy for the Preservation of Old-Time Country Music, December 1993.

—Pamela L. Shelton

Des'ree

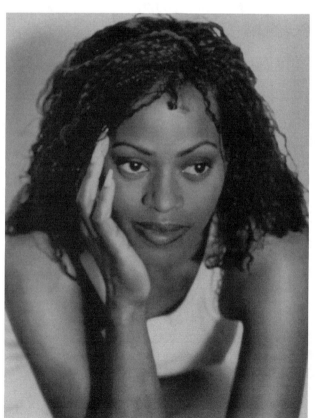

Photograph by Caterina Jebb, © 1994 Sony Music

British vocalist and songwriter Des'ree captured U.S. pop and contemporary rhythm and blues audiences in July of 1994 at the age of 25 with the hypnotically upbeat Top Five hit single "You Gotta Be." The song was featured on her second album, *I Ain't Movin'*, which eventually achieved platinum status. In addition to attracting an enthusiastic audience, the song's success led to an offer from filmmakers Spike Lee and Martin Scorsese to contribute a single to the soundtrack for their motion picture *Clockers,* as well as to a guest spot on the television show *Saturday Night Live.*

Des'ree's music has sometimes been categorized as folk/soul since her sound fluctuates between soft and sultry, pensive and thoughtful, and smoothly soulful. Des'ree blends Caribbean rhythms with American R&B, flamenco, hip-hop, and English pop to create a unique musical representation of her own musical tastes and life experience in Barbados and England. Her music has been deemed not "black enough" for extensive airplay on black radio stations in the United States, a charge that has rankled the singer. She told *Musician* magazine, "I find it very hard when people say 'You're not black enough for black radio.'... The fact that I'm not like everyone else, don't you see that as a challenge?"

Early Love of Music

Des'ree was born Desiree Weekes in 1970 in London, England, and was exposed to a wide array of music as a child. Reggae, pop, and jazz were all played in her home, and she began taking piano lessons at the age of three. She later took up the viola and abandoned piano lessons in favor of singing, writing poems, and composing music. By the time she was 13, she was writing poetic lyrics and chords. Specific early influences for Des'ree include a diverse group of musicians—Stevie Wonder, Bob Marley, Donny Hathaway, Sam Cooke, Gil Scott-Heron, and Joan Armatrading.

When Des'ree was ten years old, her family moved to Barbados, and during her three-year stay on the island, the youngster was exposed to soca, calypso, and dub music. Her parents separated there, an event that caused Des'ree to briefly question her faith in human nature, and she moved back to London with her mother and sister after the divorce. Her time in Barbados exposed her to an uplifting and powerful tradition: black pride and black accomplishment. This pervasive feeling in Barbados of strength and optimism is evident in Des'ree's songs.

At the age of 16 Des'ree took a demo tape to a major record company just to test the waters. She told *People*

For the Record . . .

Born Desiree Weekes in 1970 in London, England; daughter of Samuel Weekes (a jazz musician and insurance company director) and Annette Norma

Began taking piano lessons at age three and later took up viola, singing, and composing; signed recording contract with Sony 550/Epic and released debut album, *Mind Adventures,* 1992; toured with Simply Red, 1993; guest appearances on *The Tonight Show, The Arsenio Hall Show, Late Show with David Letterman, Soul Train, The Today Show, CBS This Morning,* and *Saturday Night Live;* embarked on world tour with Seal, 1995; made first U.S. tour as a headliner, 1995.

Awards: Platinum album award for *I Ain't Movin,* 1995.

Addresses: *Record company*—Sony 550, 550 Madison Avenue, New York, NY 10022.

magazine's Jennifer Mendelsohn that by the time she returned home, someone from the label had already called to set up a meeting. However, she decided "the time wasn't right" and waited until six years passed—when she was 22 and working at a health food store—before she tried sending out a demo tape again.

The success of her breakthrough album, *Mind Adventures,* can partially be attributed to positive thinking. In interviews she repeatedly describes herself as spiritual and a believer in the power and effectiveness of daily affirmations. Des'ree told *Entertainment Weekly's* Michele Romero, "I woke up one morning with an oddly positive feeling and I told my manager to send my demo over to the chap who signed [pop singer] Terence Trent D'Arby.... Only he would understand my music." Her intuition proved correct when three days later, she was signed by Sony 550/Epic, even though she was very young and had no connections in the music industry.

Ashley Ingram of the British soul trio Imagination told *Musician's* Barney Hoskyns that he remembered when CBS (now Sony) artisits and repertoire (A&R) representative Lincoln Elias first thought of signing Des'ree. "[Elias] played me a very rough demo of the song that later became 'Feel So High.' It's not often that a singer can present a demo tape and expect the powers-that-be to acknowledge the full wonders, but on a creative level she shone. She leapt out of the cassette."

When "Feel So High" was first played on British radio, Hoskyns wrote, "it sounded like a young [contemporary jazz/R&B singer] Anita Baker perched on your shoulder and singing directly into your ear." Des'ree's 1992 debut album, *Mind Adventures,* did not fare as well as its hit single, but it did sufficiently introduce Des'ree's vocal and songwriting talents and paved the way for her second LP.

After the introduction of her first album, Des'ree toured with the pop group Simply Red and recorded a Top Ten British single called "Delicate" with Terence Trent D'Arby. The song is featured on D'Arby's 1993 album, *Symphony or Damn.* "Delicate" provided Des'ree the opportunity to appear on *The Tonight Show* and *The Arsenio Hall Show,* which in turn made the executives at her record company more confident of her unusual brand of soul.

Employs Positive Thinking

Des'ree's "You Gotta Be" single from her second album, *I Ain't Movin',* which was released in 1994, is reminiscent of a motivational speaker's advice. The painful demise of the singer's real-life relationship with a boyfriend—who was also her manager for her debut album—jolted Des'ree into reading Shakti Gawain's *Creative Visualization,* which served as inspiration for the single and her second album. Des'ree explained the origin of her philosophy to *Us* magazine's Gregg Goldstein, "My mother always said 'Embrace the good and the bad with the same ferocity, and don't be afraid.'"

Des'ree's popularity soared. The year after *I Ain't Movin'* was released, it went platinum, and "You Gotta Be" reached the Top Five on the *Billboard* music charts. Des'ree then traveled to Ethiopia to shoot a video for her single "Little Child," which is about starvation in Africa, and embarked on a world tour with pop singer Seal. She was perhaps made especially aware of her growing fame when legendary bluesman B. B. King asked for her autograph at an airport.

Music Video Boosted Album Sales

The music video for "You Gotta Be" served to heighten Des'ree's visibility in the United States. The video was shown on the VH-1 channel longer than any video in VH-1 history. In the sophisticated black-and-white piece that features four simultaneous images of the singer, Des'ree blends the stunning beauty of a runway model, the grace of a ballet dancer, and a chic wardrobe. In markets with little radio play, it was clear that video exposure was contributing to album sales.

The success of "You Gotta Be" prompted *New York Newsday* to proclaim that for 1995, pop superstar Madonna was "out" and Des'ree was "in." The single broke into *Billboard's* Top Ten music chart at Number Seven in January of 1995, and its popularity led to more guest appearances for Des'ree, including spots on the *Late Show with David Letterman, The Today Show, Soul Train,* and *CBS This Morning.* She completed her first U.S. tour as a headliner in March of 1995, playing to full houses in 17 cities. *People's* Mendelsohn noted that in mid-1995 Des'ree was at work on a third album and a book of poetry. "I'm a restless person—I need my stimulation," the singer confided. "And now the world is my universe."

Selected discography

Mind Adventures, Sony 550/Epic, 1992.

(With Terence Trent D'Arby) "Delicate," *Symphony or Damn,* Columbia, 1993.
I Ain't Movin', Sony 550/Epic, 1994.
"Silent Hero," *Clockers,* MCA, 1995.

Sources

Billboard, September 28, 1994; January 28, 1995.
Chicago Tribune, November 10, 1994.
Entertainment Weekly, February 17, 1995.
Musician, March 1995; May 1995.
New York Newsday, December 28, 1994.
Paper, October 1994.
People, May 8, 1995.
Request, January 1995.
Rolling Stone, December 1, 1994; January 26, 1995.
Time, February 20, 1995.
Us, February 1995.

—*B. Kimberly Taylor*

Digable Planets

Rap group

While rap music sometimes strikes the uninitiated listener as monotonous rhythms and rhymes, Digable Planets' two albums have demonstrated the range of sounds rap can encompass. The group has also discovered, however, that such musical experiments can incite political debates among rap's commentators. The band's liberal use of jazz prompted mainstream music critics and many white listeners to embrace the trio's sound, declaring it a part of the "acid jazz" phenomenon. At the same time, their sound also turned away much of a black audience who equated only the stark tones of "gangsta" rap with black urban experience.

Digable Planets' first album demonstrated not only the politics that surround rap, but also how much those politics can be about race. In their follow-up album the Planets confronted their critics: They brought black power politics to the forefront in their lyrics, while still cultivating the unorthodox sound they had introduced on the first album. That is, Digable Planets insisted that their jazz/rap fusion was not on the margins of black culture, but the future of it.

When Digable Planets first appeared on MTV airwaves in 1992, they attracted attention for many reasons, not the least of which was their unorthodox appearance. While most hip-hop outfits tend to be strictly defined by gender—all men highlighting their masculinity or all women carving out their own space—the Planets presented viewers with two men *and* a woman who was not just a figurehead.

Furthermore, Digable Planets adopted neither the angry stance of gangsta rap nor the high energy rush of dance-oriented hip-hop. They were, instead, unusually muted in their stage and video persona, presenting the simpler styles of the jazz world. The group's character emerged from the chemistry of the three individuals who are Digable Planets: Ishmael Butler, also known as Butterfly; Craig Irving, also known as Doodlebug and Knowledge; and Mary Ann Vieira, also known as Ladybug and Mecca.

Band Members Exposed to Jazz in Childhood

Critics see Butterfly, more than the others, as Digable Planets' "leader," and his history appears to have had the most influence on the group's sound. "My parents were revolutionaries," he told *The Source*'s Todd Williams. In the 1960s, Butterfly's parents worked with both the Black Panthers and the Student National Coordinating Committee, the most active student organization in the civil rights movement. Butterfly apparently inherited those politics from his parents, as Williams and other

For the Record . . .

Members include **Butterfly** (born Ishmael Butler in Seattle, WA; attended University of Massachusetts); **Doodlebug** (also known as Knowledge; born Craig Irving in Philadelphia, PA); **Ladybug** (born Mary Ann Vieira in Brazil).

Group formed in New York City in early 1990s; signed contract with Pendulum Records and released debut album, *Reachin' (A New Refutation of Time and Space)*, 1992.

Awards: Grammy Award for best rap performance by a duo or group, 1993, for "Rebirth of Slick (Cool Like Dat)"; Image Award nominations, National Association for the Advancement of Colored People (NAACP); *Billboard* Music Video Award; *Soul Train* Music Award nomination for best rap album and gold album award, both for *Reachin' (A New Refutation of Time and Space)*.

Addresses: *Record company*—Pendulum Records, 1290 Avenue of the Americas, New York, NY 10104.

journalists have noticed from the contents of Butterfly's bookshelves, which include volumes by various members of the Black Panthers, leftist philosopher Karl Marx, Chinese communist leader Mao Tse-tung, and French existentialist writer Jean-Paul Sartre.

Butterfly spent his childhood in Seattle, Washington, where he was born in the early 1970s. After his parents divorced, he moved around the country with his history professor father, living in Baltimore, Maryland; Philadelphia, Pennsylvania; and Harlem and Brooklyn, New York. Butterfly's father provided him with a rich musical environment, exposing his son to an extensive jazz collection. As Butterfly grew up, he augmented that foundation with rap; he also played saxophone in his teen years. Upon completing high school, he attended the University of Massachusetts on a basketball scholarship but quit before long. He decided instead to earn an education in the music business, taking an internship with Sleeping Bag Records, a New York City-based hip-hop label, in the mid-1980s.

Relating a similar early exposure to jazz, Butterfly's band mate Doodlebug recalled the music of his childhood for Ann Powers of *Spin*. "My mother would always sit around, reading a book or the Sunday paper, and listen to jazz. My aunt taught me about [jazz legends]

Bessie Smith and Billie Holiday, she was always playing the records and talking about them," he explained. Born in the late 1960s, Doodlebug grew up in Philadelphia before moving to Washington, D.C., to attend Howard University, where he made a reputation for himself as a deejay on the college's radio station. He also mixed with local members of the religious sect Five Percent Nation of Islam, adopting some of their political ideals of black power.

Digable Planets' female member, Ladybug, though she was born in Brazil in the mid-1970s, spent her childhood mostly in Maryland. By the time she was in high school, she was a restless young woman; in four years, she attended three different schools. She told Pat Blashill of *Details* that she "didn't talk to anyone. I had, like, long-ass dreads and a nose ring and the other students weren't used to that.... I just couldn't wait to get out of high school." Powers described Ladybug as "a tomboy whose version of climbing trees was learning to rap."

Ladybug's musical influences combined rap with the Brazilian dance music her parents had always listened to. On weekends, she would make exploratory trips to Philadelphia and New York City; there she discovered the clubs and parties where artists experimented with rap and hip-hop. She and Butterfly met in D.C., soon became friends, and eventually moved to Philadelphia together.

Hip-Hop for a Liberal Freshman

By the late 1980s Butterfly had moved to Philadelphia to live with his grandmother while making a living and learning the ropes of the local music scene. He met Doodlebug on the local circuit while the latter was rapping with an outfit called Dread Poets Society, which later became the 7 OD's. Butterfly, Doodlebug, and Ladybug soon became fast friends and rapping partners. In the early days of Digable Planets, they lived together, first in Jersey City, New Jersey, and later, New York. The last move brought them into the heart of Brooklyn's black neighborhoods, where they scraped by for a while rapping and working. Ladybug, for example, was selling sneakers just before the group won its record contract in 1992. By that summer, however, they were recording the material for their first album with Pendulum Records.

Spin's Chris Norris described Digable Planets after the release of their debut album in late 1992 as "poster children for a jazzy new world." *Reachin' (A New Refutation of Time and Space)* opened on the *Billboard* charts at Number 15, thanks to the popularity of the single "Rebirth of Slick (Cool Like Dat)." The song appeared on both the Top 40 and R&B charts, went gold in a month, and received heavy rotation on MTV in video form. Powers described "Rebirth of Slick" as "a study in magic wordplay shaped with elegant reserve." The song, according to *The Source*'s Williams, "expanded hip-hop's hegemony, dragging it into previously unexpected terrain; an 'alternative' rap group had come along with 'whip appeal' for progressives ... and Afrocentric utopians."

In the *Details* interview with Blashill, Butterfly described the vision that had shaped *Reachin'*. "Hip-hop has to change all the time," he explained, "because the African-American community changes at such a rapid pace. Especially in the use of language.... That's the Digable Planets' main thing, man. To manipulate language, to use it, juxtapose it, break it down, set it back." Kevin Powell offered his blessing in a *Rolling Stone* review, in which he wrote that "*Reachin'* ... is everything hip-hop should be: artisitically sound, unabashedly conscious and downright cool." He also predicted that the album's mix of jazz and hip-hop would take some of the bitterness out of the latter for outside listeners. "Digable Planets' modus operandi," Powell claimed, "is to elevate a rebellious and oft-misunderstood music to universal recognition."

Some of the critical response to Digable Planets, however, has argued that "universal recognition" has entailed a sacrifice of the hard edge, the political confrontation rap was known for, making the genre inappropriately accessible to those who normally found it threatening. Dream Hampton pointed out in the *Village Voice* the political divide that occurred: "Along with Arrested Development, Digable became a safe, politically correct, sexually integrated space for part-time hip hop fans who wanted nothing more to do with ugliness and raised voices." A *Time* reviewer exemplified that relief when he declared, "At last, rap even a liberal freshman philosophy major could love."

Jazz and Politics

Consequently, some writers dismissed Digable Planets' jazz-inflected rap for not accurately reflecting the urban black experience. Williams commented in *The Source,* "Instead of hip-hop lauding [the Planets] for their inventive and smart rap, they were admonished for not being 'hard enough' or 'keepin' it real.'" In retrospect, Butterfly expressed discontent with the album's reputation, saying that its achievements did not reflect the group's goals. "We were sampling a lot of jazz and speaking about a lot of political issues," he told *Billboard*'s Chris Morris in September of 1994. "I felt like people sort of missed it because of that pop appeal. And

it was sort of like a misconception, like this was what we were aimin' for. It didn't bother us, but the fact that we didn't achieve all that we wanted it to, did."

> *"I'f you're an artist with any type of consciousness and you have some rudimentary understanding...you know that your political ideas are not going to be easily swallowed by a record company."*
> —Butterfly

The *Village Voice*'s Hampton, coming to the Planets' defense, argued that it was "ridiculous and condescending that Digable's intellectualism is attributed to the fact that [Butterfly's] dad has a job.... [It's] offensive because it presumes that [Butterfly] can't be 'ghetto to his marrow' if his dad can read. As if the grassroots, leftist black power movement that was [Butterfly's] ever left its base in the hood." Almost seemingly apart from such debates, the second single from the album, "Nickel Bags," fell flat in what appeared to be a bad omen for the group's future, despite the album's gold record status.

When the group was presented with a Grammy Award for best rap performance by a group for "Rebirth of Slick," Butterfly stunned viewers with an explicitly political speech. He told his listeners, as Williams recorded in *The Source,* that the Planets would "like for everybody to think about the people right outside this door that's homeless as you're sittin in these $900 and $300 seats. They not out there eatin' at all."

With that statement, Butterfly began to declaim more directly the political philosophy he believed in and that had shaped *Reachin'*. The monikers that each rapper acquired for the debut album, for example, referred to "the insect theory," which Butterfly expanded on in a *Source* article: "The insect theory is the son of socialist readings. Knowing where you stand in this society and knowing where you should stand. Like if you look at ants and their hill, they're always around it, protecting it. Cats is going out getting food, bringing it back. Think of [Karl Marx's] *The Communist Manifesto*'s last sentence, 'workers of the world unite.' In front of, 'of the world unite,' you could put anything: it's about unity." The mainstream businesses that had embraced Digable Planets, however, did not find this kind of unity appealing and took a step back.

"9th Wonder (Blackitolism)," the first single off of Digable Planets' second album, *Blowout Comb,* signaled the new angle the trio would emphasize. The message became openly political, reflecting in particular the diet of revolutionary socialism on which Butterfly had been raised. Commenting on the shift from the first to the second album, the rapper explained it as necessary to survival in the music business. "If you're an artist with any type of consciousness," he told *Spin's* Norris, "and you have some rudimentary understanding of the business, you know that your political ideas are not going to be easily swallowed by a record company. So it's sort of like an infiltration. You have to get your foot in the door. Once you get in there, make some noise, sell some records, you got some power. *Then* you can begin to be more stern and direct with the shit you saying."

When *Blowout Comb* hit the market in October of 1994, critics did hear what Digable Planets was saying. Nathan Brackett commented appreciatively on the change in *Musician,* describing the trio as having "taken a step back from ... jazz-bo posturing, opting instead for a messier, more funk-oriented approach." *Rolling Stone's* Eric Berman noted that the trio had "taken admirable chances" with the new release; specifically, he cited the group's use of live musicians along with samples, as well as the intertwining of "Five Percent Nation dialect and Planetspeak on black pride and cultural imperialism with dabblings in political philosophy ... and scenes straight outta New York City's projects." Craig Marks reviewed the album for *Spin* in December of 1994 and declared it a "beguiling, demanding, damn near revolutionary follow-up."

In *Time* Christopher John Farley offered a specific definition of the kind of politics embodied in the jazz/hip-hop hybrid of Digable Planets and their peers. "Rap is a form of rebellion," Farley wrote, "but it can be a trap when it plays into violent stereotypes. By adapting the humanism of jazz and channeling the power of rap away from anti-social braggadocia, Digable Planets ... are helping make hip-hop truly revolutionary."

Selected discography

Reachin' (A New Refutation of Time and Space; includes "Rebirth of Slick [Cool Like Dat]"), Pendulum/EMI, 1992.
Blowout Comb (includes "9th Wonder"), Pendulum/EMI, 1994.

Sources

Audio, October 1993.
Billboard, September 10, 1994.
Details, July 1993.
Down Beat, June 1993.
Entertainment Weekly, March 26, 1993.
Essence, August 1993.
Metro Times (Detroit), April 21, 1993.
Musician, July 1993; November 1994.
Noir, November 1994.
People, April 5, 1993.
Rolling Stone, February 18, 1993; March 18, 1993; December 1, 1994; May 4, 1995.
Seventeen, March 1993.
The Source, March 1993; April 1993; December 1994.
Spin, May 1993; July 1994; November 1994; December 1994.
Time, February 15, 1993; November 21, 1994.
Us, May 1993.
Village Voice, November 28, 1994.

Additional information for this profile was obtained from Pendulum Records publicity materials, 1994.

—Ondine E. Le Blanc

Dr. Dre

Rap singer, producer

Though Dr. Dre's music career hasn't always been a "'G' Thang," (the "G" stands for "gangsta"), his own recordings combined with his production work made gangsta rap among the most vital pop genres of the 1990s. Born Andre Ramelle Young in Compton, California, Dr. Dre was raised by his mother. From the time he was four years old, he loved playing DJ at her parties. In 1981, he heard a song by Grandmaster Flash that inspired him to change his name in honor of basketball star Julius "Dr. J" Erving and become a full-time DJ.

Dr. Dre began spinning records at a Los Angeles nightclub called Eve After Dark. He produced the dance tapes in the club's four-track studio during the week, then played them on the weekends. In addition to using the rap trademarks of sampling, scratching, and drum machines, he added keyboards and vocals. "I would put together this mix shelf," Dre told Jonathan Gold in *Rolling Stone,* "lots of oldies, Martha and the Vandellas and stuff like that. And where normally you go to a club and the deejays play all the hit records back to back, I would put on a serious show. People would come from everywhere, just to see Dr. Dre on the wheels of steel."

In 1982, when Dre was 17 years old, he formed the World Class Wreckin' Cru with Yella (Antoine Carraby), his fellow DJ and manager of Eve After Dark. Dre's demo, "Surgery," became the group's first independently released single and sold 50,000 copies. Dre graduated from Compton's Centennial High School in 1983. Impressed with his studies in mechanical drafting, Northrop Aircraft offered him a job, but he turned it down. Dre discovered he could make more money as a DJ, and all of his spare time was spent preparing for the release of the World Class Wreckin' Cru's second album.

The Birth of N.W.A.

Dr. Dre left the World Class Wreckin' Cru in 1984. "They wouldn't do my songs," Dre said in a Death Row Records biography. "They said they'd never get on the radio." Dre joined with Ice Cube (O'Shea Jackson), who was in a group with his cousin at the time. Together they performed live wherever they could, including dates at skating rinks, where they played in front of 2,000 people at a time.

In 1985, Dr. Dre and Eazy-E (Eric Wright) decided to start up their own record company with Eazy-E's capital and Dre's producing talent. Dre produced the label's first project, "Boyz-n-the-Hood," featuring Eazy-E as the artist. They sold about 10,000 copies out of the

For the Record . . .

Born Andre Ramelle Young, c. 1965, in Compton, CA; children: (with girlfriend, Michel'le) Marcell (son).

Rap artist; record producer for various artists, including Eazy-E, the D.O.C., and Snoop Doggy Dogg. Began career as a DJ in high school, early 1980s; formed World Class Wreckin' Cru, 1982; released two albums; joined N.W.A., 1985; released three albums and one EP; produced eight albums for Ruthless Records; cofounded Death Row Records, 1991; released first solo album, *The Chronic*, Death Row, 1993.

Awards: Grammy Award for best rap solo performance, 1994; *Source* awards for best producer, solo artist, and album, 1994; named "One of the Top Ten Artists That Mattered Most, 1985-1995" by *Spin* magazine.

Addresses: *Record company*—Death Row Records, 10900 Wilshire Blvd., Suite 1240, Los Angeles, CA 90024.

trunks of their cars and used the money to finance the first single for their newly formed group, N.W.A. (Niggaz with Attitude). N.W.A. included Dr. Dre, Ice Cube, Eazy-E, Yella, M. C. Ren (Lorenzo Patterson), and Arabian Prince. Dre wrote and produced the group's first single, "Dopeman." He also produced Eazy-E's first platinum album, *Eazy-Duz-It,* that same year.

N.W.A. began their controversial and successful career in 1987 with the release of *N.W.A. and the Posse* on Macola Records. Two years later, the group released *Straight Outta Compton* on Ruthless Records and sold more than two million copies. Of course, the controversy behind the group and the album only assisted in launching their sales. Milt Ahlerich, assistant director of the Federal Bureau of Investigation's Office of Public Affairs, wrote a letter to the group's parent record company objecting to the lyrics of the song "F— tha Police." Police throughout the country added fuel to the fire by allegedly making it standard operating procedure to pull over any car driven by African American men blaring N.W.A. "We loved the controversy," Dre said in his record company biography. "It's the reason we blew up as big as we did. It wasn't hurting us, it was helping us."

Keeping his career as a producer alive, Dre produced the D.O.C. (Tray Curry), a rapper he had discovered in

Dallas, Texas. The D.O.C.'s album, *No One Can Do It Better,* became Number One on *Billboard*'s R&B album chart, Number 20 on the pop chart, and reached platinum sales. The track titled "It's Funky Enough" became a Number One rap single. Dre also produced an album for his girlfriend, Michel'le, which went platinum and reached Number One on *Billboard*'s R&B chart.

Away from N.W.A.

In January of 1990, Ice Cube left N.W.A. over a financial dispute and started a solo career. Later that year, N.W.A. released the platinum EP *100 Miles and Runnin'* on Ruthless Records. The group's third album, *Efil4zaggin* ("Niggaz 4 Life"), hit the stores in 1991, sold over a million copies in just two weeks, and reached Number One on *Billboard*'s album chart.

N.W.A.'s success and controversy brought them lots of attention, and Dr. Dre began receiving attention for his antics outside of the recording studio. On January 27, 1991, Dre allegedly hit Denise ("Dee") Barnes, the former host of *Pump It Up,* a FOX-TV show, and tried to push her down a staircase at an L.A. nightclub. *Pump It Up* had aired a segment about the separation of Ice Cube and N.W.A., with Ice Cube and the members of the group talking about each other. N.W.A. and Dr. Dre decided the show made them look bad. After the incident, Barnes filed assault charges and a $22.75 million suit against Dr. Dre; he settled out of court.

Later in 1991, Dr. Dre and Marion "Suge" Knight inspected Dre's contract with Ruthless Records. Dre, the house producer at Ruthless Records, had watched seven of the eight albums he produced go platinum. Knight claimed Ruthless had taken advantage of Dr. Dre by paying him a substandard royalty rate and withholding back pay. Dre left Ruthless, and Knight engineered his release from his contract with the label. Ruthless Records president Eazy-E claimed that he only agreed to end the contract because Knight and two other men threatened him with baseball bats and pipes.

"I got Ice Cube his start. I also launched Eazy," Dr. Dre said in his record company biography. "There ain't no question that N.W.A. became what it was in large part because of my music and my producing. Me and Eazy had agreed from Jump Street that we was to be partners. Now Eazy says he's the owner of the record company, Ruthless. Well, let him own it then. But I was never supposed to be signed to him or owned by him." Eazy-E filed suits against Dr. Dre at the end of 1991 and late 1992 for racketeering and conspiracy. A federal judge dismissed the charges on August 9, 1993.

On Death Row

Suge Knight and Dr. Dre founded their own label, called Death Row Records, and searched for major label distribution. They had Dr. Dre's first solo effort, *The Chronic,* completed by the time they formed a partnership with Interscope Records in 1992. "People didn't want to take a chance on us, and it pissed me off," Dre said in *Newsweek.* "I mean, I had talent—talent that had already been proven with huge record sales from N.W.A.—so you had to wonder what the f— the problem was."

Dr. Dre continued to keep his name in the press and on police records before the release of his solo album. On June 5, 1992, Dre surrendered to police after they had issued a warrant for his arrest on charges that he assaulted record producer Damon Thomas. Then, in October of 1992, Dre pleaded guilty to battery of a police officer during a May 22 brawl. He served "house arrest" sentences for each charge, which necessitated his wearing a police-monitoring ankle bracelet. On a more positive note, he also became the co-host of *Yo! MTV Raps* with Ed Lover.

In 1993, *The Chronic* arrived in stores—the first release for Death Row Records. It sold three million copies and spent eight months in the Top Ten of *Billboard's* album chart. The first single, "Nuthin' But a 'G' Thang," sold more than a million copies, and "F— wit Dre Day" went gold. *The Chronic* featured other budding rap artists from Dre's "posse," including Snoop Doggy Dogg, Rage, RBX, Jewell, Nate Dogg, Daz, and Kurupt. Dr. Dre then went behind the scenes of the music video business, following the release of the album with his directorial debut, *Nuthin' But a 'G' Thang.* He also starred in the movie *Who's the Man?* with Lover, his MTV cohost.

Dre went on to produce the debut of his brother's best friend, Snoop Doggy Dogg. *Doggystyle,* released on Death Row, sold 800,000 copies in its first week. In August of 1993, Dr. Dre and other Death Row artists headlined a national tour that included Run-D.M.C., Geto Boys, Onyx, and Boss. The $200,000 stage show included a 14-piece band, a 1964 Impala, a makeshift liquor store, a garage, a 10-foot skeleton, and a 42-person entourage.

Dr. Dre found himself in serious trouble in 1994. It all began on January 10, when he led Los Angeles police through the streets on a high-speed chase. When Dre was finally apprehended, the police found his blood-alcohol level to be 0.16, twice the legal limit in California. Since he had broken his 1993 probation, he received an eight-month jail sentence, a $1,053 fine, four years summary probation, and an order to complete a 90-day alcohol education program.

Later that same year, Dre received a Grammy Award for best rap solo performance. In addition, he produced his younger brother's debut single on Death Row's *Above the Rim* compilation. By August of 1994, albums he had rapped on or produced had sold nearly 28 million copies. On September 27, 1994, Death Row Records released *Murder Was the Case,* which featured a song by Dr. Dre and Ice Cube called "Natural Born Killaz." Dre also directed an 18-minute video, starring Snoop Doggy Dogg, called *Murder Was the Case: The Movie.*

Dr. Dre and Ice Cube reunited on their album *Helter Skelter.* The first single, "You Don't Want to See Me," featured an appearance by funk founder George Clinton. However, *Helter Skelter's* release was postponed due to Dre's eight-month jail sentence, which started on January 10, 1995. In the meantime, he contributed the single "Keep Their Heads Ringin'" to the soundtrack for *Friday,* a comedy film starring Ice Cube.

Despite the setback, Dr. Dre is expected to bounce back from the adverse publicity and continue his career as a producer and recording artist. "Dre has vision," Jimmy Iovine, producer and head of Interscope Records, commented in Dr. Dre's biography. "I believe he's one of the great producers around today because his approach combines a lot of different worlds, in music and life. He can reach everyone. Because of his creativity and innovation, pushing the limits like most producers don't anymore these days—whether in rap or rock—he deserves his own label. He's that gifted."

Selected discography

With N.W.A.

N.W.A. and the Posse, Macola, 1987.
Straight Outta Compton, Ruthless, 1989.
100 Miles and Runnin', Ruthless, 1990.
Efil4zaggin, Ruthless, 1991.

Other

The Chronic, Death Row, 1993.
(Contributor) *Murder Was the Case,* Death Row, 1994.
(With Ice Cube) *Helter Skelter,* Death Row, 1995.
"Keep Their Heads Ringin'," *Friday* (soundtrack), Priority, 1995.

Sources

Books

Beckman, Janette, and B. Adler, *Rap: Portraits and Lyrics of a Generation of Black Rockers,* St. Martin's Press, 1991.
The Trouser Press Record Guide, edited by Ira A. Robbins, Collier, 1991.

Periodicals

Billboard, October 14, 1989; April 7, 1990; June 22, 1991; July 6, 1991; July 13, 1991; September 7, 1991; June 6, 1992; June 20, 1992; October 24, 1992; January 16, 1993; January 23, 1993; May 8, 1993; July 3, 1993; July 10, 1993; August 23, 1993; November 27, 1993; December 25, 1993.
Details, April 1993; May 1993.
Entertainment Weekly, February 26, 1993; December 31, 1993; November 11, 1994; February 3, 1995.

Jet, September 19, 1994.
Musician, June 1989; December 1990; March 1991; February 1994.
Newsweek, August 22, 1994; October 31, 1994.
New York Times, March 10, 1993; April 23, 1993; January 2, 1995.
People, May 23, 1994; September 19, 1994.
Rolling Stone, June 29, 1989; August 8, 1991; September 19, 1991; March 18, 1993; September 30, 1993; June 2, 1994; October 20, 1994.
The Source, September 1993; June 1995.
Spin, January 1994.

Additional information for this profile was obtained from an *MTV News* transcript, January 9, 1995, and Death Row Records press material, 1995.

—*Sonya Shelton*

Gloria Estefan

Singer, songwriter

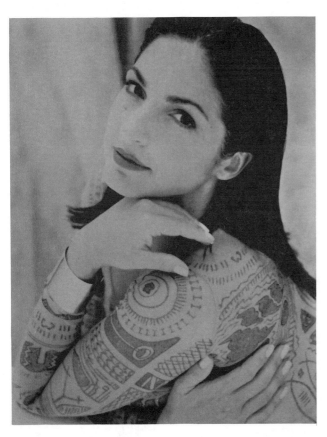

The path of Gloria Estefan's career might be best traced through the successive names of the musical ensemble of which she has been a member since the mid-1970s: she joined the Miami Latin Boys as a teen-aged vocalist; her bandmates then renamed themselves the Miami Sound Machine. Estefan eventually became their primary singer, and, in a little over a decade, her energetic fronting of the band and its burgeoning pop success led to its rechristening as Gloria Estefan and the Miami Sound Machine. By the mid-1990s, nearly twenty years into her career, the singer and songwriter had finally achieved solo billing.

Estefan was originally a Spanish-language performer but switched to English as the Miami Sound Machine began receiving more recognition. Over the years Estefan's recordings have sold millions and made her an international star. Her musical style is credited with helping make Latin-flavored pop music—based on the rhythms of her native Cuba—a tremendous crossover success. In 1993 she returned to her first language and released an album of songs in Spanish. Although Estefan's early years in the entertainment industry were marked by a terrible, recurring stage fright, she has metamorphosed into a sultry international pop star known for her showstopping performances. Estefan still lives in her hometown of Miami, Florida, where she is revered by its large Cuban American community. Adding to the drama of her rags-to-riches life story, in 1990 Estefan survived a near-fatal bus accident that could have put her in a wheelchair permanently.

Estefan was born in Cuba in 1957 to Gloria, a schoolteacher, and Jose Manuel Fajardo, who worked as a bodyguard for the country's dictatorial leader, Fulgencio Batista. When Communist forces, led by Fidel Castro, took over a year later, the Fajardo family fled to Miami; Estefan's father later went back on a military mission funded by the U.S. government and was captured by his own cousins and imprisoned. After eighteen months, President John F. Kennedy negotiated his release. Jose Fajardo then joined the U.S. military, and the family, which by then included Gloria's younger sister Becky, relocated several times as he transferred from base to base. Eventually he was sent to Vietnam.

As a child Estefan attended Catholic schools and began taking on an increasing amount of responsibility in her family. Her mother first attended college, then worked outside the home, and Gloria did many of the household chores. Her father, after returning from the war in 1968, was stricken with multiple sclerosis as a result of his exposure to Agent Orange in Vietnam. The adolescent Estefan looked after her disabled father for part of the day. She found solace from the burdens in singing. "It was my release from everything, my escape," Estefan

Born Gloria Fajardo, September 1, 1957, in Havana, Cuba; immigrated to the United States, 1959; daughter of Jose Manuel (a bodyguard to Cuban leader Fulgencio Batista) and Gloria (a schoolteacher) Fajardo; married Emilio Estefan, Jr. (a musician), September 1, 1978; children: Nayib, Emily Marie. *Education:* Received B.A. in psychology from the University of Miami.

Worked as a customs translator at Miami International Airport, mid-1970s; joined group Miami Latin Boys (also billed as the Miami Latin Kings), 1975; group's name changed to Miami Sound Machine; other members included Enrique Garcia, Juan Marcos Avila, and Emilio Estefan, Jr. Toured Latin America and Europe numerous times, 1976-84; had several hit albums in Spanish. First million-selling, English-language, American album, *Primitive Love,* 1986. Represented United States at the Pan American Games, 1987. Solo performer since the early 1990s. Founder and owner, with husband, Emilio, of Larios on the Beach, a Cuban cuisine restaurant in Miami, FL.

Awards: Songwriter of the Year, BMI, 1988; lifetime achievement award, Premio lo Nuestro Musica Latina, 1992.

Addresses: Home—Star Island, FL. *Record company*—Epic Records, 51 West 52nd St., New York, NY 10019.

told *Rolling Stone* reporter Daisann McLane. "I'd lock myself up in my room with my guitar," a birthday gift her mother had ordered from Spain. "I wouldn't cry.... I would sing for hours by myself." The popular music of the era, especially British acts like the Beatles and Gerry and the Pacemakers, were a strong influence on her.

Began Singing Career on a Lark

The singer met her future husband, Emilio Estefan, at a wedding in 1975. He was playing the disco hit "The Hustle" on an accordion. Smitten with the young Cuban emigre, Gloria, along with her cousin Merci, offered to sing in Estefan's local combo for free. Within a year, she was singing with the band—then called the Miami Latin Boys but sometimes billed as the Miami Latin Kings—at local weddings and had enrolled in the University of Miami as a psychology major. At the time, however, she was still a shy, overweight teenager; bandmate Emilio

Estefan, though, was considered "the catch of the town." His work as a percussionist and manager of the Latin Boys, soon to be renamed the Miami Sound Machine, was only a hobby for the workaholic. He worked for Bacardi, eventually rising to the post of director of Hispanic marketing for the rum importing company.

The couple began a flirtation during the hours they spent together rehearsing and performing. They married in September of 1978, after Gloria had graduated from college. Meanwhile, she was becoming a more integral member of the Sound Machine, by this time a phenomenally popular Miami act that also included Enrique Garcia and Juan Marcos Avila. Estefan further honed her vocal style, learned more about the Cuban music of her roots, and became a percussionist as well. It was also around the time of the couple's marriage that the Miami Sound Machine recorded their first album, *Renacer,* on a Miami-based label. "A rough collection of original Spanish-language ballads and disco pop, it was produced on a budget of $2000, but Estefan's warm, distinctive purr comes through," wrote McLane in *Rolling Stone.*

By 1980 Emilio Estefan had recognized that the band's sound—with its blend of Cuban rhythms and American pop sensibilities—had surefire potential. He resigned from Bacardi in order to take the Sound Machine's local success onto another level, a move that also coincided with the arrival of the couple's first child, a boy they named Nayib. As the band's full-time manager, Emilio won a recording contract with the Hispanic division of CBS Records, called Discos CBS. Estefan performed as vocalist on four of the albums the Sound Machine recorded for the company during the early 1980s and also wrote some of the band's songs.

Played to Stadium Crowds in Latin America

With such major-label backing, the Miami Sound Machine quickly became a success south of the border. Writing of this early period, McLane explained that their "sound was derivative, but for Latin American fans, Miami Sound Machine was unique—the first band that played state-of-the-art American pop rock *and* spoke the right language. In Venezuela and Peru, Panama and Honduras, their records shot to Number One." The band wielded their success in the Hispanic market when they convinced CBS to put out an English-language album.

The first crossover release for the Miami Sound Machine, and Estefan's debut record in English, was 1984's *Eyes of Innocence.* Its first single, a disco tune called "Dr. Beat," made appearances on European charts. Next, the band signed on a local trio called the Jerks—Rafael Vigil, Joe Galdo, and Lawrence Dermer—whom Emilio had met when they were recording a jingle for a commercial. The Jerks had been working on a salsa-influenced aerobics record, and some of the tracks they penned appeared on the Sound Machine's next album, 1985's *Primitive Love.* The hugely successful release catapulted both Estefan and the group into international pop superstardom with the singles "Bad Boys," "Words Get in the Way," and "Conga." At that point, Emilio left the band to take over as a full-time manager and producer.

The Jerks also worked on the Sound Machine's 1987 album, *Let It Loose,* but quit after disagreements with Emilio—also listed as producer—over creative and financial differences. Other personnel changes in the Sound Machine—including the departure of founding drummer Enrique Garcia—also plagued the group during these years. Estefan was needled by her husband to change her look and become more outgoing on stage. "Emilio saw a side of me that I didn't let people see, and he wanted that to come out to people," Estefan said of her husband in the *Rolling Stone* interview with McLane. "He was trying to make me confident, but I could've smacked him. At the beginning, everybody would always accuse me of being stuck up, 'cause I was shy. But a performer can't afford to be shy."

A Household Name by 1990

Estefan's increasing confidence and ebullience helped propel record and concert sales through the roof, success she and the band could hardly have imagined. *Let It Loose* sold 4 million copies, spurred by its hit single "1-2-3." In 1988 Estefan won the prestigious BMI Songwriter of the Year award. She penned several of the songs for *Cuts Both Ways,* a 1989 effort. It also sold well into the millions, and international tours to support the releases were often marked by sell-out crowds. By now the act was billed as Gloria Estefan and the Miami Sound Machine.

In 1990 the nonstop touring that had marked much of Estefan's career came to an abrupt halt when she was involved in a serious accident. The band's tour bus had stopped before a stalled, jackknifed semitrailer on a snowy highway in Pennsylvania one March night. The vehicle was hit from the rear by another truck, and Estefan was catapulted to the floor from the berth in which she had been sleeping. Her husband and nine-year-old son were only slightly injured, but the impact broke Estefan's back. Fans feared from early news reports that the singer might be paralyzed for life.

The public outpouring of support for the critically injured Estefan was overwhelming. Some radio stations in Miami began playing her songs nearly nonstop, and a 1-900 number was set up for well-wishers to leave messages. Cards, flowers, and presents flooded her hospital room, first in Scranton, Pennsylvania, then in New York City, where she was later transferred. Even then-President George Bush called twice to wish the singer well.

In New York, surgeons implanted two eight-inch-long titanium steel rods in her spine in an effort to fuse it back together. Although the operation was a success, it traumatized her body to such a degree that she lay nearly immobilized for weeks. Estefan returned home to Miami three months after the accident—in a plane belonging to friend Julio Iglesias—to television cameras and an emotionally charged crowd at the airport. She began intense physical therapy and had to adhere to a strict diet and a grueling exercise program to help regain her strength and mobility. For months she would awaken nearly every hour in her sleep from the lingering pain in her back and legs.

Accident Revived Memories for Estefan

The memories of caring for her increasingly disabled father, who had passed away in 1980, also pushed Estefan through the rehabilitation process. "All my life I've been afraid of becoming an invalid," she recalled to *People* reporter Steve Dougherty. "He was a very athletic, strong and handsome man. For years and years I watched him weaken and die. I saw what it did to the people around him—to his family. I've had a premonition all my life that I would become a burden to the people I love." Prior to the accident, Estefan had had an elevator installed in a house she and Emilio were building in Miami, for the ostensible purpose of moving musical equipment. "But in the back of my mind, I knew what it was really for. So when I was lying in the bus, I thought 'Here it is. This is the thing I've been waiting for.'"

Less than six months after the crash, Estefan performed in public for the first time on the annual Jerry Lewis Labor Day Muscular Dystrophy Telethon to a standing ovation. By that time, she was also working in the studio and writing songs for an upcoming album. Entitled *Into the Light,* its first single was "Coming Out of the Dark," a gospel-inspired melody that Emilio had begun to write while they were en route to the New York hospital for the surgery. Other tracks on *Into the Light* include "Nayib's Song," an ode to her son, and "Close My Eyes."

"I wanted this album to be a very freeing experience for me," Estefan told *Detroit Free Press* music writer Gary

Graff. "I wanted my vocal performance to be much more emotional, and I think they are. The emotions are right there on the surface. I was very happy when I started singing again ... and I wanted to share that feeling." Estefan embarked on another major tour for *Into the Light* only a year after her accident. Although doctors had predicted that it would take her three to five years to achieve the level of mobility and fitness that her performing schedule demanded, she soon returned to the same energetic movements onstage. "I just have to make sure I don't do crazy things, like backflips off the stage," she explained to Dougherty.

> *Estefan's musical style is credited with helping make Latin-flavored pop music—based on the rhythms of her native Cuba—a tremendous crossover success.*

Critics point to Estefan's increasing success over the years as a turning point for American pop music, helping it to reflect the nation's growing Hispanic minority and influence. Record sales hovering near the 10 million mark for the Sound Machine, and later in Estefan's solo career, seemed to have awakened major labels to the possibilities of other Spanish-language acts. In 1993 Estefan recorded and released an album of Spanish-language songs entitled *Mi Tierra*. The record, which means "My Land," achieved sales of over 1.3 million, holding at Number One on the Latin charts and Number 27 on the pop charts. The work also featured performances by percussionist Sheila E. and noted Cuban musician Tito Puente.

In early 1994 Estefan was invited by the Grammy Awards to perform a song in Spanish for the telecast, a first for the music industry ceremony. Further proof of Estefan's impact on the music business came with the success of another Cuban American performer. She and her husband had discovered a young Miami resident named Jon Secada, and Emilio became his manager. Secada went on tour with Estefan for almost a year before the release of his solo debut album, which made him an international success. "Gloria was very important to the Latin scene," Secada told *San Jose Mercury News* contributor Harry Sumrall. "She opened all the doors and set a good example to the Latin community." Late in 1993 Estefan released a holiday-themed recording of classic Christmas songs reworked with a Latin flavor. It also included a few original songs. Next, she released an album of covers in 1994 entitled *Hold Me, Thrill Me, Kiss Me*. Its title track became the first hit single, and the record included Estefan's versions of "Breaking Up Is Hard to Do" as well as the 1970s-era disco hits "Cherchez la Femme" and "Turn the Beat Around." The latter also appeared on the soundtrack to the 1994 Sylvester Stallone/Sharon Stone film *The Specialist*. A *People* review of Estefan's *Hold Me* granted that while "she does a fine job updating oldies ... most of her takes on other singers' hits sound too perfunctory to be essential."

Adored by Miami's Cuban American Community

In the mid-1990s Estefan took a hiatus from performing when she had another child. Doctors had warned her that becoming pregnant again might place too much pressure on her fused spine and endanger her life, but the pregnancy went well and daughter Emily Marie was delivered by Caesarean section in late 1994. The family—including teenaged son Nayib and two Dalmatians named Ricky and Lucy—lives in the Miami area in a residential enclave called Star Island, onetime home to actor Don Johnson and former Nicaraguan dictator Anastasio Somoza. Estefan also became involved with a Cuban restaurant she and her husband opened in the city's trendy South Beach area.

Estefan's success has made her more than just a local celebrity in her hometown. She is known as "Nuestra Glorita," or "Our Gloria," and is revered by Miami's populous Cuban community as a sort of symbol of their own success. (Nearly ostracized as newly arrived exiles to Florida only 30 years before, Cuban Americans in the 1990s had gained enormous social, political, and economic influence in the state.) While grateful for her success, Estefan herself remains philosophical about her life—and credits the brush with tragedy for changing everything about her. "It's very hard to stress me out now," the singer told *People* magazine's Dougherty. "It's hard to get me in an uproar about anything because most things have little significance compared with what I almost lost.... So many people [got] behind me and gave me a reason to want to come back fast and made me feel strong. Knowing how caring people can be, how much they gave me—that has changed me forever."

Estefan took these positive feelings to her next effort, the Spanish-language, *Abriendo Puertas* (title means "opening doors"). Although the recording features holiday-oriented songs juxtaposed against Latin American rhythms, Estefan is quick to define it as not just another Christmas album. "There's Christmas music, and then there's this record," she explained to *Billboard* magazine's John Lahnert. "Some of these songs hopefully will live on way beyond Christmas because of the positive messages and interesting rhythms." Featuring a blend of Latin American musicians, the album reflects Estefan's hopes to open even more doors for this kind of music. "You have to reach a certain level where you have a strong enough fan base where they will be curious about what you do and they'll listen to it...I think my fans are going to hopefully like the direction we've moved into and grown into, since all of these projects eventually become a part of you."

Selected discography

Eyes of Innocence, Discos CBS, 1984.
Primitive Love, Epic, 1985.
Let It Loose, Epic, 1987.
Cuts Both Ways, Epic, 1989.
Into the Light, Epic, 1991.
Greatest Hits, Epic, 1992.
Mi Tierra, Epic, 1993.
Christmas through Your Eyes, Sony/Epic, 1993.
Hold Me, Thrill Me, Kiss Me, Epic, 1994.
Abriendo Puertas, Epic, 1995.

Sources

Books

Gonzalez, Fernando, *Gloria Estefan: Cuban-American Singing Star,* Millbrook Press, 1993.

Periodicals

Billboard, September 2, 1995.
Detroit Free Press, January 27, 1991; August 21, 1991.
Detroit News, June 25, 1992; November 25, 1993; November 19, 1994.
Entertainment Weekly, June 25, 1993; July 30, 1993.
Miami Herald, November 2, 1994.
People, April 9, 1990; June 25, 1990; February 18, 1991 October 31, 1994.
Rolling Stone, June 14, 1990.
San Jose Mercury News, February 23, 1995.

Additional information for this profile was obtained from Epic press materials, 1995.

—*Carol Brennan*

Everything But The Girl

Pop duo

Courtesy of Atlantic Records

In the decade that vocalist Tracey Thorn and guitarist/keyboardist Ben Watt have been writing and recording music together as Everything But The Girl (EBTG), they have watched their jazz-influenced pop style go from unfashionable to trendy. Although several music writers have credited EBTG with parenting the trend, the duo has nevertheless remained at the periphery of success. Their names are known in their native England, where they enjoyed initial popularity with college crowds, but they've mustered only a cult following in the United States, again mostly among college students. Writing in *Seventeen* almost a decade after their first collaboration, Wif Stenger summarized EBTG's nonrise to fame thus: "Their seductive, mellow sound, perfect for lazy, hazy afternoons or steamy summer nights, wasn't exactly fashionable in 1981 (the start of the synth-pop craze). Oddly enough, it did catch on—although Ben and Tracey didn't get famous for it."

After working with two other women in a band called the Marine Girls in the early 1980s, Thorn was signed as a solo artist by independent label Cherry Red. She cut one album, *A Distant Shore,* for the label in 1982 before leaving London to begin university studies in Hull. During the same period, guitarist Ben Watt was also initiating his music career; he landed a gig at a club run by Mike Alway, who also produced records for Cherry Red. By 1982, Watt had released an EP called *Summer into Winter* on Cherry Red. Soon after, he also left for college in Hull. Alway recommended that Thorn and Watt look one another up; the result was Everything But The Girl.

Shared Penchant for Jazz

The two became friends immediately, even finding an apartment together soon after meeting. Some reporters have characterized their relationship as a romantic one, treating it as general knowledge, but neither Watt nor Thorn has confirmed the status of their private collaboration, leaving it persistently ambiguous. Their union as musical partners began somewhat experimentally, each writing songs that they would then work on together and each seeing collaboration as secondary to their solo work. They did, however, share strong interests, including a penchant for jazz and an unwillingness to produce music for the market.

They concentrated on writing jazz-influenced pop songs that were subdued and literary—not the popular musical fare of the early 1980s. When they did win attention from listeners, the notice came not for any of their own compositions, but for a cover of Cole Porter's "Night and Day." Their rendition, recorded in January 1983 and released the following June, dovetailed with a burgeon-

For the Record . . .

Members include **Tracey Thorn** (born September 26, 1962, in England; studied English at University of Hull), vocals, and **Ben Watt** (born December 6, 1962, in England; studied music at University of Hull), guitar, keyboards.

Band formed in Hull, England, c. 1982; released single "Night and Day," Cherry Disc, 1983; released debut album, *Eden,* Blanco Y Negro, 1984.

Addresses: *Record company*—Atlantic Records, 75 Rockefeller Plaza, New York, NY 10019.

ing interest in a musical style referred to as "new jazz." The single brought them to the notice of Paul Weller, an important figure in English rock from his work with the Jam and Style Council, who negotiated their first large-exposure performance in London, in early January 1983. *Melody Maker*'s Ian Pye described the stage style that would become characteristic of the duo: "Armed with acoustic guitars and their own quiet determination, they won the audience over through the simple yet endearing quality of a delicately sketched performance."

Despite the positive response prompted by their performance and single, both Watt and Thorn still viewed their solo careers as their main work. They did reveal, however, that as a duo they were receiving calls from major labels in London and Los Angeles. They responded tentatively at the time, ultimately passing over big-label sponsorship for the freedom to shape their own direction gradually. They switched labels only when they became frustrated with Cherry Red, and their original producer, Mike Alway, decided to start his own label, Blanco Y Negro. EBTG followed Alway in the spring of 1983 and became official clients in April 1984; the deal offered EBTG the artistic freedom of an independent label and the distribution of a major label, since Blanco Y Negro operated as a subsidiary of Warner Bros.

Despite the security of their new professional home, some label confusion followed during and after the transition from Cherry Red to Blanco Y Negro. By the time Watt had produced his full-length solo album, *North Marine Drive,* for Cherry Red in 1983, the duo had recorded the material for their joint debut album. But the release of that record, *Eden,* was held up until the summer of 1984, by which time the band had moved to

Blanco Y Negro. Despite its scrambled origin, reviewers and listeners greeted *Eden* with warmth, pushing it to the Number 14 spot on the U.K. charts. Paul Strange, writing for *Melody Maker* in May 1984, called it "a haunting, mellow, passionate and highly addictive debut album." The success of the album and its lead single, "Each and Every One," brought Thorn and Watt an offer to perform on BBC-TV; they had to turn it down, however, in order to take their university exams.

Influenced Chart-Topping Bands

Although EBTG grew as a name in English popular music, *Eden* would be the last moment of an uncomplicated relationship with the English music press; reviewers and interviewers quickly became critical and sometimes harsh, often dismissing the duo's relaxed, jazzy sound and intellectually deliberate lyrics. In 1986 Thorn and Watt explained to *Melody Maker* interviewer Sorrell Downer their impression of the conflict they experienced with English reviewers. Thorn told Downer that the "records were being reviewed by people a lot older then us, ... but so many people who listened to it were our age, and to them it was just fab and meant an enormous amount." Thorn also discussed the response that her withdrawn and vulnerable manner had earned from music writers, reporting, "Every time I get on stage, they bring out the knife and start running up and down screaming 'Why isn't she more tough?'" She attributed much of the trouble, paradoxically, to her outspoken feminism, explaining, "because I'm one of so few female vocalists that will stand up and say 'I'm a feminist,' write songs about women, and talk about my lyrics in a feminist way."

Despite criticism, these elements found a steady following with English youth, particularly of university background, and became a significant influence among bands that would achieve chart-topping sales and enormous popularity within a decade, actually turning the EBTG sound into an important force in the music industry. At the time their work prompted comparisons to the style of sultry singer Sade.

In 1985 Jimmy Guterman gave the band's second album, *Love Not Money,* a favorable and optimistic review in *Rolling Stone,* demonstrating the general division between American and British reviewers. Similarly, when Sire (another Warner Bros. division) released *Eden* in the United States as *Everything But The Girl* in 1984, Roy Trakin greeted it with approval in *Creem.* He credited the pair with "carving out a brand-new musical category ...: post-post-punk cocktail jazz." Like most reviewers, he focused on Thorn's voice, claiming that her "husky, tobacco-filled vocals soothe on the outside, but reward more than casual listening, too."

Drifting in Limbo

Baby, the Stars Shine Bright, released in 1986, exchanged Watt's previously spare arrangement for the lush accompaniment of a full orchestra. A *Melody Maker* review noted what appeared to be the duo's popular position at the moment, balanced between "their status as marginal indie-pop cuties" and "a wider acceptance," noting in particular attention from the United States. But two years later, *Melody Maker* reviewer David Stubbs described the band as in exactly the same place they had been at the beginning of their career; in the wake of the 1988 release of *Idlewild,* he noted that the duo "persisted and drifted into a limbo between heaven and hell" from which there seemed to be no escape, remarking, "They have painted themselves into this corner of dumb comparisons and painted thus in soft pastels with a limited repertoire of permutations and options." Nonetheless, *Idlewild* held on in the Top Twenty from March through August of that year.

The Language of Life, released in 1990 on Atlantic Records and recorded in Los Angeles, landed EBTG in the pages of many American magazines, including *Seventeen, Rolling Stone, Stereo Review,* and *Spin.* The album made it onto the American pop charts with a push from the single "Driving," which won regular radio airplay and video rotation on cable network VH-1. Rachel Pepper later noted in *Deneuve* EBTG's "recently gained widespread American musical attention," referring to the effect of *Language* and the 1991 follow-up *Worldwide.* In fact, it was generally acknowledged in the music industry that the duo was finally poised to break out of their cult vacuum with the American public. Thorn and Watt next produced an acoustic album, *Acoustic,* that recalled many previous recordings.

At that critical moment, Watt fell prey to Churg Strauss syndrome, an often fatal illness that kept him in the hospital for most of 1992. Looking back in a 1994 *Billboard* article, Jon Cummings argued that the illness "derailed much of the momentum that [Watt] and Thorn had gained at American radio." EBTG had been scheduled for a major tour of the States that year in order to maintain the excitement generated by *Language* and

to promote both *Worldwide* and *Acoustic.* Consequently, when the illness gave way, Watt and Thorn found themselves starting practically from scratch with American listeners.

Miraculously, *Amplified Heart* easily repeated the success of *Language,* winning unusually broad notice, as well as praise. Stephen Holden hailed it in the *New York Times* as "possibly their best," and Karen Schoemer claimed in *Newsweek* that *Amplified Heart* found "the perfect balance of folky simplicity and understated technology." It was this balance, she felt, that made the disc "the most beautifully mature album of their career," as well as "one of the sleeper gems of 1994."

Selected discography

Eden (includes "Each and Every One"), Blanco Y Negro, 1984, released in U.S. as *Everything But The Girl,* Sire, 1984.
Love Not Money, Blanco Y Negro/Sire, 1985.
Baby, the Stars Shine Bright, Blanco Y Negro/Sire, 1986.
Idlewild, Blanco Y Negro/Sire, 1988.
Language of Life (includes "Driving"), Blanco Y Negro/Atlantic, 1990.
Worldwide, Blanco Y Negro/Atlantic, 1991.
Acoustic, Blanco Y Negro/Atlantic, 1992.
Amplified Heart, Atlantic, 1994.

Sources

Billboard, June 11, 1994.
Creem, April 1985.
Deneuve, April 1993.
Entertainment Weekly, July 29, 1994.
Melody Maker, April 24, 1982; September 4, 1982; January 15, 1983; January 29, 1983; May 19, 1984; June 2, 1984; August 30, 1986; March 5, 1988; February 10, 1990; September 28, 1991.
Newsweek, September 5, 1994.
New York Times, September 9, 1994.
Rolling Stone, August 15, 1985; July 12, 1990.
Seventeen, July 1990.
Spin, March 1990.
Stereo Review, June 1990.
Stereoplay, December 1991.

—*Ondine E. Le Blanc*

Julia Fordham

Singer, songwriter

Photograph by Kate Garner, courtesy of Virgin Records

The earthy, sensual appeal and the emotional potency of Julia Fordham's contralto voice are what initially strike most people listening to the British pop singer. Having released four albums to British acclaim and moderate U.S. attention, Fordham has carved a niche for herself in the adult contemporary market. She writes almost all of the songs she sings, alternating between melancholy, love-centered lyrics and socially conscious ones. Influenced by Julie London and Joni Mitchell, Fordham combines ethereal background instrumentation with folk/pop sounds for the thinking listener.

Born in 1963 in Portsmouth, England, Fordham, along with her two siblings, was brought up on Hayling Island, a rural island next to the Isle of Wight. "I wanted to be a singer from the time I was a small child," she expressed to Kristine McKenna of *Musician* in 1990, "but my hopes were temporarily dashed when I couldn't get into the school choir. My voice was so low they wouldn't have me! It wasn't until I was 12 and got a guitar and spent endless hours singing in my room that I discovered I had two voices—one high and one low—that I could switch between quite easily."

Although many musicians can point to childhood performances as heralds of their later careers, Fordham actually entered the world of professional music at a very early age. At 15, she began performing in pubs, having left school to devote herself to music. She took buses off the island to sing in pubs in Portsmouth and Hampshire. "In retrospect, it's amazing my parents let me do it," Fordham exclaimed to McKenna. Not only did the singer have the courage to launch her career so young, she had the confidence to rely for the most part on her own songs. Along with her own music, Fordham mixed songs from the 1940s, such as tunes by the Mills Brothers, and pieces by Joan Armatrading.

Fordham's musical career took a shift in 1982 when she responded to an advertisement in *Melody Maker* for backup singers for Mari Wilson. As one of the Wilsations, the 19-year-old Fordham was exposed to the workings of the pop music business. "I learned a lot from Mari," Fordham explained to *Musician's* McKenna. "An intelligent woman with a great voice, but she let herself be manipulated into selling herself as a pop novelty. She took off in this big, pink bubble that eventually burst, and observing that process I came to understand that if I was gonna be successful in this business, that wasn't how I was gonna do it."

Five years later, Fordham felt she had enough experience to launch her solo career. Virgin Records agreed with her, offering the singer a contract in 1987. By 1988 Fordham's debut album was released to positive reviews in Great Britain. *Julia Fordham* generated two

Born in 1963 in Portsmouth, England.

Sang in pubs in England, beginning in late 1970s; background singer for Mari Wilson, beginning in 1982; signed contract with Virgin Records, 1987; released self-titled debut album, 1988.

Addresses: *Home*—London, England. *Record company*—Virgin Records, 338 North Foothill Road, Beverly Hills, CA 90210.

European hit singles and sold 150,000 copies. After hearing the singer's album, Jim Farber of *Rolling Stone* complimented Fordham's voice, calling it "a deep, warm instrument, rich with deliberation. Her alto is as thick and androgynous as Alison Moyet's, but she doles it out smoothly in a cool jazz style reminiscent of Sade and informs it with a self-conscious ambition suggesting Joni Mitchell." However, Farber felt that a "murky production" detracted from the impact her voice could have made.

Rolling Stone reviewer Rob Tannenbaum had few good things to say about Fordham's second album, *Porcelain,* released by Virgin in 1990. He judged her experimentation with foreign genres too casual to have more than a surface appeal and her melancholy unrelenting. "With its curious match of adolescent lyricism and contemporary musical structure, Fordham's second album is full of foolish and beautiful extremes," was the best he could find to say in his 1990 review.

Record buyers apparently disagreed, acquiring *Porcelain* to the tune of 225,000 copies and raising the album to Number 74 on the album charts. In addition, the single "Manhattan Skyline" from the album achieved substantial popularity on the VH-1 music video network. Fordham's 1991 release, *Swept,* would not fare as well, selling only 85,000 copies. Jon Cummings in *Billboard,* though, called both *Porcelain* and *Swept* "exquisitely crafted, meticulously sung pop." Fordham herself commented that her intent with the two albums was to achieve a certain kind of delivery, one that was emotive but controlled.

For her fourth album, *Falling Forward,* Fordham changed tactics, abandoning her controlled delivery for a more

spontaneous sound. She remarked to Cummings, "This time I wanted to sing my pants off." To help create an original feel for the album, Fordham looked to new producers. She left Grant Mitchell and Hugh Padgham, who had produced all three of her previous albums, and enlisted Larry Klein, Joni Mitchell's husband and collaborator. Despite the radical change in sound, Fordham claimed to be happy with how she sang on her previous albums, explaining to Cummings, "I just came to feel you can't keep doing the same things forever."

The change seemed to renew enthusiasm for Fordham's music. When the album was released in 1994 in Great Britain, it leapt to Number 21 on the British charts. Virgin Records felt the emergence of the LP on alternative and contemporary jazz radio stations would give it the boost that *Swept* did not have. Also, the label did not want to repeat what it saw as a grave mistake in the promotion of *Swept:* the lack of a U.S. tour, which it cited as the main reason for *Swept's* poor performance in the United States.

Virgin brought Fordham to the United States in the summer of 1994 to prepare for an extensive fall tour. "We're all big fans of Julia's at Virgin," product manager Jean Rousseau told *Billboard's* Cummings, "and we're expecting that all it's going to take will be to get her out in front of people and let them rediscover her."

Selected discography

Julia Fordham, Virgin, 1988.
Porcelain, Virgin, 1990.
Swept, Virgin, 1991.
Falling Forward, Virgin, 1994.

Sources

Billboard, June 4, 1994.
Entertainment Weekly, July 29, 1994.
Musician, July 1, 1990.
Rolling Stone, November 17, 1988; May 17, 1990; September 22, 1994.

Additional information for this profile was provided by Virgin Records publicity materials, 1994.

—Susan Windisch Brown

Bill Frisell

Guitarist, composer

Photograph by Deborah Feingold, courtesy of Nonesuch Records

Why would a serious jazz guitarist be interested in composing accompaniments for slapstick genius Buster Keaton's silent movies? The answer, as Gene Santoro reported in the *New York Daily News,* is that Bill Frisell specializes in the unexpected. Santoro pointed out the appeal of Frisell's unique style of playing, noting that a typical set with the guitarist's band—which features bassist Kermit Driscoll and drummer Joey Baron—"finds song fragments hurtling in and out of a continuous, unfolding narrative. Rhythms churn and change up, spaces yawn and collapse, and the leader's guitar ricochets from acoustic lyricism to airplane-level raunch." Although a talented composer himself—as evidenced by his work for Keaton—Frisell has an ability to react to others' musical texts that has made him one of the most sought-after session players in contemporary music.

Frisell's collaborative instinct carried over to his own recordings. He has utilized his formidable improvisational skills "to hone a composition style in which weepy country melodies coexist with rumbling funk bass lines and kitschy Fifties rock ... juxtaposed with graceful, surprisingly arresting dissonances," according to Tom Moon of *Rolling Stone.* His 1993 recording *Have a Little Faith* at first seems to promise the listener familiar songs, like Madonna's "Live to Tell," Bob Dylan's "Just Like a Woman," and John Hiatt's "Have a Little Faith in Me," but then treats those songs as places to begin exploration.

Discussing *Have a Little Faith'*s offerings, Frisell related in *Guitar Player,* "I've played some of these pieces, like 'When I Fall in Love' and the Sonny Rollins tune, for a really long time. In fact, the Stephen Foster song gets back to my earliest memories of music. It's almost as if there's this pool of melodies that's part of your person." That pool extends to such classical pieces as Charles Ives's "Three Places in New England" and Aaron Copland's "Billy the Kid," which helped define the American music conscious. These disparate tunes are held together by the same subtleties of texture that make Frisell instantly identifiable to listeners.

Frisell's interpretations serve to reposition listeners with respect to their musical heritage and continued with 1994's *This Land,* an extension of Frisell's journey through the American mosaic, drawing, according George Varga in the *San Diego Union-Tribune,* "from funk, rock, modern jazz, Dixieland, country and pioneering American composers." Critics such as Tom Moon have asserted that this eclectic style is governed by rock and roll's disregard for convention, and Frisell, though not a rock musician, points out that he chose in part to play the guitar because of the music he heard on the radio while growing up.

His choice of instrument has helped define the type of musician Frisell has become. In *Guitar Player* he confided, "It's harder to deny all the things that have happened on the guitar in the last 30 or 40 years than it would be if you played the saxophone. If I played the saxophone or trumpet, it would be a lot easier to fall into this classicism. Whereas with guitar, you *could* just do a Wes Montgomery thing, but if you're my age and grew up with the Beatles, Rolling Stones, and Jimi Hendrix, you'd have to be more blatant."

Yet despite his many influences, Frisell continues to be identified as a jazz musician, an association he could take or leave; he commented in *Down Beat,* "I don't really care. It doesn't matter what it's called. It bothers me that people use names to box things away. What [jazz musicians] do comes out of jazz, it has a lot of stuff that attracted me to jazz in the first place. But we don't confine ourselves to a certain era: we use everything we know. That's what all the great jazz players do."

In another *Guitar Player* piece, Frisell asserted that his best music, "writing or playing, comes from instinct. I'm just not thinking about notes. Sure, if you stop me, I can identify what note I'm playing and explain its relationship to an underlying chord, but the music I felt best about comes from somewhere else. The things I've studied intellectually have taken years to seep down, and now they come out naturally."

Born in Baltimore, Maryland, Frisell began playing clarinet ain his school marching band in Denver. According to an Elektra/Nonesuch biography, his exposure to the music of Otis Rush, B.B. King, Paul Butterfield, and Buddy Guy instilled in Frisell a passion for Chicago blues. In high school he played in bands covering James Brown tunes and other pop and soul classics, and later, after studying music at the University of Northern Colorado, he attended the Berklee College of Music in Boston. Frisell moved in 1978 to Belgium where he concentrated on writing music for a year before moving to New York City and staying for ten years.

In an interview with Joe Gore in *Guitar Player,* Frisell did not downplay his formal education, though "he disagrees with those who argue that conservatory educations hatch musical eggheads." The guitarist commented, "It's only the players' fault if they let themselves be programmed by the routines that [schools] establish. There are all kinds of things you can do with the 'rules' that a school might give you. For example, in the harmony class at Berklee, they'd have 'avoid notes,' notes you weren't supposed to use over a particular chord. Naturally, those were the first ones I'd check out."

The eclecticism and uniqueness of Frisell's playing and composing—perhaps the result of his curiosity about unconventional sounds—is the most often cited aspect of his work. His early 1990s releases, including *This Land, Have a Little Faith,* and the Buster Keaton film music collections *Go West* and *The High Sign/One Week,* earned accolades from magazines ranging from *Rolling Stone* to *Down Beat* for their refreshing experimental guitar stylings. In his 1994 review of *This Land, Rolling Stone's* Josef Woodward praised, "More than almost anyone else in the last decade, Frisell brought a new voice to the fraying realm of the electric guitar."

Frisell's virtuosic and understated playing is, for critics and listeners alike, a welcome relief in the world of contemporary music. The *San Diego Union-Tribune's* Varga declared, "An artist, not an acrobat, Frisell is one of those rare guitarists who consistently avoid fast licks and overwrought solos. In their place, he offers atmospheric swells, delightful country inflected twangs, bluesy punctuations, surging power chords and wonderfully creative lines that never go where you expect but are always perfectly timed and executed." Whether playing, writing, or leading a band, Frisell exhibits a dexterous maturity, growing out of a unique personal vision that at the same time is also open to other interpreters of the world around him.

Selected discography

Lookout for Hope, ECM, 1988.
Rambler, ECM, 1988.
ECM Works, ECM, 1989.
Before We Were Born, Elektra/Musician, 1989.
Is That You?, Elektra/Musician, 1990.

Where in the World?, Elektra/Musician, 1991.

Hal Willner Presents Weird Nightmare: Meditations on Mingus, Columbia, 1992.

Have a Little Faith, Elektra/Nonesuch, 1993.

This Land, Elektra/Nonesuch, 1994.

The High Sign/One Week: Music for the Films of Buster Keaton, Elektra/Nonesuch, 1995.

Go West: Music for the Films of Buster Keaton, Elektra/Nonesuch, 1995.

Bass Desires, ECM.

In Line, ECM.

It Should've Happened a Long Time Ago, ECM.

Later That Evening, ECM.

(With Vernon Reid) *Smash and Scatteration,* Rykodisc.

(With Hal Willner) *Stay Awake: Various Interpretations of Music for Vintage Disney Films,* A&M.

Steal This Disc, Rykodisc.

Sources

Boston Phoenix, April 1, 1994.

CMJ (College Music Journal), April 4, 1994.

Down Beat, March 1992; April 1993; August 1994; June 1995.

Guitar Player, July 1992; June 1993; May 1994.

Musician, March 1993; June 1994; November 1994.

New York Daily News, February 24, 1994; April 1, 1994.

Pulse!, June 1994.

Rolling Stone, May 13, 1993; September 22, 1994.

San Diego Union-Tribune, April 7, 1994.

Additional information for this profile was provided by Elektra/Nonesuch publicity materials, 1994.

—John Morrow

Mitchell Froom

Producer, keyboardist

Mitchell Froom has been a pivotal force behind some of the most acclaimed albums of the 1980s and 1990s, yet his is hardly a household name to those outside the music industry. A veteran keyboard player, his talents as a studio musician can be heard on the records of a variety of performers. But it is as a producer that Froom is best known among industry insiders.

Froom has served as producer for artists as diverse as the Pretenders, Richard Thompson, Los Lobos, and Suzanne Vega. "Cut the crap; get rid of extraneous elements right away," Froom described his method of production in an interview with *Rolling Stone* writer Bud Scoppa. "Keep as many generic elements out as possible. Make sure the song is right and understand the emotional level on which it works. And then, to make a song interesting, I like to think that there's the 'wild element'—what Brian Jones did for the early Stones—where you go for something unusual, but it still works."

Froom hails from Northern California and like many a musician, studied classical piano as a youngster. He also played the pipe organ, which one day he would help reintroduce as a quirky instrument of choice in late 1980s studio sessions. Froom became increasingly seduced by rock music, however, and as an adult relocated to Los Angeles to be closer to the music business. He played keyboards on one of rock musician Ronnie Montrose's solo projects in 1982, but his first real break came later that year when Froom was hired to score an artsy, X-rated independent film called *Cafe Flesh*. He was paid $2,000 for a week's worth of work that entailed putting the soundtrack together on an eight-track recorder with a drummer. In 1984, Bob Biggs, president of Slash Records, liked what he heard in *Cafe Flesh* so much that he decided to release Froom's score as an album.

From Keyboard to Mixing Board and Back Again

The resulting *Key of Cool,* Froom's only solo release, was a minor success and landed Froom another production job. This time it was a little-known Boston bar band on the Slash label, a bluesy, Hispanic rock ensemble known as the Del Fuegos. Both the label and Biggs were in a quandary about how to record the group—they feared the Del Fuegos studio sound would not be as thrilling as their live performances. Froom cut a demo with the musicians, which led to their debut album, 1984's *The Longest Day.* Slash was thrilled with the resulting sound; also impressive, Froom had done the job quickly and within budget. He was hired to produce the Del Fuegos' 1985 follow-up effort, *Boston, Mass.*

His association with Slash Records helped Froom obtain more studio work as a keyboard player. Noted musician and producer T-Bone Burnett tapped Froom to play on the single "Will the Wolf Survive?," an early hit from another group of Latino rockers—Los Lobos. At the time, Burnett was their producer. Froom also played keyboards on several tracks for Elvis Costello's lauded 1986 *King of America* release, produced by Burnett, former Plimsoul Peter Case's self-titled solo album, the best-selling 1985 release from the Bangles, *Different Light,* then *Love & Hope & Sex & Dreams* from the BoDeans, and 1985's *Downtown* from Marshall Crenshaw.

Froom's skills as a keyboardist so impressed Costello that the British rocker invited him to join the Confederates, who were backing Costello on his 1986 tour. Although Froom had a commitment to produce a third Del Fuegos album, he accepted anyway; he would fly back to Los Angeles after performances to work with the Del Fuegos. "The combination of my respect for Elvis as an artist and that band being the greatest group of musicians that I know of made it impossible to say no," Froom told *Billboard*'s Paula Parisi. Froom and T-Bone Burnett would work together on a number of other well-received projects after Costello's *King of America* album, including the aforementioned BoDeans and Marshall Crenshaw discs. Froom also became a frequent collaborator with Los Angeles recording engineer Tchad Blake.

Richard Thompson is another performer who has utilized Froom's talents for a series of recordings. The British folksinger and guitarist, formerly with Fairport Convention, often uses unusual instruments in his repertoire. Froom has managed to translate his exceptional sound onto recordings such as 1986's *Daring Adventures,* 1991's *Rumor and Sigh,* and *Mirror Blue,* Thompson's 1994 release. For *Daring Adventures,* Thompson and his musicians used medieval instruments such as the hurdy-gurdy and shawm, as well as standard folk fare like fiddles and accordions.

Musician's Point of View

At the time of *Daring Adventures*'s release in 1986, Thompson told *Billboard*'s Parisi that Froom "approaches things from a musician's point of view, so he contributes enormously to the arrangements and was instrumental in selecting the musicians." Eight years later, in a *Stereo Review* critique of *Mirror Blue,* writer Parke Puterbaugh praised Froom's expertise calling the album the duo's "best work to date." Puterbaugh nonetheless noted that on some tracks, "Froom's production signature—a dry sound with a dull finish marked by percussion that means to be unconventional but sometimes feels contrived—tosses a wet blanket over Thompson's passion," but concluded that with the combination of Thompson's "daring and Froom's production, *Mirror Blue* manages to be both timeless and up-to-date."

As he added many more successful albums to his production credits, Froom returned to the arena that had given gave him his first break, scoring films. In 1987 he did the nearly all-instrumental soundtrack for the oddball release *Slam Dance,* a movie featuring Tom Hulce, Harry Dean Stanton, and Adam Ant. He told Scoppa of the score in *Rolling Stone,* "I classify it as 'Debussy hires James Brown's horn section and records in South America.'" Froom also scored an episode for the avant-garde children's television series *Pee-Wee's Playhouse.*

In 1992 Froom produced songwriter Suzanne Vega's release *99.9,* a collaboration that led to marriage; the two have a daughter, born in 1994. Another successful debut in 1994 for Froom was the Elvis Costello album *Brutal Youth.* The work, which reunited Costello with his original band the Attractions, was co-produced by Froom and Costello; *Stereo Review*'s Puterbaugh termed it "as dense and unrelenting as anything Costello's ever recorded." Froom's longtime affiliation with Los Lobos led to a related undertaking that year—the self-titled 1994 debut from the Latin Playboys. The release, a side project with Los Lobos members David Hidalgo and Louis Perez, featured Froom and Blake as players as well as producer and engineer.

Froom's keyboard skills are often utilized on the spot in recording sessions. *Billboard* writer Parisi queried Froom as to when he actually stepped out from behind the mixing board. "Most of what I do in terms of music is atmospheric and subtle," he replied. "I don't come in with a musician's ego, saying 'Boy, would I love to play on that track.' It's more like there's a job to be done, and it's a lot simpler if I do it than to bring in another personality." When not behind the keyboards himself in the studio, Froom professes to a prejudice for recording musicians who have little experience on the instrument. "Often the best keyboardists for a given piece of music are the people who can barely play," Froom told *Keyboard* writer Paul Tingen. "You hear an individuality and emotion that is deeply rooted in the songs they've written. There's also a sense of struggle and amateurism in their performance that can provide a good tension to a track."

Prefers Vintage Instruments

Froom has also worked extensively with Australian pop ensemble Crowded House. For their 1986 self-titled release, Froom guested on electric piano and Hammond organ as well as producing. His expertise on the latter dates back to his youth and resulted in an "astonishingly contemporary effect," declared Parisi in *Billboard*. Indeed, Froom often prefers vintage instruments to the newer, high-tech models. He owns an extensive collection of electric pianos and organs, Mellotrons, and other early synthesizers. Froom contends that older instruments present artists with unusual challenges and seem to bring out their strengths.

Despite his preference for older equipment, Froom asserts that the new computer-driven technology is not wholly responsible for the chilly sound sometimes found in modern music. "It's ... the human application that too often yields such dismal results," he told *Keyboard*'s Tingen. "If more musicians would utilize the capacity for spontaneity these things provide, they might come up with weirder musical hybrids of more unusual arrangements." Froom does see the new technology eventually bringing the music industry fresh blood and fresh sounds. "Record companies aren't so sure anymore about what it takes to become successful," he remarked. Maybe some kid in Idaho will plug his fuzztone into his grandmother's home organ and make a great roaring noise that will be heard around the world."

Selected discography

(With Ronnie Montrose) *Gamma 3,* Elektra, 1982.
The Key of Cool, Slash, 1984.
(With Latin Playboys), *Latin Playboys* (also producer), Slash/ Warner Bros., 1994.

As producer

Del Fuegos, *The Longest Day,* Slash, 1984.
Del Fuegos, *Boston, Mass.,* Slash, 1985.
Crowded House, *Crowded House,* Capitol, 1986.
Richard Thompson, *Daring Adventures,* Capitol, 1986.
Crowded House, *Temple of Low Men,* Capitol, 1988.
Crowded House, *Woodface,* Capitol, 1991.
Richard Thompson, *Rumor and Sigh,* Capitol, 1991.
Elvis Costello, *Mighty Like a Rose,* Warner Bros., 1991.
Pretenders, *Packed,* Warner Bros., 1991.
Los Lobos, *Kiko,* Slash, 1992.
Suzanne Vega, *99.9,* A&M, 1992.
Peter Case, *Six Pack of Love,* Geffen, 1992.
American Music Club, *Mercury,* Reprise, 1993.
Elvis Costello, *Brutal Youth,* Warner Bros., 1994.
Richard Thompson, *Mirror Blue,* Capitol, 1994.
Ron Sexsmith, *Ron Sexsmith,* Interscope, 1995.

Sources

Billboard, November 22, 1986; March 12, 1994.
Keyboard, April 1993.
People, May 23, 1994.
Rolling Stone, December 4, 1986.
Schwann Spectrum, Winter 1994/95.
Stereo Review, May 1994; June 1994; July 1994.

—Carol Brennan

Hassan Hakmoun

Sintir player, singer

Photograph by Stephen Lovell-Davis, courtesy of Realworld Records

Moroccan-born Hassan Hakmoun is among the most eclectic of popular musicians. Though schooled in the deeply traditional sounds of the Gnawa people in his native Marrakesh, since moving to the United States in 1987, Hakmoun's music has absorbed elements from a variety of popular styles including jazz, rock, funk, and hip-hop. His fan base has broadened with his musical range. And his participation in the European-based organization WOMAD (World of Music, Art, and Dance) and collaborations with other musicians, such as the Kronos quartet, have brought him further into the spotlight.

Hakmoun's musical origins are rooted in the African folk music of the Islamic Gnawa sect. The Gnawa people are descended from West African slaves who were brought to North Africa several hundred years ago. Their music combines complicated West African syncopations with long and sinuous North African melodies. Tracing their roots back to the Bilal, the slave of the Islamic prophet Mohammed and the first to sing an Islamic call to prayer, Gnawa musicians often express their religious devotion through their music, using it to enter spiritual trance states and to heal the sick and injured. Hassan began studying the music at a very young age. As he told Gene Santoro of New York's *Daily News,* "My sister was one year old when she had burned her whole belly. The Gnawas came and played all night ... and asked for forgiveness for what she had done to cause this to happen. They healed her, which drew me into the music. I was five years old."

"Listen, Listen, Listen"

Hakmoun began to grasp the Gnawa form by rote repetition, copying the old masters. "To learn this music," he said in the *New York Times,* "you have to go and listen to the musicians playing. You cannot write this music, you have to be friends of the musicians and listen, listen, listen to it first. Then you get your instrument, and you buy a tape of the music and listen to it, and go back to the musicians, and ask how you can use your finger to get this note."

While still a youngster, Hakmoun chose the sintir as his main instrument. The sintir is a three-stringed lute with a body made of camel skin stretched over nut wood. The strings are pitched low, so the instrument can serve as the bass foundation, much like the Western string bass. But the tone of the sintir is sweet, so it is also well suited to carrying the melodic line of a composition. By drumming on the body, Hakmoun adds his own percussion, while also contributing vocals. Moreover, he is schooled in the traditional trance-inducing dances.

For the Record . . .

Born September 16, 1963, in Marrakesh, Morocco. Began formal study of Gnawa music, c. 1968; street performer in Morocco, c. 1973; formed own group, c. 1977; made American debut at Lincoln Center, New York City, 1987; worked in T-shirt factory, late 1980s; performed at Ethnic Folk Arts Center, New York City, 1988; opened World Music Institute's fall season at Symphony Space, New York City, 1989; joined group Magmouat Hakmoun, 1989; formed group Zahar; recorded with WOMAD (World of Music, Art, and Dance) artists at Real World Studios, Bath, England, 1992; toured with WOMAD, 1992—; collaborated with Kronos Quartet, 1993; with WOMAD, performed at Woodstock '94, 1994.

Addresses: *Record company*—Caroline Records, 114 West 26th Street, New York, NY 10001.

Gnawa musicians frequently earn their living on the streets, and Hassan started performing there a few years after beginning to study. "I was ten or eleven years old when I began, and it was very hard," he told Paul Roland of *Folk Roots* magazine. "At first I was just happy and excited to be playing to people, usually in front of their houses. But when I was fourteen, I formed my own group."

Performed in U.S., Then Stayed

Hakmoun first visited the United States with a group of Gnawa musicians in 1987 for a government-sponsored concert at Lincoln Center in New York. The experience was so positive that he decided to stay. He spent his first few years working at a T-shirt factory to supplement his performance income. He performed both by himself and with others. When performing by himself, he frequently would dance for his audience to a tape of his own playing.

In 1989 Hakmoun became part of the group Magmouat Hakmoun with his brother Said and two other relatives, Mohammed Bechar and Abdel Hok Dahmad. While the music they performed included both sacred and secular pieces, the emphasis was frequently on the sacred. "It is spiritual music," he told the *New York Times.* "People in Morocco cannot use [the sintir] when they are drunk or when they are not clean. It's like you're going to mosque; the words we are singing should be respect-

ed. We are singing about gods and prophets, and it is very serious." In 1989 the World Music Institute produced Hakmoun's debut album, entitled *Moroccan Gnawi Songs.*

For both musical and commercial reasons, Hakmoun began to expand his range, adding some American sounds to the Moroccan form. He told Paul Roland of *Folk Roots* magazine that he "came to America playing traditional Moroccan music, but I didn't find a large audience so I mixed it with jazz, reggae, funk and salsa and Western instruments. Then I formed my own band with the help of my new American friends, but I had to rehearse and teach them for a long time."

Continued Moroccan Fusion with Zahar

With his "new American friends," Hakmoun formed the group Zahar. An early version of the band included only Hakmoun, Hahn Rowe on electric guitar and violin, and Yuval Gabay on drums; the ensemble grew to eventually include seven musicians, among them three percussionists, Anthony Michael Petersen on electric guitar, and Sabir Rizaev on soprano saxophone. Their music fused elements of rock and jazz with African styles, resulting in a completely new sound. The *Calgary Herald* attested, "[Their music] spans centuries. It blows through the streets of New York where [Hakmoun] now lives, incorporating rock and funk, percussive Afro-jazz grooves, buoyed by wild guitar riffs and sax solos. It is exotic and yet familiar." *Newsday* called Hakmoun's work a combination of "polyrhythmic funk, harmelodic jazz, and tough dancehall-reggae attitude."

In 1992 Hakmoun joined WOMAD, which had been founded in 1980 by pop musician Peter Gabriel. Under WOMAD's wing, Hakmoun has been spreading his Moroccan fusion outside of the United States. He cut another album, *Trance,* at Gabriel's Real World Studios in Bath, England. From Bath, Hakmoun toured Europe, the Middle East, and the United States with other WOMAD artists. In 1994, he performed under the group's auspices at the Woodstock '94 festival before a huge audience. In fact, Hakmoun's increased exposure has resulted in letters of admiration from former New York City Mayor David Dinkins, television host Jay Leno, and saxophonist David Sanborn, as well as from executives of the *New York Times* and British Broadcasting Corporation.

Despite the stylistic growth of Hakmoun's music, he remains committed to the traditional sounds of his childhood. "Traditional music is like my key," he said in the *New York Daily News,* "and I can't get home if I lose it. It's my best friend, my gift from God." Of his popularity outside of Morocco, Hakmoun explained, "People follow me ... and afterward they feel good, even though they don't understand the words I'm singing."

Selected discography

Moroccan Gnawi Songs, World Music Institute, 1989.
Gift of the Gnawa, Flying Fish Records, 1991.
Trance, Realworld/Virgin, 1993.
(With Kronos Quartet), *Pieces of Africa,* Elektra Nonesuch, 1993.

Sources

Billboard, September 5, 1992.
Calgary Herald (Alberta, Canada), December 19, 1993.
Detroit Free Press, June 3, 1994.
Folk Roots, September 1993.
Newsday, October 17, 1989; March 22, 1994.
New York Daily News, January 14, 1994.
New York Times, January 26, 1988; September 29, 1989; June 1, 1990; June 4, 1991; December 13, 1993.
USA Today, July 12, 1994.
Washington Post, October 2, 1989.

Additional information for this profile was provided by Caroline/Real World Records.

—Robin Armstrong

Roy Hargrove

Jazz trumpeter

Photograph by James Minchin, courtesy of Verve Records

After recording his highly acclaimed first album at age 20, Roy Hargrove became a charter member of a precocious group of jazz prodigies known as "The Young Lions." Hargrove, along with fellow trumpeters Nicholas Peyton and Marlon Jordan, saxophonists Antonio Hart and Joshua Redman, bassist Christian McBride, and a host of other young players, ignited a global resurgence in the popularity of jazz. Intelligent, well-educated, and articulate, with a strong sense of jazz's rich history, these musicians were signed by major recording labels and supported by the kind of publicity formerly reserved for pop stars.

In an astonishingly brief time, Hargrove arose as one of the most influential artists of this young generation. He developed an extremely personal style that tempered brilliant virtuosity with grace and passion. Tom Masland of *Newsweek* remarked of Hargrove, "He plays with a sweetness that speaks of a world of hurt." Even early in his career, Hargrove's work showed a sense of order that many players take decades to achieve. As *New York Times* writer Richard B. Woodward put it, his solos are a "string of sentences that read as paragraphs."

Inspired by Early Teacher

Hargrove was surrounded by music from an early age, but it was his elementary and high school band director, Dean Hill, who sparked his interest in a performing career. Hill not only guided Hargrove's development as an improviser, but introduced him to a variety of great jazz musicians, including David "Fathead" Newman, a legendary sax player who many years later joined Hargrove on his eighth album, *Family*.

While working with Hill, Hargrove discovered the music of Clifford Brown, a brilliant trumpeter who recorded extensively in the 1950s; he died at age 25. It was Brown's example, Hargrove told *Rocky Mountain News* writer Norman Provizer, that gave the young trumpeter confidence in his own musical gifts. "That was the key that opened the door for me," he recalled. "There have always been musicians who could play no matter what age they were. If you love it, you will search it out regardless of your age."

Like many jazz musicians of his generation, Hargrove also owed an important debt to trumpeter Wynton Marsalis. After hearing Hargrove perform at Dallas's Arts Magnet High School, Marsalis invited him to sit in with his group at the Caravan of Dreams Performing Arts Center in Fort Worth, Texas. The performance effectively launched Hargrove's career, and though some writers later tried to promote competition between Hargrove and his mentor, the younger musician has dem-

Born October 16, 1969, in Waco, TX; son of Roy Allan (a musician and member of the U.S. Air Force) and Velera Hargrove. *Education:* Attended Berklee School of Music, 1988-90; attended New School for Social Research Jazz and Contemporary Music Program, beginning 1990.

"Discovered" by trumpeter Wynton Marsalis, Dallas, TX, 1986; toured Japan and Europe; formed quintet and released first album, *Diamond in the Rough,* Novus, 1990; appeared with saxophonist Sonny Rollins at Carnegie Hall concert, New York City, 1991; premiered first extended composition, *The Love Suite in Mahogany,* Lincoln Center, New York City, 1993; participated in Verve Records 50th anniversary celebration, Carnegie Hall, 1994; offered series of master classes and clinics in the New York City public schools, 1994.

Awards: *Down Beat* Student Music Award, 1988; first place, 1992 *Jazz Times* Readers' Poll; voted "Talent Deserving Wider Recognition" in *Down Beat's* 1993 Critics' Poll.

Addresses: *Record company*—Verve Records, Worldwide Plaza, 825 Eighth Avenue, New York, NY 10019.

onstrated nothing but respect and admiration for Marsalis. "I really dig Wynton's place in society," he told *New York Times* contributor Woodward. "He's a tremendously dedicated person." In 1995 Hargrove put all rumors of a feud to rest by inviting Marsalis to join him on his *Family* album.

Formed Quintet, Released Debut

Hargrove's debut at the Caravan of Dreams led to extensive tours of the U.S. and Europe. In 1990, after two years at Boston's prestigious Berklee School of Music, he moved to New York City, formed his first quintet, and released his debut album, *Diamond in the Rough.* This album, and the three succeeding recordings Hargrove made for the Novus label, were among the most commercially successful jazz recordings of the early 1990s, and made the young trumpeter one of the music's hottest properties. Still, unimpressed by stardom, Hargrove continued to develop his craft by performing with jazz giants such as saxophonist Sonny Rollins and trumpeter Dizzy Gillespie.

As Hargrove's talents as a soloist matured, so did his strength as a bandleader. During the early 1990s Hargrove experimented with a variety of personnel, trying to build a tightly focused ensemble. As he told *Rocky Mountain News* writer Provizer, "No matter how many people you have in a group, you need to think as one." In 1992 he laid the foundation for future groups by hiring bassist Rodney Whitaker and drummer Gregory Hutchinson, who together comprised one of the finest rhythm units in modern jazz. By the release of 1993's *Of Kindred Souls,* Hargrove's exacting taste and hard work had paid off: in the words of *San Francisco Chronicle* writer Derk Richardson, he had found "the kind of unified group feeling that has distinguished the most fondly remembered acoustic jazz units, from the Max Roach-Clifford Brown Quintet, through the classic Miles Davis bands of the 1960s."

Collaborated with "Lions" on Tribute to Family

In 1994 Hargrove made a widely publicized move to Verve Records and released *The Roy Hargrove Quintet with the Tenors of Our Time.* The concept for the recording was unique: Hargrove's own quintet, featuring sax player Ron Blake and pianist Cyrus Chestnut, in addition to Whitaker and Hutchinson, was joined by some of jazz's greatest tenor sax players, both veterans such as Joe Henderson and Stanley Turrentine, and relative newcomers like Branford Marsalis (Wynton's brother) and Joshua Redman. But unlike other "all-star" jam recordings, the album presented each guest soloist individually, in repertory specially chosen to illustrate his talents. The recording, dubbed "a jazz classic" by *Star-Ledger* critic George Kanzler, was one of the best-selling jazz albums of 1994.

In June of 1995 Hargrove released his second recording for Verve, *Family.* As the title suggests, the album paid tribute to the musicians and relatives who played a significant role in the trumpeter's life. Like *The Tenors of Our Time, Family* featured a variety of guest artists. "Young Lions" such as Christian McBride and sax player Jesse Davis, as well as established figures including pianist John Hicks and drummer Jimmy Cobb once again joined Hargrove's quintet. The result was an exciting and heart-felt look at jazz's past, present, and future.

Family also showcased several of Hargrove's own works. "The Trial" was a dark and intense movement from his extended composition *The Love Suite in Mahogany,* which had been premiered at New York City's Lincoln Center in September, 1993. The piece featured an imaginative duet for bowed bass and soprano sax. The Latin-tinged "Another Level" placed the innovative solos of Hargrove, Blake, and pianist Stephen Scott against a complex background of shifting rhythmic patterns. And "Trilogy" painted brief portraits of three of Hargrove's family members: the lush, tender "Velera" paid homage to Hargrove's mother; "Roy Allan" evoked the sousaphone playing of Hargrove's father with an infectious, driving bass line; and the looping melody of the blues number "Brian's Bounce" was inspired by Hargrove's energetic brother.

As Hargrove's star continued to ascend, he also dedicated himself to spreading jazz's affirmative message to a new generation of musicians. Following Wynton Marsalis's lead, he began giving workshops for jazz musicians in high schools throughout the U.S. "There is a positive aspect to playing music, and it makes a difference when you can reach young people around the country and tell them about jazz," he told *Down Beat* columnist June Lehman. "You may inspire a young person to do great things just by having music in their life."

Selected discography

Diamond in the Rough, Novus, 1990.
Public Eye, Novus, 1991.
(Contributor) Antonio Hart, *For the First Time*, Novus, 1991.
(Contributor) Sonny Rollins, *Here's to the People*, Milestone, 1991.
(Contributor) Stephen Scott, *Something to Consider*, Verve, 1991.
(Contributor) *New York Stories*, Capitol, 1992.
The Vibe, Novus, 1992.
Roy Hargrove and Antonio Hart: The Tokyo Sessions, Novus, 1992.
Of Kindred Souls, Novus, 1993.
Approaching Standards, Novus, 1994.
Roy Hargrove Quintet with the Tenors of Our Time, Verve, 1994.

(Contributor) Johnny Griffin, *Chicago, New York, Paris*, Verve, 1995.
(Contributor) Christian McBride, *Gettin' to It*, Verve, 1995.
(Contributor) Teodross Avery, *In Other Words*, GRP, 1995.
(Contributor) David Sanchez, *Sketches of Dreams*, Columbia, 1995.
Family, Verve, 1995.
(With Christian McBride and Stephen Scott) *Parker's Mood*, Verve, 1995.

Selected compositions

The Love Suite in Mahogany, 1993.
Trilogy, 1995.

Sources

Billboard, April 2, 1994; July 8, 1995.
Chicago Sun-Times, June 12, 1994.
Detroit Free Press, Sept. 24, 1993.
Down Beat, July 1994; August 1994; September 1994; August 1995.
Essence, December 1991.
Los Angeles Times, January 19, 1995.
Metro Times (Detroit), September 2, 1992.
Newsweek, December 12, 1994.
New York Post, April 4, 1994.
New York Times, June 23, 1994; September 7, 1994.
Rocky Mountain News (Denver), February 16, 1994.
San Francisco Chronicle, May 14, 1994.
Star-Ledger, June 5, 1994.
Washington Post, March 4, 1995.

Additional information for this profile was obtained from Verve Records, 1995.

—*Jeffrey Taylor*

Eddie Harris

Saxophonist, singer, inventor

Courtesy of Rhino Records

One of the few jazzmen to land a million-selling hit, Eddie Harris has emerged over the last four decades as a standard-bearer of hard bop, an inventor of several musical instruments, and an important exponent of soul and fusion jazz. Like his former contemporary trumpeter Miles Davis, Harris has explored numerous musical paths, absorbing the sounds of gospel, electric blues, funk, and rap. Labeling himself an "experimentalist," he puts musical expression before popular and critical recognition. His uncompromising artistic vision has won the praise of musicians and listeners throughout the world.

Eddie Harris was born on October 20, 1936, in Chicago, Illinois. The son of a religious mother, Harris began singing in church at age four; a year later he started taking piano lessons from a cousin, a church keyboardist. At Du Sable High School, famous for producing a number of talented jazz musicians, he played sports and continued to study music. Unable to afford an instrument, the school's band instructor, Walter "Captain" Dyette, selected Harris to play the marimba. Despite the youngster's request to play saxophone, Dyette, a strict instructor and disciplinarian, insisted he then play clarinet. Soon Harris rejoined the band playing an inexpensive pawn-shop clarinet. Twice kicked out of the band for defying Dyette, he eventually switched schools and finished his secondary studies at Hyde Park High School.

Sat in at Chicago Clubs

Harris longed to attend a southern college on a sports scholarship, but his mother, fearful of the culminating racial tensions in the Deep South, opposed the idea. Harris remained in Chicago and studied music at Roosevelt University. During the evenings, Harris visited nightclubs around the city, performing with such jazz greats as Lester Young, Charlie Parker, and Roy Eldridge. The multitalented young man accompanied musicians on reed instruments as well as bass and drums. While still in high school, he made his professional debut on piano, playing a one-nighter with saxophonist Gene Ammons. "I used to be like Erroll Garner," recalled Harris in the liner notes to *The Eddie Harris Anthology,* "I played everything by ear." By the early 1950s Harris had taken up tenor saxophone as his primary instrument, often practicing with future sax giant John Coltrane, who visited him during his trips through Chicago.

In the late 1950s, Harris was drafted into the army. With the help of trumpeter Don Ellis, he was able to join the 7th Army Symphony Orchestra and Soldier's Show Company, a musical ensemble featuring a jazz band that included such talent as pianist Cedar Walton and sax-

For the Record . . .

Born October 20, 1936, in Chicago, IL. *Education:* Attended Roosevelt University, mid-1950s.

Began singing in church choir, c. 1940; studied piano; played first professional engagement, as pianist, with saxophonist Gene Ammons, c. early 1950s; member of 7th Army Symphony Orchestra, late 1950s; signed with Chicago-based Vee-Jay label and recorded "Exodus," 1961; signed with Atlantic, 1965, and recorded numerous LPs throughout the late 1960s; performed in Ghana, 1970; toured and recorded with guitarist John Scofield, 1994. Author of numerous books on music theory and business.

Addresses: *Record company*—Rhino Records, 10635 Santa Monica Blvd., Los Angeles, CA 90025-1900.

ophonist Leo Wright. Despite his early opposition to joining the army, Harris explained in *The Eddie Harris Anthology* how the military "was the best thing that ever happened to me ... because I got a chance to travel and meet people of different cultures." While stationed in Germany, he toured France and played at jazz jam sessions in Frankfurt and Munich.

After finishing his military service, Harris returned to the Chicago music scene, then traveled to New York, where he worked seven nights a week performing in numerous musical settings, including club work with pianists Thelonious Monk and Duke Jordan. During this time, he also played with saxophonists Stan Getz, Wardell Grey, and Sonny Stitt.

Scored Hit with "Exodus"

Back in Chicago, Harris turned down a job touring with trumpeter Quincy Jones's band to cut an album on the Chicago-based Vee-Jay label. The night before the recording session, in April 1961, Harris was in a restaurant listening to the jukebox when he heard Ferrante & Teicher's film soundtrack piece "Exodus." Drawn to the melody, he put two dollars in the machine, borrowed a pen, and began writing an arrangement of the number on a tablecloth. The next day he cut the arrangement, playing tenor saxophone. Within weeks his version of "Exodus" had sold more than a million copies.

Harris's commercial success, however, brought criticism. As he later explained to Steven Marks in *Down*

Beat, "Exodus actually cost me a lot of jobs. Club owners would think about John Coltrane or Cannonball Adderly, but when my name came up, they'd say, 'Who, that commercial cat?' And many musicians felt the same way." During this period, Harris and pianist Richard Abrams headed a Chicago-based avant-garde ensemble, the Experimental Jazz Band.

In 1965 Harris signed with Atlantic Records and released "Freedom Jazz Dance," a composition he described in *the Eddie Harris Anthology* "as an exercise ... on how to approach chords without running up and down the scales. By 'Jazz Dance' I was incorporating a constant rhythm, something uninhibited people can dance to. It's a fusion of rhythm and avant-garde." With a cover version recorded by Miles Davis, "Freedom Jazz Dance" became a standard among modern jazz ensembles.

Harris's 1966 LP *Tender Storm* featured his debut on the electric saxophone—the use of a conventional instrument played through a signal processor, the Varitone. Though Sonny Stitt initially recorded with this device, Harris's technique furthered the creative use of the instrument. As Marks pointed out in *Down Beat,* despite the opposition of many traditional jazzmen to the amplification of the saxophone, "Harris [made] the instrument and all of its electrical accoutrements a focal part of his music."

From Jazz to Funk then Back to Bop

In 1968 Harris recorded the Top Ten hit "Listen Here," a funk-style number accompanied by the Latin percussion of Ray Baretto and Joe Wohletz. "Listen Here" ushered in a new phase of Harris's career. As he explained in *The Eddie Harris Anthology,* "All of a sudden I went from being a jazz artist to funk artist." A year later, Harris's group performed at the Montreux Jazz Festival in Switzerland. During the week of the concert, Harris agreed to join pianist Les McCann and trumpeter Benny Bailey onstage for an unrehearsed performance. Their effort, released as the live recording *Swiss Movement,* featured the numbers "Cold Duck Time" and the near-militant anthem "Compared to What?" The LP enjoyed substantial commercial success and became one of the most popular soul-jazz albums of the late 1960s.

Harris continued his path of musical and cultural exploration into the next decade. In 1970 he traveled to Ghana with a number of other African American musicians to celebrate the country's 14 years of independence. His albums *Is It In, Get on Down,* and *I Need Some Money* spotlighted the use of the electric saxophone. During this time Harris also experimented with self-made instruments: trumpet and trombones fitted with reed mouthpieces, and saxophones fitted with brass mouthpieces. Throughout the 1970s, he published several books such as *How to Play the Reed Trumpet, The Intervalistic Concept for Single Line Instruments,* and *Do You Want to Be a Musician?* These works addressed musical theory and aspects of the music business.

Though Harris had begun a return to a more traditional bop style by the mid-1970s, he maintained his experiments with various self-fabricated instruments into the following decade. His 1980 album *Playing with Myself,* for example, featured him on acoustic and electric sax, reed trumpet, and Yamaha grand piano. By the early 1990s Harris had published his seventh book, *Jazz Astrology, Numerology, and Information.*

Harris has appeared on over 70 albums, many of which have been collaborative efforts with musicians of diverse musical styles. His 1990 release *There Was a Time (Echo of Harlem)* marked a return to his earlier jazz roots, showcasing noted sideman such as pianist Kenny Barron, bassist Cecil McBee, and legendary pianist Thelonious Monk's former bandmember drummer Ben Riley. The 1993 LP *Listen Here* displayed Harris's mastery of electronic instruments, funk rhythms, and vocals that, like his horn style, exhibit a broad palette of musical influences. His original compositions "I Need Some Money" and "People Get Funny When They Get a Little Money" reach into the musical realms of jazz, funk, and the sounds of the black church.

Though his name has faded from the forefront of popular music in recent decades, Harris has not gone unheralded among musicians, as evidenced in bassist Ron Carter's statement in *Down Beat:* "I've always enjoyed listening to Eddie Harris. He was probably the forerunner in the use of electronic devices played by other musicians today, and he is certainly a fine saxophone player." Harris has prided himself on his versatility and intent on playing music, as he explained in *Down Beat,* simply "for the enjoyment." He is musically adept in the complex modal textures of hard bop as well as the idioms of traditional swing and funk. Perhaps Harris's impact on the current music scene was best summed up by saxophonist and bandleader Branford Marsalis when he told Todd Barkan, as quoted in the liner notes to *There Once Was a Time (Echo in Harlem),* "Make no mistake about it: there is no badder cat around than Eddie Harris."

Selected discography

Exodus to Jazz, Vee-Jay, 1961.
The Lost Album and the Better Half, Vee-Jay.
Mighty Like a Rose, Vee-Jay.
In the Sound, Atlantic, 1965.
Mean Greens, Atlantic, 1966.
The Tender Storm, Atlantic, 1966.
The Electrifying Eddie Harris, Atlantic, 1968.
Plug Me In, Atlantic, 1968.
Silver Cycles, Atlantic, 1969.
Free Speech, Atlantic, 1970.
Eddie Harris Sings the Blues, Atlantic, 1972.
Is It In, Atlantic, 1973.
Excursions, Atlantic, 1973.
I Need Some Money, Atlantic, 1975.
That's Why You're Overweight, Atlantic, 1976.
Eddie Who?, Impulse, 1986.
Playing with Myself, RCA, 1980.
There Was a Time (Echo in Harlem), Enja, 1990.
A Tale of Two Cities, Night Records, 1991.
Artist's Choice: The Eddie Harris Anthology, Rhino/Atlantic, 1993.
Listen Here!, Enja, 1993.
The Best of Eddie Harris, Rhino/Atlantic.

With others

Les McCann & Eddie Harris, *Swiss Movement,* Atlantic, 1969.
Horace Silver, *It's Got to Be Funky,* Columbia, 1993.
John Scofield, *Hand Jive,* Blue Note, 1994.

Sources

Books

Feather, Leonard, *From Satchmo to Miles,* Stein & Day, 1972.
Thomas, J. C., *Chasin' the Trane: The Music and Mystique of John Coltrane,* Da Capo, 1976.

Periodicals

Down Beat, August 6, 1970; February 7, 1972; January 1975; December 1975; March 1980.

Additional information for this profile was obtained from liner notes by Todd Barkan to *There Once Was a Time (Echo in Harlem),* Enja, 1991, and by Joel Dorn to *Artist's Choice: The Eddie Harris Anthology,* Rhino/Atlantic, 1993.

—*John Cohassey*

Helmet

Rock band

Aggressive yet precise, Helmet doesn't fit the "typical" post-punk band mold. Blending extensive musical training with intellect and brute force, the band quickly took off on an upward curve toward success in the early 1990s. "Helmets are put on when you want to prevent a good pounding. Helmet is put on when you want to get one," said Craig Tomashoff of *People*.

Singer and guitarist Page Hamilton brought Helmet together in early 1989 in New York, after leaving avant-garde luminaries Band of Susans. Originally from Medford, Oregon, Hamilton wasn't always interested in music. While growing up, he worked at a local logging mill by day, and during the evenings he lit smudge pots under trees in the Harry and David fruit orchard to keep the buds from freezing. "I was just a really nice little small-town geek who wanted to play baseball and football," Hamilton told *Rolling Stone*. But in his senior year of high school, the music of *Led Zeppelin IV*—combined with what he now calls excessive marijuana smoking—completely changed Hamilton's direction. He started learning to play guitar.

Photograph by John Falls, © 1994 Interscope Records

After graduating from the University of Oregon with a major in jazz and classical guitar, Hamilton moved to New York to get his master's degree in jazz guitar at the Manhattan School of Music. He had never heard of New York's popular rock clubs like the Mudd Club or CBGB, but he did frequent the Village Vanguard, where his hero, jazz artist John Coltrane, had played. Hamilton soon hooked up with minimalist composer Glenn Branca's famous guitar orchestra and then went on to play with wall-of-sound, Branca-influenced Band of Susans. He played on the album *Love Agenda* and toured with the band before forming Helmet.

Combined Genres

"Band of Susans and the whole distortion thing got me back into rock," Hamilton explained in *Rolling Stone.* "I wanted to write songs and be part of the group, but they didn't want it. I brought in some four-track demos of my stuff, and they said they liked the songs, but they weren't right for the band, so I decided to leave." Hamilton found a "whole new fun world" in the post-punk scene, but he also clung to his earlier musical influences. He decided to combine the two genres to form the basis of his new band.

"If you're a dedicated musician, you're interested in learning everything you can about music, so for me it's never been a matter of some sort of 'purity of punk' that you shouldn't play well," Hamilton told *Guitar Player.* "I've never believed in that ... and I never will. It's really limiting. That's why the idea of one 'scene' or another doesn't really interest me—it's about music."

Reyne Cuccuro, a friend of Hamilton's who worked at the music-trade magazine *Rockpool,* liked the demos that Band of Susans had rejected. She offered to pay for Hamilton's classified ads in the *Village Voice* to search for bandmembers, and she introduced him to her then-husband, Peter Mengede, who became Helmet's original guitarist. Mengede had moved to New York from Australia and joined Hamilton in the search for the remaining members. Through their classified ads, they found drummer John Stanier and bassist Henry Bogdan.

Originally from Portland, Oregon, Bogdan had played with Portland's punk pioneers Poison Idea. When he saw Hamilton and Mengede's ad, he was already disillusioned with rock, preferring to concentrate on his career as a scenic artist and studio assistant to the minimalist painter Frank Stella. Still, he decided to reply to the ad because of his interest in Branca, the Cramps, and the early No Wave post-punk scene influence that Helmet offered.

Drummer John Stanier had moved to New York from Fort Lauderdale, Florida. After he graduated from high school, Stanier studied orchestral percussion at the University of Miami and then dropped out. He developed a combination of control, power, and endurance through years of playing with the drum and bugle corps in his hometown. He performed with Fort Lauderdale hardcore bands while building his technique in the nationally known corps Florida Wave and Sunco Sound.

Once the band cemented, they considered names such as Tuna Lorenzo and Froth Albument before someone suggested Helmut, which they soon modified to Helmet. They recorded a demo tape that got the attention of Tom Hazelmeyer, the owner of the Minneapolis-based independent label Amphetamine Reptile Records. He decided to sign Helmet to his label. They released their first single, "Born Annoying" and "Rumble," six months after the band had formed.

Record Contract Controversy

In 1990, Helmet went on to release their debut album, *Strap It On,* on Amphetamine Reptile and met with a fervent audience reception on their tour of the United Kingdom and other countries in Europe. They released their next single, "Unsung" and "Your Head," in October of 1991, and the buzz began. Though *Strap It On* had only sold 10,000 copies, eight different major labels started courting Helmet in 1992. They ended up signing a controversial million-dollar-plus contract with Interscope Records. The contract allowed the band complete creative control and generous royalty rates.

Helmet released *Meantime* in June of 1992, and "Unsung" took off as their first hit single. After recording the album, Hamilton went to Seville, Spain, to join his old friend and bandmate Glenn Branca for a live performance of Branca's *Symphony No. 8.* Then, Helmet traveled to Japan, Australia, and Hawaii to kick off the tour for *Meantime.* Though their record contract had generated skepticism and controversy, Helmet's success rocketed. *Meantime* reached gold status, and in 1993, *Guitar World* published a cover story naming Page Hamilton a central figure of a new generation of players.

Interscope Records re-released *Strap It On* in December of 1992, while Helmet prepared the final leg of their tour before heading back into the recording studio. On February 17, 1993, just before the tour began, the band asked guitarist Mengede to resign. "The relationship with Peter got increasingly strained," Hamilton told *Rolling Stone.* "My take on it is that he became resentful of the fact that I was writing songs that the three of us were capable of playing, and he wasn't as capable. A good musical thing can't survive in that kind of vibe."

"Until February 17, 1993," Mengede replied in *Rolling Stone,* "it was four individuals contributing musically and in other ways. You're in a partnership based on trust.... Page said my dismissal was due to our worsening personal relationship, which he said was largely his fault. I think that's legitimate." Mengede didn't think everything about his dismissal was legitimate, however. He filed a suit against the band in Manhattan Federal Court, alleging, among other things, their failure to supply accounting records and their withholding of royalties.

New Guitarist Brought New Beginnings

In March of 1993, Mengede was replaced by Rob Echeverria, who had played in some early New York hardcore bands including Straight Ahead and Rest in Pieces. After finishing their '93 tour, Helmet made their break into film soundtracks. They collaborated with House of Pain for the song "Just Another Victim" on the *Judgment Night* soundtrack, which was released in September of 1993. They then recorded the original version of "Milquetoast" for *The Crow* soundtrack.

In the summer of 1994, Helmet released their third album, *Betty,* produced by T. Ray. When *Rolling Stone* asked Hamilton about Helmet's musical progression to *Betty,* he commented, "*Strap It On* was kind of an accident—we'd stumbled upon this thing we could all do well together. The next album was a little more metal. On this album, we were all aware we liked the groove aspect of things."

Helmet continued their contribution to film soundtracks with a song for *Johnny Mnemonic,* featuring Henry Rollins and Ice-T. And they appeared in the *Jerky Boys* movie as a rock band, with veteran rocker Ozzy Osbourne playing their manager. The band recorded Black Sabbath's "Symptom of the Universe" and "Lord of This World" for the movie, but only "Symptom of the Universe" made it in. "Lord of This World" appeared as a giveaway with an English magazine called *Volume.* In addition, Helmet recorded their version of "Custard Pie" for the Led Zeppelin tribute album.

Helmet has grown and changed considerably since 1989, but Hamilton maintains that the band remains dedicated to their music. "Whatever anyone's doing, they should do it with incredible passion," he told *Rolling Stone.* "It's the process itself, it's trying to assert yourself with some discipline and reach something higher. That, to me, is critical."

Selected discography

Singles; on Amphetamine Reptile

"Born Annoying"/"Rumble," 1989, reissued with "Shirley MacLaine" and "Taken," Interscope, 1993.
"Unsung"/"Your Head," 1991.
"In the Meantime"/"No Nicky No," 1992.
"Primitive"/"Born Annoying," 1993.

Albums

Strap It On, Amphetamine Reptile, 1990, reissued, Interscope, 1992.
Meantime, Interscope, 1992.
Betty, Interscope, 1994.
(Contributors) *Judgment Night* (soundtrack), 1993.
(Contributors) *The Crow* (soundtrack), 1994.
(Contributors) *Johnny Mnemonic* (soundtrack), 1995.
(Contributors) *Jerky Boys* (soundtrack).

Sources

Books

The Trouser Press Record Guide, edited by Ira A. Robbins, Collier, 1991.

Periodicals

Billboard, June 27, 1992; September 12, 1992.
Entertainment Weekly, June 24-July 1, 1994.
Guitar Player, October 1992; August 1994.

Metro Times (Detroit), June 22-28, 1994.

Musician, February 1993; July 1994.

New York Times, July 24, 1994; August 22, 1994.

People, July 4, 1994.

Pulse!, July 1994.

RIP Magazine, September 1994; January 1995.

Rolling Stone, January 9, 1992; August 20, 1992; August 25, 1994.

Spin, August 1994; September 1994.

Stereo Review, December 1992.

Time, September 14, 1992.

Additional information for this profile was obtained from Interscope Records publicity materials, 1994.

—*Sonya Shelton*

Harlan Howard

Songwriter

In Nashville's country music star system, everyone is in service to the song—including the singer, the musician, the producer, the promoter, and the executive. It follows, then, that Nashville is bursting with songwriters, yet most are broke, transient, or not long for the vagaries of Music Row. One thing, though, is consistently true: All of those songwriters persist because of the legacy of Harlan Howard, thought by many to be the greatest of country songwriters.

Sometimes called the dean of country songwriting or even Nashville's answer to Irving Berlin, Howard has accomplished feats that seem impossible. Of the nearly 5,000 songs he has penned, 2,000 have been recorded and more than 40 have reached the Top Ten of *Billboard's* country chart. Three of Howard's most enduring titles—"Heartaches by the Numbers," "I Fall to Pieces," and "Busted"—crossed over into the Top Ten of the pop charts.

Because of his extraordinary success, Howard is continually asked if he employs a formula when he is creates songs. He has responded with humility, even a tinge of guilt. "I've got a kind of system," he explained in a *Country Music* interview, "and it's always been that way. But really it's just doodling on a legal pad. I like to find a good title. Then I study it for a while, think about what stories I could write from that title. Then I'll pick out the one that I think most people would like, the most commercial story. Then I'll either reject the idea as not strong enough, or I'll keep thinking about it, and all of a sudden I'm thinking that we've got to have a little chorus here and a line pops to mind. When I get about halfway through, I pick the guitar up and I mess around with a melody. Finally I judge it against other things I've written."

Howard was born in Kentucky on September 8, 1929, and his family moved to Detroit in the early 1930s in pursuit of car magnate Henry Ford's five-dollar-a-day-factory-work promise. In the predominantly white ghetto where the family lived, young Harlan was able to hear the sounds of hillbilly country as well as the rhythm and blues from the nearby black ghetto. He especially loved the clear, hard sound of Ernest Tubbs, then country's most prominent practitioner.

In 1947 Harlan joined the army and was stationed at Fort Benning in the 11th Airborne Division. While in the service he learned to play the guitar, jotting down derivative lyrics in his spare time. In 1954 he moved to Tucson, Arizona, to find factory work. He ended up becoming more serious about his music, writing "Keeper of the Key," his first mature effort.

In 1955 Howard took a job driving a fork truck at Pacific Pressing in Los Angeles. He would often write songs

Born September 8, 1929, in Kentucky; married first wife, Lula Johnson (later known as Jan Howard), 1958 (marriage dissolved).

Songwriter. Learned to play guitar while in the army; moved to Tucson and wrote songs while working hourly jobs, 1954; moved to Los Angeles and worked at a paper mill while writing songs with Tex Ritter and Buck Owens, 1955; wrote "You Took Her off My Hands" and "Above and Beyond" for Wynn Stewart, 1957; wrote "Heartaches by the Numbers" for Ray Price, 1959, re-recorded by Guy Mitchell and became Number One hit on *Billboard* pop charts, 1960; moved to Nashville, TN, 1960; released first album, 1964; established Wilderness Publishing, 1965, then sold it to Tree Publishing, Nashville, 1967; wrote nearly 30 Top Ten hits, 1965-80; took a three-year sabbatical, 1980-83; inaugurated annual Birthday Bash and Guitar Pull, 1988; contributed to *Signatures II,* a songwriter's compilation, 1993. *Military service:* Joined U.S. Army, 1947.

Selected awards: Ten Broadcast Music Inc. (BMI) awards, 1961; Grammy Award, 1963, for "Busted"; inducted into Country Music Hall of Fame, 1991; Robert J. Burton Award for most performed song for "Blame It on Your Heart," BMI, 1994.

Addresses: *Publishing company*—Harlan Howard Songs, Inc., 1902 Wedgewood Ave., Nashville, TN 37212.

between loads, at times ending his day with three finished lyrics. Through honky tonk singer Skeets McDonald, Howard met a young and struggling Buck Owens, with whom Howard soon began writing. Howard also became friends with Johnny Bonds and Tex Ritter, co-owners of Vidor Music, Howard's first publisher. In 1956 Howard met and later married Lula Johnson, who would gain fame as Grand Ole Opry star Jan Howard.

Howard and Owens had a couple of songs—"You Took Her off My Hands" and "Above and Beyond"—recorded by Wynn Stewart, who was then a star on the West Coast. Later, in 1958, Charlie Walker cut Howard's "Pick Me up on Your Way Down," which became a Number Two country hit. More importantly, the song was heard by Ray Price, the most influential country singer alive at the time. He called Howard, looking for songs; a nervous Howard quickly sent him a new song, "Heartaches

by the Number." In May of 1959 Price released the song, which stayed on the charts for 41 weeks. Singer Guy Mitchell took it to Number One on the pop charts a year later. The song has since been cut more than 200 times.

In June of 1960, Howard quit the his job at the Los Angeles paper mill and moved to Nashville. Upon arriving he hit the ground running, and would eventually rack up a significant string of song credits between the years 1960 and 1975. In 1965 he opened his own publishing company, Wilderness Music, but quickly sold it to the conglomerate Tree Publishing when he found the business end of creating songs tiresome. The majority of Howard's tunes since that time have been administered by the firm Pamper, Combine and Central.

In the early 1960s Howard bonded with a small group of other wild and hugely talented songwriters—Roger Miller, Willie Nelson, and Hank Cochran. Along with legendary country crooner Patsy Cline (who recorded Howard's "I Fall to Pieces"), they were regulars at Tootsies Orchid Lounge, located just across the street from Ryman Auditorium. "We were all young and poor," Howard commented in *USA Today* in 1992. "Looking back I now know that we were really happening. We didn't know it but we were hot as hell."

In the mid-1960s Howard recorded the first of five albums of his own. He never considered himself a performer, and in fact, he performed only once, in Houston, Texas, on a bill with Johnny Cash. His songwriting, though, earned him numerous awards, including ten from Broadcast Music Inc. (BMI) in just one year.

Howard's oeuvre is not just a compilation of popular country songs. He in effect galvanized the country sensibility, establishing an emphasis on words above melody, using the melancholy nature of male/female relationships as a theme, and letting the songs suggest an entire way of living. Howard's songs have been recorded by everyone from Ray Charles to Bing Crosby to Mel Tillis to Pam Tillis.

Having reached his mid-sixties in the mid-1990s, Harlan has slowed his pace, as he noted in *Country Music,* to about "12-15 songs a year, which also includes some co-writing. I want to stay pretty active from here on out." He continues every September to hold his famous Birthday Bash and Guitar Pull, a bit of reverie that features proven and unproven songwriters alike.

"I've lost my confidence before," Howard admitted in *Country Music,* "but I've always fought my way back. I've always just really bore down, and even if I had to write a few terrible songs, I eventually worked my way back to the mark. I don't quite understand it myself. I know when I was a kid, I admired not only the people in country music, but also the old Tin Pan Alley masters, and I always wanted to be like them. I considered that if I ever got in this profession, I was going to do it for the rest of my life."

Selected songs

"Pick Me up on Your Way Down," Charlie Walker, 1957.
"Mommy for a Day," Kitty Wells, 1959.
"Heartaches by the Numbers," Ray Price, 1959; Guy Mitchell, 1960.
"Above and Beyond," Buck Owens, 1960.
"I Fall to Pieces," Patsy Cline, 1961.
"Busted," John Conlee, 1961; Ray Charles, 1963.
"I Don't Remember Loving You," John Conlee, 1962.
"Too Many Rivers," Brenda Lee, 1963; Forester Sisters, 1987.
"You Comb Her Hair," George Jones, 1964.
"Tiger by the Tail," Buck Owens, 1965.
"The Chokin' Kind," Waylon Jennings, 1967.
"Yours Love," 1969.
"Life Turned Her That Way," Ricky Van Shelton, 1985.
"Somebody Should Leave," Reba McEntire, 1985.
(With Kostas) "Blame It on Your Heart," Patty Loveless.

Sources

Books

Biracree, Tim, *Country Music Almanac,* Prentice Hall, 1993.
DeCurtis, Anthony, James Henke, and Holly George-Warren, editors, *Rolling Stone Album Guide,* Straight Arrow, 1992.
Guralnick, Peter, *Lost Highway,* Vintage Books, 1982.
Marsh, Dave, *Rolling Stone Record Guide,* Rolling Stone Press, 1979.
Pareles, Jon, and Patricia Romanowski, *Rolling Stone Encyclopedia of Rock & Roll,* Rolling Stone Press, 1983.
Rees, Dafydd, and Luke Crampton, *Rock Movers and Shakers,* Billboard Books, 1991.
Whitburn, Joel, *Top Billboard Country Singles, 1942-88,* Billboard Books, 1990.

Periodicals

Billboard, October 29, 1994.
Country Music, January/February 1994.
Country Music Parade, May 1993.
Los Angeles Times, June 14, 1992.
USA Today, May 8, 1991.

—*Stewart Francke*

Inner Circle

Reggae band

Photograph by Daniel Hastings, courtesy of Atlantic Recordings

Apparently one fan *can* make a difference in a band's career, if Inner Circle's recent success is any indication. Since the mid-1970s, the reggae band Inner Circle had been plugging away, remaining relatively unknown outside their native Jamaica. It wasn't until a fan—who happened to be a field producer for a new television show—suggested the group's song "Bad Boys" for the show's theme that their music went through the roof, bringing reggae and Inner Circle into homes across the globe.

In the early 1970s, brothers Ian and Roger Lewis played in various Top 40 bands around their hometown of Kingston, Jamaica. In 1975 they joined forces with keyboardist Bernard "Touter" Harvey. Neighbor Jacob "Killer" Miller used to stop by rehearsals and ridicule the band, jeering at their singers. Roger Lewis recalled in a Big Beat/Atlantic press release that Miller would "tell us that one day we were going to need him, because he was a great singer; sometimes he would try to grab the mike. He was a real prankster." Soon Miller grabbed the microphone and kept it, joining what had become Inner Circle.

Lead Singer's Death Halted Success

During their maiden U.S. tour in 1975, the band realized that original reggae tunes were the way to make it big, having witnessed the thunderous reception for reggae superstars such as Toots & the Maytals and Dennis Brown. Inner Circle quickly looked to their roots in soul and R&B vocals and rhythms, and they incorporated them into an extensive catalog of reggae originals. Opening for more famous groups and often singing backup for them gained Inner Circle widespread popularity. Soon, they established their own Top Ranking label and recorded songs like "Tenement Yard," "All Night Till Daylight," and "Tired fe Lick Weed in a Bush"—all considered classics according to *Vibe* magazine.

A taste of overseas success came when the band was signed by Capitol Records in 1976, but the truly big break came when they performed for over 40,000 fans in the famous Jamaican Peace Festival of 1978. The long-running film *Heartland Reggae* documented this reggae version of Woodstock, which included such artists as Bob Marley, Peter Tosh, Jimmy Cliff, and Bunny Wailer. English entrepreneur Chris Blackwell, who started Marley's career rolling, spotted the band at the festival and signed them to his Island Records label.

Inner Circle's 1978 Island debut *Everything Is Great* hit the Top 20 in the United Kingdom and the Top Ten in

For the Record . . .

Members include **Calton Coffie** (born February 27, c. 1950s, in London, England; joined group c. 1985), lead and backing vocals; **Lance Hall** (born February 7, c. 1950s, in Kingston, Jamaica; joined group c. 1985), drums and percussion; **Bernard "Touter" Harvey** (born October 25, c. 1954, in Kingston), keyboards and backing vocals; **Ian Lewis** (born November 1, c. early 1950s, in Kingston), bass and guitar; **Roger Lewis** (born June 29, c. early 1950s, in Kingston), rhythm guitar; **Jacob "Killer" Miller** (born May 4, 1954, in Kingston; died in a car accident, March 23, 1980), lead singer.

Band formed in Kingston, Jamaica, 1975; signed with Capitol Records, 1976; performed at the Jamaican Peace Festival, signed with Island Records, and released *Everything Is Great,* 1978; Jacob Miller killed in auto accident and group disbanded, 1980; group reunited in Miami, FL, 1986; released *One Way* on RAS Records, 1987; signed with Big Beat/Atlantic; released reconfigured *Bad to the Bone* as *Bad Boys;* single and TV theme song, "Bad Boys," became international hit, 1993.

Awards: Gold record for *Bad Boys,* 1993; Grammy Award for best reggae album and Caribbean Music Awards in the best group and best reggae album categories, all for *Bad Boys,* 1994.

Addresses: *Record company*—Big Beat/Atlantic Records, 75 Rockefeller Plaza, New York, NY 10019.

France. The title track was a Euro-smash, as were the hit singles "Mary, Mary" and "Music Machine." But all of this burgeoning success came to a halt in 1980, when lead singer Jacob Miller was killed in a car accident. In the band's press materials Roger Lewis noted, "Jacob was like family and it wasn't the kind of thing where you could go out and just find another singer to replace him."

After Miller's death, Ian Lewis and Harvey moved to Miami, Florida, and built a recording studio. There they worked with artists such as soul singer Joe Tex and rappers 2 Live Crew. Roger Lewis joined them there in 1985. The passing years had helped to heal the wounds left by the death of Miller; the band was eager to get back to their music. With new lead singer Calton Coffie and drummer Lance Hall, Inner Circle was rehearsing again by 1986. In no time the band was signed by RAS

Records, and their 1987 album, *One Way,* was receiving critical acclaim.

While touring in Europe, Inner Circle discovered that a single of theirs, "Bad Boys," was becoming a huge hit in Sweden. An independent Swedish label had apparently released the song with neither a contract nor Inner Circle's knowledge. The label went bankrupt, but the song was picked up by WEA Scandinavia's Metronome label and went on to become one of that territory's bestselling singles of 1991.

Television Show Brought Worldwide Fame

At the same time a field producer for the brand-new, globally syndicated, "real-life" television show *Cops* suggested "Bad Boys" as the show's theme song. *Cops* became immensely popular worldwide, and that, coupled with radio airplay, made "Bad Boys" and Inner Circle a global sensation. The 1993 album of the same name eventually sold over 3 million copies and earned the group a Grammy Award for best reggae album as well as Caribbean Music Awards in the best group and best reggae album categories. *Bad Boys* contained two Top 20 singles, and the title track was certified gold.

Prior to the release of *Bad Boys,* Inner Circle took a break from touring, returned to Miami, and released 1992's *Bad to the Bone.* The band then signed with Big Beat/Atlantic and reconfigured their album—with some track changes—creating 1993's *Bad Boys.* Following on the heels of "Bad Boys," the song "Sweat (A La La La La Long) broke in Sweden and then went on to top radio play lists in Denmark, Finland, Holland, Belgium, Israel, Portugal, Switzerland, Austria, and Germany. In Germany the band made history, holding the Number One pop slot for 13 weeks, garnering the most German airplay of any record ever over a given period.

After such a long time on the music scene, huge success was new to Inner Circle. "We've never really been through this before," Ian Lewis told *Billboard* contributor Gil Griffin. "'Bad Boys' helped us go into new areas where people only knew of reggae through Bob Marley." Lance Hall furthered that discussion of reggae's popularity in *Rap Masters Presents:* "A lot of people have the misconception that reggae is popular now. Reggae was popular when Bob Marley was around. But Bob Marley and *only* Bob Marley got the exposure. Now that you have Inner Circle, Shabba Ranks, Maxi Priest gettin' exposure, these other artists are getting the best response." And commenting on their jump to the larger Big Beat/Atlantic label, "Basically, it's the conglomerates getting behind reggae music," Ian Lewis pointed out in *Vibe.* "Everywhere you look nowadays is red, gold, and green [the colors of the Jamaican flag]. But reggae music is not something that just come to blow in the wind. It's something here to stay and it must be respected."

With Success Came Controversy

With the worldwide success of Inner Circle came controversy. Ian Lewis told Griffin: "Some of our black fans have come to us and told us 'Cops' is a negative show. We have heard that some black radio stations didn't play the song because of the association with 'Cops.' We were told by the producers, when they asked if they could use the song, that it was a docu-drama. The song isn't about telling the police to lock people up or beat them up; it's about troubled kids who have problems at home." It's a theme that Lewis, a father, often delves into in his music.

In 1994 Inner Circle released the much-awaited *Reggae Dancer,* and although it did not touch the success of *Bad Boys,* it received mostly good reviews. This album represents what the band has been through since their success. As Ian Lewis told *Vibe,* "We chose songs that were kind of personal in our struggle." *BRE* felt that "the reggae beat suits [the first single, "Games People Play,"—a remake of Joe South's 1969 hit] well and has a really happy vibe about it. All ages will find it hard to ignore the seductive influence it has. Maybe not as traditional a reggae cut as some of Inner Circle's previous cuts, but it still pleases."

Entertainment Weekly didn't find that "happy vibe" a good thing. Their Chuck Eddy gave *Reggae Dancer* a C+, noting that "the fattest reggae band in the land is also noted for its blandness.... But Inner Circle mostly sticks to ingratiating feel-good reggae with upbeat early '70s soul influences, guaranteed not to upset baby boomers." *Cash Box* urged, "Let's not forget that [Inner Circle] make some very accessible reggae music without pandering to current urban styles." One single, "Summer Jammin'," got an extra boost when it was featured in a scene in "Beverly Hills Cop III" and appeared on the film's soundtrack.

The future is uncertain for Inner Circle as the world waits for another *Bad Boys.* In 1993 Cema Records put out a *Best of Inner Circle 1976-1977* in order to capitalize on the success of that song; it didn't do well. The influence of *Reggae Dancer* remains to be seen. But as Ian Lewis waxed hopeful in their press materials, "We're still building and America is coming around.... We're working for the music. You have to if there's to be a future. Bob Marley laid the seeds, and we are honored to be carrying the banner right now."

Selected discography

Everything Is Great (includes "Mary, Mary" and "Music Machine"), Island Records, 1978.
One Way, RAS Records, 1987.
Bad to the Bone (includes "Bad Boys"), 1992.
Bad Boys (includes "Bad Boys"), Big Beat/Atlantic, 1993.
Best of Inner Circle 1976-1977, Cema Records, 1993.
Reggae Dancer, Big Beat/Atlantic, 1994.
(Contributors) *Beverly Hills Cop III* (soundtrack), MCA, 1994.

Sources

Billboard, February 12, 1994; July 2, 1994.
BRE, August 5, 1994; August 26, 1994.
Cashbox, August 20, 1994; September 3, 1994.
Daily News (Los Angeles, CA), August 5, 1994.
Entertainment Weekly, August 19, 1994.
Factor-X, October 1994.
Hitmakers, November 19, 1993.
Hollywood Reporter, August 1, 1994.
Network Forty, January 28, 1994; September 30, 1994.
Rap Masters Presents, December 1994.
Spokesman-Review (Spokane, WA), July 29, 1994; August 1, 1994.
Terry Marshall's Daily Insider, March 4, 1994.
Vibe, November 1994.

Additional information for this profile was obtained from Big Beat/Atlantic publicity materials, 1993 and 1994.

—*Joanna Rubiner*

Milt Jackson

Vibraphonist

AP/Wide World Photos

Jazz vibraphonist Milt Jackson is probably most recognized for his membership in the Modern Jazz Quartet (MJQ), but he has also forged a long and formidable solo career spanning five decades. His articulate two-mallet attack and deep blues approach represents a stylistic departure from earlier jazz vibists; unlike swing vibist Lionel Hampton, Jackson is known for slowing down the motor of his vibraharp (an instrument that is larger than a vibraphone). "The result," wrote Thomas Owens in *Bebop: The Music and Its Players,* "is that his long notes have a beautiful, subtle style instead of the nervous shimmy that originally was the norm of the vibraphone." A performer and composer, Jackson serves as an inspiration to an entire generation of vibists who owe a tremendous debt to his inventive reinterpretation of his instrument.

One of six sons, Milton Jackson was born January 1, 1923, in Detroit, Michigan, to a devoutly religious mother and a musically talented father. (His brother became a professional drummer.) As a child, Jackson sang in church. He was later quoted in *Jazz Masters of the Fifties* as saying: "In my case, I believe that what I heard and felt in the music of my church ... was the most powerful influence of my musical career. The music I heard there was open, relaxed, impromptu—soul music." At seven Jackson took up guitar, and around age 11 he began to take piano lessons. At Miller High School, an institution reputed for producing a number of important jazz musicians, he played drums, timpani, violin, xylophone, and sang in the glee club. When he was 16, his high school music instructor, Mr. Goldberg, encouraged him to take up vibes. Around the same time, Jackson was also performing in a gospel group and a dance band.

Watching Hampton's live shows at the Michigan State Fairgrounds and Detroit's Graystone Ballroom further inspired Jackson to study vibes. Though he appreciated Hampton's musicianship, Jackson did not seek to play in the same style; rather, as a member of a younger generation growing up in the 1940s, he received his main musical inspiration from innovative bebop jazz musicians, especially modern pianists and horn players.

Though Jackson had intended to join the band of pianist Earl Hines, he was inducted into the armed forces in 1942. Out of the service in 1944, Jackson returned to Detroit and formed a commercial based music group, the Four Sharps, which included pianist Willie Anderson, bassist Miller Clover, and guitarist Emmit Flay. In the quartet, he sang and played piano, guitar, and vibes. It was at this time that he received the nickname "Bags." In the liner notes to *Plenty, Plenty Soul,* Jackson explained: "I did a lot of celebrating with a lot of late night hours, and so I had little bags under my eyes. The musicians called me 'Bags' and it stuck." In Detroit, Jackson found a flourishing jazz community. "The environment of the '40s in Detroit was very similar to the environment of 52nd Street when I first came to New York," he related in *Jazz Talk.* "In Detroit we had Al McKibbon, Howard McGhee, Teddy Edwards ... [and] the Jones brothers [Hank and Elvin]."

Bebop Invasion of the West

In 1945 Dizzy Gillespie recruited Jackson for his West Coast engagement at Billy Bergs on 1356 Vine Street in Los Angeles. Added as a sixth member to Gillespie's initial quintet, Jackson joined the ensemble as a possible replacement for the group's chronically unpredictable saxophonist, Charlie Parker. In his memoir *To Be or Not to Bop,* Gillespie recounted how "Milt Jackson, on vibes, was someone new and coming up fast in our music, very rhythmic, soulfully deep, and definitely one of my most prized pupils." Though Gillespie's stint at Bergs has been viewed by music critics as a "disaster," the stage performances and live radio broadcasts from the club did expose a great number of bebop fans and intellectuals to authentic modernist jazz.

In March of 1945 Jackson opened with Gillespie's group at New York's Spotlite on 52nd Street with pianist Al Haig, bassist Ray Brown, and drummer Stan Levey.

Despite numerous personnel changes over the next months, Jackson remained a steady member of Gillespie's quintet, which eventually became the core of the trumpeter's second big band. In *To Be or Not to Bop,* Jackson paid tribute to his mentor: "He's dynamic with a big band. I learned how to play good music, this particular kind of music, because he's the father of it.... I love his philosophy of music, and his philosophy of life, modern progressive development."

Two months after his debut at the Spotlite, Jackson played piano on Gillespie's big band recording of Tadd Dameron's "Our Delight"; he also played vibes on the now-classic "Things to Come." The next winter, Jackson joined the band on the Victor sides "Anthropology," "A Night in Tunisia," and "52nd Street Theme." He later recorded for the Musicraft label with Gillespie's alumni saxophonist Sonny Stitt and drummer Kenny Clarke, cutting the numbers "Oop Bop Sh'Bam," "That's Earl," and "One Bass Hit."

Musical Explorations with Monk

Leaving Gillespie in 1947, Jackson teamed up with pianist Thelonious Monk. Together, they recorded for the Blue Note label over the next two years. In 1948 Jackson and Monk, along with bassist John Simmons and drummer Shadow Wilson, produced the numbers "Evidence," "Mysterioso," "Epistrophy," and "I Mean You." Several years later, accompanied by drummer Art Blakey and bassist Al McKibbon, Jackson recorded such arrangements as "Four in One," "Criss Cross," "Ask Me Now," and "Straight No Chaser."

In 1949 Jackson joined the big band of Woody Herman and toured nationally. With Herman's small ensemble, the Woodchoppers, he appeared at the Tropicana in Havana, Cuba. When the audience was unresponsive to the group's modernist repertoire, Herman called upon Jackson to supply some popular standards. In the liner notes for Jackson's *Plenty, Plenty Soul,* Herman described Jackson's remarkable memory for arrangements: "He's a fantastic musician. And one of the things about him that impressed me was his great knowledge of tunes. He was ... a young man, but he remembers songs I've long forgotten. He remembers all about a song, the bridge, the right changes. That depth of repertoire is a long-lost quality with most young players, but not with Milt."

Jackson rejoined Gillespie from 1951 to 1952. For Gillespie's Detroit-based Dee Gee label, he recorded sessions with John Coltrane and Kenny Burrell. The rhythm section of Gillespie's big band—pianist John Lewis, bassist Ray Brown and drummer Kenny Clarke—soon broke off to form a group with Jackson. As the Milt Jackson Quartet, they recorded sessions for Dee Gee, Savoy, and Blue Note.

MJQ and Beyond

In 1952 Jackson's quartet—with exception of Brown, who was replaced by Percy Heath—incorporated themselves as the Modern Jazz Quartet (MJQ). The ensemble performed a format of jazz standards, classically-based originals written by Lewis, the group's music director, and numerous blues compositions written by Jackson. As Ralph J. Gleason wrote in the liner notes to The Modern Jazz Quartet, "Milt Jackson remained the star of the rhythm section because he is a natural soloist and also because it was such a blindingly unique style of playing he brought forth." This observation was shared by Lewis, who explained in Plenty, Plenty Soul, "Milt is not only a fine soloist improviser, but he is an excellent group player too. And he keeps on developing. In all areas."

Throughout the 1950s Jackson performed with the MJQ and continued to record under his own name, collaborating with musicians such as Coleman Hawkins, Art Farmer, Harry "Sweets" Edison, Jimmy Heath, and Ray Brown. A guest musician on the 1954 album Miles Davis and the Modern Jazz Giants, Jackson provided Davis's LP with two takes of his classic minor-blues number, "Bags' Groove" in a session that evoked the now-legendary controversy concerning Davis's demand that Monk "lay out" during his trumpet solos. Five years later, Jackson co-led a session for Atlantic with John Coltrane, Bags and Trane, which brought together two powerful voices of the modern age of jazz.

The 1960s saw Jackson continuing his solo efforts. His 1958 collaboration with Ray Charles, Soul Brothers, for Atlantic, was followed by the 1961 release Soul Meeting. Atlantic producer Jerry Wexler recalled the two musicians' creative interaction: "Dialoguing like two long lost friends, Milt and Ray were soul brothers indeed—relaxed, chatty, honest, respectful of each other's time, patient listeners with nowhere to go except further into the landscape of their pasts and sorrowful joys of their songs." That same year, Jackson teamed up with guitarist Wes Montgomery to record Bags Meets Wes!, featuring pianist Wynton Kelly and drummer Philly Joe Jones.

The breakup of the Modern Jazz Quartet in 1974 enabled Jackson to pursue a full-time solo career. In 1975 he signed with Pablo Records and made several Montreux Jazz Festival appearances. Outside of performing, Jackson has devoted himself to lecturing on the history of music. The MJQ reformed in 1981 for a tour of Japan, and he has subsequently made several albums with the group. Featuring backup by Cedar Walton and Billy Higgins, Jackson's 1994 release, The Prophet Speaks, is a testament to his timelessness. In a career that began with the birth of bebop and included collaborations with nearly every influential name in jazz music, Jackson has made substantial contributions to nearly a half century of African American musical development.

Selected discography

Solo releases

Milt Jackson, Blue Note, 1952.
Wizard of the Vibes, Blue Note, 1952.
What's New?, Blue Note, 1952.
Milt Jackson Quartet, OJC, 1955.
Roll 'em Bags, Savoy, 1955.
Jackson's Ville, Savoy, 1956.
Plenty, Plenty Soul, Atlantic, 1958.
Bags' Opus, Blue Note, 1958.
Bags and Flutes, Atlantic, 1961.
Big Bags, OJC, 1962.
Olinga, CTI, 1974.
Mostly Duke, Pablo, 1975.
Brother Jim, OJC, 1976.
Feelings, OJC, 1976.
Fuji Mama, West Wind, 1976.
Montreux '77, OJC, 1977.
Sings and Plays "Soul Believer," OJC, 1978.
Bags' Bag, Pablo, 1980.
Ain't But a Few of Us Left, Pablo, 1983.
It Don't Mean a Thing if You Can't Tap Your Foot to It, Pablo, 1984.
Reverence and Compassion, Qwest, 1993.
The Prophet Speaks, Qwest, 1994.
Meet Milt Jackson, Savoy.
Opus de Jazz, Savoy.
The First Q, Savoy.
The Jazz Skyline, Savoy.
All Star Bags, Blue Note.
Memories of Thelonious Monk, Pablo.

With Modern Jazz Quartet

Fontessa, Atlantic, 1956.
The Modern Jazz Quartet, Atlantic, 1957.
The Modern Jazz Quartet and Orchestra, Atlantic, 1960.
A Quartet is a Quartet is a Quartet, Atlantic, 1963.
Blues at Carnegie Hall, Atlantic, 1966.
The Last Concert, Atlantic, 1974.
For Ellington, East West, 1988.
MJQ40 (Boxed Set), Atlantic, 1991.

Compilations

Big Band Jazz: From the Beginning to the Fifties, Smithsonian Collection of Recordings.

As co-leader

(With Sonny Stitt) *In the Beginning,* OJC, 1948.
(With J. J. Johnson) *Milt Jackson & J. J. Johnson: A Date in New York,* Inner City, 1958.
(With Ray Charles) *Soul Brothers,* Atlantic, 1958.
(With John Coltrane) *Bags and Trane,* Atlantic, 1959.
(With Ray Charles) *Soul Meeting,* Atlantic, 1961.
(With Wes Montgomery) *Bags Meets Wes!,* Riverside, 1961.
(With Count Basie) *Milt Jackson + Count Basie + the Big Band,* Pablo, 1978.
(With Ray Brown) *Ray Brown—Milt Jackson,* Verve.

As sideman

Dizzy Gillespie, *A Night in Tunisia,* Victor, 1946.
Dizzy Gillespie, *Anthropology,* Victor, 1946.
Thelonious Monk, *Misterioso,* Blue Note, 1948.
Cannonball Adderly, *Things Are Getting Better,* Riverside, 1958
Oscar Peterson, *Very Tall,* Verve, 1962.
Benny Carter, *The King,* Pablo, 1976.

Sources

Books

Clancy, William D., *Woody Herman: Chronicles of the Herds,* Schirmer Books, 1995.
Gillespie, Dizzy, and Al Fraser, *To Be or Not to Bop: Memoirs of Dizzy Gillespie,* Doubleday, 1979.
Goldberg, J., *Jazz Masters of the Fifties,* Da Capo, 1983.
Owens, Thomas, *Bebop: The Music and Its Players,* Oxford University Press, 1995.
Rusch, Robert D., *Jazz Talk: The Cadence of Interviews,* Lyle Stewart, 1984.
Wexler, Jerry, and David Ritz, *Rhythm and the Blues: A Life in American Music,* Alfred A. Knopf, 1993.

Periodicals

Down Beat, May 19, 1977; August 1994.

Additional information for this profile was obtained from the liner notes to *The Modern Jazz Quartet* by Ralph J. Gleason, Atlantic, 1957; the notes to *Plenty, Plenty Soul* by Nat Hentoff, Atlantic, 1958.

—John Cohassey

The Jayhawks

Rock band

Reminiscent of country-rock bands of the late 1960s and early 1970s, the Jayhawks have become in the 1990s one of the most critically acclaimed performers of a blend of down-to-earth rock, country, and folk music. Their songs sketch life from the perspective of the common man; their music can shift from a rowdy good-time feel to touching melancholy within a few bars. "We're between the seams of different rock systems," singer and lead guitarist Gary Louris told the Detroit *Metro Times*. "We do have American influences, but we don't analyze what we do—almost to a fault. In Europe they keep trying to put us up as this band symbolizing America. We write songs because we have things that are calling out to be expressed."

When singer and guitarist Mark Olson was growing up in California and Minneapolis, Minnesota, his musical tastes leaned toward performers like seminal folksinger Woody Guthrie, country vocalist Emmylou Harris, blue-grass's Louvin Brothers, and traditional blues musicians. For a while he played bass fiddle with a rockabilly band called Stagger Lee; it was with that outfit that he

Courtesy of American Recordings

began performing his own songs. In the mid-1980s Olson met guitarist Marc Perlman, who had previously played with the Neglecters. Olson and Perlman decided to form a new band, with the latter switching to bass. The twosome was joined by drummer Norm Rogers, formerly of the Cows.

For his part, Louris got a late start as an electric guitarist, not purchasing his first instrument until graduating from college in 1977. He began playing lead at twenty-five, after which he established some local presence playing with two Minnesota bands, Schnauzer and Safety Last. Louris joined Olson, Perlman, and Rogers after seeing them perform in Minneapolis in February of 1985.

Honed Country-Folk-Rock on Club Circuit

Calling themselves the Jayhawks, the group honed their country-folk sound and won over an audience playing the club circuit. They recorded their first album, *The Jayhawks,* independently in 1986. Though only a few thousand copies of the album were made, the release helped expand the Jayhawks' reputation outside of the Minneapolis area. Critics began labeling the group "the new Flying Burrito Brothers," after the legendary country-rock band of the late 1960s and early 1970s, according to American Recordings press materials.

Olson and Louris clicked as a songwriting team, but the group was unable to earn a living from music alone. They continued playing gigs at night while working at day jobs. Sometimes they would grind out three sets a night in run-down watering holes and sleep on the floors of friends or strangers when they played outside of their hometown. Rogers was replaced on drums by Thad Spencer. Then, in the fall of 1988, Louris was almost fatally injured in an automobile accident. The group disbanded to reassess their musical direction.

Dave Ayers, an executive with Twin Tone Records, which had released debut albums by the Replacements and Soul Asylum—stalwarts of the underground rock scene who would go on to great prominence—recommended that the group put their demo tapes together to form an album. The result was *Blue Earth,* released on Twin Tone in 1989. *Blue Earth* featured a broader sound than was found on the Jayhawks' previous release, and was received with some enthusiasm.

Seduced Critics with Major Label Debut

After recovering from his injuries Louris rejoined the group, and the Jayhawks became a full-time act. Another new drummer, Ken Callahan, brought a harder rock sound to the band, and frequent touring helped to build awareness of the group. As the story goes, George Drakoulias, a producer with Def American Recordings who had hit it big with an Atlanta band called the Black Crowes, was talking on the phone to Ayers and heard *Blue Earth* in the background. Impressed by the group's sound, Drakoulias signed the Jayhawks to Def American (which would later drop the "Def" from its name).

The partnership with Drakoulias led to the group's breakthrough 1992 recording, *Hollywood Town Hall.* Featuring a bigger, more developed sound and contributions from noted keyboardists Nicky Hopkins, who had worked with the Rolling Stones, and Benmont Tench of Tom Petty's Heartbreakers, it provided the songs of Olson and Louris with a considerably richer presentation.

Critical praise for *Hollywood Town Hall* was virtually universal. In *Guitar Player,* Heidi Siegmund wrote, "The Jayhawks' tough, country-tinged rock recalls the plain-spoken emotion of Neil Young's earliest solo albums." *Entertainment Weekly* reported that the album offered "blatant old-wave country rock" and "earnest, rugged songs about the travails of forlorn love and salvation." Stewart Francke of the *Metro Times* described the band's work as "taut, emotional music that falls somewhere between Bill Monroe's hill-top country and the melancholy, myth-drenched rock of the Band."

Particular attention was paid to *Hollywood's* lyrics. Demonstrating a contentment drawn from tradition and hope for a better future, the poetry of the Jayhawks' stood in stark contrast to the alienation and rage of the so-called grunge bands that were claimed youthful audiences in 1992. "The Jayhawks' sincerity is refreshing: it implies a mode of acceptance and affirmation when all around is satire and rejection," remarked Francke. Louris told him, "The lyrics are intentionally oblique. Maybe it's our midwestern embarrassment at having to actually speak our minds. It's easier for us to hide things in imagery." The most popular song from the album was the lead single, "Waiting for the Sun," for which the group filmed a video that earned airplay on the cable giant MTV. "Crowded in the Wings," "Wichita," and "Take Me with You (When You Go)" also received radio play.

In yet another change behind the drum kit, Tim O'Reagan replaced Callahan in 1993. While touring, the group added keyboardist Karen Grotberg, who had been playing with a weekend band called the Ranchtones. The Jayhawks spent 18 months on the road after the release of *Hollywood Town Hall,* sometimes opening for the Black Crowes, who were vocal supporters of the band. Various bandmembers also contributed songs or session work to albums by former Lone Justice singer Maria McKee and Rolling Stone Mick Jagger. The group also appeared at the benefit concert Farm Aid VI. Finally back in Minneapolis, Olson and Louris began working on songs for a new album.

Broadened Sound on *Green Grass*

Spring of 1994 saw the band's return to the studio. This time Olson, Louris, Perlman, Grotberg, Tench, and former Lone Justice drummer Don Heffington serving as the basic recording unit. Experimenting with their sound, the group steered slightly away from their country tendencies. The addition of strings—arranged by Paul Buckmaster, highly regarded for his work on Elton John's early albums—added new texture to several songs.

Tomorrow the Green Grass was released in February of 1995. Reflecting a widely held view, tastemaker Lorraine Ali said of the record in *Rolling Stone,* "This may be the album that breaks the Minneapolis-born band beyond its base of critics and country-rock connoisseurs." She called *Tomorrow* "the finest album in their nine-year history," remarking that it "still delivers sweet vocal harmonies and heartbreaking melodies, but this time around there's more bite to all the pure prettiness." Ali singled out the cut *Nothing Left to Borrow* for its "stunning yet uninhibited vocals."

"We had a retro tag, but I don't think anything on this record sounds like old stuff," Olson told Ali. "In fact, it doesn't even sound like our last album." Two songs in particular, "Blue" and "I'd Run Away," clearly crossed the line from country-rock to pop. Still, the band retained a connection to their roots with "See Him on the Street," which sounded to some like it would have been comfortable on *Blue Earth.*

Touring to promote the album proved somewhat disillusioning; as opening act for the enormously popular Tom Petty, the Jayhawks frequently found themselves playing in large arenas where much of the crowd, there to see Petty, did not disguise their disinterest. "What I don't like about these tours is the pressure to make some sort of an impression, to sell ourselves night in, night out," Olson told *Entertainment Weekly.* Despite their appearance on such a high-profile tour, meanwhile, members of the group did not appear eager to become a "mainstream" act. Nor did they think it likely. Said Perlman in *Entertainment Weekly,* "Maybe we'll have a huge hit some day, but I think our stuff is too quirky and not straightforward enough."

In fact, as 1995 wore on, the Jayhawks seemed as dedicated as ever to their rough-hewn version of what has become known as "roots" rock. Though they have not achieved the commercial success that many of their supporters believe is inevitable, they are intent on making music their way or not at all. "We have our thing that we do, and we don't really pay attention to what's happening tomorrow," said Olson in the band's press biography. "We just play what seems melodic and right to us."

Selected discography

The Jayhawks, Bunkhouse, 1986.
Blue Earth, Twin Tone, 1989.
Hollywood Town Hall, Def American, 1992.
Tomorrow the Green Grass, American Recordings, 1995.

Sources

Billboard, January 7, 1995.
Entertainment Weekly, December 25, 1992; April 28, 1995.
Guitar Player, February 1993; April 1995.
Metro Times (Detroit), April 28, 1993.
Musician, June 1995.
Rolling Stone, December 15, 1994.

Additional information for this profile was obtained from American Recordings publicity materials, 1995.

—*Ed Decker*

Hank Jones

Pianist, conductor, composer

Eloquent, lyrical, and impeccable—these are words musicians and critics use to describe the jazz piano style of Hank Jones. From nightclubs to the Broadway stage, Jones has accompanied nearly every major name in jazz. Since his New York debut with trumpeter Oran "Hot Lips" Page in 1944, Jones has appeared as a guest artist, soloist, and bandleader on hundreds of studio sessions. Melding the piano styles of Art Tatum and Teddy Wilson with "bebop," an innovative jazz form known for its complex constructs, Jones has honed a refined technique filled with inventive chordal texture and flowing single-line passages. "[Jones's] light, harp-like touch," wrote David Rosenthal in *Hard Bop: Jazz and Black Music, 1955-1965,* "as though he were plucking the piano's strings instead of striking its keys, and his gracefully restrained single-note style are a reformulation of their aesthetic in modern jazz."

Born in Vicksburg, Mississippi, on July 31, 1918, Henry "Hank" Jones moved to Pontiac, Michigan, where his father, a Baptist deacon, bought a three-story brick home. One of seven children, Jones was raised in a musical family. His mother sang; his two older sisters studied piano; and his two younger brothers—Thad, a trumpeter, and Elvin, a drummer—became world famous jazz musicians. As Thad recalled in *The Jazz Scene: An Informal History from New Orleans to 1991,* "There was always the sound of the piano in the home and, naturally, the sound of the radio." As the eldest son, Hank was the first to receive piano instruction. In *Down Beat* he reflected on his introduction to the piano: "I started with classical training. I never did sit down and practice of my own volition. I always had to be forced. They'd say, 'Hey, you practice that lesson! Teacher's coming next week and you got four pages to go.'"

Over time, however, Jones developed an affinity for the keyboard. His musical education went beyond formal studies: "I listened to a lot of Duke Ellington, Fats Waller, Earl Hines—and there was an awful lot of blues which found its way into our house for one reason or another," he told Andrew Sussman in *Down Beat.* On Sundays, he and his brothers listened to radio broadcasts of the Detroit Symphony. Years later, Elvin recalled his early musical rapport with his older brother in a *Down Beat* interview, stating: "I used to listen to Hank practice. He'd put on an Art Tatum record on our windup Victrola and tell me to play along on a book."

By the age of 13, Jones began playing in local groups in high school. He then joined the Detroit-based territory bands of Benny Carew and altoist Ted Buckner, traveling throughout Michigan and Ohio. While playing on the road in Lansing and Grand Rapids, Michigan, he met Detroit-born tenor saxophonist Lucky Thompson, who

For the Record . . .

Born Henry Jones, July 31, 1918, in Vicksburg, MS; son of a Baptist deacon and lumber inspector.

Began performing with Detroit-based big bands, c. 1931; went to New York to join the band of trumpeter Oran "Hot Lips" Page, 1944; performed with Jazz at the Philharmonic series, 1947-50; freelanced with numerous groups throughout 1950s and 1960s; member of the CBS Orchestra, 1959-74; performed in Broadway stage production *Ain't Misbehavin'* in the 1970s; played in duo piano combination with several artists, including John Lewis and Tommy Flanagan, during the 1980s.

Addresses: *Record company*—Verve Records, Worldwide Plaza, 825 Eighth Ave., New York, NY 10019.

invited him out to New York to play with trumpeter "Hot Lips" Page.

In 1944 Jones joined Page's band at the Onyx Club on 52nd Street in New York. His arrival in the city at the height of the bebop movement brought Jones in contact with a new modernist conception of jazz keyboard. He first heard the Dizzy Gillespie-Charlie Parker group with pianist Al Haig. In *Swing to Bop: An Oral History of the Transition in Jazz in the 1940s,* Jones noted that Haig's "style of playing was quite a departure from what I had previously been trying to play. That style—as I look back on it—I suppose the style came about mainly because these pianists rarely, if ever, played solo. I think they played with groups, and with groups it was not necessary for them to use a lot of left hand."

By listening to other modern pianists like Bud Powell, Jones began to adapt himself to the melodies and harmonic changes of bebop. "Everyone was talkin' 'bout Bud back then," explained piano legend Ray Charles, as quoted in *Rhythm and the Blues: A Life in American Music,* "but I actually preferred Hank Jones. I liked his touch, and I had a great feeling for his solo work. With all his wonderful taste, he reminded me of Nat Cole."

While Jones received an education in the art of bebop, he continued to perform with several major big band talents such as Andy Kirk and Billy Eckstine. In the autumn of 1947, he began a three-year stint touring with Norman Granz's Jazz at the Philharmonic (JATP) concerts, which afforded him the opportunity to play with Roy Eldridge, Charlie Parker, and Max Roach. During the 1950s, he toured Europe with saxophonist Coleman Hawkins and trumpeter Howard McGhee; then he recorded with Parker, who was already a legendary saxophonist. Bob Blumenthal described Jones's piano work on Parker's 1952 recording of "Cosmic Rays" in the liner notes for *Charlie Parker: The Verve Years (1952-1954):* "As always, Hank Jones is elegant, lyrical, [a] model of grace without pressure."

Not long after, Jones became the accompanist for singer Ella Fitzgerald. As Savoy Records' "house pianist," he appeared on hundreds of sides and later in the 1950s began recording on several labels under his own name. He also recorded with Lester Young and Milt Jackson as a sideman. On Cannonball Adderly's 1958 release *Somethin' Else,* he provided brilliant harmonic support behind the horns of Adderly and Miles Davis.

Jones joined the CBS Orchestra in 1959 and remained until the ensemble disbanded in 1974. He performed primarily with big bands and even worked as a pit-pianist with Ray Bloch on the *Ed Sullivan Show.* During the 1960s, he bided his time between television performances, studio sessions, and jazz dates. Throughout the 1970s, he conducted and performed in the Tony Award-winning Broadway musical *Ain't Misbehavin'.* An international talent, Jones has also recorded numerous albums on Japanese and French labels. His various projects in the 1980s included duo performances with pianists John Lewis and Detroit-born bebop veteran Tommy Flanagan who, in *Jazz Spoken Here,* lauded Jones as "a great solo pianist" and "a great accompanist." Jones continued to record in the 1990s. In 1991 he joined forces with bassist Dave Holland and drummer Billy Higgins on the album *The Oracle.*

Describing Jones's ability to perform in a variety of musical settings, a music critic wrote in *Down Beat,* "The enigma of Hank Jones simply is that there's more than one of him. Jones the classicist, Jones the bopper, and Jones the modern jazzer." This versatility has made Jones one of the most active jazz musicians in the business. "I think jazz has proven itself over the past several decades," stated Jones in *Down Beat.* "I don't think you have to go to any great lengths to prove the validity of jazz." Like his inherent faith in his music, Jones has proved himself a true artist. He is widely regarded as a musician's musician—one of the greatest living masters of jazz piano.

Selected discography

Solo releases

The Jazz Trio of Hank Jones, Savoy, 1955.
Just for Fun, Original Jazz Classics, 1977.

Tiptoe Tapdance, Original Jazz Classics, 1978.
Moods Unlimited, Evidence, 1982.
The Oracle, Verve, 1991.
Handful of Keys: ... "Fats" Waller, Verve, 1993.
Upon Reflection—The Music of Thad Jones, Verve, 1994.
Bluebird, Savoy.
Quartet-Quintet, Savoy.
Bluesette, Black & Blue.
I Remember You, Black & Blue.
Lazy Afternoon, Concord.
Rockin' in Rhythm, Concord.

With others

Cannonball Adderly, *Somethin' Else,* Blue Note, 1958.
Gato Barbieri, *El Gato,* Flying Dutchman, 1975.
Kenny Burrell: Bluesin' Around, Columbia, 1983.
Lionel Hampton and the Golden Men of Jazz Live at the Blue Note, Telarc, 1991.
Grover Washington, Jr., *All My Tomorrows,* Columbia, 1992.
Telarchives: Lionel Hampton and Friends, Telarc, 1992.
Benny Carter: Legends, Music Makers, 1993.
Charlie Parker: 1949 Jazz at the Philharmonic, Verve.
Charlie Parker Plays the Blues, Verve.
Charlie Parker: The Verve Years (1952-1954), Verve.

Sources

Books

Enstice, Wayne, and Paul Rubin, *Jazz Spoken Here: Conversations with Twenty-two Musicians,* Louisiana State University Press, 1992.
Gitler, Ira, *Swing to Bop: An Oral History of the Transition in Jazz in the 1940s,* Oxford University Press, 1985.
Rosenthal, David, *Hard Bop: Jazz and Black Music, 1955-1965,* Oxford University Press, 1992.
Stokes, Royal W., *The Jazz Scene: An Informal History from New Orleans to 1991,* Oxford University Press, 1991.
Wexler, Jerry, and David Ritz, *Rhythm and the Blues: A Life in American Music,* Alfred A. Knopf, 1993.

Periodicals

Down Beat, April 1980; May 1981; November 1994.

Additional information for this profile was obtained from liner notes by Bob Blumenthal to *Charlie Parker: The Verve Years (1952-1954).*

—John Cohassey

John P. Kee

Singer, songwriter

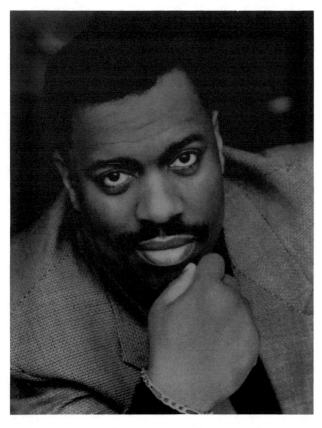

Photo by Tar, courtesy of Verity Records

Prolific gospel singer John P. Kee, who has built an avid fan base within the realm of gospel music, infiltrated the secular rhythm and blues industry in 1994 with his eleventh album, *Show Up!,* by combining church choir harmonies with hip-hop sounds. Kee has often been compared to gospel music legend the Reverend James Cleveland, and the sheer power of Kee's voice is reminiscent of Shirley Ceaser and Edwin Hawkins. Kee described his music to *BRE* magazine's Ruth Robinson as "simple Sunday morning hip-hop, it's got the thing that makes the kids move."

Born on June 4, 1962, in Charlotte, North Carolina, John Prince Kee was the last of six boys born into a family of 16 children. Kee's father was a religious man who insisted that his children embrace religion early in life, and all 16 kids were gifted singers who were members of gospel choirs. At the age of 13, Kee formed his first gospel choir, and by the time he went off to study voice and classical music at the North Carolina School of the Arts in Winston-Salem, he was six-feet-one-inch and had already amassed five years of solid performing and conducting experience. His early musical influences were Thomas Dorsey and Frank Williams.

While Kee was in college he performed with such groups as Cameo and Donald Byrd & the Blackbirds. His formative college years were turbulent after he was lured into using and selling cocaine regularly; Kee even operated his drug racket out of a church at one time. It was only after he witnessed the slaying of a close friend in a drug deal that he turned wholeheartedly to religion and gospel music for solace and inspiration. Ironically, it was Kee's experience trafficking and using drugs that helped him relate to and feel comfortable with fans from all walks of life and of all ages.

In 1981 Kee formed the New Life Community Choir in Charlotte, which consists of 30 young inner city recruits. His ministry is aimed at attracting the young and providing a safe place for them to flourish spiritually. The singer told *BRE*'s Robinson, "I thought we should go down to the police station and get mug shots of all the people in the choir who have been arrested and put them on the back of an album." Like Kee, most of the choir members struggled with drug abuse at one time and eventually turned their lives around through religion and their devotion to gospel music.

In 1985, at the age of 23, Kee became the first artist to record lead vocals on two selections for James Cleveland's Gospel Music Workshop of America's (GMWA) annual mass choir recording. Kee's songs were "Jesus Can Do It All" and "He's My All and All." He confided to Teresa Hairston of *Score* magazine, "James opened the door for me through the GMWA." Kee's songwriting

Born John Prince Kee, June 4, 1962, in Charlotte, NC; divorced from first wife; children: Christopher, Shannon. *Education:* Studied voice and classical music at North Carolina School of the Arts, Winston-Salem, NC, and Yuba College Conservatory School of Music, Marysville, CA.

While a teenager, performed with groups Cameo and Donald Byrd & the Blackbirds; formed New Life Community Choir, 1981; provided lead vocals on two songs for James Cleveland's Gospel Music Workshop of America's (GMWA) annual mass choir recording; wrote and recorded "Jesus Lives in Me" for Edwin Hawkins Music & Arts Seminar album *Give Us Peace;* signed with Tyscot Records and released debut album, *Yes Lord,* 1987; tours U.S. with New Life Community Choir, 1990—.

Selected awards: Stellar awards, 1989, for album of the year for *Wait on Him,* best traditional choir, and song of the year for "It Will Be Alright"; Image Award nomination for best gospel artist, National Association for the Advancement of Colored People (NAACP), 1989; Stellar Award for best male solo performance for *Just Me This Time,* contemporary producer of the year citation from GMWA, and Dove Award for traditional black gospel recorded song, all 1990; two Stellar awards and five GMWA Excellence awards for *Wash Me,* all 1991; four GMWA awards for *Never Shall Forget,* 1991; two Billboard music awards and four GMWA awards for *We Walk by Faith,* all 1992; Dove Award for traditional black gospel album of the year and Stellar Award for best traditional album, both 1993; two GMWA awards, Inside Gospel Award, and Stellar Award, all for *Colorblind,* all 1994; Dove Award for contemporary black gospel recorded song of the year for "It Could Have Been Me," 1994.

Addresses: *Record company*—Verity Records, 137 W. 25th Street, New York, NY 10001.

In 1989 Kee released *Wait on Him* with the New Life Community Choir. The LP was awarded three Stellar Awards, for album of the year, best traditional choir, and song of the year for "It Will Be Alright." The recording served to propel Kee to the forefront of the gospel realm.

The following year Kee and his choir released *There Is Hope.* A portion of the album's proceeds was donated for AIDS research and to a foundation that assists battered children. The album earned Kee a nomination for a National Association for the Advancement of Colored People (NAACP) Image Award in the best gospel artist category. Later in 1990 Kee recorded his first solo album, *Just Me This Time,* which garnered the singer a Stellar Award for best male solo performance and a contemporary producer of the year award from the GMWA. *Just Me This Time* was also nominated for a Dove Award in the category of traditional black gospel recorded song.

In 1991 Kee and the New Life Community Choir released *Wash Me,* which received two Stellar awards and five GMWA Excellence awards. That same year Kee wrote *I Can Call Him* for the East Coast Regional Mass and recorded *Never Shall Forget* with the Victory in Praise Mass Choir. The latter album reflects the culmination of nightly services and workshops at an annual conference for gospel delegates and was awarded four GMWA Excellence awards. Later in 1991 Kee produced *Surrender,* an LP comprised of performances by New Life's female choir members.

A video for *Wash Me* was released in 1992 and earned a Stellar Award for best music video and a GMWA Excellence Award for best video concert. That same year *We Walk by Faith* was released; it won two *Billboard* music awards and four GMWA excellence awards. *Lily in the Valley,* released in 1993, is a second recording by the Victory in Praise Mass Choir. This won a Dove Award for traditional black gospel album of the year and a Stellar Award for best traditional album.

Colorblind, an album that tackles such contemporary issues as prejudice, was released in 1994 and was Kee's second solo effort and first release on the Verity Records label. It was the recipient of two GMWA Excellence awards, an Inside Gospel Award, and a Stellar Award. The album was also nominated for a Dove Award.

Show Up!, Kee's crossover LP, appeared in 1995 and features Kee backed by the New Life Community Choir. It debuted at Number Seven on the *Billboard* Heatseeker's Chart, the highest debut for a gospel album in the chart's history. Robinson commented in a *BRE* review, "The album might be filled with ole' time religion, but it's

and singing career began to bloom soon after the recording; he subsequently wrote and performed on "Jesus Lives In Me" for the Edwin Hawkins Music & Arts Seminar album *Give Us Peace.* Kee was then able to finance a demo tape and was signed to the Tyscot Records label. In 1987 he released his debut album, *Yes Lord,* which was a low-budget effort marked by production glitches.

not full of solemn, sober pleas to the Lord. This is a foot-stomping, hand-clapping sho' nuff shout to the Heavens."

When Kee isn't producing, writing, and performing for his New Life Productions, he oversees an inner-city youth program in Charlotte. Divorced from his first wife, he keeps in close contact with his two children: a son, Christopher, and daughter, Shannon. In addition to music and ministry, Kee has pursued such philanthropic interests as building an inner-city playground, donating $3000 to an urban reading program, providing anti-drug counseling, and creating the Victory in Praise Music & Arts Convention.

Kee declared to *Score* magazine's Hairston, "[The New Life Choir wants] to be unique. The only way we can do that is for people to be able to identify with who we are and what we stand for. That's the key to where we are and where God is taking us."

Selected discography

Yes Lord, Tyscot, 1987.
Wait on Him, Tyscot, 1989.
There Is Hope, Tyscot, 1990.
Just Me This Time, Tyscot, 1990.
Wash Me, Tyscot, 1991.
Never Shall Forget, Tyscot, 1991.
We Walk by Faith, Tyscot, 1992.
Lily in the Valley, Tyscot, 1993.
Colorblind, Verity/Jive, 1994.
Show Up!, Verity/Jive, 1995.

Sources

Billboard, February 25, 1995.
Blues & Soul, May 17, 1994.
BRE, January 20, 1995.
GMMC (*Gospel Music and Ministry Connection*), February/March 1995.
Jack the Rapper, February 15, 1995.
Music Review, July/August 1994.
Score, July/August 1993; July/August 1994.

Additional information for this profile was provided by Verity/Jive publicity materials, 1995.

—B. Kimberly Taylor

Sammy Kershaw

Singer

Photograph by Victoria Pearson, courtesy of PolyGram Records

Benefiting as much from his confident, extroverted stage presence as from a voice that echoes the style of country music legend George Jones, Sammy Kershaw became one of the top country performers of the early 1990s. While carrying the flag of tears-in-your-beer honky-tonk to a new generation of listeners, Kershaw has also managed to gain the allegiance of country music's old guard. He only performs songs he can relate to on a personal level, and his warm, sensitive, soulful renditions of love-gone-wrong ballads combined with his exuberant, up-tempo approach to life have made him one of the most consistently popular country music stars of the decade.

Born February 24, 1958, and raised in Kaplan, Louisiana, the heart of bayou country, Sammy Kershaw is the third cousin of notable fiddle-wielding Cajun Doug Kershaw. When he was just seven years old, Kershaw fell under the spell of George Jones after hearing his mother play "Things Have Gone to Pieces" on the family's stereo turntable. Four years later, after his father died of lung cancer, Kershaw was taken under the wing of family friend J. B. Perry, a well-known country bandleader.

Perry focused the troubled youngster's energy on music; by the time he was twelve, Kershaw was working with Perry's band after school and singing in local clubs on the weekends. In addition to broadening his vocal skills by opening shows for famous country performers like Jones, Charlie Rich, Cal Smith, and Ray Charles, Kershaw learned about showmanship. "J. B., he was one of the best showmen I ever saw ... as far as gettin' with the people," Kershaw told *Country Music*'s Michael Bane. "That's what it's all about and that's what I learned from J. B. Those people in the audience, they're people just like you are, and you're people just like them. That's the whole thing, just having fun with them. Once they see you're having fun, they're going to have fun. And, boy, do I have fun."

Despite Perry's influence, Kershaw constantly flirted with life in the fast lane throughout his teen years; he had parted company with J. B. and the band by the time he was twenty. Not willing to give up music for a more responsible lifestyle, Kershaw ferried through a period of hard living, several marriages that didn't make it, substance abuse, bankruptcies, and stints in numerous bands. He also deejayed, worked in a rice mill, as a carpenter, a welder, a stand-up comic, and even managed a dry cleaning store for a while.

Finally, in 1988, Kershaw pulled himself out of the downward spiral and took a full-time job as a building remodeling contractor for the Wal-Mart Corporation. He worked overtime for two years while trying to gain some stability in his life and in his family. Then, in 1989, out of

Born February 24, 1958, in Abbeville (one source says Kaplan), LA; son of Minos (a carpenter) and Emily Rachal Cashat; married third wife, Kim, 1988: children: Erin, Emily, Ryan (stepson).

Began playing with J. B. Perry and his band in Kaplan, LA, c. 1970; worked as a sometime musician, 1978-88; Wal-Mart Corporation, building renovation contractor throughout the southern United States, 1988-90; signed with Mercury Records, 1990; released debut EP *Don't Go Near the Water,* 1991; made acting debut in *Fall Time,* 1994. Sponsor of a National Association for Stock Car Auto Racing (NASCAR) team.

Awards: Horizon Award nomination, Country Music Association (CMA), 1993.

Addresses: *Record company*—Mercury Records, 66 Music Square West, Nashville, TN 37203. *Management*—James Dowell Management, 50 Music Square West, Nashville, TN 37203.

the blue, Kershaw got *the* phone-call. "This guy had seen me ten years ago in a nightclub in Lafayette called 'Cowboy's,'" he told Bane. "[He] wanted me to send a tape and picture up to Nashville to show to some people. So I did that." After an audition for several Mercury Records A&R representatives, Kershaw landed a record deal; he signed with Mercury in 1990, put down his hammer, and hasn't looked back.

It is no surprise that Mercury wanted to put the then-unknown singer under contract; Kershaw's vocal style is so like that of his musical hero, George Jones, that it's almost uncanny: he possesses "a set of elastic, vowel-bending, liquid-drawl vocal cords that can make even a gray lyric sound like a sunburst," noted *Country America*'s Neil Pond. And nowhere was this retro-Jones styling heard to better effect than on Kershaw's debut album, *Don't Go Near the Water,* released in 1991. In addition to containing several Number One hits, including the tongue-in-cheek "Cadillac Style" and the sassy title cut, the album includes a cover of the Jones hit "What Am I Worth"—just to drive the vocal likeness home. Each of the EP's tracks, taken together, add up to the kind of classic fifties and sixties country sound that Jones cultivated in his heyday, but despite that similarity, Kershaw's own talent transcends the vocal parallel. As Bob Allen noted in *Country Music,* "Kershaw makes it clear ... that he fully understands the difference

between mimicking one's influences and using them as a basis for innovation."

In a Nashville full of young singers who rattle off the names of "country greats" influences as if they were required courses, Kershaw's insistence that he came by his pipes honestly created suspicion among some. "There's nothing I can do about that," the singer exclaimed in his 1994 Mercury press release. "The only thing I can do is try to select material that might be different, that will help the vocal go into its own style." With 1993's *Haunted Heart,* Kershaw did just that; he took a step away from the classic Jones stylings of his debut and moved toward a more original hard-country approach to his songs. With a fresh, contemporary eye on honky-tonk, Kershaw infuses the entire album with the same low-key humor and fun that marked his debut effort—and to good effect: his first two albums for Mercury went platinum, and *Haunted Heart* produced the Top Ten singles "She Don't Know She's Beautiful," as well as the poignant "I Can't Reach Her Anymore."

The next year's *Feelin' Good Train* took Kershaw another giant step off the hardcore country track, once again proving his unique talent and showcasing his own rhythm and blues influences. However, Kershaw and Jones did team up for a duet on the album. The rollicking "Never Bit a Bullet Like This" is almost Jones-on-Jones. For Kershaw, a duet with "The Possum" is like stopping back home after you're grown and gone. Still, no matter how many times Kershaw may renew his bond with his musical mentor, it is clear that he is going his own way. As he noted in a Mercury Records press release, "I can't sing a song unless *I've* lived it. And at one time or another, I guess I've lived 'em all. The best way to put it is, 'You can't program ol' Sammy.' Whatever I sing—whatever I say—at least you know it's gonna be me, it's gonna be honest."

Selected discography

Don't Go Near the Water (includes "Cadillac Style" and "Don't Go Near the Water") Mercury, 1991.
Haunted Heart (includes "She Don't Know She's Beautiful" and "I Can't Reach Her Anymore"), Mercury, 1993.
Feelin' Good Train, Mercury, 1994.
Christmas Time's a Comin', Mercury, 1994.

Sources

Books

Comprehensive Country Music Encyclopedia, Random House, 1994.

Periodicals

Country America, June 1993.
Country Music, January/February 1993; March/April 1993;
    September/October 1994; July/August 1995.
Nashville Banner, May 14, 1993.
People (*People Country* special issue), fall 1994.
Stereo Review, September 1994.

Additional information for this profile was obtained from Mercury Records publicity materials, 1993 and 1994.

—Pamela L. Shelton

The Kinks

Rock band

Few rock bands can boast a lifetime of more than 30 years, especially those whose members exhibit such open enmity as do Ray and Dave Davies of the Kinks. Yet not only have the seminal garage-rockers accomplished this incredible feat, they have also managed to have a hit song on the charts in every decade since their formation in London, England, in the mid-1960s. For reasons unknown, however, the super-stardom accorded to most rock bands of similar longevity and influence has somehow escaped the Davies brothers and their assorted bandmates. While almost everyone even slightly familiar with rock music has heard of the Beatles and the Rolling Stones, for example, those who know of the Kinks are comparatively few. This disparity is compounded by the fact that many people who do not recognize the group's name are familiar with their songs, especially their breakthrough 1964 hit, the much-covered and now-classic "You Really Got Me."

Ray Davies waxes philosophic when reflecting on his band's second-rate status. "I just take it with a pinch of

AP/Wide World Photos

For the Record...

Members include **David Russell Gordon Davies** (born February 3, 1947, in Muswell Hill, London, England), lead guitar and vocals; **Raymond Douglas Davies** (born June 21, 1944, in Muswell Hill, London, England), lead vocals and guitar; **Bob Henrit** (born May 2, 1945), drums; **Jim Rodford** (born July 7, 1945), bass guitar.

Former members include **Michael Charles "Mick" Avory** (born February 15, 1944, in Hampton Court, London, England), drums; **John Dalton**, bass guitar; **Gordon Edwards**, keyboards; **Ian Gibbons**, keyboards; **John Gosling**, keyboards; **Mark Haley**, keyboards; **Andy Pyle**, bass guitar; **Peter Alexander Greenlaw Quaife** (born December 31, 1943, in Tavistock, Devon, England), bass guitar.

Group formed in England in mid-1960s; scored first worldwide hit with "You Really Got Me," 1964; other hit songs include "Lola," 1970, and "Come Dancing," 1983. Ray Davies wrote and directed the film *Return to Waterloo*, 1985, and wrote a musical version of *Around the World in Eighty Days*, 1988, and the novel *X-Ray*, 1995.

Awards: Inducted into Rock and Roll Hall of Fame, 1990.

Addresses: *Record company*—Columbia, 550 Madison Avenue, New York, NY 10022-3211.

---

salt," he told *Musician* in 1990. "I think we're in our own space and we'll be judged accordingly. I don't think people have really appraised or valued our work yet. 'Cause maybe the work cycle hasn't completed itself. It's only when you get to the point where you can't do any more that people actually can reappraise it."

Birth of a Band

The Kinks' original lineup consisted of Ray Davies as lead vocalist and rhythm guitarist, Dave Davies on lead guitar, Peter Quaife on bass guitar, and Mick Avory on drums. Ray had been bouncing around as the guitar player for various bands when he heard about younger brother Dave's new group and decided to join. Ray's obvious vocal and songwriting talent quickly earned him the status of the band's frontman. Calling them-

selves the Kinks—because of their often bizarre, "kinky" stage costumes—the band jumped into the club circuit and released a few relatively unsuccessful singles. The turning point came when in 1964, fighting record company pressure every step of the way, the Kinks released an iconoclastic, proto-punk paean to adolescent sexual frustration titled "You Really Got Me," which Ray had written on the piano in his parents' sitting room. Millions of transistor radios the world over were soon to echo with Dave Davies's raw, distorted power chords and raging guitar solo as the song immediately shot to the peak of the British and U.S. charts.

As is the case with many songs that end up becoming hugely popular, "You Really Got Me" almost didn't get released. The original version, produced by American Shel Talmy, was slower and weighed down with heavy instrumentation. The Kinks expressed their dissatisfaction and their desire to re-record it. Their record company, however, stingily demanded that the group pay for the studio time themselves. The four scraped together the requisite 200 British pounds and banged the tune out in just a few takes.

The One that Really Got 'Em

"You Really Got Me" managed to become one of only a few milestone songs in the history of rock music. *Rolling Stone* magazine voted it Number 15 on its list of Top 100 singles from the years 1964 to 1988, writing, "The fierce, machine-gun-like stutter of Dave Davies"s fuzzed-up guitar ... is arguably the most influential and imitated riff of rock's last quarter century." Indeed, the Kinks themselves were to recycle the riff in their next few hit singles, "All Day and All of the Night," "Tired of Waiting for You," and "Till the End of the Day."

Never content to simply ride the wave of success, the Kinks soon proved they were something more than the average mid-1960s one-hit wonder. Ray's talent for writing meaningful lyrics and infectious melodies gave the band a series of smash singles in England in the late 1960s, including "Sunny Afternoon," "A Well-Respected Man," "Death of a Clown" (written by Dave), "Autumn Almanac," "Where Have All the Good Times Gone," "Set Me Free," and "Waterloo Sunset," among others.

Unfortunately, for reasons somewhat unclear, during their first U.S. tour in 1965 the Kinks had an altercation with the American Federation of Television and Recording Artists and were barred from playing live in the United States until 1969. As a result, their American chart singles were few in number during this period. The group did not spend this time dormant, however.

When they finally did return to the United States, it was with a level of sophistication hardly before seen in the pop world.

The record-buying public, however, was sometimes ill prepared to deal with the Kinks' new worldliness. Ray, a "genuine and brilliant neurotic in a landscape full of sham psychotics," according to Fred Schruers of *Rolling Stone,* had begun to move in strange new directions. "Lola," perhaps the Kinks' second-most-famous single, is generally considered to be the only Top Ten U.S. song to deal openly with transvestism and homosexuality.

"Give the People What They Want"

Around this time the Kinks also began a short but unhappy relationship with music-industry giant RCA Records. Instead of delivering hit singles as expected, the band began to churn out unconventional concept albums. Ray's fascination with the theater and film led to elaborately staged—and critically faulted—concerts and records, such as *Preservation, Everybody's in Showbiz, Everybody's a Star,* and *Soap Opera.* Dave, on the other hand, was growing increasingly dissatisfied with the road the Kinks were taking, and his relationship with his brother sank to a new low. Ray's alcoholic consumption, both onstage and off, escalated dangerously during this period, and he threatened to quit the band several times throughout the decade. Dave took this one step further and actually did depart in 1973, not to return until 1975.

By the close of the 1970s, however, the Kinks had a new record label, Arista, and a new outlook on both life and music. Ray and Dave bandaged their wounds and rejuvenated their slipshod live show. Ray also made a sincere and reasonably successful effort to get his group back on the charts. The nostalgic "Come Dancing" and "Don"t Forget to Dance" scored big for the Kinks in this era, as well as such quintessential pop singles as "(Wish I Could Fly Like) Superman" and "A Rock "n" Roll Fantasy."

Following their stint with Arista, the Kinks jumped to MCA and then to Columbia, releasing a series of well-made and under-appreciated albums throughout the 1980s and early 1990s. During this period Ray, especially, also devoted much of his time to solo projects, such as a musical version of Jules Verne's novel *Around the World in Eighty Days,* which had a limited run in California in 1988; the 1985 film *Return to Waterloo,* which he wrote and directed and for which he recorded a soundtrack; and a semiautobiographical detective novel titled *X-Ray,* published in 1995, concerning the recollections of a retired rock and roller

turned hermit of north London named Ray Davies. Perhaps his extensive extracurricular activities have enabled angst-ridden artist Ray Davies to step back and assess his career, both past and future, with a new perspective. "Music is becoming more and more important to me the older I get," he revealed in *Pulse!* in 1993. "The Kinks have got this tremendous catalog now, but it still feels like a work-in-progress. I'll sit back and listen to it and recognize the connections and get the feeling that it isn't quite finished yet. And I suppose it won't bother me *too* much if my epitaph just says, 'The guy who sang with the Kinks.'"

Dave Davies, on the other hand, is much more pragmatic. He commented in *Pulse!,* "I don't know much about [the Kinks'] place in history, I'm just interested in getting on with it. I don't have any reasons or excuses for why we're still [making music]. I'm just glad that we still are, and I'm feeling ready for a fight." If the younger Davies's relentless attitude is any indicator, one day soon the Kinks just may come into their own.

Selected discography

The Kinks, Pye, 1964.
You Really Got Me, Pye, 1964.
Kinks-Size, Pye, 1965.
Kinda Kinks, Pye, 1966.
Face to Face, Reprise, 1966.
The Live Kinks, Reprise, 1967.
Kinkdom, Reprise, 1967.
Greatest Hits, Reprise, 1968.
Something Else by the Kinks, Reprise, 1968.
*The Kinks Are the Village Green Preservation Society,,*Reprise, 1969.
Arthur (or the Decline and Fall of the British Empire), Reprise, 1969.
Lola Versus Powerman and the Moneygoround, Part One, Reprise, 1970.
Percy, Pye, 1971.
Muswell Hillbillies, Reprise, 1971, re-released, Rhino, 1990.
The Kink Kronikles, Reprise, 1972.
Everybody's in Showbiz, Everybody's a Star, Reprise, 1972, re-released, Rhino, 1990.
Preservation, Act One, RCA, 1973.
Preservation, Act Two, RCA, 1974.
Soap Opera, RCA, 1975, re-released, Rhino, 1990.
Schoolboys in Disgrace, RCA, 1975, re-released, Rhino, 1990.
Greatest Hits—Celluloid Heroes, RCA, 1976.
Sleepwalker, Arista, 1977.
Misfits, Arista, 1978.
Low Budget, Arista, 1979.
One for the Road, Arista, 1980.
Second Time Around, RCA, 1980.

Give the People What They Want, Arista, 1981.
State of Confusion, Arista, 1983.
Word of Mouth, Arista, 1984.
Come Dancing with the Kinks, Arista, 1986.
Think Visual, MCA, 1987.
Live: the Road, MCA, 1988.
Kinda Kinks, Rhino, 1988.
Kinks-Size Kinkdom, Rhino, 1988.
You Really Got Me, Rhino, 1988.
Greatest Hits, Rhino, 1989.
Lost and Found, MCA, 1989.
UK Jive, MCA, 1989.
Preservation (A Play in Two Acts), Rhino, 1991.

Did Ya (EP), Columbia, 1991.
Phobia, Columbia, 1993.
To the Bone, Konk, 1994.

Sources

Musician, January 1987; March 1990.
Newsweek, July 5, 1993.
Pulse!, May 1993.
Rolling Stone, November 2, 1978; September 8, 1988; May 13, 1993; April 20, 1995.

—*Alan Glenn*

Suge Knight

Record company executive

A large and imposing figure in the music industry, Suge Knight, also known as "Sugar Bear," is the cofounder of Death Row Records and a major force in 1990s rap music. Knight's Death Row musicians garnered three multiplatinum albums between the company's founding in 1991 and 1994. Grammy-winning Dr. Dre's *The Chronic,* Snoop Doggy Dogg's *Doggy Style,* and the *Above the Rim* soundtrack effectively placed Knight and the burgeoning, multimillion dollar Death Row enterprise on the very tip of the rap music mountain.

Born Marion Knight, Jr., in 1966, Suge was raised in a two-bedroom house in the rough Compton area of Los Angeles. His father, a truck driver originally from Mississippi, was a former college football tackle and R&B singer who inspired Suge's passion for music and sports. As a child, Knight was given the nickname "Suge" by his father because of his sweet, good-natured temperament. Knight's mother, Maxine, told *Spin* magazine's Chuck Philips, "My son is the type of person who still sends me roses all the time."

When Knight was in high school, he devoted most of his energy to playing football and securing an athletic scholarship to college, which he hoped would lead to a National Football League (NFL) contract. Knight made the dean's list at the University of Nevada in Las Vegas, and he won the Rookie of the Year title there in 1985 on defense. His former coach told Philips, "He was Super Bowl material, the kind of guy you love having on your side." After college, Knight went to Japan with the Los Angeles Rams. He quit football, though, in favor of concert promotion work when it became clear that he would not have a stellar career in the NFL.

Success and Probation

Knight's promising future was almost derailed in 1987, when he was arrested for auto theft, carrying a concealed weapon, and attempted murder. He pleaded no contest and was placed on probation. Knight was arrested again in 1990 for battery with a deadly weapon, but the charges were dismissed. He told Philips, "Ain't nobody perfect in this world except God. We all make mistakes. Sometimes you end up in the wrong place at the wrong time."

After working as a bodyguard and making a name for himself on the concert circuit for a while, Knight formed a music publishing company in 1989 and assigned composition work to a small group of unknown songwriters. Within a year, he made a significant amount of money from ownership rights to several songs on Vanilla Ice's successful debut album, which were written by composer Mario Johnson in Texas.

Born Marion Knight, Jr., April 19, 1966, in Los Angeles, CA; professionally known as "Suge" or "Sugar Bear" Knight; son of Marion (a truck driver, former college football tackle, and R&B singer) and Maxine Knight; married wife Sheritha (a rap manager); children: one daughter. *Education:* Attended University of Nevada, Las Vegas.

Cofounder and CEO of Death Row Records, 1991—; founder of Suge Knight Management. Football player in high school and at University of Nevada, Las Vegas; named Rookie of the Year, 1985; worked as a bodyguard and a concert promoter; formed a music publishing company, 1989; held ownership rights to several songs on Vanilla Ice's debut album; expanded into the artist management field and founded Death Row Records with rapper Dr. Dre, 1991; joined forces with Interscope Records; adapted *Murder Was the Case* single from Snoop Doggy Dogg's *Doggy Style* album into a short film, 1994.

Death Row musicians garnered three multiplatinum albums between the company's founding in 1991 and 1994: Grammy-winning Dr. Dre's *The Chronic,* Snoop Doggy Dogg's *Doggy Style* and the *Above the Rim* soundtrack. Artists including Mary J. Bilge, Jodeci, and DeVante Swing signed on with Suge Knight Management, 1994.

Addresses: *Record company*—Death Row Records, 10900 Wilshire Blvd., Suite 1240, Los Angeles, CA 90024.

Knight then expanded into the artist management realm of the music business, representing rapper musicians DJ Quik and the D.O.C. Through these musicians, Knight met Dr. Dre, who was then a member of the rap group N.W.A. Dre was popular for creating and producing the material on N.W.A.'s albums *Straight Outta Compton* and *Efil4zaggin; Efil4zaggin* was the first hardcore rap album to reach the Number One mark on the nation's pop chart.

Hood or Robin Hood?

According to Knight, Dre's contributions had garnered N.W.A.'s record label, Ruthless Records, over six million units in sales, yet both Ice Cube and Dre were short on cash. Ice Cube quit N.W.A. because he felt he wasn't being compensated properly for his work. Knight somehow obtained a copy of Dre's contract agreement, which verified what Ice Cube had suspected; Knight also discovered that other Ruthless musicians were being paid less than the standard industry rate for their contributions. He then bypassed Ruthless management and negotiated a deal with their distributor, Priority Records, in 1990.

Knight was able to secure releases for Dre and two other Ruthless musicians which, in the long run, would benefit all of them handsomely. However, the manner in which Knight engineered the releases was a point of contention. Eric "Eazy-E" Wright, president of the Ruthless label, claimed in court that he signed the release contracts under duress after Knight and two henchmen had threatened him—as well as his general manager—with pipes and baseball bats. Musician DeVante Swing was quick to come to Knight's defense when speaking with Philips: "I know Suge's got this reputation for being a guy who goes around strong-arming, but I think those rumors just come from jealous people. The thing is, he's a real sharp negotiator, and he won't let anybody walk over him or any of his artists—and a lot of people resent that."

Shining Knight

After Dre was released from his obligations at Ruthless, he and Knight founded Death Row Records. For almost a year, they searched for a major label willing to distribute their product, eventually landing with Interscope Records. In 1993 the label grossed more than $60 million and released two of the most significant albums of the year: Dre's *The Chronic* and Snoop Doggy Dogg's *Doggy Style.* In 1994 Death Row released the soundtrack to *Above the Rim,* which featured Dre's younger brother, Warren G., and went double-platinum.

Knight was able to convince musicians Mary J. Bilge, Jodeci, and DeVante Swing of MCA-owned Uptown Records to sign West Coast management deals with him. He secured greater creative control for the musicians, landed them substantial retroactive back payments, upgraded their contracts, and doubled their royalty rates. Knight also tossed in a $250,000 white Lamborghini for one of the musicians to sweeten the deal. Snoop Doggy Dogg asserted in the interview with Philips, "Suge is the best businessman I could have ever hoped to hook up with.... He keeps the music real.... He's got an ear to the street."

Among Knight's many plans for the future are the formation of a union for rap musicians and an organization for veteran soul musicians who need financial assistance. Death Row hosted a Mother's Day celebration in Beverly Hills for 500 single mothers and sponsored toy giveaways at churches and hospitals during the 1994 Christmas holiday. In addition, Knight is working on an anti-gang foundation in Compton and hopes to establish an organization that would put young unemployed people to work in the black community.

Dre began working on an album called *Helter Skelter* with Ice Cube, his former N.W.A. partner, in late 1994, and the pairing is almost certain to produce double-platinum material for Death Row in 1995. In the meantime, Knight has dabbled in marketing and worked on the adaptation of *Murder Was the Case*—originally a popular cut from Snoop Doggy Dogg's *Doggy Style* album—into an 18-minute film, complemented by a new-and-improved soundtrack album. Knight is also thinking of publishing a magazine called *Death Row Uncut.* "I make my own rules," Knight told *The Source* in 1995.

Sources

Newsweek, October 31, 1994.
The Source, January 1995; May 1995.
Spin, August 1994.
Time, July 31, 1995.

—*B. Kimberly Taylor*

Robert Krasnow

Record company executive

Music mogul David Geffen proclaimed in *The Los Angeles Times* in 1994, "Bob Krasnow is one of the smartest and most talented executives working in the music business these days.... His track record as a talent scout is impeccable." Indeed, with over 30 years of experience in the record industry, Bob Krasnow is renowned for his keen ear, bold decision making, and eclectic tastes. In 1994, after a 20-year stint with the Warner Bros. family of labels, Krasnow began his own company, Krasnow Entertainment, with plans to tackle film and television as well music. The entertainment industry expected great things from this man renowned for discovering and developing new artists.

Robert Krasnow dropped out of high school at age 17 to join the navy. Constantly on the lookout for new educational experiences, he gravitated toward the record industry. In 1957 he took a job as a sales representative for Decca Records. A year later he landed the position of branch manager for King Records in San Francisco. There Krasnow was exposed to legends of rhythm and blues like Little Willie John, Hank Ballard, the Five Royales, and James Brown. Fascinated by the innovations developed by these artists, Krasnow began producing their records. His first project, for which he shared production credit with Brown, resulted in the monumental breakthrough hit "Papa's Got a Brand New Bag." With a string of successes under his belt, Krasnow moved to Los Angeles in 1964 to form his own R&B label, Loma, which would be distributed by Warner Bros. Records.

In 1966 Krasnow went on to become vice-president of Kama Sutra Records and later helped found Buddha Records. He left Buddha in 1968 to create the highly adventurous Blue Thumb Label, which he sold in 1974 to return to the Warner Bros. fold. There he accepted the post of vice-president of talent, which was created especially for him. In 1983 Krasnow took command of the Elektra/Asylum/Nonesuch record labels—all distributed by Warners—where he reigned until his sudden departure in 1994.

As chairman of what eventually became the Time Warner corporation's Elektra Entertainment, Krasnow made crucial decisions regarding both mainstream and underground music. In 1984 Elektra was the first record company to publicly acknowledge an exclusive arrangement to supply videos to cable television's music video channel MTV. Krasnow agonized over the decision, but he believed it was in the industry's best interest to support MTV. Quoted in *Billboard,* Krasnow said he felt that MTV had "an almost fanatical sympathy to the music industry," suggesting that the network's commitment to music video surpassed that of other video outlets. To strengthen his support of music video, Kras-

For the Record . . .

Born Robert A. Krasnow, c. 1935, in Rochester, NY; wife's name is Sandy; children: three.

Sales representative, Decca Records, 1957-58; branch manager, King Records, 1958-64; founded, and directed Loma Records, 1964-66; vice-president, Kama Sutra Records, c. 1966-67; helped found, and headed Buddha Records, c. 1967-68; created Blue Thumb Label, and served as director, 1968-74; vice-president/talent, Warner Bros. Records, 1974-83; chairman, Elektra/Asylum/Nonesuch Records (name later changed to Elektra Entertainment), 1983-94; created Krasnow Entertainment, 1994.

Member: Member of board of directors of City Center (New York City theater for independent choreography); member of board of directors and president's council, Brooklyn Academy of Music; co-president, French Music Office; national committee member, March of Dimes; executive vice-president, Paul Taylor Dance Company; member of board of directors, Wadleigh School (New York).

Selected awards: Winner of March of Dimes Personality Cook-Off, 1981; named T. J. Martell Cancer Research Man of the Year, 1984, 1989; Nordoff Robbins Music Therapy honoree, 1989; Ellis Island Medal of Honor, 1992.

Addresses: *Office*—Krasnow Entertainment, 1755 Broadway, Eighth Floor, New York, NY 10019.

now created a home video wing at Elektra, developing new markets for the then-fledgling art form.

Krasnow further expanded Elektra by developing its classical music sector. By adding Germany's Teldec and France's Erato labels to the Nonesuch imprint, Elektra Entertainment's International Classics became a major force within the genre. Krasnow also entered into a distribution pact with a new Disney label, Hollywood Records, which would expand the Elektra catalog with releases ranging from soundtracks to rock albums.

Krasnow effectively rescued Elektra from a decline into which it had fallen during the early 1980s. "The first eighteen months were the hardest," he told *Rolling Stone*'s Fred Goodman. Krasnow spent over ten million dollars buying out artists' contracts and moving the company's headquarters back to New York City, where it had been born in the 1950s. Krasnow followed a "small but beautiful" philosophy as he reduced the label's roster from 120 to 46 acts. Goodman asserted that this downsizing of talent "made Elektra the only major record company that can approach such disparate acts as [urban folksinger Tracy] Chapman, [heavy metal giants] Metallica, and [flamenco group] the Gypsy Kings with the same intensity and dedication." By following this tack, Elektra became famous for its eclecticism and reputation as "the artist's label."

While at Elektra Krasnow oversaw the release of music by such creative visionaries as the Icelandic alternative rock group the Sugarcubes, British socialist/punk troubadour Billy Bragg, and Latin activist bandleader Rubén Blades, as well as major moneymakers like alternative pop band 10,000 Maniacs, R&B chanteuse Anita Baker, and pop singer Natalie Cole. As he told Goodman, "There's a big difference between being a record label and a record company. Anybody can have a hit record. You stay in this business long enough, you have deep enough pockets, and you put out enough records, you're going to have hit records. But that's a mercurial way of trying to make a living and build something."

Krasnow took the art of developing talent seriously and preached his beliefs widely. At the 1991 New Music Seminar in New York City he warned in his keynote address, as reported by *Billboard,* "The record business finds itself dangerously close to creative stagnation. There's so much money lying around the corporate bank accounts that it's seemingly easier to buy a band or label than it is to take the time and let something develop." Worrying that the industry's profits had made executives lazy, he counseled, "Your goal must be to seek out and promote great innovation. Your challenge is to do so in spite of the difficulties and temptations offered by an over-prosperous industry."

In 1994 Krasnow abruptly stepped down as chairman and CEO of Elektra Entertainment. Warner Music Group had just announced a corporate realignment that required Krasnow to report to former Atlantic Group chairman Doug Morris, who was elevated to the top spot of Time Warner's new domestic music division (of which both Elektra and Atlantic Records were part). Sources for the *Los Angeles Times* said that Krasnow blamed his departure on his exclusion from the new corporate inner circle. Others suggested that he regarded himself as a more seasoned executive than Morris and was simply smarting at being passed over for promotion. Some pointed out that Krasnow had recently been dogged by Elektra's lackluster chart and fiscal performance. As the *Los Angeles Times* put it, "Once the toast of the industry, the eclectic New York label has been sorely lagging behind its sister companies, Atlantic Group and Warner Bros. Records."

Krasnow immediately began negotiations to start a new label at rival MCA Music Entertainment Group. In December of 1994 MCA and Krasnow's recently developed entertainment company, Krasnow Entertainment, confirmed an arrangement to jointly create a new record label under the MCA Records banner. "I am delighted to be in business with Bob Krasnow," MCA Entertainment head Al Teller stated in a press release announcing the deal. "He is one of the rare executives in the music business with the unique ability to attract top-flight artists and to discover the best new talent." With his start-up company preparing to make waves in film and television, as well as the music industry, Krasnow told *Billboard* he had no plans to amend his basic operating methods: "I've had a low-volume, high-quality philosophy for the last 20 years, and I'm not changing."

Though not absent from the music scene for long, Krasnow said to Chuck Philips in the *Los Angeles Times,* "I'm back and I'm ready to do business. What I'm selling is specialized individual attention and dedicated commitment to each act I sign." Krasnow has always backed such sentiment with substance, so much so that some artists pledged their allegiance to him personally and not to the company for which they recorded. When he summarily departed Elektra, superstars Metallica, one of the Time Warner family's most profitable bands, filed a lawsuit severing their decade-long association with the label, citing their strong relationship with the departed Krasnow as a

factor in the move (the lawsuit was later settled, with Metallica remaining at Elektra).

The man who signed soul diva Chaka Khan, jazz guitarist George Benson, funk pioneer George Clinton, and pop powerhouse the Cure, among a host of others throughout his years in the industry, has always put the artist first. As he insisted in MCA press materials, "I am committed to nurturing and shepherding the careers of influential artists from both the mainstream and the underground, and to identifying and cultivating changing musical tastes from one generation to the next."

Sources

Billboard, August 25, 1984; January 11, 1986; July 27, 1991; July 23, 1994; July 30, 1994; September 25, 1994; December 10, 1994; June 3, 1995.
Entertainment Weekly, October 30, 1992.
Los Angeles Times, July 13, 1994; August 2, 1994; October 21, 1994; December 2, 1994.
New York Times, December 2, 1994.
Rolling Stone, February 9, 1989; September 25, 1994.
Variety, January 19, 1983; November 4, 1991; July 25, 1994.
Wall Street Journal, July 13, 1994; July 20, 1994; November 1, 1994; December 2, 1994.

Additional information for this profile was obtained from publicity materials provided by Elektra Entertainment, 1990 and 1992, and MCA Music Entertainment Group, 1994.

—*Joanna Rubiner*

Love and Rockets

Rock band

The history of Love and Rockets reaches back almost to the very beginning of its member's lives. Drummer Kevin Haskins and bassist David J are brothers, and guitarist Daniel Ash first met David J in kindergarten. The three did not start playing together, however, until their teenage years in their hometown of Northampton, England.

The Haskins, J, and Ash joined with singer Peter Murphy in the late 1970s to form the band Bauhaus, which became the biggest influence in the black-draped, gothic music scene of the late 1970s and early 1980s. Songs like "Bela Lugosi's Dead," "Terror Couple Kill Colonel," and "Stigmata Martyr" defined the era's post-punk, dark, gothic rock music. Despite their dedicated following, Bauhaus broke up in 1983, after the release of their third album.

"I think Danny and Dave needed to have a break from each other," Haskins recalled in *Musician*. "They've both got very strong personalities, and they're at opposite extremes in their musical tastes and the way they

For the Record . . .

Members include **Daniel Ash**, guitar, vocals; **David J**, bass guitar, vocals; and **Kevin Haskins**, drums.

Group originally formed as Bauhaus with Peter Murphy as lead vocalist, late 1970s; re-formed without Murphy as Love and Rockets, 1985; released debut album, *Seventh Dream of Teenage Heaven,* in U.K., 1985, released in U.S. on Beggars Banquet/RCA, 1986; released *Hot Trip to Heaven,* American Recordings, 1994. Daniel Ash and David J have released solo albums.

Addresses: *Record company*—American Recordings, 3500 West Olive Ave., Suite 1550, Burbank, CA 91505.

form songs." Murphy went on to establish a duo called Dali's Car and then pursued a solo career. Daniel Ash and Kevin Haskins founded the band Tones on Tail, and David J played bass for Jazz Butcher and released his own solo albums.

During that break, Tones on Tail produced two albums. Ash and Haskins completely dismissed their dark Bauhaus days by purposely dressing only in white during their performances. "I'm generally very proud of the Tones on Tail stuff," Ash told Joe Gore in *Guitar Player.* "I was being myself more than ever then, because there were no commercial pressures whatsoever. I love the idea of music that sounds like it comes from another world, but you can still tap your foot to it."

But due to musical differences, Tones on Tail disbanded in 1985. "At that point, David, Danny, and I had been socializing," Haskins told Alan di Perna in *Musician.* "We looked back on that last period of Bauhaus and realized that there was a special chemistry there. And that's what decided us to get back together again." The same year Tones on Tail broke up the three former Bauhaus members and longtime friends launched Love and Rockets, named after the chic, adult comic book by Los Angeles's Hernandez brothers. Daniel Ash and David J shared both the songwriting and lead vocals for the band.

The members of Love and Rockets came up with a story about how they came together. They said they were "discovered" by the Bubblemen, space aliens from the planet Girl. Later, the trio recorded a 12-inch rap single under the name Bubblemen, in tribute to their space alien alter egos, whom Love and Rockets described as "very nice beings" and "saviors of the world." "Contrary to popular belief," Ash told Jeffrey Ressner in *Rolling Stone,* "Glenn Miller was abducted by a Bubblemen flying saucer in the 1940s, and they whisked him to a small nightclub on their planet." In reality, Daniel Ash created the characters from doodles that he had drawn during the latter period of Bauhaus.

Love and Rockets released their debut album, *Seventh Dream of Teenage Heaven,* in Great Britain in 1985. But the LP did not arrive in the United States until after the release of the band's second album, *Express. Express* reached Number 72 on the U.S. charts and featured the singles "Kundalini Express," "All in My Mind," and a cover of the Motown group the Temptations' "Ball of Confusion."

Though their reputation with Bauhaus preceded them, Love and Rockets pursued their own style of music while leaving room for experimentation. "You can't pigeonhole us," Ash told Elizabeth Royle in *Rolling Stone* after *Express* arrived in the United States. "It's a little of everything, '60s, '70s influences and the present."

The following year, Love and Rockets released *Earth, Sun, Moon* on Beggars Banquet/RCA Records, which contained the single "No New Tale to Tell." The band, though, would not achieve major commercial success until their self-titled 1989 effort. The T-Rex-influenced single "So Alive" hit Number Three on *Billboard's* singles charts, while *Love and Rockets* reached Number 14 on the U.S. charts. With their career boosted, the band toured throughout the country and saw the video for "So Alive" given heavy rotation on MTV.

With *Love and Rockets,* the group further displayed their tendency to experiment with music. After the restrictive dark sound of Bauhaus, Love and Rockets extended their musical limits and followed their creative whims. "They're 'anything goes' artistic creed has made their four-album catalog a study in stylistic schizophrenia," commented a reviewer in *Musician.*

After their brush with commercial success, Love and Rockets disappeared from the new release schedule for five years. Daniel Ash used the time to release two solo albums. Then, in 1994, the band returned with *Hot Trip to Heaven,* an album targeted to anything but commercialism. "We didn't want to come back with another *Earth, Sun, Moon,* and doing the orthodox song thing would just be repeating ourselves," Ash told *Guitar Player's* Gore. "In the past, we've always gone into the studio with finished songs, but this time, we deliberately went in with nothing. It's not a daytime/ radio/MTV record. Try it at 2 AM, after you've had a couple of drinks and a spliff—it will set you up fine!"

Throughout all of their projects together, the members of Love and Rockets have clearly avoided being predictable. Their longevity has stemmed from their lifetime friendship and their dedication to leaving the band open to any direction their creativity—or the world-saving Bubblemen's dictation—would lead them.

Selected discography

As Bauhaus

Burning from the Inside (reissue), A&M, 1989.
The Sky's Gone Out (reissue), A&M, 1989.
Swing the Heartache (live recordings from 1980-83; reissue), Beggars Banquet, 1989.

As Love and Rockets

Seventh Dream of Teenage Heaven, Beggars Banquet/RCA, 1986.
Express, Big Time Records, 1986.
Earth, Sun, Moon, Beggars Banquet/RCA, 1987.
Love and Rockets, Beggars Banquet/RCA, 1989.
Hot Trip to Heaven, American Recordings, 1994.

Solo releases by Daniel Ash

Coming Down, Beggars Banquet, 1991.
Foolish Thing Desire, Columbia, 1992.

Solo releases by David J

Songs from Another Season, RCA, 1990.
Urban Urbane MCA, 1992.

Sources

Books

Rees, Dafydd, and Luke Crampton, editors, *Rock Movers and Shakers,* Billboard Books, 1991.

Periodicals

Audio, November 1989.
Billboard, December 27, 1986; July 15, 1989.
Guitar Player, November 1994.
Musician, January 1987, October 1989.
People, June 19, 1989; June 26, 1989; September 25, 1989.
Rolling Stone, March 12, 1987; May 21, 1987; September 21, 1989; October 5, 1989; June 1, 1995.
Stereo Review, October 1989.

Additional information for this profile was obtained from the on-line *All-Music Guide,* 1994.

—*Thaddeus Wawro*

The Mavericks

Country band

The Mavericks, a country band whose neo-honky-tonk tunes hark back to the 1950s and 1960s, found success in Nashville with the release of their second major label album, *What a Crying Shame,* in 1994. The album's breakthrough helped to introduce country fans to the group's poetic, socially-conscious worldview and raucous, rock-influenced delivery. "To players as seasoned as the Mavericks, the simple chord changes and boom-chicka-boom bass lines of country music aren't exactly rocket science," wrote Doug Adrianson in the *Miami Herald.* "What grabs your attention are the instantly unforgettable melodies ... and the unanimous vigor of the band's playing." Adrianson added that the Mavericks' rockabilly twang provides "the freshest sound in town."

Odd success stories are a Nashville staple, but few can top that of the Mavericks, who formed in Miami in 1989, attracted a loyal following in the trendy rock clubs of Miami's South Beach, and emerged as stars after their first major-label album sold less than 20,000 copies. Lead vocalist and songwriter Raul Malo told the *Char-*

Photograph by Jim Herrington, courtesy of MCA Nashville

---

lotte Observer that he wrote a more commercially appealing mix of songs for the group's second album in order to "keep this band and this music alive." He added: "That was always on the back of our mind, but you try not to let that cloud your judgment too much. The so-called integrity thing is so subjective, but I know we can sleep well at night with what we've done."

Country Meets Thrash

Some critics have accused the Mavericks of lightening up their message and style in order to appeal to a wider range of listeners. In fact, the band owes its very success to its members' insistence upon artistic integrity at a time when they couldn't even make a subsistence wage as performers. The group was founded in 1989 by Malo, a Cuban American and native of Miami whose parents had fled the regime of Cuban revolutionary Fidel Castro. Malo, who grew up listening to his parents' collection of country records, gravitated to pop music as a teen. He played in Miami pop-rock bands, including the Tomboys and the Basics, until the night he heard Rodney Crowell perform at a club in Miami Beach. He told the *Miami Herald:* "I knew at that moment that he was doing exactly what I wanted to do." Malo quit the Basics to form a new band of his own.

First Malo recruited acoustic guitar player Ben Peeler—himself a classically trained college music student. After several months with various backup players, the duo approached bassist Robert Reynolds and drum-

mer Paul Deakin, two close friends who had also been playing in pop bands. The quartet quickly adopted the Mavericks as a good name for their band, and small wonder—they found work not in the numerous country music clubs in Broward County but in the rock venues of South Beach. The country music clubs spurned them because they wanted to play original songs rather than merely covering other stars' hits.

"The greatest thing about the band is that it was started for the right reasons: to play, with no idea of what was going to happen," Malo explained in the *Miami Herald.* "We started playing around town with no real expectations. People started coming out, and before you knew it every place we played was packed. We'd get these thrash kids—the punks, heavy metal kids with mohawks—thinking we were the hippest thing in town. And we'd get these older people coming out because we were playing country music."

Debut Flopped, Second Effort Went Platinum

For more than two years the Mavericks reveled in their local popularity, augmenting their meager earnings as performers with day jobs and occasional appearances with more conventional bands. Gradually—as Malo added more and more songs he had written to their play list—they began to ponder the possibilities of landing a recording contract with a big Nashville record company. In 1991 the group scraped together $7,000 and recorded a 13-song album that was released by the Miami-based Yesterday & Today Records. The idea was not to sell a massive number of albums—in fact, only about 5,000 were produced—but to interest a bigger company in the band's sound and style.

The ploy was a common one, but for the Mavericks it worked like a charm. Executives at several Nashville studios competed with one another to sign the group. Late in 1991 MCA Records arranged for the Mavericks to play a concert in Nashville. Producer Tony Brown signed the band to a multiple record deal—so the story goes—before the musicians had even finished their sound check. The Mavericks' first MCA album, *From Hell to Paradise,* was released in the spring of 1992.

Dark and poetic with songs about child abuse, rundown neighborhoods, and the plight of political refugees, *From Hell to Paradise* won rave reviews for the Mavericks from record critics. But country radio stations failed to play the singles MCA released from the album. As a result, sales of *From Hell to Paradise* failed even to cover production costs, and the Mavericks found themselves booked into hotel lounges and country fairs. They still had the multiple-record deal, though, and

Malo decided his band was well worth preserving. He teamed with some of Nashville's most successful songwriters, including Kostas and Harlan Howard, and wrote a new group of songs in the time-honored honky-tonk tradition of love lost and found.

The resulting work, *What a Crying Shame,* brought the Mavericks the exposure they had hoped for. With some hard work by the radio promotions department at MCA, the title song became a hit; the album was certified gold in sales just a few months after its 1994 release. (It later went platinum.) The Mavericks, with new lead guitarist Nick Kane, found commercial success without compromising their rowdy rockabilly sound. *Miami Herald* music critic Fernando Gonzalez wrote: "The lyrics of the newer songs might be more in the conventional ... country fare, but in their delivery, the Mavericks deftly undercut sentimentality with no-nonsense urgency. This band doesn't exactly wallow in emotion. Malo says his piece and moves on—broken heart or not."

Crossing the Lines

Having established themselves in Music City, the Mavericks embarked on the standard record-and-tour lifestyle of major country artists. Reynolds married singer Trisha Yearwood in 1994, and he and the other members of the group have all moved to Nashville. "If you dug old country music like we did, and were so far away from the place it originated," Reynolds told the *Philadelphia Daily News,* "then moved to this town and were living blocks from the Ryman Auditorium [home of the original Grand Ole Opry], you start thinking just pure good ol' country music."

Malo, whose engaging tenor vocals serve to anchor the group, added that he plans to continue melding traditional and novel sounds in his songs. "You know that fine line between rock 'n' roll and country?" he asked in the *Philadelphia Daily News.* "We just kind of want to make it a little wider so we can walk on it." When asked about the group's future efforts, Malo told *Country Music* contributor Patrick Carr, "I'm a little reluctant to use the term 'ballroom country,' but that's what I have in mind, something very swinging and sophisticated."

Selected discography

The Mavericks, Yesterday & Today, 1991.
From Hell to Paradise, MCA, 1992.
What a Crying Shame, MCA, 1994.

Sources

Charlotte Observer, November 10, 1994.
Country Music, March/April 1995.
Lexington Herald-Leader, February 10, 1994.
Miami Herald, April 21, 1990; December 7, 1990; November 2, 1991; August 15, 1993; October 27, 1994; November 2, 1994.
Philadelphia Daily News, April 16, 1994.

Additional information for this profile was obtained from MCA Nashville publicity materials.

—Anne Janette Johnson

Del McCoury

Guitarist, banjoist, singer, songwriter

Photograph by Señor McGuire, courtesy of Keith Case & Associates

From out of the revolving ranks of the now-legendary Blue Grass Boys—the crack band backing blue-grass music founder Bill Monroe—have come a legion of talented musicians: Lester Flatt, Earl Scruggs, Jimmy Martin, Sonny Osborne, Vassar Clements, and, in 1964, a young musician named Del McCoury. From his start as guitarist and lead singer for Monroe during the early 1960s, McCoury has gone on to make his mark on modern bluegrass as one of the most popular perform-ers of the now-classic "Monroe" sound that first set fire to audiences during the 1940s. Nashville promoter Lance Leroy once commented, "As a bluegrass purist, you could get papers on Del McCoury," and not many would disagree. With an engaging confidence, a dis-tinctive tenor that essentially defines the "high lone-some" sound, and an unflaggingly energetic approach to his music, it is no wonder that McCoury and his talented band are considered "bluegrasser's bluegrass-ers," respected by their musical peers and performing at the peak of their profession.

Delano Floyd McCoury was born on February 1, 1939, in Bakersfield, North Carolina. When young McCoury was two, he moved with his parents, two brothers, and three sisters to York County, Pennsylvania, where he was raised around "old-time music"—music from rural Kentucky and Tennessee. When his older brother brought home a 78 rpm record by a hot new country act called Bill Monroe and the Blue Grass Boys, young Del finally sat up and listened. "As a kid I liked music," he recalled in an interview with *Contemporary Musicians* (*CM*). "I can remember singing when I was just little. But when G.C. [Grover Cleveland McCoury, Del's older brother] bought that record—it was Earl Scruggs—when I heard him pick I thought, 'This is really something.' And I just couldn't get that out of my head." McCoury was soon devoting most of his free time to learning Scruggs's banjo licks.

Life in the Fast Lane, Bluegrass-Style

After graduating from high school in 1956, McCoury joined the Blue Ridge Ramblers as a banjoist. From there he moved to Baltimore, Maryland, and picked with Jack Cooke, a former bass player with the Blue Grass Boys. The job playing alongside Cooke would provide young McCoury with the opportunity to earn his Ph.D. in bluegrass. When Monroe stopped at Cooke's Baltimore bluegrass club on the way up to perform in New York state in 1963, he was in need of a banjo player. Im-pressed with the then-22-year-old McCoury, Monroe offered the young banjoist a full-time spot with the Bluegrass Boys.

McCoury took some time making up his mind to move south; meanwhile Monroe had lined up banjo player Bill

Born Delano Floyd McCoury, February 1, 1939, in Bakersfield, NC; married, 1964; wife's name, Jean; children: Ronnie, Rhonda, Robbie.

Guitarist, banjoist, singer, and songwriter, 1956—. Banjoist with Keith Daniels and the Blue Ridge Ramblers, 1956; played with Jack Cooke, Baltimore, MD, c. 1960; member of Bill Monroe and the Blue Grass Boys, 1963-64; joined Golden State Boys, Los Angeles, CA; returned to Pennsylvania and recorded with Bill Keith and Jerry McCoury as the Shady Valley Boys; formed Del McCoury and the Dixie Pals, 1967; son Ronnie McCoury became a bandmember, 1981; toured Europe, 1983; son Robbie McCoury became a member and group renamed Del McCoury Band, 1987; signed with Rounder Records, 1990. Has toured extensively, playing at festivals, concerts, and clubs throughout the U.S., Canada, Japan, Great Britain, and Europe; appeared in film *Great Moments in Bluegrass*, 1994; made television appearances on *American Music Shop, Crook & Chase, Country Music News,* all the Nashville Network, and *Ronnie Reno's Old Time Music Festival,* Americana Network.

Awards: International Bluegrass Music Association awards for male vocalist of the year, 1990, 1991, and 1992; record event of the year, 1990, for *Don't Stop the Music,* and 1991 (with the Parmleys) for *Families of Tradition;* entertainer of the year, 1994; and album of the year, 1994, for *A Deeper Shade of Blue;* named best traditional male vocalist, Society for the Preservation of Bluegrass Music in America, 1992.

Addresses: *Agent*—Keith Case & Associates, 59 Music Square West, Nashville, TN 37203. *Record company*—Rounder Records, One Camp Street, Cambridge, MA 02140.

Keith. "Monroe needed a lead singer in the worst way," McCoury recounted for *CM.* "More than anything, he depended on them pretty heavy. And he asked me. I said, 'Man, I don't know if I could do that or not,' you know. But I auditioned on his guitar, singin' lead for him. I didn't know all of his songs—I knew choruses but I didn't know all the verses. I sang what I did know, and played the guitar. And he said, 'Well, I tell you what. I'll try you for two weeks. If it sounds pretty good, I'll get you in the union here.' I thought, 'Well, I don't know if this is gonna work out.' I wasn't sure if I wanted to do it anyway,

you know. But I kinda liked it and after about two weeks, they took me down to the union hall and signed me up."

McCoury played with Monroe for a year, recording one LP with the band. While he loved touring and got along well with the sometimes taciturn Monroe, being lead singer for a prolific songwriter like Monroe was no simple task. "My hardest problem was learning those words," McCoury explained to *CM.* "All of those words, all at one time. I had sung since I was a little kid and sung every part. But all those lyrics—now that was a different story. It was hard to jam all those songs in your head at one time. Lots of times I would sing wrong words, but I never would stop; I would keep it going somehow."

McCoury continued in his *CM* interview, "Monroe made a new record while I was with him. And that kinda helped me because I knew he wanted to do these new songs. So I learned all those songs off that one album. But then I still had to do old things because Bill, he just don't say 'Now, okay, today we're gonna do this song, or that song.' He just gets on stage and does what he wants. And if somebody requests something that he recorded 20 years ago, he'll do it. And," McCoury laughed, "you gotta know it."

Enter the Dixie Pals

After he left Monroe in 1964, McCoury, along with his new wife, Jean, moved from Tennessee to Los Angeles, where he and fiddler Billy Baker played with the Golden State Boys. The couple would return to their familiar Pennsylvania after less than a year, and by 1967 Del had formed the Dixie Pals, drawing fine instrumentalists from the area to begin building the blues-based, soulful sound for which he would become known. The group's first album, *High on a Mountain,* recorded for Rounder in 1972, firmly established them as a top act on the bluegrass festival circuit.

Throughout the 1970s and 1980s, McCoury and the Dixie Pals stuck to the traditional bluegrass style popularized by Monroe, but with a difference. "You know, what excited me back when I first heard [bluegrass] was the way that it was done," McCoury told *CM.* "The way that five-piece band was, the sound they got. And it still does. It excites me to listen to the old stuff that I first heard. And so through the years I didn't want to change the structure of that band. I wanted to keep that same sound. When I went out on my own, I knew that I had to get different songs, and write songs, because I couldn't play shows with other bluegrass artists and do their songs like I had done Bill Monroe's and Flatt & Scruggs's before that. I imagine my taste for songs is a little different than somebody else's. And I think that's how you develop a sound, you know, with the songs you record." In addition to reworking songs by others, McCoury includes several self-penned numbers on each of his albums. "This Kind of Life" and "Dreams" are two of his most popular tunes; his "Rain Please Go Away" has become a bluegrass standard.

Stage Became a Family Tradition

In 1981 McCoury's elder son, Ronnie, joined the band as mandolinist and was followed in 1987 by his younger brother, Robbie, who was then still in high school. Eventually considered two of the most talented instrumentalists within the bluegrass community, Ronnie and Robbie were both inspired at an early age to follow their father's lead. "We're as proud of dad as he is of us," award-winning mandolinist Ronnie told Brett F. Devan in *Bluegrass Unlimited*. "I guess he was my best inspiration in learning the mandolin."

As the decade of the 1980s neared a close, McCoury was fast approaching the musical chemistry that would make his popularity skyrocket in 1989. Now flanked onstage by his sons, he began focusing on the blues and country influences that caught his ear. In 1987 the band decided that a name change was in order; by 1990 they would have achieved widespread national prominence as the Del McCoury Band. Since then their momentum has been unstoppable. In 1992 bassist Mike Bub and fiddler Jason Carter added their strong instrumental and vocal talents to round out the band's timeless bluegrass sound.

Led by McCoury's bluesy, high-pitched tenor voice and rhythmic guitar, the talented group has followed both the letter and the law of the original Blue Grass Boys lineup—the sound born of Monroe's mandolin, Scruggs's banjo, Lester Flatt's guitar, Chubby Wise's fiddle, and the bass playing of comedian Cedric Rainwater. "This remains the bedrock sound of the music," noted Devan in *Bluegrass Unlimited* in 1990, "almost 45 years after the now legendary coalition finalized its form and first introduced it to millions of ... Grand Ole Opry listeners. The McCourys and their compatriots are now reminding us of how good it really was."

McCoury's voice is the trademark of the Del McCoury Band; it is "what fans love—and detractors hate—about bluegrass," as Jim Patterson put it in the *Tennessean*. "[McCoury] sings it high and lonesome, and is as legendary a vocalist in bluegrass as George Jones is in country music." McCoury is also one of those rare musicians who has allowed his style to mature as he has. "It's funny about singing," he told *CM.* "I can do more with a song now than I could before. And I think it's

because I have these young musicians backing me up. My sons got on stage with me, and all of a sudden the other guys in the band are [my sons'] age. And that helps keep the spark up. And then I can sing better. It keeps me from gettin' older too."

Within McCoury's broad-ranging tenor vocals resonate the mournful wail of wasted lives, love lost, and the raw hurt of living. But the effect is far from depressing; a subtle humor is never far away. "McCoury's vocals are the icing that makes the cake," commented Jim Ridley, reviewing the musician's 1993 release, *A Deeper Shade of Blue*, in *New Country*. "Whether he's cackling Lefty Frizzell's 'If You've Got the Money Honey' in randy high spirits or romping through Willie Nelson's 'Man with the Blues,' [McCoury] infuses every tune with joyous vitality, no matter how sad the song. Where Jerry Lee Lewis wailed 'What Made Milwaukee Famous' with a drawl that said 'go to hell,' McCoury sings it as though he's thankful to Heaven to still be making noise."

While his role in modern bluegrass has been to carry the Monroe traditions forward into the next century, McCoury looks forward to the continued evolution of the music. "It's bound to change some," he noted of the bluegrass sound. "I know the stuff that I first heard was really excitin' to me. But maybe to somebody else it wouldn't be, like younger people. But that first band, that Bill Monroe, Flatt & Scruggs, Rainwater, and Chubby Wise [group]: it's still good music. That music will probably stand forever." With his traditional appeal, McCoury has received numerous awards from the International Bluegrass Music Association (IBMA); "I always thought I could sing a little," he deadpanned to the audience of the 1994 IBMA Awards Show, during which he was voted entertainer of the year by the professional bluegrass community. "But I didn't know I could entertain people. I can't dance. Bill Monroe can dance."

Selected discography

(With brother, Jerry McCoury) *The McCoury Brothers,* Rounder, 1987.
(With David Grisman) *Home Is Where the Heart Is*, Rounder, 1988.
(With Don and David Parmley) *Families of Tradition*, BGC, 1990.

As Del McCoury and the Dixie Pals

High on a Mountaintop, Rounder, 1972.
(With Hershel Sizemore) *Strictly Bluegrass Live,* Japanese Trio, 1979.
Sawmill, Rebel, 1984.

As the Del McCoury Band

Don't Stop the Music, Rounder, 1990.
Blue Side of Town (includes "High on a Mountain" and "You Need a Fool"), Rounder, 1992.
A Deeper Shade of Blue (includes "True Love Never Dies" and "What Made Milwaukee Famous"), Rounder, 1993.

Sources

Books

Comprehensive Country Music Encyclopedia, edited by Russell D. Barnard, Times Books, 1994.
Rosenberg, Neil V., *Bluegrass: A History,* University of Illinois Press, 1985.

Periodicals

Billboard, October 8, 1994.
Bluegrass Canada, May/June 1994.
Bluegrass Unlimited, August 1990.
Columbia Flier, November 7, 1991.
Dirty Linen, June/July 1994.
Nashville Banner, December 21, 1993; September 23, 1994.
New Country Music, April 1994.
Owensboro Messenger-Inquirer, September 23, 1994.
Sing Out!, May-July 1994.
Tennessean, July 4, 1994.

Contemporary Musicians interviewed Del McCoury in October, 1994.

—*Pamela L. Shelton*

Neal McCoy

Singer

Photograph by Mark Tucker, courtesy of Atlantic Records

Country music singer Neal McCoy achieved huge popularity in 1994 with his third album, *No Doubt about It,* which was certified gold and rose to Number 13 on *Billboard's* country chart. The album generated two Number One hit singles, "No Doubt About It" and "Wink," as well as a third single, "The City Put the Country Back in Me," that reached the Number Five slot on the music charts. McCoy had the distinctive honor of having a hit single, "Wink," occupy the Number One position on the music charts for a month and remain on the charts longer than any other single in 1994.

McCoy was born Hubert Neal McGaughey, Jr., on July 30, 1960, in Jacksonville, Texas, where he spent most of his adult life. Because he found that McGaughey was difficult for people to pronounce, he changed his name first to McGoy in 1982, then to McCoy in 1991. Country music was not McCoy's sole preference when growing up; he liked pop and disco sounds in addition to the Texas twang of Jacksonville's brand of country music. He confided to the *Cincinnati Post's* Mary Jo DiLonardo that pop icon Michael Jackson was one of his main influences. Seeing such a young performer as Jackson, McCoy said, "put the spark in me and made me think, 'That's what I wanna do someday.'"

Pride Acted as a Mentor

McCoy sang in school and church choirs, musicals, and quartets throughout his high school years and, after earning his diploma, attended a junior college close to home. He tried his hand at various jobs in order to support himself before becoming a successful singer and musician. He sold women's shoes in a local mall, sang with a combo at local restaurants, and mowed lawns to make ends meet. In 1980 McCoy met his wife, Melinda, when she came into the shoe store where he worked. They married the following year, and several years later would have a daughter and a son.

In 1981, at the age of 21, McCoy entered a talent contest at the Belle Star nightclub in Dallas, Texas, where country star Janie Fricke served as a judge. She was employed at singer Charley Pride's management company at the time and was sufficiently impressed with McCoy to introduce him to Pride. Pride saw McCoy perform at another local country music contest and quickly decided to take the young singer under his wing.

McCoy's friendship with Pride proved to be fortuitous. McCoy was invited to open shows for Pride, which provided a much larger audience than he was accustomed to, and he began to perform before thousands of people on the weekends while mowing lawns for his livelihood during the week. When Pride left RCA Records in favor of a new Nashville label called 16th Avenue Records, McCoy was signed by 16th Avenue as well.

The new label did not fare well and let McCoy go after one year. The singer continued to tour with Charley Pride, and the two eventually parted amicably in 1990 after working together for almost six years. In 1991 McCoy signed with Atlantic Records. Company executive Rick Blackburn asked McCoy to change his surname to McCoy since fans were already pronouncing "McGoy" as "McCoy." The singer's early records, *At This Moment,* released in 1991, and *Where Forever Begins,* released the following year, generated scant fanfare, and McCoy feared a repeat of his dismal experience with 16th Avenue Records. Atlantic was just then breaking into the country music market with a new office in Nashville, and it was not until the label paired McCoy with a third producer, Barry Beckett, that the singer's talent began to shine.

A Natural Showman

Atlantic Records in Nashville eventually achieved enormous success with new stars Tracy Lawrence, John Michael Montgomery, and Confederate Railroad. Beckett, McCoy's third producer, had done work for Confederate Railroad, and Atlantic hoped he could assist, guide, and ultimately market McCoy with similar success.

McCoy told the *Chicago Tribune's* Jack Hurst, "Barry [Beckett] and I went out to dinner, just us two, and we

really hit it off. I'm pretty loud and obnoxious and outgoing and he's the opposite, so I really listened to what he had to say." Beckett's approach was to let McCoy go into the studio and be himself, although he did help to make McCoy more commercially viable in the country music realm. Also, Beckett's R&B background—he had worked with Muscle Shoals—melded perfectly with McCoy's diverse musical influences, and together the two were able to choose songs that best suited McCoy's voice. McCoy told *The Tennessean's* Robert Oermann, "I don't write songs. I'm not an instrumentalist at all, not a musician.... I'm an entertainer."

Atlantic's Blackburn told Hurst, "McCoy's a natural entertainer, a guy who was working 250 dates a year without a hit, and you can't abandon somebody like that." Part of the reason Blackburn and Beckett stood by McCoy through the lean early years was McCoy's ability to bring an audience roaring to its feet and clamoring for more music. The singer's performances onstage were down-to-earth, natural, and marked by an appealing diversity. His raucous, knee-slapping laugh, Texas drawl, and polite demeanor served to endear him to audiences.

Charm and Energy Captured on Records

McCoy often intersperses pop standards, blues, swing, and big band with country fare during live performances, drawing upon such unlikely influences as Quincy Jones and James Ingram. He is also noted for making appearances without a set list; he prefers instead to tailor his material to a specific audience. The memorable antics, humor, Las Vegas-style acrobatics, and spontaneity in which audiences take delight had been honed while McCoy toured with Charley Pride.

Most Nashville record executives in the early 1990s were dropping aspiring country music stars after only a brief shot or two, but Blackburn and Beckett sensed that if they could stick with McCoy and find a way to translate his charm and energy while performing before an audience onto a record, they would have a hit on their hands. Blackburn told Hurst in the *Chicago Tribune,* "We always thought he could maybe be our biggest act, and I had no intention of not staying with him."

When *No Doubt about It* was released in 1994, the country music market was already flooded with aspiring Nashville stars. McCoy felt that if his third album failed to generate notice, he should probably move to Las Vegas with his wife to pursue work as a live entertainer, instead of continuing to record albums. His fears and doubts were soon dispelled with the astounding success of three of the album's singles. *No Doubt about It* was effective in highlighting McCoy's vocals in a deeper, more soulful manner. What kept the singer optimistic about the success of the recording was that, toward the end of the run of his second album, *Where Forever Begins,* a single titled "Now I Pray for Rain" had managed to crack the Top 20 of the music charts and peak at Number 19.

McCoy made his television debut on *The Tonight Show* with Jay Leno in July of 1994. *You Gotta Love That* was released in January of 1995, with Beckett as the producer, and the album's debut single, "For a Change," hit Number 33 in its fourth week on *Billboard's* Hot Country Singles and Tracks chart. In July "They're Playin' Our Song" held the Number Seven position, while *You Gotta Love That* was ranked at Number 39 on the albums chart. Also in 1995, McCoy embarked on a tour with the band Alabama. The singer told *Billboard's* Peter Cronin, "I'm still not as home in the studio as I'd like to be, but entertaining is really more important to me than the other aspects of this business. I live for that part."

Selected discography

At This Moment, Atlantic, 1991.
Where Forever Begins, Atlantic, 1992.
No Doubt about It, Atlantic, 1994.
You Gotta Love That, Atlantic, 1995.

Sources

Baltimore Sun, May 13, 1994.
Billboard, June 18, 1994; January 7, 1995.
Chicago Tribune, July 31, 1994.
Cincinnati Post, July 7, 1994.
Country Music Magazine, July 1994.
Tennessean, July 23, 1994.

Additional information for this profile was obtained from Atlantic Records publicity materials, 1995.

—*B. Kimberly Taylor*

Sylvia McNair

Opera singer

Sylvia McNair is one of the most promising young singers in classical music. Since the early 1980s, a radiant but disciplined performing style has carried her to the front ranks of her profession, buoyed on a wave of audience and critical acclaim. Initially making her mark as an orchestral soloist, McNair has also achieved considerable repute in the world of opera, interpreting a wide-ranging repertoire from the classic to the contemporary with invariable success. In the mid-1990s, with her vocal talents approaching their peak and a solid schedule of performances and recording dates before her, she seemed poised to take her place among the top sopranos of the twentieth century.

McNair was born in Mansfield, Ohio, on June 23, 1956, the daughter of George McNair, a chemical engineer, and Marilou McNair, a music teacher. Between her mother's profession and her father's hobbies of playing the violin and singing in the church choir, there was a decidedly musical atmosphere in the McNair household; Sylvia's musical education started at age three with piano lessons from her mother. At age seven, she began playing violin, and though she also sang in the choir throughout her childhood and adolescence, instrumental music remained her first love.

In 1974 McNair enrolled in the music program at Wheaton College in Illinois, intending to concentrate in violin performance, with the ultimate goal of making a career as an orchestral musician. Opera was perhaps the furthest thing from her mind; in fact, she found it repellant, as she recalled in an interview with *BBC Music Magazine:* "My first experience of opera was playing in the orchestra.... I just couldn't believe how ridiculous it was. I thought, what a ludicrous art form this is!"

Became a Singer by Chance

Given this adverse initial reaction to opera, it seems odd that McNair should excel in that very discipline. It was purely by coincidence that she did. While at Wheaton, one of her violin instructors suggested she take voice lessons to refine her instrumental technique. Discovering that she enjoyed singing more than playing the violin, McNair modified her career plans, and in 1978 enrolled in the master's program in vocal music at the University of Indiana. Under the guidance of her voice teachers, who included the renowned opera singer and teacher Virginia McWatters, she applied the technical precision and musical exactitude she'd learned from playing the violin to singing, developing quickly into a first-rate vocalist.

In 1980 Robert Shaw, conductor of the Atlanta Symphony, visited Indiana to direct a performance of

For the Record . . .

Born June 23, 1956, in Mansfield, OH; daughter of George (a chemical engineer) and Marilou (a music teacher) McNair; married Hal France (a conductor), 1986. *Education:* B.A. in music, Wheaton College, 1978; M.A. in vocal performance, University of Indiana, 1982.

Appeared with Atlanta Symphony, 1980; appeared with Boston Symphony, Berlin Philharmonic, Academy of Saint-Martin-in-the-Fields, and San Francisco Symphony; released first recording, *Gloria,* Telarc, 1982; debuted at Opera Theater of Saint Louis, 1983, Schwetzingen Palace Festival, 1984, Glyndebourne Opera Festival, 1989, Royal Opera, 1990, and Metropolitan Opera, 1992.

Awards: National Metropolitan Opera Auditions, first place, 1982; Marion Anderson Award, 1992; four albums on which McNair has appeared have received Grammy Award nominations, with Deutsche Grammophon's *Semele* winning the award in 1993.

Addresses: *Home*—Old Tappan, NY. *Agent*—Colbert Artists Management, 111 West 57th St., New York, NY 10019. *Record company*—Philips Classics/PolyGram, 825 Eighth Avenue, New York, NY 10019.

Bach's *B-minor Mass* with McNair singing the soprano solo. Shaw was impressed by her abilities, so much so that McNair began making guest appearances with the Atlanta Symphony and recording on the Telarc label before even finishing her degree. In 1982, she won the National Metropolitan Opera Auditions, made her London concert debut as part of the American Artists' Series, and received a Grammy nomination for her *first* recording, Poulenc's *Gloria.* Such on-the-job training was to prove invaluable; without having to undergo the struggle for recognition faced by many young artists trying to establish themselves on the classical music scene, McNair received immediate professional and critical exposure, enabling her to work full-time as a singer from the moment she left school.

Singing and recording with orchestras as a soloist proved a staple in the 1980s for McNair. In addition to her work with the Atlanta Symphony, she appeared with the Boston Symphony under Seiji Ozawa and Kurt Masur, the Academy of Saint Martin-in-the-Fields under Neville Mariner, the Berlin Philharmonic under Jeffrey Tate, and the San Francisco Symphony. Working in this distinguished company, she became widely known for her interpretation of oratorios, choral works with a scriptural basis, particularly those of Mozart. The most significant factor in her success was the tone of her voice; perhaps as a result of her prior training on the violin, it had a strongly instrumental quality to it, which seemed to naturally complement the playing of an orchestra. McNair acknowledged this in a *New York Times* interview, explaining, "Because I'm still an instrumentalist at heart, I tend to respond most strongly to singing that sounds like brilliant instrumental playing."

Debut at Carnegie Hall

In 1985 McNair made her Carnegie Hall debut in a concert performance of Handel's *Semele.* Soon after, she had her first major label release, a Philips Classics recording of Mozart's *Mass in C Minor* with the Monteverdi Choir and Orchestra under John Eliot Gardiner. Performing as a soloist with orchestras also had an impact on McNair's personal life; in 1984 she met Hal France, a conductor on the American regional opera and symphony circuit, at a rehearsal of Handel's *Messiah.* They wed 16 months later. The couple currently make their home in New York's Hudson Valley, though the demands of their respective careers often keep them apart for prolonged periods.

In the field of opera, McNair was slower to make a name for herself, initially performing largely on regional stages. In 1983 she appeared to highly favorable reviews in the role of Hero for an Opera Theater of Saint Louis production of Berlioz's *Beatrice and Benedict.* McNair became something of a favorite with this company and subsequently returned to perform in Mozart's *The Magic Flute* and *Idomeneo,* Handel's *Alcina,* and Purcell's *King Arthur.* The following year, she made her European opera debut at the Schwetzingen Palace Festival, playing the title role in the world premiere of *Ophelia,* an opera by contemporary Swiss composer Rudolf Kelterborn. Other appearances by her in Europe included playing Ilia in *Idomeneo* in Strasbourg and Lyon, France, Susanna in Mozart's *Le Nozze di Figaro* with the Netherlands Opera and the Vienna State Opera, and Pamina in Mozart's *The Magic Flute* with the Deutsch Oper of Berlin.

The turning point in McNair's opera career came in 1989 and, like her decision to take up singing, was more by chance than design. While in New Mexico to perform in *The Magic Flute* with the Santa Fe Opera, she happened to play tennis with Brian Dickie, artistic director of England's prestigious Glyndebourne Opera Festival. Dickie accidentally hit her in the face with a hard serve, her face became swollen and, by her account, Dickie felt so remorseful that he offered her the part of Anne Truelove in a Glyndebourne production of Stravinsky's *The Rake's Progress*. Whatever the case, her performance of the role was a triumph, garnering critical acclaim for her simplicity and purity of tone. Max Loppert, reviewing her performance for *Opera*, stated that McNair sang "with a candid radiance and a limpid sweetness of tone that kept one spellbound."

Prefers Intimacy of Small Concert Halls

In the wake of her international exposure in one of opera's foremost venues, other opportunities were quick in coming. In 1990 McNair scored a fresh success in her debut at the Royal Opera in London as Ilia in a new production of *Idomeneo*. This role has become a hallmark for her, and she repeated it for her first appearances at the Salzburg Festival in Salzburg, Austria, and the Bastille Opera in Paris. In the same year, she was the first winner of the Marian Anderson Award and later embarked on a recital tour of the United States and Europe. For the bicentennial of Mozart's death in 1991, she sang his *Requiem* at Carnegie Hall in New York. The following year saw her debut at the Metropolitan Opera in New York—a milestone for any rising star—as Marzelline in Beethoven's *Fidelio,* and in 1993 she returned as Pamina in *The Magic Flute*. The 1992/93 season also featured her debut with the San Francisco Opera as Tytania in Benjamin Britten's *A Midsummer Night's Dream*.

Just as important as her work on opera's top stages was a substantial increase in McNair's recorded output. Beginning in 1982, she appeared on more than two dozen recordings, primarily from the late 1980s on. In 1991 she signed a long-term contract with Philips Classics to record a wide range of operatic and choral works, some of which would fall outside of the traditional classical repertoire. Reflecting McNair's strong interest in twentieth-century American choral music, her releases through the mid-1990s included an album of songs by Jerome Kern, the Broadway songwriter and composer, with piano accompaniment by Andre Previn, himself a noted composer and arranger. Four albums on which she was featured have been nominated for Grammy awards, including Deutsche Grammophon's *Semele,* which won a Grammy in 1993.

Having reached the musical pinnacle at a relatively young age, McNair's future seems bright, and the only real limits to her potential are self-imposed. She understands that her voice lacks the size and power necessary for some roles, and as a result, is extremely careful in choosing those to which she feels ideally suited. McNair has also expressed a dislike for singing in large venues such as New York's Metropolitan Opera, preferring the intimacy of small concert halls where, as she stated in a *New York Times* interview, "you can see the whites of people's eyes." Wherever she may choose to sing, the quality of McNair's voice, the perfected and flawlessly pure tone that is her hallmark, is sure to inspire awe in her listeners.

Selected discography

Gloria, Telarc, 1982.
Messiah, Telarc, 1984.
Symphony of Psalms, Telarc, 1985.
Mass in C Minor, K. 427, Philips Classics, 1986.
La Marseillaise & Other Berlioz Favorites, Telarc, 1988.
Missa Solemnis, Telarc, 1988.
Mass in B Minor, Telarc Digital, 1990.
La clemenza di Tito, Archiv Produktion, 1991.
Peer Gynt, Angel/EMI, 1991.
Il Re Pastore, Philips Classics, 1991.
Requiem, K. 626, Philips Classics, 1991.
Idomeneo, Archiv Produktion, 1991.
Missa KV 317, Deutsche Grammophon, 1992.
Le martyre de Saint Sebastien, Sony Classical, 1992.
Messiah, Philips Classics, 1992.
Beatrice et Benedict, Musifrance, 1992.
Music of Samuel Barber, Telarc, 1992.
Semele, Deutsche Grammophon, 1993.
Symphony No. 9 Choral, Philips Classics, 1993.
The Yeoman of the Guard, Philips Classics, 1993.
Orfeo ed Euridice, Philips Classics, 1993.
Exsultate Jubilate, Philips Classics, 1993.
Symphony No. 4, Philips Classics, 1993.
Sure Thing: The Jerome Kern Songbook, Philips Classics, 1994.

Sources

BBC Music Magazine, November 1994.
High Fidelity/Musical America, January 1985.
New Yorker, July 18, 1983.
New York Times, November 27, 1994.
Ovation, March 1989.
Opera, Annual 1989.
Opera News, July 1983.
Village Voice, August 1, 1989.

Additional information for this profile was provided by Colbert Artists Management, Philips Classics, and Telarc Records press materials, 1994.

—*Daniel Hodges*

Marian McPartland

Pianist, composer, educator, radio commentator

Photograph by Barbara Bordnick, courtesy of Concord Jazz, Inc.

Few women in jazz have become as successful an instrumentalist as pianist Marian McPartland, who has been a mainstay on the American jazz scene since moving to the United States from England in the 1940s. As a white female who was not a native American, McPartland had to overcome a number of prejudices in the jazz world in order to make her mark.

Known for having very fast fingers and using the whole keyboard when playing, McPartland has mastered every style of jazz from bebop to avant garde to romantic. She is noted for her improvisational skills and her keen ear for the latest trends in contemporary music.

McPartland's playing has placed her in the same ranks as other great jazz pianists, including George Shearing, Teddy Wilson, and Billy Taylor. She is also a gifted arranger and has composed a number of highly regarded jazz pieces, usually with a bittersweet and nostalgic flavor. Her works include "In the Days of Our Love" (recorded by Peggy Lee), "Twilight World" (recorded by Johnny Mercer), and others songs recorded by Tony Bennett, Sarah Vaughan, Gary Burton, George Shearing, Cleo Laine, and the Thad Jones/Mel Lewis band.

Despite her talent as a performer, McPartland is best known to the public as the host of a popular radio series called *Piano Jazz,* which profiles major jazz artists. Her radio show has had a major impact on developing awareness of both famous and little-known jazz musicians. As Peter Watrous noted in the *New York Times,* "Marian McPartland is an important jazz figure not so much for her piano-playing as for her articulate advocacy of the form." Referring to this radio series in another *Times* article, George Wein was quoted during the 1991 JVC Jazz Festival in New York City as saying, "Marian McPartland has done more for jazz pianists than anyone in the entire world."

Switched from Classical to Jazz

A number of McPartland's cousins in England were musically inclined, and she began studying voice, violin, and classical piano as a child at the Guildhall School of Music. Piano became her main instrument in her teens, and at that time she developed an interest in jazz music that defied her parents' wishes. She left her classical training to perform in a four-piano vaudeville act that was the led by Billy Mayer, playing under the stage name of Marian Page because of her parents' disapproval.

During World War II, she often entertained British and American troops with ENSA, the British equivalent of the American USO. In 1944 she met well-known American

Born Margaret Marian Turner, March 20, 1920, in Slough, England; immigrated to the United States, 1946; married Jimmy McPartland (a cornetist), 1945 (divorced, then remarried McPartland, 1991). *Education:* Attended Guildhall School of Music, England.

Studied classical piano, violin, and voice as a child; played piano with vaudeville act, 1930s; performed for troops during World War II, 1940s; played solo and with husband, Jimmy McPartland, at clubs in New York City, 1940s; formed own trio, 1951; established long-term playing residence at Hickory House, New York City, 1952; began recording for Savoy and Capitol, early 1950s; began teaching jazz to schoolchildren, 1955; toured with Benny Goodman's Sextet, 1963; wrote articles and reviews for *Down Beat,* c. 1960s; established own record company, Halcyon, 1970; wrote soundtracks for two educational films, *Mural* and *The Light Fantastic Picture Show;* performed at Cafe Carlyle, New York City, 1974; appeared at Newport Jazz Festival with husband, 1978; began hosting own nationally syndicated radio show, *Piano Jazz,* 1979; performed classical repertoire, 1980s; published collection of writings on jazz and jazz artists, *All in Good Time,* Oxford University Press, 1987.

Awards: International Radio Festival of New York Gold Medal, Corporation for Public Broadcasting Program Award, Southern Educational Communication Association Award, ASCAP/Deems Taylor Award, and Peabody Award, 1980, all for *Piano Jazz;* named Jazz Educator of the Year, National Association of Jazz Educators, 1986; Lifetime Achievement Award, *Down Beat,* 1994; awards for soundtrack *Mark,* Edinburgh and Venice Film Festivals; honorary doctorates from Union, Bates, and Ithaca colleges.

Addresses: *Record company*—Concord Jazz, P.O. Box 845, Concord, CA 94522.

cornetist Jimmy McPartland while jamming with American musicians of the U.S. Army Special Service in Belgium. The next year, the two were married in Aachen, Germany.

After moving to the States with her new husband in 1946, McPartland had a battle ahead of her to win acceptance as a serious jazz musician. Since jazz originated in the United States, outsiders who attempted to enter the genre were often viewed with suspicion by American practitioners. Being white and a woman also hampered McPartland's assimilation into the jazz world. However, being married to an established American musician put her in the right circles to develop her talent and helped her land gigs she otherwise might not have been offered.

Formed Popular Trio

McPartland worked steadily as a performer throughout the 1940s and 1950s, playing some engagements with her husband and solo spots at Condon's and other jazz clubs. Her career took a giant leap forward after she formed her own trio with Bill Brow on bass and Joe Morello on drums in 1951. The trio played a variety of club dates, including a legendary run at Hickory House in New York City that started in 1952 and continued on and off for a decade.

In the early 1950s McPartland began recording albums for Savoy and Capitol. She entered another phase of her musical career in 1955, when she started teaching jazz to schoolchildren. Since that time she has both played and taught jazz at grade schools, high schools, and colleges. "I was so afraid rock & roll was going to kill jazz that I went into the schools," she told *Down Beat* in 1994. "I couldn't fight rock & roll but I wanted kids to know that there's another music."

Among McPartland's later teaching activities was a nine-week stint in 1974 teaching jazz to children in Washington, D.C. "Working with students diminishes my inhibitions and lubricates my creativity," she said in a Concord Jazz press kit. The impact of her jazz education efforts was acknowledged in 1986 when she became the first woman to be named Jazz Educator of the Year by the National Association of Jazz Educators.

Started Own Record Company

Along with playing in her trio, McPartland has performed in duets with Joe Venuti and with fellow pianists Wilson and Shearing. In the 1960s she toured with Benny Goodman's sextet and wrote a series of articles and reviews for *Down Beat.* Her soundtrack for *Mark,* an art film, won awards at both the Edinburgh and Venice Film Festivals in that decade.

When the 1960s ended, McPartland felt that she was being ignored by the major record companies. She solved the problem by forming her own company, which she called Halcyon. Her first album on her new label was *Interplay.* A recording of her own composition, "Ambiance," earned her a Grammy nomination.

During the 1960s and 1970s McPartland maintained an active performing schedule. She played frequently at jazz festivals in Nice, Montreux, Antibes, Berlin, and Monterey, as well as at the JVC Jazz Festival in New York City and the Kansas City Women's Jazzfest. Over the years she has also performed with the New York Pops, New Amsterdam Symphony, and major symphony orchestras in London, St. Louis, and New Orleans. After their divorce, she and Jimmy McPartland continued to play together, including an appearance at the 1978 Newport Jazz Festival.

Hosted Hit Radio Show

McPartland's visibility increased dramatically in 1974, when Bobby Short asked her to fill in for him at New York City's posh Cafe Carlyle while he was on vacation. Another major turning point took place in 1979, when William Hay of South Carolina Educational Radio asked her to host a 13-week radio series to be distributed by National Public Radio (NPR). McPartland had been recommended by her friend, pianist Alec Wilder.

The show's format of two pianists who talk and play, both solo and as a duet, was determined by McPartland. She dubbed the show *Piano Jazz* and had noted pianist Mary Lou Williams as her first guest. A year after its first airing, *Piano Jazz* won a Peabody Award and a number of other prestigious honors. By the 1990s the show had expanded to 39 weeks a year and had logged an impressive lineup of guests from all corners of the jazz world.

After addressing almost every aspect of jazz piano on her radio program, McPartland branched out by inviting singers, saxophonists, trumpeters, and other instrumentalists onto the show. As of the mid-1990s, the show had featured over 300 guests, including Tony Bennett, Wynton and Branford Marsalis, Dizzy Gillespie, Ray Charles, Eubie Blake, Gerry Mulligan, Rosemary Clooney, Steve Allen, Dudley Moore, and younger artists such as Benny Green, Geoff Keezer, Allen Farham, and Geri Allen. "I want to do the right thing with *Piano Jazz*," she said in a Concord Jazz press release. "I have a responsibility to make it good. It's an historical record." McPartland also made a number of popular live recordings of her shows.

Further confirming her versatility, McPartland ventured successfully into the realm of classical music in the 1980s. In concerts across the United States, she performed twentieth-century American composer George Gershwin's *Rhapsody in Blue*, nineteenth-century Norwegian composer Edvard Grieg's *Piano Concerto*, and popular songs arranged for piano and orchestrated by

Robert Farnon. In the 1990s she gained further exposure by appearing on the *Today* show, various PBS specials, and the television series *Live at Wolf Trap* with George Shearing. She has also served as moderator for the series *Women in Jazz* on the Arts & Entertainment (A&E) cable network.

Past the age of seventy, McPartland managed to keep her talent at a high level. In the CD liner notes to *Marian McPartland's Piano Jazz with Guest Milton Hinton,* which was recorded live in 1991, reviewer Phil Sheridan commented: "Each time [McPartland] plays, her approach to the material is inquisitive and probing, as if it were new, yet has the confidence of an artist whose lines flow in the creativity generated by an intimate familiarity with the scene at hand." And *JazzTimes* contributor Leslie Gourse, writing in the liner notes to *Marian McPartland Live at Maybeck Recital Hall, Volume Nine,* declared: "Her technique and repertoire show how she has imbibed every important innuendo in jazz's development."

McPartland remarried her ex-husband, Jimmy McPartland, in 1991. He died later that year, and in 1993 McPartland honored him with a CD, *In My Life,* dedicated to his memory. Showing no signs of slowing down in the 1990s, McPartland maintains an active schedule of playing and lecturing. In 1994 she recorded an album of Mary Lou Williams compositions, backed by Bill Douglass on bass and Omar Clay on drums. In the liner notes for the CD, Chris Albertson of *Stereo Review* wrote, "Actually, Marian does her own thing throughout this set, capturing—with charm and a healthy measure of swing—the flavor and diversity that characterized the music of Mary Lou Williams."

Perhaps McPartland's ultimate honor came in 1994, when *Down Beat* awarded her its Lifetime Achievement Award. But even this career high note was not enough to make her consider retirement. As she said at age 74, as quoted in Concord Jazz press materials, "I still want to improve, experiment, and keep up with what's happening."

Selected discography

Jazz at the Hickory House, Savoy, 1952-53.
With You in My Mind, Capitol, 1957.
At the London House, Argo, 1958.
Ambiance, Halcyon, 1970.
From This Moment On, Concord Jazz, 1978.
At the Festival, Concord Jazz, 1979.
Willow Creek and Other Ballads, Concord Jazz, 1985.
Plays the Music of Billy Strayhorn, Concord Jazz, 1987.
Marian McPartland Plays the Benny Carter Songbook, Concord Jazz, 1990.

Marian McPartland Live at Maybeck Recital Hall, Volume Nine, Concord Jazz, 1991.
Marian McPartland's Piano Jazz with Guest Milt Hinton, Jazz Alliance, 1991.
In My Life, Concord Jazz, 1993.
Marian McPartland's Piano Jazz with Guest Dave Brubeck, Jazz Alliance, 1993.
Great Britain's, Savoy Jazz, 1993.
Marian McPartland's Piano Jazz with Guest Teddy Wilson, Jazz Alliance, 1993.
Marian McPartland Plays the Music of Mary Lou Williams, Concord Jazz, 1994.
Personal Choice (recorded 1982), Concord Jazz.
Interplay, Halcyon.

Selected compositions

"In the Days of Our Love."
"Twilight World."
"So Many Things."
"With You in My Mind."
"Ambiance."

Sources

Books

Cook, Richard, and Brian Morton, *The Penguin Guide to Jazz on CD, LP and Cassette,* Penguin, 1992.

The Guinness Encyclopedia of Popular Music, volume 3, edited by Colin Larkin, Guinness Publishing, 1992.
McPartland, Marian, *All in Good Time,* Oxford University Press, 1987.
The New Grove Dictionary of American Music, volume 3, edited by H. Wiley Hitchcock and Stanley Sadie, Macmillan, 1980.
The Oxford Companion to Popular Music, edited by Peter Gammond, Oxford University Press, 1991.

Periodicals

Atlantic, September 1991.
Audio, May 1991.
Down Beat, December 1988; October 1990; October 1992; September 1994; July 1995.
Jazziz, May 1994.
JazzNow, October 1994.
New York Times, June 30, 1991; March 7, 1994.
Stereo Review, October 1990.

Additional information for this profile was obtained from Concord Jazz publicity materials and the liner notes to *Marian McPartland Live at Maybeck Recital Hall, Volume Nine; Marian McPartland's Piano Jazz with Guest Milt Hinton;* and *Marian McPartland Plays the Music of Mary Lou Williams.*

—Ed Decker

The Mekons

Rock band

In the mid-1990s, two decades after their formation, the U.K. rock band the Mekons were still struggling to pull their career together. Once again, they seemed on the verge of breaking through into the mass market. They released an album in 1993 titled *I ♥ Mekons,* which recalled the ferocious despair that first sparked England's punk movement. Sometimes dismissed as remnants of the punk flameout in the 1980s, the Mekons lost a few musicians since their debut in 1977. In the 1990s the group had a new label, Quarterstick/Touch and Go, after years of static and, according to the band, neglect from other record companies. They followed the prickly romance cycle *I ♥ Mekons* with the 1994 effort *Retreat from Memphis,* chronicling their rear guard action against the musical establishment.

Lead singer Sally Timms is a willowy blonde with a broken glass voice. Guitarist Tom Greenhalgh supports her with tenor harmonies. Jon Langford, lead guitarist and cofounder of the group with Greenhalgh—they were both art students in Leeds, England—lends exuberance to the stew. Back in the days when "New Wave"

Photograph by Michael Levine, courtesy of Stick Records

was being invented, the Mekons wrote a cynically humorous response to the Clash's "White Riot" entitled "Never Been in a Riot." Released in 1977, it was their first "hit" single.

The Mekons are an urban guerrilla band in a bleak, moonlit landscape. The band's *nom de plume* comes from an English comic strip, *The Eagle,* in which imperialist adventurer Dan Dare flees evil space invaders called Mekons. The band scorns the commercial romance favored by their older British compatriots, Paul McCartney and Phil Collins. When the Mekons speak of love, the word is ironic but somehow innocent, like badly applied lipstick. In the song "Millionaire," Timms croons, "Everybody's so in love, but they don't touch or meet." The band's attitude recalls the political outrage that spawned punk—the anger now tempered with grief.

It is difficult to pigeonhole the Mekons' sound. Early in their career, the band featured dissonant anti-music— guitars crunched into sledgehammer drums. The Leeds bar scene also produced bands such as Gang of Four with similar orchestrations. The Mekons' first album was *The Quality of Mercy Is Not Strnen,* a play on words echoing the aphorism that a monkey could create the works of Shakespeare if given enough time. In the punk ethos, it did not matter if rockers could sing or play their instruments better than the members of the audience. The theory was that people on stage were the same as their listeners, a deliberate revulsion from the rock-star syndrome.

Later, the Mekons became more polished, added the soulful Timms in 1986, and used keyboards, horns, and drum machines. They incorporated the sounds of reggae, blues, folk and American country. In some incarnations, the Mekons abandoned their trademark confrontational blasts of sound but invariably pushed the boundaries of convention. At times, the band exhibited a demented honky-tonk style with fiddles and country and western embellishments, as in 1987's *Honky Tonkin'.*

The later albums with Timms exude a baleful intelligence. There are always punk echoes, but a melodic interest that salutes the great songsmiths of Tin Pan Alley and Nashville is also evident. The Mekons changed their methods frequently, searching for a formula that combine pop and punk. *Fear and Whiskey,* released in 1985, spat out a message of hallucinated gloom: "darkness and doubt just follow us about." *Rock and Roll* (1989) was an electric blitzkrieg through the corridors of industry power and the mirrors along them. *Curse of the Mekons* (1991) employed a more subdued acoustic mix with banjo, violin, accordion, and bagpipes.

Bassist Sarah Corina, as quoted in *Interview* magazine, has stated that if you love the Mekons, "you could take it as loving an alien," a practice she viewed as good for extraterrestrial relations. Many reviewers have loved the Mekons throughout their career. Dave Jennings of *Melody Maker* described the *I ♥ Mekons* album as "simultaneously a brilliant, exhilarating pop record and an exploration of the assumptions behind other people's pop records." The band bewailed its distance from success, turning it into a metaphor for the failures of the heart.

Most critics agree that it is rare to find a rock band that considers ideas in its music. The Mekons persistently challenge the demise of rock as a spiritual quest that involves the mind as well as the viscera. The band asserts passion as the fundamental human condition and resists social conditioning and hero worship. While acknowledging the band's intellectual side, Langford still likes the "sonic stuff," according to *Net* magazine. He pointed to the band's celebrated live performances as his ideal mode, stripped to guitars, drums, and bandmember Susie Honeyman's violin. In their headbanging guise, driving for "truth, justice and Led Zeppelin," as the chorus from the song "Amnesia" puts it, the band could shake the rafters for its devoted following. "Memphis, Egypt," one of their standard set numbers, advises: "Destroy your safe and happy lives before it is too late." The audience howls its assent.

Greenhalgh tried to summarize the band's cerebral-*cum*-intestinal style for *Request* magazine: "The whole punk-rock approach has a certain distance; it's not as simple as early rock 'n' roll. So coming from that background, it makes sense to have a certain distance in the way you work.... The real world is infinitely more complex than we can ever imagine."

Selected discography

The Quality of Mercy Is Not Strnen, Virgin.
Mekons, Redmek, 1980.
Fear and Whiskey, 1985.
Honky Tonkin', 1987.
The Mekons' Rock and Roll, A&M, 1989.
Mekons New York, ROIR, 1990.
Curse of the Mekons, Blast First, 1991.
I ♥ Mekons, Quarterstick/Touch and Go, 1993.
Retreat from Memphis, Quarterstick/Touch and Go, 1994.
(Contributors) *You Are What You Shoot*, 1995.

Sources

Billboard, January 27, 1990; December 8, 1990.
CMJ, September 27, 1993.
Entertainment Weekly, October 22, 1993; May 6, 1994.
Interview, November 1993.
Metro Times (Detroit), June 1994.
Net, October 1993.
People, December 18, 1989.
Pulse!, December 1993.
Request, November 1993.
Rolling Stone, July 2, 1987; October 14, 1993; February 10, 1994; June 1, 1995.
Spin, November 1993.
Stereo Review, September 1987.

—*Paul E. Anderson*

Ennio Morricone

Film composer

Ennio Morricone is one of the most eclectic and prolific film composers of the twentieth century. He began composing scores for Italian westerns (often called "spaghetti westerns") in the 1960s and over the course of his career, has created soundtracks for over 350 films and television productions released in English, Italian, and French. In addition to westerns, he has composed highly melodic scores for mystery thrillers, romantic dramas, comedies, and epics, including *The Untouchables, La Cage aux Folles, The Mission,* and *Disclosure.*

In an interview with Fred Karlin, author of *Listening to Movies,* Morricone discussed his humble beginnings, stating, "My first films were light comedies or costume movies that required simple musical scores that were easily created, a genre that I never completely abandoned even when I went on to much more important films with major directors."

Songs for a "Man with No Name"

Yet these "simple musical scores" were inherently ingenious, immediately setting Morricone apart from his contemporaries. The compositions were marked by a blend of rock, jazz, folk, blues, and classical music and "found" sounds—birdcalls, gunshots, footsteps, the lash of a whip, rolling baby carriages, animal noises, and most notably, the human whistle. Writing for *The Village Voice* in 1986, Peter Watrous remarked, "[Morricone] has an acute sense for sound, and if it means using lower-class instruments—electric guitars, cheezo keyboards—to gain a specific effect, he'll do it." Morricone's work with director Sergio Leone on the classic 1960s "man with no name" trilogy vaulted both Morricone and actor Clint Eastwood to instant cult stardom. In scores for *A Fistful of Dollars, For a Few Dollars More,* and *The Good, the Bad, and the Ugly,* Morricone mirrored the violence, irony, and campy humor pervading the classic Eastwood western.

Though westerns established Morricone as a "name" in the film-score business, his work with major directors such as Franco Zefferelli, Federico Fellini, Roman Polanski, and Roland Joffe put him on par with composers like John Williams, the man who dominated film music in the 1980s with memorable themes to *Jaws, Close Encounters of the Third Kind,* and *Star Wars.*

In the 1990s, roughly a quarter-century after he first attained prominence, moviegoers would be moved by Morricone's dramatic swells in big-screen epics such as *City of Joy* and startled by his jagged strings in thrillers like *Wolf.* "Morricone, in short, is a postmodernist," wrote Harlan Kennedy in a 1991 interview in *Ameri-*

For the Record...

Born November 10, 1928, in Rome Italy. *Education*: Diplomas in trombone, orchestra direction, and composition, Santa Cecilia Conservatory; studied with Goffredo Petrassi.

Composed first film score, for *The Fascist,* 1961; scored "spaghetti westerns" of Sergio Leone, beginning mid-1960s; has composed more than 350 scores for music and television. Also composer of classical works, chamber music, a ballet, and music for theater, radio, and television. Contributor to periodicals, including *Soundtrack!, Positif, Cinefantastique,* and *Cinema Papers.*

Awards: Nominated for five Academy awards for best score; British Academy awards for *Days of Heaven,* 1979, *Once upon a Time in America,* 1984, *The Mission,* 1986, and *The Untouchables,* 1987; Golden Globe Award, 1986, for *The Mission;* Top Box Office Film Award from American Society of Composers, Authors and Publishers for *Wolf,* 1995.

Addresses: *Record company*—Rhino Records, 10635 Santa Monica Blvd., Los Angeles, CA 90025-4900.

can Film. "Every acoustic gewgaw is grist for his mill; every period of musical history may be ransacked for inspiration. No wonder that in the 1990s, at the peak of his form, he's become the musical general in the Italian invasion of American cinema." Still, Morricone is loath to define himself in any category of film composers. He said in *American Film,* "I can't classify myself. Others must do it. Others, if they wish, can analyze my works."

"The Musical Sounds of Life"

Born in Rome in 1928, Morricone started writing music at the age of six. He holds diplomas in composition, trombone, and orchestra direction from the Santa Cecilia Conservatory in Rome, and he still plays trombone with a local music group called Nuova Consonaza. Along with his classical compositions, he has composed a ballet (*Requiem for Destiny*) but little other non-film music. His first full-length film composition was for Luciano Salce's *Il federale* (The Fascist) in 1961, though his fame was not established until Leone's mid-1960s trilogy and 1968's *Once upon a Time in the West,* perhaps Morricone's best-known score.

Morricone has often described his music as being about the pain inside a character. He told *American Film* contributor Kennedy that the screams, whistles, bells, and whips used in the "man with no name" trilogy were essential because they underlined the quirks of the character played by Eastwood. "I do only what I think is correct," he said. "A composer has the obligation to 'invent and capture' noises, the musical sounds of life."

Perhaps Morricone's most famous single "invention" is the theme song for *The Good, the Bad, and the Ugly,* which topped the American charts after it was borrowed and slightly altered by Hugo Montenegro—a slight that still irritates the composer. And though he writes almost exclusively for events onscreen, Morricone's soundtracks have endured on their own when released separately, often topping album charts.

Musical Solutions

Director Leone once told Kennedy that in the beginning of their collaboration, he would invite Morricone to his house and have him work on a piano that was out of tune because "if a score is good, it must rise above a bad instrument." For the most part, Morricone begins his work on a film score by consulting the director about problem spots in the film and suggesting musical solutions. Only after this collaboration takes place does Morricone begin his work with an orchestra. The *Village Voice's* Watrous explained of his signature style, "Where Morricone comments on the action, it's wildly imaginative kitsch.... Even without the visuals, the soundtracks are perfectly formed, if small, bits of music reeking sleaze." This down-and-dirty aspect of his work has attracted a devoted following among other musicians, including experimentalist John Zorn, who made his own "cover" versions of some of Morricone's work in the 1980s.

Despite the suggestion that Morricone's music needs no visual accompaniment, the composer told *Listening to Movies* author Karlin, "Actually, people are little concerned with the musical element if they are watching a film, except when the music is ... particularly emphasized." In fact, Morricone is usually brought in only after a film is completed. Because at this point it is effectively too late to alter the look of the film, some directors rely on the score to smooth over any weak points in the drama. Many films depend heavily on music to establish suspense, for example. Ultimately, the composer is confronted with having his score cut to fit precise moments of the film. (To counter this, Morricone has become active in the release of his works as they were initially conceived, the composer personally overseeing selection and arrangements.)

Musically enhanced cinematic moments, nonetheless, can carry a film. In a 1992 review of the movie *Bugsy*, an *Entertainment Weekly* reviewer stated, "Morricone achieves something here that [very few] even try: music that's as integral to the movie's very conception as the dialogue, camera work, and performances." In *American Film*, Morricone supports this statement by insisting that music in a film add depth to the story and characters; it must "say all that the dialogue, images, effects, etc., cannot say."

If Morricone has a weakness, it is his incredible productivity, which inevitably leads to the occasionally listless score; this was the critical consensus about his work on the generally forgettable films *So Fine, Butterfly,* and *The Thing.* Writing for *Melody Maker,* Frank Owen found the soundtrack to *The Mission* "just plain dull," calling it a "post-dinner aid to digestion. The sonic equivalent of a ... mint."

Rising at five every morning, Morricone locks himself in his room to keep from becoming distracted by the hubbub of his Italian household. Alluding to his massive body of work, Kennedy asked the composer, who often publishes music under the pseudonym Loe Nichols or Nicola Piovanti, if he ever grows weary of scoring film after film. To this Morricone responded, "I'm not tired of writing music. It's the only thing that I know how to do."

Selected scores

Italian titles translated into English

The Fascist, 1961.
Crazy Desire, 1962.
The Little Nuns, 1963.
A Fistful of Dollars, 1964.
Before the Revolution, 1964.
Nightmare Castle, 1965.
Fist in his Pocket, 1965.
For a Few Dollars More, 1965.
The Hawks and the Sparrows, 1966.
The Good, the Bad, and the Ugly, 1966.
The Battle of Algiers, 1966.
The Hills Run Red, 1966.
Navajo Joe, 1966.
Wake Up and Die, 1966.
The Witches, 1967.
The Girl and the General, 1967.
Death Rides a Horse, 1967.
The Big Gundown, 1967.
Dirty Heroes, 1968.
Come Play with Me, 1968.
A Fine Pair, 1968.

Once upon a Time in the West, 1968.
The Mercenary, 1968.
Dirty Angels, 1968.
Brief Season, 1969.
The Bird with the Crystal Plumage, 1969.
Hornet's Nest, 1970.
Two Mules for Sister Sara, 1970.
Lulu the Tool, 1971.
The Burglars, 1971.
Devil in the Brain, 1972.
Duck You Sucker, 1971.
Far West Story, 1972.
Hearts and Minds, 1973.
Revolver, 1973.
The Devil Is a Woman, 1974.
Night Caller, 1974.
A Thousand and One Nights, 1974.
Space 1999, 1974.
The End of the Game, 1975.
Salo—the 120 Days of Sodom, 1975.
The Sunday Woman, 1975.
1900, 1976.
The Inheritance, 1976.
Down the Ancient Stairs, 1976.
Exorcist II, 1977.
The Heretic, 1977.
Orca—Killer Whale, 1977.
La Cage aux Folles, 1978.
Days of Heaven, 1978.
Bloodline, 1979.
The Meadow, 1979.
The Thief, 1979.
Windows, 1979.
So Fine, 1980.
The Island, 1980.
So Fine, 1980.
The True Story of Camille, 1980.
The Professional, 1981.
The Thing, 1982.
Butterfly, 1983.
The Scarlet and the Black, 1983.
Order of Death (Cop Killer), 1983.
A Time to Die, 1983.
Once upon a Time in America, 1984.
The Seven, 1984.
The Trap, 1985.
Red Sonja, 1985.
Fred and Ginger, 1986.
Good Morning Babylon, 1986.
The Untouchables, 1987.
Frantic, 1987.
Cinema Paradiso, 1988.
Casualties of War, 1989.
Tie Me Up! Tie Me Down!, 1989.
State of Grace, 1990.
Hamlet, 1990.

Voices of the Moon, 1990.
Money, 1991.
Bugsy, 1991.
City of Joy, 1992.
In the Line of Fire, 1993.
Wolf, 1994.
Disclosure, 1994.
A Pure Formality, 1995.

Selected discography

The Good, the Bad, and the Ugly, EMI, 1966.
Once upon a Time in the West, RCA, 1968.
Sacco and Vanzetti, Omega, 1971.
Sahara, Intrada, 1983.
The Untouchables, A&M, 1987.
Hamlet, Virgin, 1990.
State of Grace, MCA, 1990.
Bugsy, Epic, 1991.
City of Joy, Epic, 1992.
In the Line of Fire, Epic, 1993.
Movie Music, Sony Music Italy, 1993.
Wolf, Sony, 1994.
Disclosure, Virgin, 1995.

A Fistful of Film Music: The Ennio Morricone Anthology, Rhino, 1995.
Film Music, Vol. 1, Virgin.
Film Music Vol. 2, Virgin.
Ennio Morricone: His Greatest Themes, Accord.
Legendary Italian Westerns, RCA.

Sources

Books

Karlin, Fred, Listening to Music, Schirmer, 1994.

Periodicals

American Film, February 1994.
Billboard, April 4, 1993.
Entertainment Weekly, February 7, 1992; July 21, 1995.
Film Review, September 1976.
Melody Maker, November 8, 1986.
Newsweek, July 2, 1993.
Village Voice, November 18, 1986.

—Sarah Messer

M
People

Contemporary dance group

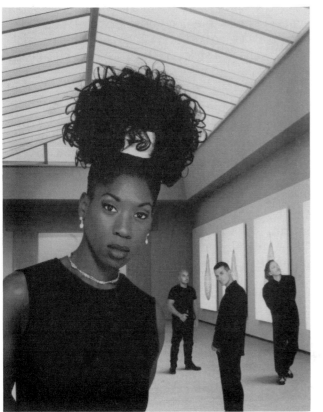

Photograph by Norbert Schoerner, © 1995 Sony Music

In a 1993 issue of *Melody Maker,* Paul Mathur distinguished dance group M People from their colleagues by saying, "More than mere trance chancers, they're fairly keen on things you can hum in the bath." Dance music in the 1990s had for the most part developed a character that was, to some degree, stale and faceless.

As house, techno, and rave music took over European dance floors in the 1980s, it drove out the disco bands of the 1970s, replacing them with electronic beats and sampled voices controlled by a deejay; musical creativity stemmed from the mixing board or turntables, and the only "face" was that of the deejay. Dance "bands" were often flexible collections of musicians combined in the recording studio for each single; there wasn't really a "band" in the celebrity sense to command a following. Consequently, when M People won Britain's prestigious Mercury Music Prize in 1993—pushing aside numerous popular rock outfits—more than a few jaws dropped. Although M People was started in 1991 by deejay Mike Pickering, the group had emerged not just as a powerful force on the dance floor, but as a band with a human presence.

Pickering People

For much of Pickering's working life, deejaying was just another one of the odd jobs he pursued occasionally; he juggled a wide array of callings, some musical and some not—including training as a cook. He got his start in the music business in the 1980s as a roadie for some of England's most important post-punk electronic dance bands, including Joy Division and Kraftwerk. He went on to serve that function for rock band Supertramp, Swedish dance popsters Abba, and Spanish crooner Julio Iglesias. Not content to offer his contribution only behind the scenes, he also played saxophone with a band called Quando Quango. He polished his deejaying skills in Holland, where he moved after the suicide of singer Ian Curtis dissolved Joy Division in 1980. Struck by an absence of dance venues, Pickering decided to open his own club, Rotterdam Must Dance, and in the words of *Detail*'s William Shaw, he "taught the Dutch how to do the electric boogaloo."

Rotterdam Must Dance, however, coincided with a day job that sent Pickering back to England. Washing windows in Rotterdam, he found himself dangling from the side of a skyscraper one day and decided it was time to return home and devote himself to the deejay booth. The Hacienda Club in Manchester, owned by the members of New Order, which had sprung from the remains of Joy Division, offered him a venue to spin records and, ultimately, to build a following. During this time Pickering also had the opportunity to handle the business side of

For the Record . . .

Members include **Paul Heard** (born October 5, 1960, in London, England), bass; **Michael Pickering** (born in 1958 in Manchester, England), deejay; **Shovell**, percussion; and **Heather Small** (born January 20, 1965, in London), vocals.

Group formed with shifting lineup by Pickering in Manchester, 1991; Heard and Small joined permanently, c. 1992; released first album, *Northern Soul,* deConstruction, 1992; signed with Epic label in the U.S., 1994; Shovell joined as permanent percussionist, c. 1994.

Awards: Brit awards for best dance act, 1992 and 1993, and for album of the year, 1993, for *Elegant Slumming*; Mercury Music Prize, 1994.

Addresses: *Record company*—Epic Records, 550 Madison Ave., New York, NY 10022-3211.

music as an A&R (artists and repertoire, the talent scouting area of a record label) representative at Factory Records, the company that had released records by Quando Quango.

Probably of the most use to his future with M People, however, was the remixing work he did for the deConstruction label; here, he cut beat-heavy house singles using the name T-Coy. Not surprisingly, his success as a mixer hinted at other possibilities—rather than reworking other people's compositions, he could create his own. Thus, he decided to embark on M People—or Mike People—in 1991.

Initially, Pickering expected to be the only stable element of M People. He would write the songs and manage the recording, bringing in different musicians to work with him as the need arose. Soon after he began work with Paul Heard and Heather Small, however, that plan changed. Pickering described the band's history to Larry Flick in *Billboard:* "I was looking to collaborate with someone who was very musical when I met Paul. We became great friends and formed a partnership. I wrote 'Colour My Life,' our first club hit, for Heather, though, at the time, I didn't think she'd join us permanently. While we were working on the track, we fell in like family. We became completely connected to one another." Heard, an erstwhile teacher, played bass, which he had done in the past for a string of bands, including Working Week, Strawberry Switchblade, and Orange Juice. Small had less practical experience than either of

her bandmates, but a good deal of obvious vocal talent. She had worked with a soul band called Hot House that drew heavily on her deep, powerful voice, which *Melody Maker* contributor Richard Smith would describe as "at once dignified, desolate and delirious." Small had also worked as an administrative assistant in the Wandsworth Council offices and at the Hammersmith Job Centre.

Released Debut to Immediate Praise

Appropriately, the trio gave their first live performance at the Hacienda Club, where Pickering would continue to deejay even as M People's star rose. M People's debut album, *Northern Soul,* was released in 1992 on deConstruction, which *Melody Maker* contributor Mathur described in March of 1993 as "the most broadly thrilling dance label in the country." The single "Colour My Life"—which *Melody Maker's* Andrew Smith described as "a luxuriant, gently pulsating soul workout lifted by some appealingly funksome piano and singer Heather Small's velveteen voice"—had led the way for the album.

When Mathur reviewed *Northern Soul* for *Melody Maker* the following spring, he applauded the artists for "successfully incorporating the heavenly swish of seventies soul and disco into a nineties musical environment, genuinely reinventing the genre rather than just papering over cracks in a once glittery empire." He further remarked that "almost every track is a potential single, but the variety of styles are held together by immaculately assured production." In fact, both "Colour My Life" and "How Can I Love You More" made the Top Ten and enjoyed extensive club play. Despite this excitement, Mathur would be forced to argue a year later that "M People deserve far more critical respect than is currently lobbed their way."

The group's second effort, however, far outstripped the success of the first. With *Elegant Slumming,* released in October of 1993, M People scored a trio of Top Ten singles—"One Night in Heaven," "Movin' on Up," and "Don't Look Any Further"—which combined to push the album to the Number Two position on the charts. At the Brit Awards that year, M People took home album of the year laurels. They were also named best dance act, the second time they were so honored. In September of 1994, *Elegant Slumming* was named best album of the year at the Mercury Music Prize ceremony.

Billboard's Flick, who had been an M People fan for some time, greeted the release of the second U.K. album with a declaration that the group had "struck a near perfect balance between hip dance culture and radio-savvy pop/soul." He had taken note of M People's dance singles as they were released in England and had encouraged his readers to get to the import bins. Commenting that it "boggles the brain that M People have yet to secure a U.S. major-label deal," Flick urged, "Wake up, folks, it rarely gets better than this." The strength of *Elegant Slumming* did eventually bring the group to the attention of American labels. Epic offered a suitable contract and released a version of *Elegant Slumming* in the U.S. in 1994 that combined cuts from both of M People's British releases.

American audiences, and crowds at dance clubs in particular, drove "Movin' on Up" up the dance charts. As Flick had predicted, "One Night in Heaven" also climbed the rankings, making it to the Number One position on *Billboard*'s Hot Dance Music/Club Play chart. Even before American dance fans began picking up on the M People vibe, Pickering had told Flick, "Although I do feel that our popularity has been slowly building over time, I think we're all a little surprised by the fast success of [*Elegant Slumming*]." At the time Pickering also revealed to Flick his "plan to establish the act as a creatively viable and commercially competitive entity for more than a couple of hit singles."

"Pan-European Purveyors of Soul-Studded Dance"

With *Elegant Slumming*'s release in the U.S., American critics joined Flick in taking notice. Anderson Jones granted it an "A" in his *Entertainment Weekly* review, quipping, "[the] British trio rips through broad pop-soul territory with the voraciousness of a Range Rover." Michael Freedberg waxed poetic in the *Village Voice*, naming "Movin' on Up" "the silkiest danceable diva music." He saved his greatest praise, however, for Small's voice, about which he said, "If Small's high-pressured tenor recovers the luscious anxieties of ... 1950s rhythm and gospel, she's also rocketing atop Mike Pickering's sound effects and tiptoe rhythms direct to enthronement as the queen of clubland."

A tour of the U.K. and Europe in support of *Elegant Slumming* added to the group's already strong tour resume; 1992 had introduced them to enthusiastic audiences at clubs and universities throughout Europe. The group also appeared at a twentieth anniversary party for a London paper, prompting *Melody Maker*'s Mathur to rave anew, contending that the group were "entertainers of the first water and the classiest pan-European purveyors of soul-studded dance."

Not everyone, however, was thrilled with the face M People had put on dance music; some viewed it as a step backward. One critic unimpressed by the M People sound was Richard Smith, who took *Elegant Slumming* to task in *Melody Maker*. "They still do all those things that most dance acts threw in the box marked 'boring' years ago" he wrote, "pushing their personalities, writing songs with verses and choruses and going on tour. Such things are forgivable when they can turn out a funky little monster like 'Movin' on Up,' but most of this album is just soul muzak."

Nonetheless, Pickering kept to his vision for his group, telling Flick: "Dance music does not have to be disposable. You need to be focused on being a real band; the kind that can come up with good, solid songs, and can play them live. A few years ago, you could get away with ... a 'Who sings? Who cares?' attitude. These days, people do care."

By the spring of 1995, M People had expanded to a quartet—bringing drummer Shovell in permanently—and had produced its third album, *Bizarre Fruit*. The first single, "Open Your Heart," entered the Top Five on U.S. dance charts, reflecting its popularity in the clubs. By this time, however, the album had already achieved platinum status in the U.K. (one million copies sold). *Elle*'s Adele Sulcas called the album "a juicy set of tightly structured songs," while Jeremy Helligar reported in *People* that the group "stuffs in all the best elements of timeless R&B: soaring melodies, gospel backdrops, joy in repetition and big, distinctive vocals." Concluded Jonathan Gold in *Vanity Fair*, "'Bizarre Fruit' threatens to make [M People] the most popular British dance group in the U.S."

Selected discography

Northern Soul (includes "Colour My Life"), deConstruction, 1992.
Elegant Slumming (includes "One Night in Heaven," "Movin' on Up," and "Don't Look Any Further"), deConstruction, 1993, Epic, 1994.
Bizarre Fruit (includes "Open Your Heart"), Epic, 1995.

Sources

Billboard, June 5, 1993; October 23, 1993; September 24, 1994; June 24, 1995.
Details, May 1995.
Elle, June 1995.
Entertainment Weekly, July 15, 1994.
Melody Maker, June 1, 1991; March 28, 1992; March 27, 1993; June 12, 1993; July 17, 1993; October 30, 1993.

Out, May 1995.
People, May 22, 1995.
Rolling Stone, August 10, 1995.
Vanity Fair, May 1995.
Village Voice, August 23, 1994.

Additional information for this profile was obtained from Epic Records publicity materials, 1995.

—Ondine E. Le Blanc

Michael Nyman

Film composer

Photograph by Nigel Parry, courtesy of Decca Records

As if describing his own musical career, composer Michael Nyman told *Time* magazine, "music is power, passion, pulse, pain." Indeed, he has reached the "power" of commercial success. He has exemplified the "passion" of composition—and has reacted passionately to the lack of respect he has sometimes received from British critics and contemporary composers. His long list of compositions has proved the nonstop "pulse" of his creative output. And despite his accomplishments, Nyman has discussed how the music community once defined him as a film composer and the "pains" he went through to break out of that confinement to gain recognition as a multitalented, crossover composer.

Nyman's interest in music began in childhood. At the age of eight, his talent earned the attention of his instructor, Leslie J. Winters, at the Chase Lane School in Northeast London. "I couldn't sing or play, but he saw some quality in me no one had noticed before," Nyman told Timothy White in *Billboard.* "It's one of the mysteries of my life."

Nyman went on to study at the Royal Academy of Music and at King's College in London. His mentors in school included English harpsichordist Thurston Dart and the composer Alan Bush. Nyman's instructors purported the idea that serial music—music founded on a set of tones displaying a particular pattern and disregarding traditional tonality—was the only music worth writing. Nyman attempted to write serial pieces, but he eventually gave up composing in 1964. Instead, he went to work as a music writer and critic for the *Listener, New Statesman,* and *Spectator.*

From Critic to Composer

In 1968 Nyman introduced the term "minimalism" to musical parlance in a review of English composer Cornelius Cardew's *The Great Learning.* Nyman published a book on minimalism in 1974 titled *Experimental Music—Cage and Beyond.* In his book, Nyman explained how the work of English experimentalists like John Cage and John White ventured into new areas of composing. He wrote that these composers gave permission to use a single phrase from a classical piece of the past as a resource for an entire composition. In fact, Nyman would later use this same technique in some of his own musical compositions.

Two years after Nyman's book was released, Henry Birtwistle, the director of music at the National Theatre in England, asked Nyman to arrange the music for a production of *Il Campiello* by Italian librettist Carlo Goldoni. Nyman formed a band for the stage production

For the Record . . .

Born March 23, 1944, in London, England; son of Mark and Jeanette Nyman; married, wife's name, Aet. *Education*: Graduated from Royal Academy of Music and King's College.

Music writer, 1964-76; wrote book *Experimental Music—Cage and Beyond*, 1974; began composing professionally with *Il Campiello*, 1976; released first film soundtrack, *One to One-Hundred*, 1976; composed opera *The Man Who Mistook His Wife for a Hat*, 1986; composed soundtrack for film *The Piano*, 1993.

Addresses: *Record company*—Argo, Worldwide Plaza, 825 Eighth Ave., New York, NY 10019.

which featured a combination of period instruments, including rebecs and sackbuts, as well as other instruments, like the banjo and saxophone. During his participation in *Il Campiello*, Nyman composed some incidental music that effectively revived his composition career. He continued working with the band he'd formed, later known as the Michael Nyman Band, and found his own minimalist style in his composition of *In Re Don Giovanni*.

Nyman began his long collaborative relationship with filmmaker Peter Greenaway in the mid-1970s, writing the musical scores for Greenaway's sequence of British Film Institute shorts. The two released the first of their 18 short and feature films, *One to One-Hundred*, in 1976. Unlike most film composers, Nyman wrote the music for Greenaway's films in long, continuous streams before the film began shooting. Once Greenaway finished filming, he would trim the music to fit the visual images, making Nyman's music an integral part of the production.

A Decade of New Beginnings

In 1977 Nyman released two of his works on the Obscure Records British music collection. *Bell Set No. 1* and *One to One-Hundred* filled an entire side of *Obscure 6: Decay Music*. His music achieved international notoriety with the soundtrack for the Greenaway film *The Draughtsman's Contract* in 1982. Nyman and Greenaway continued their collaborative relationship throughout the 1980s, scoring films like *A Zed and Two Noughts*, *Drowning by Numbers*, and *The Cook, the Thief, His Wife and Her Lover*.

During the mid-1980s, Nyman wrote his first string quartet, *String Quartet No. 1*, for the Arditti Quartet. The

foundation for this piece came from Schoenberg's *String Quartet No. 2*. He followed with *String Quartet No. 2* and *String Quartet No. 3* in 1988 and 1990, respectively.

Another first in Nyman's career came in 1986 when he released his own opera, titled *The Man Who Mistook His Wife for a Hat*. He based the story on a book by American neurologist Oliver Sacks about a music professor, Dr. P, who suffers from visual agnosia (the inability to recognize what he sees). Dr. P depended on certain songs to guide him through his disorder—eating songs, dressing songs, bathing songs. "When I performed that piece for the first time in October 1986," Nyman told *Billboard*, "I came off stage shaking with emotion. My attitude when writing it was very cool, analytical, yet I somehow injected the material with great empathy."

Commercial Success and Critical Remarks

Nyman ended his long partnership with Peter Greenaway after the release of the film *Prospero's Books*, based on William Shakespeare's play *The Tempest*. Nyman used three singers from different genres—rock, opera, and cabaret—in the work. *Prospero's Books* was the first musical collaboration between Nyman and German cabaret singer Ute Lemper. It was the last of his pairings with Greenaway, however, because of changes and additions Greenaway made to Nyman's original score.

In 1991 Nyman produced a flood of new compositions. In a single year, he signed a new record deal, with Argo/Decca/London; wrote *Songbook*, which included the "Six Celan Songs" that he wrote for Ute Lemper and with whom he performed them all over the world; and wrote six song-texts called *Letters, Riddles and Writs*, a music-theater piece for the BBC's "Not Mozart" series. The music for "Not Mozart" actually consists of reworkings from Mozart's *Magic Flute*, *Don Giovanni*, and portions of his string quartets. The words came from letters written by Mozart and his father to each other. Nyman explained in the *Independent* why he feels such a connection to Mozart, a connection critics had not detected: "Did Mozart write for love? No. He wrote for money. And he had a father who was more of a PR agent than I've ever had: a man who walked around with his son's manuscripts in his back pocket ready to show off to any likely patron. No one held that against Mozart as they would against me."

Despite his break with Greenaway, Nyman continued to write for film. In 1992 he wrote the score for the French film *The Hairdresser's Husband*, directed by Pierre Leconte. The film score that gained Nyman international commercial success, however, was *The Piano*, released in 1993. *The Piano* soundtrack reached gold record status in the U.S. and sold over 1.5 million copies worldwide.

Nyman celebrated his 50th birthday in 1994 with five orchestral commissions; two LPs, *The Piano Concerto and MGV* and *Breaking the Rules;* and the Michael Nyman Band's North American debut tour. The following year, he released the score for the dance opera *The Princess of Milan* by Karine Saporta. Like *Prospero's Books,* the story line is based on Shakespeare's *The Tempest.* In early 1995, Nyman was working on a possible U.S. commission for his cherished operatic version of *Tristam Shandy,* which he describes as the ultimate "stackable" opera.

Despite his warm manner with close friends, reported *ABC Radio 24 Hours,* Nyman can seem aloof and confesses to a certain shyness. "Work is a great avoidance mechanism," he explained, "it allows me to distance myself from humans." Nyman's long and prolific musical career has brought him prosperity. He lives in an eighteenth-century farmhouse in the French Pyrenees with his wife, Aet, and composes in a converted barn. He also maintains a four-story Victorian home in London with a studio on the top floor. "I don't write music to grab a large audience, though I'm pleased that I do," Nyman told *Time.* "But success doesn't exactly help you confront that terrible blank page. When I sit down to write a piece of music, it's still the same old Michael Nyman, excited and terrified at the same time."

Selected discography

One to One-Hundred, Argo, 1976.
Obscure 6: Decay Music (compilation), Obscure, 1977.
The Draughtsman's Contract, Argo, 1982.
String Quartet No. 1, Argo, 1985.
A Zed and Two Noughts, Virgin, 1985.
And They Do, That's Entertainment, 1986.
The Man Who Mistook His Wife for a Hat, CBS, 1986.
Zoo Caprices, That's Entertainment, 1986.
Drowning by Numbers, Virgin, 1987.
String Quartet No. 2, Argo, 1988.
The Cook, the Thief, His Wife and Her Lover, Virgin, 1989.
Out of the Ruins, Silva Screen, 1989.
String Quartet No. 3, Argo, 1990.
Prospero's Books, Decca/London, 1991.
Flugel and Piano: For Flugelhorn & Piano, Virgin, 1991.
String Quartets 1-3, Argo, 1991.

The Convertibility of Lute Strings for Harpsichord, Argo, 1992.
For John Cage: For Brass Ensemble, Argo, 1992.
Time Will Pronounce, Argo, 1992.
The Essential Michael Nyman Band, Argo, 1992.
(With Ute Lemper) *Songbook,* Argo, 1992.
The Piano, Virgin, 1993.
The Piano Concerto and MGV ("Musique a Grande Vitesse"), Argo, 1994.
Breaking the Rules, Virgin, 1994.
The Princess of Milan, Argo, 1995.

Sources

Books

Mertens, Wim, *American Minimal Music,* Alexander Broude, Inc., 1983.
Nyman, Michael, *Experimental Music: Cage and Beyond,* Schirmer Books, 1974.

Periodicals

ABC Radio 24 Hours, June 1993.
BBC Music Magazine, April 1993.
Billboard, October 23, 1993; September 10, 1994; October 1, 1994.
Classic CD, March 1992.
Gramophone, August 1991; July 1993.
Guardian, October 5, 1993; November 12, 1993.
Independent, November 8, 1991; December 1, 1993.
Keyboard, October 1993.
Music & Musicians, September 1969; October 1971; January 1977.
Musical Events, December 1969.
Musical Times, December 1973.
New Republic, July 27, 1992.
New York Times, May 5, 1991; March 15, 1992.
Observer Life, February 20, 1994.
Opera, July 1980; January 1987; June 1987; August 1987; October 1987; March 1990; September 1992.
Pulse!, May 1993.
Q Magazine, September 1993.
Sunday Times (London), January 9, 1994.
Sunday Times Magazine (London), October 31, 1993.
Time, November 14, 1994.
Wire, July 1993.

Additional information for this profile was obtained from Virgin Records and Argo Records press materials, 1995.

—Sonya Shelton

King Oliver

Cornetist, trumpeter

Archive Photos/Frank Driggs Collection

Billed as the "World's Greatest Cornetist," Joe "King" Oliver reigned as the premier trumpeter of jazz during the early 1920s. The famed musical mentor of Louis Armstrong, Oliver is perhaps best remembered for bringing the young New Orleans hornman to Chicago in 1922. With Armstrong on second cornet, Oliver performed double-cornet breaks that sent shock waves through the jazz world. Years later, Armstrong paid tribute to his elder, noting, as quoted in the liner notes to *King Oliver "Papa Joe" (1926-1928),* that "if it had not been for Joe Oliver, jazz would not be what it is today."

Joseph "King" Oliver was born around New Orleans, Louisiana, on May 11, 1885. Over the next several years, his family moved a number of times, primarily throughout New Orleans's Garden District, a section filled with large antebellum homes and high-walled courtyards. After the death of his mother in 1900, Oliver was raised by his older half-sister, Victoria Davis. He first performed on cornet with a children's brass band under the direction of a man named Kenhen, who frequently took the ensemble on out-of-state tours. While on the road with the band, Oliver got into a fight that left him with a noticeable scar over his left eye. (The white cataract on the same eye was supposedly caused by a childhood accident.)

Like most New Orleans musicians in the early twentieth century, Oliver could not support himself solely by music. While working as a butler, his employers allowed him to hire an occasional substitute so that he could play with local brass bands that performed at picnics, funerals, and dances in the area. For over a decade, he appeared with a number of march-oriented brass bands, including the Eagle Band, the Onward Brass Band, the Melrose Brass Band, the Magnolia Band, the Original Superior, and Allen's Brass Band. As a member of these ensembles, Oliver established connections with a number of musicians, many of whom, like fellow Melrose bandmate Honoré Dutrey, would become members of his famous Chicago-based group.

The King of Storyville

In the evenings, Oliver played at cabarets and dance halls throughout New Orleans. Early in his career, he performed with pianist Richard M. Jones's Four Hot Hounds at the Abadie Cabaret. In 1911 society bandleader-violinist A. S. Piron took over leadership of the Olympia Band and hired Oliver to fill the band's trumpet chair, which was formerly occupied by departing leader Freddie Keppard. Over the next decade, Oliver worked at Billy Phillip's 101 Ranch and at Storyville establishments like Pete Lala's Cafe and the Big 25. In an interview for *Jazz Panorama,* a resident of New Orleans

Born May 11, 1885, in New Orleans (some sources say Donaldsville), LA; died April 8, 1938, in Savannah, GA.

Cornetist, trumpeter. Began playing in children's brass band; while a youngster worked as a yard boy and later as a butler; performed with a number of New Orleans brass bands, including the Eagle, Onward, Melrose, Magnolia, and Original Superior; played at nightspots in and around Storyville, LA; went to Chicago with Jimmy Noone to join bassist Bill Johnson's band and doubled in a band led by Lawrence Duhé, 1918; led own band at the Dreamland, 1920; took his band to San Francisco to play the Pergola Dance Pavilion, 1921, and also played gigs in Los Angeles; returned to Chicago in April of 1922 and led own Creole Jazz Band at the Lincoln Gardens; recruited Louis Armstrong to play in the band, 1922; briefly joined Dave Peyton's Symphonic Syncopators, 1924; led his Dixie Syncopators at Plantation Cafe, 1925-27; performed on recordings with Clarence Williams, 1928; formed another band and toured, 1930-37.

named Edmond Souchon recalled seeing King Oliver outside the Big 25: "I'll never forget how big and tough he looked! His brown derby was tilted low over one eye, his shirt collar was open at the neck, and a bright red undershirt peeked out at the V. Wide suspenders held up an expanse of trousers of unbelievable width."

Oliver's musical reputation soon began to match his imposing stature, and by 1917 he became a formidable figure on the New Orleans music scene. His forceful melodic phrasing and use of assorted trumpet mutes earned him the title of "King." In his autobiography *Pops Foster*, New Orleans bassist Foster related how "Joe had all kinds of things he put on his horn. He used to shove a kazoo in the bell to give it a different effect." Because of Oliver's unorthodox use of objects to mute his horn, trumpeter Mutt Carey, as quoted in *Hear Me Talkin' to Ya*, referred to Oliver as a "freak trumpeter" who "did most of his playing with cups, glasses, buckets, and mutes."

Along with his passion for music, Oliver possessed an equally voracious appetite for food. His diet consisted of sugar sandwiches made from whole loaves of bread, which he chased down with a pot of tea or a pitcher of sugar water. Foster recalled how Oliver would eat six hamburgers and a quart of milk in one sitting or how—with one dip of a finger—he would pull out an entire

pouch of tobacco and chew it while blowing his horn. Affectionately known as "Papa Joe" by musicians, he was also called "Tenderfoot" because of the painful corns that covered his feet.

In 1918 bassist Bill Johnson invited Oliver to join his band at Chicago's Royal Gardens. He accepted the offer and left for Chicago with clarinetist Jimmy Noone. Housed in a large building on 31st Street, the Royal Gardens—soon to be renamed the Lincoln Gardens—had an upstairs balcony and a spotlighted crystal chandelier that reflected on the dance floor. While playing the Gardens, Oliver doubled in another group at the Dreamland Cafe led by Lawrence Duhé. By 1920 he was leading King Oliver's Creole Jazz Band at the Dreamland and playing a second engagement from one till six in the morning at a State Street gangster hangout. During the following year, his band played a brief engagement at the Pergola Dance Pavilion in San Francisco. From the Pergola, the band traveled southward to perform in Los Angeles.

Armstrong Arrives

Returning to Chicago in 1922, Oliver booked his Creole Jazz Band at the Lincoln Gardens. That autumn he decided to add a second cornet to his band and sent a telegram to Louis Armstrong in New Orleans, inviting him to join the group. A devout student of the Oliver style, Armstrong went north to play with the band in 1922. In *Selections from the Gutter*, Oliver's drummer, Baby Dodds, recalled the impact of Armstong's arrival: "I was pleased because I had a chance to work with Louis again. Our music was appreciated in Chicago and it made you free and easy. We played so much music that I dreamed about it at night and woke up thinking about it." Musicians from Paul Whiteman to Guy Lombardo came to study the music of Oliver's ensemble. Some musicians even took notes on their shirt sleeves.

"From the testimony of musicians (and fans) who heard the 1922-1924 Oliver band live," wrote Dan Morganstern in the liner notes to *Louis Armstrong: Portrait of the Artist as a Young Man, 1923-1934*, "its most potent attraction was the unique cornet team." Though Oliver and Armstrong's double-breaks appeared to exhibit a natural sense of spontaneity and interplay, they "were in fact worked out in a most ingenious way: at a given point in the preceding collective band chorus, Oliver would play what he intended to use as his part in the break, and Armstrong, lightning-quick on the up-take, would memorize it and devise his own second part—which always fit to perfection." As Armstrong explained in his autobiography, *Louis Armstrong—A Self Portrait,*

"Whatever Mister Joe played, I just put notes to it trying to make it sound as pretty as I could. I never blew my horn over Joe Oliver at no time unless he said, 'Take it!' Never. Papa Joe was a creator—always some little idea—and he exercised them beautifully."

"If it had not been for Joe Oliver, jazz would not be what it is today."
—Louis Armstrong

On March 31, 1923, the Oliver Band entered the Gennet Recording Company Studios in Richmond, Indiana. Along with trumpeter Armstrong, clarinetist Johnny Dodds, pianist Lil Hardin, bassist Bill Johnson, and drummer Baby Dodds, Oliver created some of the most memorable sides in jazz history. The Gennet session produced several classics, including the legendary "Dipper Mouth Blues," a title taken from Armstrong's nickname. In describing the Gennet sides, Martin Williams wrote in *Jazz Masters of New Orleans,* "They do not have merely historical or documentary interest, and their emotional impact cuts across the years." Williams added, "The most immediately impressive characteristic of the music of King Oliver's Creole Jazz Band is its unity, the wonderful integration of parts with which the individual players contribute to a dense, often heterophonic texture of improvised melodies. The tempos are right, the excitement of the music is projected with firmness and ease, and the peaks and climaxes come with musical excitement rather than personal frenzy, with each individual in exact control of what he is about."

In 1924 Oliver's band toured the Orpheum Theater circuit throughout the Midwest, including stops in Wisconsin, Ohio, Michigan, and Pennsylvania. Urged on by his then-wife and fellow Oliver bandmember Lil Hardin, Armstrong left the group in June to join the Fletcher Henderson Orchestra. Then, on Christmas Eve of the same year, the burning of the Lincoln Gardens resulted in the disbanding of Oliver's Creole Jazz Band. Oliver took a temporary job at the Plantation Club with Dave Peyton's Symphonic Syncopators. Soon thereafter, he brought a number of talented New Orleans musicians—including reedmen Albert Nicholas and Barney Bigard, drummer Paul Barbarin, and trumpeter Tommy Ladnier—into Peyton's band. By 1925 Oliver had taken over the band. Billed as the Dixie Syncopators, the band was reorganized; with the addition of three saxophones, the Syncopators began a two-year job at the Plantation Club.

Despite the band's wealth of talent, the Dixie Syncopators experienced problems as they expanded. After 1925 the group relied primarily on stock arrangements. In the studio, the larger band—once able to rely on intuitive group discipline—faced the problem of allowing for more individuality among members. As Williams observed in *Jazz Masters of New Orleans,* "The Syncopators' rhythms are usually heavy, the horns and percussion are often unsure, the ensembles are sometimes sloppy. One passage will swing beautifully, the next will flounder." On record the band did experience occasional moments of brilliance, especially with the presence of saxophonist-arranger Billy Paige, who contributed to the 1926 sides "Too Bad" and "Snag It."

After the police closed down the Plantation Club in 1927, Oliver and his band played short engagements in Milwaukee and Detroit. These appearances were followed by a two-week stint at the Savoy Ballroom in New York City. Though the newspapers hailed Oliver's visit, the Syncopators did not take the city by storm. The band received a warm reception, but Oliver's invasion of the East had come too late. After the arrival of Armstrong and others, New York City's music scene began to lose interest in authentic New Orleans music. Though he was offered a job at the soon-to-be famous nightspot the Cotton Club, Oliver, dissatisfied with the financial arrangement, declined the engagement. The position went to a young pianist named Edward Kennedy "Duke" Ellington.

After the visit to New York, Oliver sustained himself and his bands with money from a recording contract he had established with the Victor company in 1928. Unlike his earlier label, Vocalion-Brunswick, which allowed him a great deal of creative freedom, Victor limited Oliver's creative input. By 1930 the contract with Victor had expired, and the group disbanded.

The Descent of the King

In 1931 Oliver assembled another band composed of younger musicians and toured the South and Southwest. For the next several years, he struggled with personnel changes, broken-down buses, canceled engagements, and jobs played without compensation. A proud man, Oliver always made sure his band took the stage neatly dressed and organized. But behind the scenes, his health began to decline. By 1935 he could no longer play the trumpet: pyorrhea had caused the loss of his teeth and painful bleeding of his gums. The next year, he moved to Savannah, Georgia. Unable to play his horn, he is said to have appeared at his last engagements sitting in a chair—often wearing slippers. Bankrupt and nearly forgotten, Oliver spent the last year of his life in Savannah running a fruit stand and working as a poolhall janitor. He died in Savannah on April 8, 1938.

Oliver's body was taken to New York for burial, where his stepsister spent her rent money to pay for the funeral—an occasion that attracted Armstrong and a number of musicians who never forgot their debt to Papa Joe Oliver.

With time, perhaps Oliver's musical legacy will overshadow the story of his tragic downfall and early death—and once again bring recognition to a man who ruled New Orleans and Chicago's South Side as the king of the jazz trumpet. Though his recordings remain crude by today's standards, they represent moving portraits of sound that provide the listener with audible passages into American cultural history. As musician and writer Gunther Schuller wrote in *Early Jazz: Its Roots and Musical Development,* "Oliver's Creole Jazz Band represents one of jazz's great achievements. It is worthy of our close attention, not only for its own merits, but for the lessons it can still teach us."

Selected discography

King Oliver and His Dixie Syncopators: Sugar Foot Stomp, MCA & GRP Records, 1992.
Jazz Classics in Digital Stereo: Vol. 1, New Orleans, Smithsonian Folkways.
Jazz Classics in Digital Stereo: Vol. 2, Chicago, Smithsonian Folkways.
King Oliver "Papa Joe" (1926-1928), Decca.
Louis Armstrong and King Oliver, Milestone Records.
RCA-Victor Jazz: The First Half Century—The Twenties through the Sixties, RCA.
The Riverside History of Classic Jazz, Riverside.
Sound of the Trumpets, GRP Records.

Sources

Armstrong, Louis, *Louis Armstrong—A Self Portrait: An Interview by Richard Merryman,* Eakins Press, 1971.
Foster, Pops, *Pops Foster: The Autobiography of a New Orleans Jazzman As Told to Tom Stoddard,* University of California Press, 1971.
Hear Me Talkin' to Ya: The Story of Jazz As Told by the Men Who Made It, edited by Nat Shapiro and Nat Hentoff, Dover Publications, 1955.
Jazz Panorama: From the Birth to Dixieland to the Latest "Third Stream" Innovations—The Sounds of Jazz and the Men Who Make Them, edited by Martin Williams, Collier Books, 1964.
Schuller, Gunther, *Early Jazz: Its Roots and Musical Development,* Oxford University Press, 1986.
Selections from the Gutter: Jazz Portraits from the "Jazz Record," edited by Art Hodes and Chadwick Hansen, 1977.
Williams, Martin, *Jazz Masters of New Orleans,* Macmillan, 1967.
Williams, *Kings of Jazz: King Oliver,* A. S. Barnes and Company, 1961.

Additional information for this profile was obtained from the liner notes to *Louis Armstrong: Portrait of the Artist as a Young Man, 1923-1934,* by Dan Morganstern, Columbia/Legacy, 1994, and the notes to *King Oliver "Papa Joe" (1926-1928),* Decca, by Panassié Hugues.

—John Cohassey

Tony Orlando

Singer

In some circumstances, popular songs can take on a significance far beyond their melody or lyrics alone. Such was the case for "Tie a Yellow Ribbon 'Round the Old Oak Tree," the second Number One hit for Tony Orlando and Dawn. This simple, upbeat tune was released in the early 1970s when American families were anxiously awaiting news about soldiers missing in the Vietnam War. Later it resurfaced when U.S. citizens were held hostage in Iran. By the time American troops participated in Operation Desert Storm in 1990, the image of yellow ribbons worn in hopes of the return of a loved one had become a national norm—a testament to the power of even the simplest pop music piece.

Tony Orlando, a songwriter, music publisher, and performer, admits that the works he recorded with Telma Louise Hopkins and Joyce Vincent-Wilson as Tony Orlando and Dawn were "corny." He told *Newsweek:* "I kept wondering who would listen to that crap." But it seemed as if all America listened in the early 1970s, as Orlando and his two comely backup vocalists turned out hits such as "Knock Three Times," "Candida," "Tie a Yellow Ribbon," and "He Don't Love You (Like I Love You)." Tony Orlando and Dawn posted nearly 30 million in record sales, released two platinum albums, and won two American Music Awards. Scorned by the critics, this unconventional interracial trio found a permanent place in the annals of pop music—and in the psyche of Middle America.

Born Michael Anthony Orlando Cassavitis in New York City in 1944, Tony Orlando grew up in a straight-laced family that was beset with enormous burdens. His father was a furrier of Greek ancestry, his mother was an immigrant from Puerto Rico. Orlando's only sibling, a sister named Rhonda Marie, was mentally retarded. He spent much of his youth caring for her, so he managed to avoid the pitfalls of alcohol and drugs that were threatening his working-class neighborhood.

While still a teenager, Orlando began performing, cutting demo tapes with composers and searching for rock and roll tunes that he could parlay into hits. At 16 he auditioned for producer Don Kirshner, who helped him to record the singles "Halfway to Paradise" and "Bless You." The latter song reached Number 15 on the pop charts in 1961. Orlando was unable to sustain his performing career in the mid-1960s, however, so he found work in the publishing sector of the business. By 1967 he was manager of April-Blackwood Music, a subsidiary of Columbia Records.

In 1970 a friend of Orlando's asked him to overdub the lead vocals for a new song by a group named Dawn out of Detroit. Orlando had never met the members of Dawn, and when he heard the song "Candida," he

For the Record . . .

Born Michael Anthony Orlando Cassavitis, April 3, 1944, in New York City; married second wife Frannie Amormino, 1991; children: (first marriage) Jon; (second marriage) Jenny Rose.

Pop singer, beginning 1960; manager of April-Blackwood Music (publishing arm of Columbia Records), 1967-71; member (with Telma Louise Hopkins and Joyce Elaine Vincent-Wilson) of Tony Orlando and Dawn, beginning 1971; group played briefly in 1971 as Dawn, featuring Tony Orlando. Hit singles include "Halfway to Paradise," 1961; "Bless You," 1961; "Candida," 1971; "Knock Three Times," 1971; "Tie a Yellow Ribbon 'Round the Old Oak Tree," 1973; and "He Don't Love You (Like I Love You)," 1975.

Principal television work includes *Tony Orlando and Dawn* (variety series), CBS, 1974-76; episodes of *Chico and the Man* and *The Tonight Show*; specials *The Johnny Cash Christmas Special,* 1976, and *Bob Hope Presents a Celebration with Stars of Comedy and Music,* 1981. Principal stage work includes *Barnum,* St. James Theatre, New York City, 1981.

Selected awards: Two Grammy Award nominations for vocal performance with a group; two American Music Awards for vocal performance with a group.

Addresses: *Record company*—Rhino Records, 10635 Santa Monica Blvd., Los Angeles, CA 90025-1900.

thought it would disappear from the charts without a trace. He did the vocals as a favor to his friend, and "Candida" became a Number Three hit on the Billboard pop charts in 1971. The song's success led Orlando to quit his music publishing job. He teamed with the young women in Dawn, and together they recorded a string of numbers with the same catchy optimism as "Candida."

Tony Orlando and Dawn became one of the best-known pop groups in America during the last years of the Vietnam War. In 1971 the trio had a Number One hit with "Knock Three Times," a cheerful take on love in an apartment building. The group's biggest hit found the charts in 1973—"Tie a Yellow Ribbon," a ballad about a paroled prisoner looking for a sign of affection from his sweetheart. In ordinary times the song might have had little relevance beyond its catchy pop sound, but as Americans agonized over the fate of missing soldiers in Vietnam, the hit's gentle tale of faithful love came to symbolize the homefront devotion to missing comrades. That same spirit of devotion gave the song a second life when Americans were taken hostage in Iran later in the 1970s. "Tie a Yellow Ribbon 'Round the Old Oak Tree" was the biggest-selling single of 1973.

Other Tony Orlando and Dawn hits included "Say Has Anybody Seen My Sweet Gypsy Rose" in 1973 and "He Don't Love You (Like I Love You)" in 1975. The group's middle-of-the-road appeal helped them to land a prime-time television variety show, *Tony Orlando and Dawn,* that ran from 1974 until 1976. Then, amidst reports that Hopkins and Vincent-Wilson were dissatisfied with their contracts, the show was cancelled and the group disbanded.

For Orlando, 1977 marked the low point in his career and personal life. He was stunned by the deaths of his beloved sister and his best friend, comedian-actor Freddie Prinze, who had hit it big as the star of the sitcom *Chico and the Man* before taking his own life. Orlando also later admitted to abusing cocaine and to driving himself to the point of exhaustion for the television variety show. Finally he suffered a complete nervous breakdown and retired from show business for an extended period. After a long recuperation, he began to accept engagements again, including an appearance in the Broadway play *Barnum* in 1981.

In 1988 Orlando teamed with Hopkins and Vincent-Wilson again, and the trio performed their old hits and other similar tunes in a popular nightclub act. They still do occasional shows together. Reflecting on his work with his two singing partners, Orlando told *Jet* magazine: "There is a unique feeling with Telma and Joyce that is separate from the music. That wonderful sense—that rush that only harmony can give you. There is something about those two voices and being that middle voice in that pocket of harmony."

Tony Orlando and Dawn proved that pop music need not only appeal to the young. Their vaudeville-styled numbers with their shameless Tin Pan Alley lyrics found an audience that broke the barriers of age and race. Few multiracial groups have enjoyed more commercial success, and fewer still have left a lasting cultural legacy with such irrepressibly cheerful music.

Selected discography

Candida, Bell, 1970.
Tony Orlando and Dawn's Greatest Hits, Arista, 1975.
The Best of Tony Orlando and Dawn, Rhino, 1994.

Sources

Books

Contemporary Theatre, Film, and Television, Volume 6, Gale, 1989.

Periodicals

Entertainment Weekly, August 12, 1994.
Jet, October 10, 1988.
Newsweek, January 27, 1975.
People, May 11, 1981; July 17, 1995.

—*Anne Janette Johnson*

Eddie Palmieri

Percussionist, pianist, composer

Photograph by Joel Meyerowitz, courtesy of Berkely Agency

Eddie Palmieri, also known as "The Latin Sun King," is a vital force in Latin music's Afro-Caribbean jazz movement and vibrant, drum-anchored improvisational salsa. Palmieri is often credited with creating modern salsa music—a hybrid of rhythm and blues, jazz, and rock 'n' roll; his band La Perfecta defined the lively sound of Latin New York in the 1960s. But he told *New York Latino* contributor Larry Birnbaum: "We have to eliminate the word salsa.... It's Afro-Caribbean music. Musicians have been playing this type of music in America for more than fifty years—ever since a Cuban drummer named Chano Pozo turned Dizzy Gillespie's whole orchestra around in 1947."

Having garnered five Grammy Awards between 1975 and 1994, Palmieri has fought tirelessly to bring recognition to Latin and Afro-Caribbean music. He was appointed to the board of governors of the New York chapter of the National Association of Recording Arts & Sciences (NARAS) in 1993. In addition, Palmieri has been instrumental in expanding the coverage of Latin music at the Grammy Awards. He helped institute the Latin/African-Caribbean Jazz category, beginning in 1995.

Palmieri was born in New York City's East Harlem section in 1936. He was raised in the South Bronx, where his father, an electrician by trade, ran a luncheonette called El Mambo. Palmieri's mother, a seamstress, believed that music was an important part of a child's education, so Palmieri began taking piano lessons at the age of eight, following in his older brother Charlie's footsteps. But his true love was reserved for percussion.

"I am a percussionist," Palmieri told *Columbus Dispatch* contributor Bill Eichenberger. "[I] work with complex African rhythmic patterns that are centuries old. The intriguing thing for me is to layer jazz phrasings and harmony on top of those patterns." Percussionist Tito Puente was Palmieri's greatest influence and idol, along with Tito Rodriguez and the Machito Orchestra, who gained popularity in the 1940s.

The Birth of "Salsa"

At the age of thirteen, Palmieri played timbales in Chino y sus Almas Tropicales, a band led by his uncle. New York City was exploding with Afro-Cuban dance music at the time. The blending of mambo and cha-cha rhythms with R&B, jazz, and rock gave birth to what would eventually be called "salsa." In 1951 Palmieri switched from timbales to piano and founded a nine-piece group with singer Joe Quijano. Four years later, Palmieri—not yet 20 years old—replaced his brother Charlie as a pianist in Johnny Segui's band. Then, in 1958, he joined Tito Rodriguez's mambo orchestra.

For the Record...

Born Edward Palmieri, December 15, 1936, in East Harlem, NY; raised in the South Bronx; son of an electrician/luncheonette owner and a seamstress; married; wife's name, Iraida; children: five.

Began playing piano and timbales at age eight; played timbales with Chino y sus Almas Tropicales (a band led by his uncle), 1949; switched to piano, 1951, and founded a nine-piece group with singer Joe Quijano; replaced his brother, Charlie, as a pianist in Johnny Segui's band, 1955; joined Tito Rodriguez's mambo orchestra, 1958; organized first band, La Perfecta, 1961, and recorded self-titled debut album; band played New York City's Palladium for five years; bandmembers included Manny Oquendo (timbales), Tommy Lopez (congas), Barry Rogers (trombone), George Castro (flute), and Ishmael Quintana (vocals).

La Perfecta disbanded, 1968; Palmieri recorded civil rights anthems and "boogaloos" with Harlem River Drive; formed Eddie Palmieri Orchestra in Puerto Rico, early 1980s; returned to New York City, late 1980s; recorded *Sueno, Intuition,* and *Llego la India,* Soho Sounds, both 1989; signed with Nonesuch Records; released *Palmas,* 1994; contributed to *Breaking the Silence,* a video about HIV and AIDS aimed at women in the Latin community, 1994; host of lecture/performance *The Evolution of the Afro-Caribbean Rhythm Section,* 1994.

Awards: Grammy Award for best Latin album, 1975, for *The Sun of Latin Music;* 1976, for *Unfinished Masterpiece;* 1983, for *Palo Pa' Rumba;* 1984, for *Solito;* and 1987, for *La Verdad;* voted "beyond artist of the year" in a *Down Beat* critics' poll, 1995.

Addresses: *Record company*—Elektra/Nonesuch, 75 Rockefeller Plaza, New York, NY 10019. *Publicity*—Maria Echeverria, D. L. Media, 155 E. 23rd St., Suite 607, New York, NY 10010.

Palmieri organized his first band, La Perfecta, in 1961, when he was just 25. Around the same time, he acquired the nickname "Pancho Rompeteclas," meaning "Jack the keyboards-buster." La Perfecta altered the course of Latin dance music by adding trombones to the brass section of the traditional "conjunto" format. Critics were stunned by this new "trombanga" line, which replaced traditional trumpets. Barry Rogers and Jose Rodriguez played trombones in La Perfecta, which came to be known as "the band of the crazy roaring elephants." Their trombone sound was widely imitated within the realm of salsa music, and the distinctive innovation established Palmieri as a serious new artist.

La Perfecta played four sets a night at New York City's Palladium, four nights a week, for $72 per musician in the early 1960s. The engagement lasted for five years, until the club closed in 1966. Palmieri and La Perfecta recorded *El Sonido Nuevo* in 1966, featuring Latin jazz vibraphonist Cal Tjader. Other bandmembers included Manny Oquendo (timbales), Tommy Lopez (congas), Barry Rogers (trombone), George Castro (flute), and Ishmael Quintana (vocals). "Manny is the one I ... learned my Cuban music from. I could never thank him enough for that," Palmieri told Birnbaum.

Difficulty and Fame in Puerto Rico

Palmieri's 1962 album *El Molestoso* ("The Bothersome One"), was titled in recognition of his reputation as a person willing to butt heads in order to fulfill a vision or retain his creativity. *Mambo con Conga es Mozambique,* released three years later, was never heard by most Americans because major radio stations deemed it too "communist" in nature and refused to play it. Palmieri recorded the album to pay a homage to Latin music's Afro-Cuban roots and rhythms.

La Perfecta disbanded in 1968, and Palmieri went on to record civil rights anthems and "boogaloos" with the group Harlem River Drive, fusing his Afro-Caribbean sound with rhythm and blues. When the salsa movement gained momentum in the early 1970s, Palmieri turned his attention again to Latin tracks and recorded *Vamonos Pa'l Monte* with his brother Charlie on the organ and Chocolate Armenteros on the trumpet.

In 1973 Palmieri accepted an assignment from Fania Records to record an album with Cheo Feliciano called *Champagne.* He flew to Puerto Rico to work on the album but still needed to find a vocalist. He eventually discovered a young singer named Lalo Rodriguez, who would appear on other albums as well. Palmieri followed *Vamonos Pa'l Monte* and *Champagne* with *The Sun of Latin Music,* featuring Rodriguez on vocals. In 1975 Palmieri won his first of five Grammy Awards for best Latin album. A year later, he won a Grammy for *Unfinished Masterpiece.*

Palmieri spent five years in Puerto Rico in the early 1980s. Salsa's popularity was waning in New York City at the time, and Palmieri's brother had suffered a heart attack. Palmieri went to Puerto Rico to take care of his ailing mother. There he formed a band called the Eddie Palmieri Orchestra, recorded *Palo Pa' Rumba* in 1983, *Solito* in 1984, and *La Verdad* in 1987, and won three Grammy awards—one for each album. But working in Puerto Rico was stressful for Palmieri. "I felt completely oppressed over there," he told Birnbaum. "I tried to get a helping hand from the orchestras in Puerto Rico, but I just frightened them away.... It was quite difficult. We were hurting for employment.... [The local musicians] wouldn't allow me in."

Classical Aspirations

After returning to New York City in the late 1980s, Palmieri recorded *Sueno* in 1989 for Intuition, a German record label, as well as *Llego la India* for Soho Sounds. Soon after, he signed with Nonesuch Records, a label noted for classical music rather than Latin or jazz recordings. In the mid-1990s Palmieri was at work on a project that sought to weave Afro-Caribbean rhythms into the classical compositions of Johann Sebastian Bach and Ludwig van Beethoven. In 1994 he released *Palmas*. Palmieri told *Down Beat* contributor Howard Mandel: "*Palmas* sets a precedent for how to extend jazz into the most incredible rhythmic patterns, the most exciting in the world, 40,000 years old!"

Brian de Palma's 1993 film, *Carlito's Way*, starring Al Pacino, featured Palmieri's hit single *Muneca*. The track *Puerto Rico* was included in Spike Lee's *Crooklyn* soundtrack the next year. Palmieri also contributed to *Breaking the Silence*, a 1994 video about HIV and AIDS aimed at women in the Latin community.

In his long, prolific career as a percussionist, pianist, composer, and orchestra leader, Palmieri played with an extensive list of masterful jazz and salsa musicians. Alto saxophonist Donald Harrison told Mandel: "One thing I love about Eddie is his free spirit. He goes for the music and listens to the musicians, the same way Art Blakey did, and of course, Duke Ellington, too."

Selected discography

La Perfecta, Alegre, 1961.
El Molestoso, Alegre, 1962.
Echando Pa' Lante, Tico, 1963.
Mambo con Conga es Mozambique, Tico, 1965.
Palmieri & Tjader: El Sonido Nuevo, Verve, 1966.
Molasses, Tico, 1967.
Palmieri & Tjader: Bamboleate, Tico, 1969.
Champagne, Tico, 1973.
Justicia, Tico, 1973.
Harlem River Drive, Roulette, 1974.
Vamonos Pa'l Monte, Tico, 1974.
Sentido, Coco, 1974.
The Sun of Latin Music, Coco, 1975.
Unfinished Masterpiece, Coco, 1976.
Lucumi Macumba Voodoo, Epic, 1977.
Eddie Palmieri, Barbaro, 1981.
Palo Pa' Rumba, Musica Latina, 1983.
Solito, Musica Latina, 1984.
La Verdad, Sonido, 1987.
Sueno, Intuition, 1989.
Llego la India via Eddie Palmieri, Soho Sounds, 1989.
(Contributor) *Carlito's Way* (soundtrack), 1993.
(Contributor) *Crooklyn* (soundtrack), 1994.
Palmas, Elektra/Nonesuch, 1994.

Sources

Billboard, April 23, 1994.
Cal Performances (University of California at Berkeley), 1993-94 season.
Columbus Dispatch, July 23, 1992.
Down Beat, August 1994.
Elle, September 1989.
JazzTimes, October 1994.
Musician, July 1994.
New York Latino, spring 1994.

—B. Kimberly Taylor

Lee Roy Parnell

Singer, songwriter, guitarist

Lee Roy Parnell has achieved success as a country music star without compromising his eclectic blend of Texas-influenced blues, rock, and jazz. An expert slide guitar player who is happiest when out on the road performing live, Parnell has unleashed a string of hits with Arista Records while establishing himself in the Nashville mainstream by virtue of his instrumental talents and vocal integrity. "Parnell's career has been an ideal example of effective artist development," wrote Peter Cronin in *Billboard.* "Rather than try to fit his square-peg music cleverly into the round hole of country radio, Parnell and company chose to focus on the music, buffing it to the high gloss necessary for country airplay and getting closer to Parnell's musical essence in the process."

Parnell has been a working musician throughout his entire adult life. When artists speak of "paying dues"—of laboring long years in anonymity—no one knows the lifestyle better than he does. Reflecting on nearly two decades spent on the road, playing three sets per night at clubs all over the South, Parnell told *Country Music:* "I burned the candle at both ends, as hard and as fast as I could." Now, having finally found the level of success he always wanted, he approaches his life's work with maturity. "I feel more relaxed, more self-confident about the music and about myself," he said. "I really love the way it all came down. I love my life so much more now than I did when I was younger. It's pretty amazing, the timing of it all."

Musically Diverse Roots

Lee Roy Parnell was born and raised in Texas. He had an early introduction to music and never really considered any other career. His father was a close friend of Texas bandleader Bob Wills, and often as a youngster Parnell would be treated to private concerts by Wills and his bandmembers. The singer told *Guitar Player:* "Texans have a history of mixing music. I'm a product of my environment. I like all kinds of music. When I was growing up in Texas, there were no boundaries. It was open season. Bob Wills was my introduction to music, and his band had a blues and jazz vocabulary in addition to their country leanings. The attitude is similar to the music I make—a country lyric with a bluesy feel." Parnell's other early influences included the Allman Brothers, Willie Nelson, and Jerry Jeff Walker, as well as California-based guitarists like Ry Cooder and David Lindley.

As soon as Parnell graduated from high school, he moved to Nashville. There he lived recklessly, playing in bars and indulging himself in a no-holds-barred party lifestyle. For a time he worked with a Southern rock

For the Record . . .

Born c. 1957 in Abilene, TX; married; wife's name, Kim; children: (previous marriages) Blake, Allison.

Country singer, songwriter, slide guitar player, 1975—. Member of band Panama Red, c. 1975-77. Signed with Arista Records, 1989; released first solo album, *Lee Roy Parnell,* 1990.

Addresses: *Record company*—Arista Records, 7 Music Circle N., Nashville, TN 37203. *Agent*—Shock Ink, 1108 16th Ave. S., Nashville, TN 37212.

group named Panama Red, but that band never quite found success. Finally Parnell returned to Texas, where he wrote his own songs and performed in the Austin area. According to Michael McCall in *Country Music,* it was in his home state that Parnell began to explore "a personal brand of roots music that merged jumpin' blues rhythms, slide guitar and soulful country vocals."

Parnell told *Billboard* that his music was inspired by the "cotton country" where he grew up. "The music came with the blacks and the whites all living together.... It is a black thing and a black culture," he said. "That's where Jimmie Rodgers got his stuff. So if he was, in fact, the father of country music, the grandfather was certainly the blues." The blues, of course, perfectly suited Parnell when he chose to make the slide guitar his performance tool of choice.

A Niche in New Country

In 1987 Parnell went back to Nashville. He began performing weekly at the high-profile Bluebird Cafe, and shortly thereafter he was invited to be the opening act for Bonnie Raitt at a large Nashville club. That exposure helped him to secure a recording contract with the Arista label, newly arrived in Music City at the time. In 1990 he released his first album, *Lee Roy Parnell,* an energetic, rhythm & blues-influenced country-rock collection that did not sell particularly well. Critics, who favored the work, christened Parnell's style as "country soul."

The artist told *Billboard* that his debut work was a learning experience and that after the album failed to sell he began to re-evaluate his style and material. "There has been a lot of weeding, but thank God my record company has been good about letting me hang myself. They let me make my first record the way I did.

It's a good record, and I don't regret a minute of it, but commercially I fell on my butt."

Parnell consulted with his Arista producers and decided to highlight his distinctive tenor voice and slide guitar in future recordings. The result has been a move toward the Nashville mainstream—but still a uniquely soulful sound. A *Country Music* reviewer noted that Parnell "takes decent songs and finds a way to make them shine like rare gems.... His tenor is comfortable, unaffected and packed with life, and perhaps only Dennis Robbins comes close to playing slide guitar with such gusto." Parnell's second album, *Love without Mercy,* yielded four Top Ten country hits and was considered the artist's breakthrough to country radio.

His niche in Nashville now firmly established, Parnell is able to indulge himself in the pastime he likes the most— performing live. "I sometimes think they pay me to do all the extra things outside of playing the music," he told *Country Music,* "because getting on a bus and going out playing for people, I absolutely love that part. I love it more today than the day I began."

Creating His Own Sound

Although he came to Nashville with more than 100 songs he had written himself, Parnell has never recorded any of them; he prefers to collaborate with Nashville's established songwriters, offering his own take on the melody or the rhythm. "My songs begin with a lyric idea," he explained in *Guitar Player.* "I think the music must follow the mood of the lyric. I learned from God that your eraser can be your best friend. After a while you develop an editor who lives inside your head. I have also learned that divine inspiration is great, but it's hard to come by. There really is no substitute for hard work. The craft part comes from elbow grease."

Also in *Guitar Player,* Parnell explained his motivation for his work. "I'm not doing this because of the fame," he said. "I'm driven by that primal need that I had when I picked up a guitar in the very beginning. The guitar continues to take me to places that I've never been before."

Parnell has not only sought new experiences through his guitar playing, but also in the business end of his music career. In 1995 he became the first artist to release an album—called *We All Get Lucky Sometimes*—on a new Arista label, Career. With his road band, the Hot Links, the singer has fashioned a recording that he feels, according to *Billboard,* "captures the Texas roadhouse style of his live shows." Commenting on the fact that he refused to compromise his artistic standards on *We All Get Lucky Sometimes* to prompt better sales than those of his past recordings, Parnell told *Billboard,* "I have a responsibility to my audience. People are intuitive about what's real and what's not. If I do something I don't believe in, it will leave them cold."

Selected discography

Lee Roy Parnell, Arista, 1990.
Love without Mercy, Arista, 1992.
On the Road, Arista, 1994.
We All Get Lucky Sometimes, Career/Arista, 1995.

Sources

Billboard, November 13, 1993; July 8, 1995.
Country Music, January/February 1994; July/August 1994.
Guitar Player, June 1994.
New York Times, April 10, 1994.

Additional information for this profile was obtained from Arista Records publicity materials.

—*Anne Janette Johnson*

Joe Pass

Guitarist

Photograph by Phil Bray, courtesy of Pablo Records

Throughout nearly 50 years as a professional guitarist, Joe Pass managed to break through many barriers and obstacles in music as well as in his own life. Born Joseph Anthony Jacobi Passalaqua, the eldest of five brothers in New Brunswick, New Jersey, his parents moved to Johnstown, Pennsylvania, while he was still a child. Pass became interested in guitar after he saw "singing cowboy" Gene Autry in the film *Ride Tenderfoot Ride.* Autry sparked his curiosity about the instrument and motivated him to ask for a guitar for his birthday.

When he turned nine years old in 1938, Pass's father, Mariano Passalaqua, gave him a $17 Harmony steel-string flat-top guitar. Soon, Passalaqua pushed his son to practice the guitar for at least five hours a day. "My father thought I showed signs of being able to play," Pass said in *Down Beat.* "And his object in life was not to have his kids do the same thing he did—work in a steel mill. He wanted them all to have a better education, or some better kind of livelihood. My father would go to the music store, and if he saw any book that said 'guitar' on it, he brought it home."

By the time Pass turned 14 years old, he had joined a band called the Gentlemen of Rhythm that patterned itself after the music of the legendary Gypsy guitarist Django Reinhardt. The group performed at parties and dances, and Pass earned three to five dollars per night. His talent grabbed the attention of saxophone player and bandleader Tony Pastor, who let him play with his band at a local concert. Pastor wanted to take him on the road with him, but Pass couldn't quit school to do so.

Downward Spiral of Drugs

A year later Pass's parents sent him to New York to study with the highly respected studio guitar player Harry Volpe. When Volpe realized that Pass improvised better than he did, he focused on teaching Pass to sight read music. But Pass became frustrated with his lessons and returned to Johnstown—though not for long. When his father became ill, he dropped out of the tenth grade and moved to New York.

"My father was very strict, but he got sick, and he could no longer exercise any restraint," Pass told *Rolling Stone.* "That was my chance to get out. I came to New York, and I was here in 1944 and '45 hangin' around. I played some gigs, heard Bird [saxophonist Charlie Parker] and [pianist] Art Tatum. Then, I got involved in drugs."

Pass's drug addiction, in fact, began to lead his life. He moved to New Orleans for a year, where he played bebop for strippers. "In New Orleans, I had kind of a nervous breakdown," Pass revealed in *Rolling Stone,* "because I had access to every kind of drug there and was up for days. I would always hock my guitar. I would come to New York a lot, then get strung out and leave."

The following year, Pass began to travel from place to place, performing wherever he could. In 1949 he joined bandleader Ray McKinley, but quit when he discovered the arrangements were beyond his reading abilities. During the early 1950s, Pass played in Las Vegas and other cities throughout the country. At the same time, he was in and out of jail for narcotics violations. "Staying high was my first priority," Pass told Robert Palmer in *Rolling Stone,* "playing was second; girls were third. But the first thing really took all my energy."

Restarted Career after Rehab

In 1954 Pass was arrested on drug charges and sent to the U.S. Public Health Service Hospital in Fort Worth, Texas. He spent four years there, then went back to Las Vegas to join accordion player Dick Contino's trio. Late in 1960, he entered Synanon, a narcotics rehabilitation center in Santa Monica, California. Two years later he played on the *Sounds of Synanon* compilation, released on World Pacific Records.

After three years at Synanon, Pass became more aware and appreciative of his musical abilities and started taking his career more seriously. "A lot of kids think that in order to be a guitarist, they've gotta go out and be a

junkie for 10 years, and that's just not true," Pass told *Down Beat.* "I can't credit any of that time, saying that's when I *really* learned. I spent most of those years just being a bum, doing nothing. It was a *great* waste of time."

When Pass left Synanon in 1963, he recorded *Catch Me,* his first album as a bandleader, with drummer Colin Bailey, pianist Clare Fischer, and bassist Albert Stinson. The following year, he recorded a tribute to Django Reinhardt called *For Django,* which was followed by *Simplicity* two years later. He also did studio work, performed with television show bands, and from 1965 to 1967, played with pianist George Shearing.

From the mid-1960s to the mid-1970s, Pass put his career into high gear. He recorded three albums in Germany and played on releases with jazz artists Earl Bostie, Julie London, Eddie "Cleanhead" Vinson, Chet Baker, and Carmen McRae. He worked as a sideman for pop stars Frank Sinatra, Donald O'Connor, Della Reese, Leslie Uggams, Steve Allen, and Johnny Mathis. Pass also subbed on the *Merv Griffin Show* when regular guitarist Herb Ellis couldn't make it.

The Final Decades

In 1971 Pass suggested a collaboration of his bebop guitar licks with Ellis's bluesy approach. The two formed a team and became one of the most famous and influential two-guitar ensembles in jazz history. Carl Jefferson invited Pass and Ellis to perform at the 1972 Concord Jazz Festival, which led to the recording of *Jazz Concord,* Concord Records' first release. At the 1973 Concord Jazz Festival, Pass and Ellis recorded *Seven Come Eleven.*

That year legendary bandleader Benny Goodman asked Pass to substitute for his guitarist at a concert. Pass's performance so impressed Goodman that he asked him to join his tour of Australia. When he returned from the tour, Pass signed a record deal with Norman Granz's newly formed Pablo label and immediately started recording *Virtuoso,* his first solo album. The album launched a series of *Virtuoso* LPs and made Pass the golden boy of jazz in 1975. Also around that time, Pass teamed up with pianist Oscar Peterson for a jazz version of George Gershwin's *Porgy and Bess.* In 1974 he had shared the Grammy Award for best jazz performance by a group with Peterson and Neils-Henning Orsted Pederson for their work on *The Trio.*

During the 1970s and 1980s, Pass became the most recorded jazz guitarist, producing solo records as well as accompanying other jazz greats like Duke Ellington,

Count Basie, Ella Fitzgerald, Sarah Vaughn, Stephane Grappelli, Oscar Peterson, Milt Jackson, Zoot Sims, Ray Brown, and others. In 1989 Pass reunited with the group that had recorded *For Django*—rhythm guitarist John Pisano, drummer Bailey, and bassist Jim Hugbart—to record *Summer Night*. They went on to release *Appassionato* in 1992.

Early in 1992 Pass discovered that he had liver cancer. He responded well to treatment at first, and continued to perform until early 1993. But his declining health forced him to withdraw from his tour with Pepe Romero, Paco Pena, and Leo Kottke. He released his last album, *Joe Pass & Co.,* with guitarist Pisano, bassist Monty Budwig, and Bailey, in 1993. On May 7, 1994, Pass played his last performance, with Pisano at a nightclub in Los Angeles. "He sounded better than most guitarists," Pisano told *Guitar Player,* "but afterwards, he looked at me with a tear in his eye and said, 'I can't play anymore.' It was like a knife in my heart."

Joe Pass died on May 23, 1994. In a *Guitar Player* tribute, writer Jim Ferguson summed up Pass's career as a guitarist: "Bebop, Latin, ballads, blues, originals, solos, duos, trios, big ensembles—Joe did it all. No player in recent memory has made so many recordings in so many styles and contexts.... In all probability, Joe Pass [was] the most versatile, well-rounded, mainstream guitarist in history."

Selected discography

(Contributor) *Sounds of Synanon,* World Pacific, 1962.
Catch Me, World Pacific, 1963.
For Django, Pacific Jazz, 1964.
A Sign of the Times, World Pacific, 1965.
The Stones Jazz, World Pacific, 1966.
(Contributor) *Jazz Concord,* Concord, 1972.
Virtuoso, Pablo, 1973.
Best of Joe Pass, Pablo, 1973.
(With Herb Ellis) *Seven Come Eleven,* Concord, 1973.
Joe Pass at Akron University, Pablo, 1974.
Live at Dante's, Pablo, 1974.
Portraits of Duke Ellington, Pablo, 1974.
Two for the Road, Pablo, 1974.
(With Oscar Peterson and Neils-Henning Orsted Pederson) *The Trio,* 1974.
At the Montreux Jazz Festival, Pablo, 1975.
Virtuoso—Volume 2, Pablo, 1976.
Guitar Interludes, Discovery, 1977.
Montreux '77 Live! Pablo, 1977.

Quadrant, Pablo, 1977.
Virtuoso—Volume 3, Pablo, 1977.
Tudo Bem!, Pablo, 1978.
Chops, Pablo, 1978.
Virtuoso—Volume 4, Pablo, 1978.
Northsea Nights, Pablo, 1979.
Checkmate, Pablo, 1981.
Eximious, Pablo, 1982.
Live at Long Bay Beach College, Pablo, 1984.
We'll Be Together Again, Pablo, 1984.
Whitestone, Pablo, 1985.
At Akron University, Pablo, 1986.
Blues for Fred, Pablo, 1988.
One for My Baby, Pablo, 1988.
Summer Nights, Pablo, 1989.
Virtuoso—Live!, Pablo, 1991.
Appassionato, Pablo, 1992.
Joe Pass Quartet Live at Yoshi's, Pablo, 1992.
My Song, Telarc, 1993.
Finally: Live in Stockholm, Verve, 1993.
Joe Pass & Co., Pablo, 1993.

Sources

Books

Clarke, Donald, *Penguin Encyclopedia of Popular Music,* Penguin Books, 1990.
Feather, Leonard, and Ira Gitler, *The Encyclopedia of Jazz in the Seventies,* Horizon Press, 1976.

Periodicals

Billboard, May 22, 1976; November 27, 1976; March 4, 1978; February 24, 1979; October 30, 1982; June 4, 1994.
Down Beat, August 1, 1963; November 21, 1963; June 8, 1972; February 13, 1975; March 13, 1975; February 26, 1976; December 2, 1976; February 24, 1977; April 6, 1978; July 1982; March 1984; May 1988; August 1994.
GFA Soundboard, Fall 1994.
Guitar Player, April 1983; August 1986; August 1992; September 1994; October 1994.
Musician, August 1984; November 1994.
Rolling Stone, December 13, 1979.
Time, June 6, 1994.

Additional information for this profile was obtained from the on-line All-Music Guide, Matrix Software, 1994.

—*Thaddeus Wawro*

CeCe Peniston

Singer, songwriter

Photograph by Michael Levine, courtesy of A&M Records

Dance club diva CeCe Peniston decided at a very young age that she would be an entertainer. Her dedication, ambition, and talent, combined with her "right place at the right time" charm, led her to the limelight by the time she reached her early twenties.

Peniston was born in Dayton, Ohio, but she spent the majority of her formative years in Phoenix, Arizona. She lists among her musical influences Patti LaBelle, Minnie Ripperton, Luther Vandross, and Shirley Murdock. As a grade school student, Peniston was cast in a class musical production, and her fascination with music then began to blossom. "I always told my mother that I wanted to sing," Peniston recalled in an A&M Records biography, "but it wasn't until that show that she realized I really could. From that point on, I got a lot of support from my parents because they saw I was serious." Young CeCe's parents realized what a talented singer they had in their family, and unlike many musicians' families, they supported her choice to pursue an entertainment career.

As she reached her teens, Peniston saw others beyond her immediate family offer support for her career pursuits. When she was 13 years old, her grandmother sent her a Baldwin upright piano as a surprise Christmas present. "I really wanted to take piano lessons," Peniston told *Upscale*, "but I didn't have a way to practice my lessons at home, and [my grandmother] was able to get me a piano. I was so happy; I couldn't believe it.... I still have the piano—it's at my mom's house because I have so much stuff. But it's a sentimental thing. I've written things on it, and even when I'm home, I'll play little key stuff on it—like I'll work out my melodies and little stuff like that on it."

When Peniston reached her mid-teens, she landed a part in a local theater group's production of *Bubblin' Brown Sugar*. She also participated in athletics and set several track records in high school. Once she earned her diploma, she went on to attend Phoenix College. During her first year as a college student, Peniston was crowned Miss Black Arizona.

In January of 1991 record producer Felipe "DJ Wax Dawg" DelGado, who was also based in Phoenix, asked Peniston to sing background vocals on rapper Overweight Pooch's *Female Preacher* album for A&M Records. When Manny Lehman, A&M's director of artists and repertoire, heard Peniston sing, he wanted to meet with her immediately. A&M then commissioned DelGado to produce a track featuring Peniston as a solo artist.

Peniston was 21 years old when she and DelGado produced her first single, "Finally," which became an

Born in Dayton, Ohio; divorced. *Education:* Attended Phoenix College, Arizona.

Began performing in school; recorded background vocals for Overweight Pooch's album *Female Preacher,* A&M, 1991; released first single, "Finally," 1991; released debut album, *Finally,* A&M, 1992; toured with R. Kelly, Levert, and Joe Public and the Cover Girls, 1992.

Awards: Gold album award for *Finally,* 1992.

Addresses: *Record company*—A&M Records, 1416 La Brea Ave., Hollywood, CA 90028.

instant dance club hit in the United States. By the fall of 1991 "Finally" began its rise on the U.S. pop and R&B charts and had become a Top Five single in Great Britain. With her song climbing the charts, Peniston headed into the studio to record a full album. *Finally* would eventually reach the Top Five of the pop, R&B, and dance album charts and earn gold certification.

"Having a hit was a real shock to me," exclaimed Peniston in her A&M biography. "We had two months to pull the whole album together.... I guess I didn't realize the impact the record was having until it reached the top five. I didn't know how hard it was for a new artist to start out that way ... it seemed like everything happened so quickly."

Peniston's next hit, "We Got a Love Thang," rocketed to Number One on *Billboard's* Club Play chart within a month of its release. With another hit single on the charts, Peniston began a year of touring clubs and small theaters in both the United States and abroad in support of *Finally.* Her tour started with a series of shows in the Philippines, Japan, Great Britain, Germany, Spain, and Italy. When she returned to the United States, Peniston toured with such R&B acts as Joe Public and the Cover Girls, R. Kelly, and Levert. While on tour she saw "Inside That I Cried," "Crazy Love," and "Keep on Walkin'" join the list of hits from her debut album.

Determined not to become a one-hit wonder with *Finally,* Peniston went right back into the studio after her tour to begin work on her sophomore effort. She released *Thought 'Ya Knew* on A&M Records, along with the first single, "I'm in the Mood," in 1993. "I guess the title tells you where I'm coming from with the new album," Peniston stated in her A&M biography. "It's like I thought ya

knew I could do it, that I was coming right backatcha, real and honest."

Though "Finally" was the only song on her debut album that Peniston wrote, she got more involved in the songwriting for the second album. She co-wrote three tracks for *Thought 'Ya Knew*—"Whatever It Is," "Give What I'm Givin'," and "Maybe It's the Way." "People are expecting a lot from me," the singer commented to *Billboard* about the release of *Thought 'Ya Knew.* "They want to know whether or not I'm a one-hit wonder or something. But to be honest, I sort of like the pressure; it keeps me motivated and challenges me. I take my work very seriously, and ultimately, I do feel really good about the decisions [that were made] while I was making this record."

The pressure of living up to the success of *Finally* wasn't the only thing hanging over Peniston's head while she recorded her second album. She had the turmoil of her personal life to contend with as well. Between the release of *Finally* and *Thought 'Ya Knew,* Peniston was married and then soon divorced. Her emotional distress perhaps shows through on the matured approach to *Thought 'Ya Knew,* compared to the bubbly style of *Finally.* "I've grown a lot in the past few years, musically and personally, and I wanted that to show," Peniston explained to Ray Rogers in *Out.*

Throughout all the transitions in her career and in her life, Peniston has said she wants her fans to be able to identify with her and with her music. She described herself in her A&M biography as "sensitive, sentimental, and understanding ... although I can also be sassy and earthy! And that's how I want people to relate to me, as someone who's down-to-earth, who has fun with life!"

Selected discography

Finally, A&M, 1992.
Thought 'Ya Knew, A&M, 1993.
(Contributor) *Ready to Wear* (soundtrack), Columbia, 1994.

Sources

Billboard, June 20, 1992; December 18, 1993.
Out, February/March, 1994.
People, February 7, 1994.
Upscale, May 1994; November 1994.
Vibe, February 1994.

Additional information for this profile was obtained from A&M Records publicity materials, 1994.

—Sonya Shelton

Webb Pierce

Singer, songwriter, guitarist

AP/Wide World Photos

One of country music's most passionate vocalists, Webb Pierce inherited the reins of the honky-tonk legacy after the death of legend Hank Williams in 1953. Considered one of the most distinctive stylists of the electrified country sound of the early 1950s and the embodiment of the rhinestone-encrusted crooning cowboy, Pierce was noted for his high, nasal voice, his hound-dog whine, and the uncluttered instrumental arrangements of such classics as "Back Street Affair" and "There Stands the Glass."

One of the few performers to land recordings on the country music charts during four successive decades, Pierce boasted a twangy tenor that would influence a generation of country artists, including Mel Tillis, Faron Young, and Willie Nelson. Experiencing a decline after the smooth, pop-based Nashville Sound gained mass favor in the 1960s, Pierce continued to epitomize the raw enthusiasm and lack of city-bred sophistication characteristic of his era. His guitar-shaped swimming pool, colorful suits, and outlandishly outfitted automobiles were popular with tourists and notorious among native Nashvillians throughout the 1970s and 1980s.

Pierce was born August 8, 1921, in West Monroe, Louisiana. The stepson of a farmer (his biological father died three months after he was born), he spent his childhood in the fields and didn't pick up a guitar until age 12. While his family was not musical, Pierce was inspired by his mother's collection of country music recordings. He worked hard at his guitar technique and, by the age of 16, was playing local gigs and hosting his own radio show, *Songs by Webb Pierce*. After a stint as a regular performer on Monroe's KMLB radio and a three-year turn in the U.S. Army, he moved to Shreveport, Louisiana, in 1944.

Pursued Radio while Working at Sears

Securing a job at Sears Roebuck Company, Pierce began an early-morning show on KTBS called *Webb Pierce with Betty Jane, the Singing Sweetheart,* on which the young man and his bride performed mostly gospel numbers. A year after the popular *Louisiana Hayride* radio show began airing on KWKH in 1948, Pierce was asked aboard. His early band, the Southern Valley Boys, numbered several musicians who would later achieve fame, among them Floyd Cramer, Tillman Franks, Jimmy Day, and Faron Young. Still working as a floor manager for Sears while courting fame on the *Louisiana Hayride,* Pierce also recorded several singles on the Four Star label in 1949.

Pierce signed a deal with Decca Records in 1951 and was soon hard at work recording such singles as

"Wondering," "That Heart Belongs to Me," and "Back Street Affair," all of which would reach Number One on the *Billboard* charts. Needless to say, this increase in popularity changed Pierce's career track; he quickly tendered his resignation at Sears and moved to Nashville with longtime friend Red Sovine. There, Pierce topped the charts with two more songs and joined the Grand Ole Opry.

In 1954 Pierce recorded "Slowly," now considered a classic country love song. It spent a record 36 weeks at Number One, in part due to the innovative work of pedal steel soloist Bud Isaacs. "There Stands the Glass," recorded the same year, showcased Pierce's nasal vibrato, a vocal style that would be an inspiration to later singers like Willie Nelson. "Webb had the most unique way of phrasing," friend Max Powell told *Chicago Sun-Times* contributor David Hoekstra. "He knew how to pull one word out of a line and tear your heart out with it. His phrasing was *excellent.*"

Between 1951, when "Wondering," his first record to hit the charts, zoomed to Number One, and 1955, Pierce scored a total of 11 Number One singles, including that year's "In the Jailhouse Now," "I Don't Care," and "Love, Love, Love." He would chart with a dozen Number One records out of a total of 55 Top Ten hits during his long career.

Savvy in the Studio and the Office

One of Pierce's many talents was his innate sense of what made a good country song; he spent a great deal of time looking for top-notch material. Even after a tune had been recorded, he would play it for a live audience to see if their reaction was favorable before it was released. His perfectionism was no less exacting in the studio. The recording of "There Stands the Glass," still considered *the* country drinking song, was a typical case: it was cut four times before Pierce felt it worthy of release.

Like many popular artists of the period, Pierce also took advantage of new recording technology and later remade his early Decca hits in stereo, adding the background vocals that had become all the rage by the late 1950s. He knew what his fans wanted; in 1958, when an average order for most records was 100 copies, a Webb Pierce recording was stocked in upwards of 1,000. Still, the original hit versions best showcase the reason for Pierce's phenomenal popularity. His unique sound, achieved through fiddle and electric guitar played in unison and backed by pedal steel, along with Pierce's high tenor voice, had gained him the bulk of his loyal following in those initial years with Decca.

Very early in his career Pierce became heavily involved in the business side of country music, demonstrating a clear head for marketing and finance not shared by many of his contemporaries. As he noted in an interview with *Country Music's* Patrick Carr: "I went into the business just hoping that one more hit would come up, and looking way ahead as to what I'd do when it was over. You see, I was still very young, but I had that knowledge, that business training I got through Sears & Roebuck, so I never woke up broke, owing the government ... millions." While on the *Louisiana Hayride* in 1950, Pierce developed a partnership in both the Pacemaker recording studio and the Ark-La-Tex music publishing company with then-*Hayride* director Horace Logan.

Establishing a good working relationship with country radio from the start was another area in which Pierce's investment of energy received maximum return; he was a constant fixture at annual disc jockey conventions, and his consistent wooing of prominent disc jockeys made sure that his music was played—and played a lot. He was savvy to invest in the publishing rights to many of the songs he made into hits, thereby reaping double rewards from his successes on the charts (he already received a percentage of revenues from each record sold). The influential Cedarwood Publishing company, which Pierce co-founded with former Grand Ole Opry manager Jim Denny in 1953, represented such song-writing talent as Danny Dill, Red Sovine, Mel Tillis, Marijohn Wilkin, John D. Loudermilk, and Wayne Walker. At one time Pierce held financial assets that included a record company, five radio stations, several publishing companies, a grocery store, a restaurant, and an auditorium.

> *One of the few performers to land recordings on the country music charts during four successive decades, Pierce boasted a twangy tenor that would influence a generation of country artists.*

The Gibson Guitar Company's Les Paul electric guitar was changing the traditional country acoustic sound in the late 1940s, and by the early 1950s, the rock and roll influences generated by a young man named Elvis Presley were beginning to shake the foundations of country music. Rockabilly, the fusion of country music and this new electrified sound, gained momentum in the mid-1950s, and its energy was quick to capture Pierce's interest. He wooed the new teen audience with ballads like "I Don't Care" and "Love, Love, Love" and also began to incorporate a yearning vibrato to his vocal style, though he retained his southern inflection.

"Teenage Boogie" was one such attempt to capture this new market, and it was characteristic of Pierce's later songs in its use of rockabilly guitar licks. Recorded three times before Pierce felt he had gotten it right, the instrumental backup bore the mark of Nashville's finest: Hank "Sugarfoot" Garland on lead guitar, Sonny Burnette on pedal steel, Buddy Harman on drums, and the Jordannaires contributing backup vocals to the final

session in August of 1956, that was released by Decca. A moderate crossover hit at the time, this remains one of Pierce's most collectible recordings.

Peaked in the Early 1960s

In 1956 Pierce and Sovine collaborated on the top-selling duets "Why Baby, Why" and "Little Rosa," and Pierce continued to court the rockabilly market with songs like "Teenage Boogie." Near the end of the decade, he released a cover version of the Everly Brothers' "Bye Bye, Love," but this 1957 remake did not enjoy nearly the success of the original. This was a precursor of things to come. By 1958, despite the wealth of good material coming from a young songwriter named Mel Tillis with which Pierce would continue to top the charts throughout the 1960s—songs like "Crazy Wild Desire," "Sands of Gold," and "Those Wonderful Years" would all make the Top Ten in the early years of the decade—Pierce's career as a country musician had peaked.

During the 1960s Pierce remained one of the most popular country singers in the nation, carried along on his successes of the previous decade. He toured the United States and Canada and appeared on several television shows, as well as on the Opry stage. But by the late 1960s, Pierce had begun to lose popularity on the country charts, as the slick "Nashville Sound" pumped out of Chet Atkins's RCA studios began to win over country music listeners. Pierce's last Top Ten hit would be "Fool, Fool, Fool," which charted in 1967.

Constantly flaunting his wealth for the enjoyment of his fans, in the early 1960s Pierce became the first Nashville resident to construct a guitar-shaped swimming pool in the backyard of his suburban residence. It proved to be a $40,000 home improvement project that angered his Oak Hill, Tennessee, neighbors when their quiet city became the second-biggest stopping point for the thousands of tour buses that travelled to Nashville each year. While Pierce took advantage of the situation, spending many hours by the pool autographing albums for his fans, his neighbors were angered to the point of litigation. Pierce lost these law suits, the buses were prohibited, and he was resigned to building another such pool near his offices on Music Row.

In 1962 Pierce decided it was time for some new wheels and invested the incredible amount of $20,000 in the first of what would be a pair of the fanciest cars ever seen driving the streets of Nashville. Loaded with ornamental rifles, studded with over 1,000 silver dollars, and upholstered in hand-tooled leather, the cream-colored Pontiac Bonneville's interior was designed by

Nudie Cohen, a North Hollywood tailor famous for a heavy hand with the glitz in stagewear known as "Nudie suits."

Even though most of his time was now spent basking in the adoration of his loyal fans, Pierce was not through with music. Chalking up several smaller successes on the charts throughout the early 1970s, Pierce made *Billboard's* rankings one last time in 1982, when a revival of his 1955 hit "In the Jailhouse Now," sung with Willie Nelson, made it to Number 72. Still, Pierce's characteristically country voice would not harmonize well with an industry bent on courting a pop audience with crossover hits, and he eventually withdrew from the recording studio altogether. During his later years, Pierce was frequently hospitalized with heart problems; in 1990 he was diagnosed with pancreatic cancer. He died a year later, at the age of 69, in Nashville.

Despite the prolific and incredibly popular nature of his recording history, Pierce has been largely ignored by Nashville and is not even represented in the Country Music Hall of Fame. While his flashy lifestyle was indeed an embarrassment to a Nashville society trying to glean an aura of "respectability" and escape country music's "just off the farm" image, more significant perhaps is the fact that Pierce attempted to remain in the public eye too long after his heyday, becoming almost a caricature of himself. But during the 1950s, more than any other star, Pierce embodied the hard-driving honky-tonk music that helped country music survive into the rock 'n' roll era. "Maybe the flamboyance hurt him," admitted his friend Max Powell. "[But] that's what the public loves. He wasn't doing flamboyance for the people connected with the Country Music Association. He was doing it for his fans—and that's what an artist should do."

Selected discography

Wondering Boy, Decca, 1958.
Webb with a Beat, Decca, 1960.
I've Got a New Heartache, Decca, 1963.
Country Music Time, Decca, 1965.
Webb Pierce: The Wondering Boy, 1951-58, Bear Family, 1990.
King of the Honky Tonk, Country Music Foundation, 1994.
I Ain't Never, Charly.
Cross Country, Decca.

Sources

Books

Biracree, Tom, *The Country Music Almanac,* Prentice Hall, 1993.
Cackett, Alan, *Harmony Illustrated Encyclopedia of Country Music,* Crown, 1994.
Encyclopedia of Folk, Country & Western Music, edited by Grelun Landon and Irwin Stambler, St. Martin's, 1983.

Periodicals

Billboard, March 9, 1991.
Chicago Sun-Times, October 28, 1990.
Country Music, June 1986; May/June 1991; September/October 1994; March/April 1995.
Country Music Review, November/December 1964.
Nashville Banner, February 25, 1991.

Additional information for this profile was obtained from liner notes by Otto Kitsinger to *Webb Pierce: The Wondering Boy, 1951-1958,* Bear Family Records, 1990.

—*Pamela L. Shelton*

Bud Powell

Jazz pianist

Although pianist Bud Powell succumbed in 1966 at the age of only 41 to the illnesses that had been haunting him for years, he managed to change the face of jazz music. Powell was one of the few musicians—including, among others, saxophonist Charlie "Bird" Parker, trumpeter Dizzy Gillespie, and fellow pianist Thelonious Monk—to revolutionize jazz during the 1940s by inventing bebop, a modern sound that broke out of the confines of swing and established the musicians as not only entertainers, but artists as well. To commemorate Powell's achievements and the seventieth anniversary of his birth in 1994, the Blue Note and Verve record labels released comprehensive compact disc boxed sets of his work: *Bud Powell: The Complete Blue Note and Roost Recordings* and *The Complete Bud Powell on Verve*.

Powell struggled to create his music in the midst of such personal demons as alcoholism, mental illness, and tuberculosis, as well as a largely unappreciative U.S. audience. He suffered a debilitating beating by police in 1945 in Philadelphia, which set off his subse-

For the Record . . .

Born Earl Randolph Powell, September 27, 1924, in New York, NY; died of tuberculosis, July 31 (one source says August 1), 1966, in Brooklyn, NY; son of a pianist; married Audrey Hill, 1953 (divorced); married Altevia Edwards ("Buttercup"), c. 1955 (marriage dissolved); children: (with Mary Frances Barnes) Celia, (with Edwards) John.

First appeared onstage as teen in Harlem, NY, 1939; played with Thelonious Monk at Harlem's Minton's Playhouse, early 1940s; toured U.S. and recorded with Cootie Williams's orchestra, 1942-44; recorded with Dexter Gordon and Charlie Parker, mid-1940s; led trio Bud Powell and His Modernists, 1949-51; appeared regularly at Birdland in New York City; played with Charlie Parker, Dizzy Gillespie, Charles Mingus, Max Roach, Sonny Rollins, J. J. Johnson, Sonny Stitt, and Fats Navarro in clubs and concert halls in New York City and Toronto, Canada, and on tour, late 1940s-1950s; played and recorded with Kenny Clarke, Pierre Michelot, and Niels-Henning Orsted-Pedersen, Paris, France, 1959-64.

quent lifelong health problems. Still, Powell—whose turbulent life was later used, along with that of saxophonist Lester Young, as a model for the character Dale Turner in the 1986 film *Round Midnight*—led his own bands, played for five years in exile in Paris, and pioneered a new style. One of his successors, pianist Herbie Hancock, noted Powell's lasting significance in *Down Beat:* "He was the foundation out of which stemmed the whole edifice of modern jazz piano; every jazz pianist since Bud either came through him or is deliberately attempting to get away from playing like him."

Began Career as a Teen at Minton's Playhouse

Earl Randolph Powell was born on September 27, 1924, in New York City. The son of a man talented as a stride pianist, he began learning classical music as a child from his father. Powell left school at age 15 to devote himself professionally to his own piano playing and first appeared onstage as a teen in spots around Harlem and Coney Island, Brooklyn. Thelonious Monk, also not yet famous, tutored Powell at Harlem's Minton's Playhouse, where Powell became a regular feature and launched his career.

In the 1940s, Powell established himself as one of the leading figures of bebop. He began the decade, from 1942 to 1944, touring and recording with trumpeter Cootie Williams's orchestra. In 1946, he recorded with Dexter Gordon, on *Long Tall Dexter,* and contributed to two cuts, "Cheryl" and "Buzzy," on Charlie Parker's Savoy sessions. Three years later, Powell found himself invited by the young Blue Note label to lead a group, Bud Powell and His Modernists, to produce albums for the label. Backed by drummer Max Roach and bassist Curley Russell, Powell recorded the five-volume *Amazing Bud Powell.*

Overcame Critically Hard Times

If Powell made his name in the jazz community during the 1940s, he also suffered a pivotal crisis. James T. Jones IV of *USA Today* described the incident: "In 1945, a 21-year-old Powell received a Rodney King-like cop beating after he tried to help his pal and mentor, Monk, who was being harassed by police." Most of 1945 passed with Powell recovering in the hospital from his severe head injury. From then on, the musician found himself shadowed by excruciating headaches, seizures, and generally erratic behavior that led him in and out of sanitariums, where, according to *Time* and *New York Newsday,* he experienced electroshock therapy and was once sprayed with water mixed with ammonia. He also developed a drinking problem, worsening later physical ailments.

Meanwhile, Powell and other modern jazz musicians were receiving an ambivalent response from American audiences. Many young white artists, intellectuals, and bohemians embraced bebop; in fact, they adopted the music as the theme of their "Beat generation" in the 1950s. Black youth, however, largely overlooked the modern jazz revolution in the 1940s and turned toward other forms, such as rock and doo-wop. In a reaction parallel to that of the bebop musicians themselves, these potential listeners rebelled against an earlier generation of jazz musicians—Louis Armstrong and Fats Waller, for instance—whom they believed represented "the old style of comic darky with rolling eyes and flamboyant manner," according to James Lincoln Collier in *Jazz: The American Theme Song.* Black listeners would return to the genre in the mid- to late 1950s, when jazz musicians put forth a more consciously African American-centered, bluesy, and "hot," or "hard," sound.

Despite his crisis in 1945, Powell would become a leading jazz pianist in the decade following World War II. His trio, the Modernists, anticipated in their own 1949 sessions the hard bop style that would emerge later in the fifties. The records *Bud's Bubble* (also called *Craze-*

ology) and *Indiana* from those sessions showcase Powell's own combination of right-hand melodies over complex and unpredictable left-hand harmonies. *Un Poco Loco, Night in Tunisia,* and *Parisian Thoroughfare* also shine brightly. "Frequently the face of his music is like a lie constructed out of bebop acrobatics, convoluted triplets, and finger-buckling scales attacked from as many angles as a Schoenbergian row," wrote *Village Voice* jazz critic Gary Giddins.

Powell was one of the descendants of ragtime piano. Ragtime evolved from the Creole clarinet style and found its place in a number of schools across the country, including the New Orleans school, represented by the legendary Jelly Roll Morton; the "Pittsburgh circle," starring Mary Lou Williams and modernist Errol Garner; and the "Eastern," or "Harlem," group, which included James P. Johnson and Fats Waller and from which emerged modernists Powell and Monk. "On the one hand,... players attempted the feat of adapting the piano to the vocalizing style of the other instruments (the so-called 'trumpet style');... [on] the other hand, players exploited the capacity of the piano for a combination of technical brilliance and original harmonic experiments, which led logically to the modern pianists' styles," commented jazz historian Eric Hobsbawm in *The Jazz Scene.*

The Greatest Jazz Concert Ever

Powell's Modernists brought in a number of star jazz players for their 1949 sessions. Trumpeter Fats Navarro, saxophonist Sonny Rollins, bassist Tommy Potter, and drummer Roy Haynes, for example, came together for the recordings *Bouncing with Bud* and *Dance of the Infidels.* Although Powell spent much of the years from 1951 to 1953 in a hospital, by 1953 he was once again playing and recording. A highlight from Powell's career was a concert at Massey Hall in Toronto, Ontario, with Charlie Parker, Dizzy Gillespie, Max Roach, and Charles Mingus, recorded as *The Greatest Jazz Concert Ever.*

Toward the late 1950s, Powell began growing abusive and hostile toward his fellow musicians, and his relationships worsened. After another brief hospitalization in 1959, he moved to Paris to a glorious reception from the European jazz community. After three years playing there with American drummer Kenny Clarke and bassist Pierre Michelot, however, Powell again fell ill. The pianist's new wife, Altevia Edwards, nicknamed "Buttercup," and his friends in Paris, particularly the young graphic artist Francis Paudras, took care of him, but his health problems worsened. Powell contracted tuberculosis in 1963, his marriage broke up, and he again required treatment in a hospital. Homesick for New

York, where many leading bop musicians performed a benefit concert at Birdland to help pay his medical expenses, Powell returned in 1964.

In his playing during his later years Powell still achieved a high level of artistry. Released almost a decade after his death, *Bud in Paris* demonstrates his changing moods. More than a ballad, "Autumn in New York" is a "minor epic," according to Gary Giddins in the *Village Voice.* In contrast, "Crossing the Channel" presents what Giddins called "the urgent storytelling of a most idiosyncratic and argumentative artist." The reviewer had only praise for the musician's later sessions: "On those occasions, he made clear once again that he was ... a volatile and original voice with an unmistakable urgency and diction of his own." Powell's playing reflected his physical condition. Although he had flashes of brilliance, he also floundered, barely keeping up with the melody. He died on July 31, 1966, soon after his return to New York.

The broad range of Powell's musical opus was made available in 1994 on two archival compact disc sets from Powell's two main labels, Blue Note and Verve. *Los Angeles Times* writer Leonard Reed reviewed the accomplishment presented on these collections, *Bud Powell: The Complete Blue Note and Roost Recordings* and *The Complete Bud Powell on Verve:* "These releases, in some cases wobbly and thin in their pre-stereo and pre-digital technologies, contain some of the most rigorously conceived and executed jazz ever recorded." The promotion and distribution of the CDs marked Powell's increased recognition from diverse audiences beyond jazz musicians and from devotees in the United States in the 1990s as well.

Selected discography

(With Dexter Gordon) *Long Tall Dexter,* Savoy, 1946.
(With Charlie Parker) *Bird/The Savoy Recordings* (includes "Cheryl" and "Buzzy") Savoy, 1946.
Bud's Bubble (*Crazeology*), Roost, 1947.
Indiana, Roost, 1947.
Bouncing with Bud, Blue Note, 1949.
Dance of the Infidels, Blue Note, 1949.
Tempus Fugue-it, Clef, 1949.
All God's Chillun Got Rhythm, Clef, 1949.
Hallucinations, Clef, 1950.
Un Poco Loco, Blue Note, 1951.
Night in Tunisia, Blue Note, 1951.
Parisian Thoroughfare, Blue Note, 1951.
Tea for Two, Alto, 1953.
Autumn in New York, Blue Note, 1953.
The Glass Enclosure, Blue Note, 1953.
Jazz at Massey Hall, Fantasy/OJC, 1953.

The Bud Powell Trio: The Verve Sessions, Verve, 1955.
(With Niels-Henning Orsted-Pedersen) Bouncing with Bud, Delmark, 1962.
Bud in Paris, Xanadu, 1975.
The Amazing Bud Powell, Volumes 1 & 2, (1949-53), Blue Note, 1989.
The Amazing Bud Powell, Volume 3, (1949-53), Blue Note, 1989.
Bud Powell: The Complete Blue Note and Roost Recordings, Blue Note, 1994.
The Complete Bud Powell on Verve, Verve, 1994.
The Genius of Bud Powell, Verve.
The Greatest Jazz Concert Ever, Prestige.

Sources

Books

Collier, James Lincoln, Jazz: The American Theme Song, Oxford University Press, 1993.
Groves, Alan, and Alyn Shipton, The Glass Enclosure: The Life of Bud Powell, Bayou Press, 1993.
Hobsbawm, Eric, The Jazz Scene, Pantheon Books, 1993 (first edition published by MacGibbon and Kee, 1959).

Lyons, Len, and Don Perlo, Jazz Portraits: The Lives and Music of the Jazz Masters, Morrow, 1989.

Periodicals

Dayton Daily News (OH), November 13, 1994.
Down Beat, September 8, 1966; September 22, 1966; October 20, 1966.
Jazz Journal, October 1966.
Jazz Journal International, June 1993.
Keyboard, October 1989.
Los Angeles Times, November 13, 1994.
Melody Maker, August 13, 1966.
New York Newsday, October 16, 1994.
New York Times, August 2, 1966; October 12, 1986.
Chicago Sun-Times , November 13, 1994.
Time, October 31, 1994.
USA Today, October 11, 1994.
Village Voice, December 8, 1975.

Additional information for this profile was obtained from Blue Note Records publicity materials.

—Nicholas Patti

Prefab Sprout

Pop band

Paddy McAloon, visionary and front man of England's Prefab Sprout, has been called a clever bastard, a god, an eccentric genius, and a wimp; critics either adore or abhor him. McAloon has been compared to everyone from immortal bard William Shakespeare to soul singer Marvin Gaye. "Suddenly," said London's *Independent on Sunday* of McAloon's appearance on the music scene, "[he] was [British Pop icon] Elvis Costello with a sweet tooth, or he was [former Beatle] Paul McCartney with a degree in English and either way he was the smartest alec pop had seen in years." *New Musical Experience* put it bluntly, stating, "Though it is *de rigeur* among self-styled rock pigs to feign hatred and contempt for Prefab Sprout, the truth is *Everybody* likes them." Regardless of whether or not he is worshipped or vilified, this "last pop genius"—as *Rolling Stone* called McAloon—has been plugging away for over a decade, constantly reaching for the perfect pop hit.

McAloon and his brother Martin invented their band's odd moniker in 1971 after hearing of strangely named bands such as Grand Funk Railroad and Tyrannosaurus Rex (later T. Rex). If ever they had a band, they would call it Prefab Sprout, the McAloon brothers decided. They also considered Grappled Institution, Dry Axe, and Village Bus. "I love our name because I know the naiveté it came out of," Paddy told *Rolling Stone*.

Perfect Pop and Petrol

Still, it wasn't until the early 1980s that the boys got to use the name. Between pumping gas at their father's filling station in Consett, County Durham, a small town outside of Newcastle upon Tyne in northeast England, they would play cover tunes behind the garage. As Paddy's confidence in his own songwriting grew, they enlisted school chum Michael Salmon to play drums, while Martin played bass and Paddy took lead guitar and vocals. After that, all Paddy ever wanted to do was pump gas and write songs. McAloon's early influences included T. Rex, Free, The Who, and the Beatles; the classy pop songs of Jimmy Webb, Burt Bacharach, and Hal David; and staples of Broadway, especially Stephen Sondheim.

In 1982 gigs at local pubs earned Prefab Sprout enough cash to record a single, "Lions in My Own Garden," on their own label, Candle. The single and its "simply ears ahead" poster caught the attention of the independent label Kitchenware Records, which released "Lions" nationally.

Meanwhile, local school girl Wendy Smith had fallen for the band after seeing their early shows. McAloon asked her and a friend to sing on their next single, and Wendy just kept on singing with the Sprout. Her first recorded appearance came on Prefab Sprout's second single release, "The Devil Has All the Best Tunes." The band recorded their first album, *Swoon,* in 1983. It so impressed Kitchenware that the label took it to the considerably larger CBS Records (later purchased by Sony), which signed the band for an eight-album deal. *Swoon* was released in 1984, went straight into the Top 20, and started the music media's passions rolling.

Swoon Impassioned Critics

Kitchenware had publicized the band a great deal and the notoriously temperamental British press was waiting to pounce, knives at the ready. In *Melody Maker,* Adam Sweeting deemed *Swoon* "virtually unbearable," calling it "drivel" and "a gigantic folly, a tour de force of self-indulgence." He concluded his remarks with, "As you can tell, I'm horrified." *Melody Maker's* Ian Pye felt *Swoon* "suffered from a self-conscious desire to impress," and many others called it too clever. Yet Colin Irwin, also writing for *Melody Maker,* ventured, "All that anguish, preciousness and contrived wit took a bit of stomaching ... but *Swoon* nevertheless still wielded an elusive, nagging magic that has continued to drag me back to it throughout the last year."

This apparently exasperating music has been described in a variety of ways. Sylvie Simmons of *Creem* called

McAloon "a sort of Marc Bolan [of T. Rex] spirit in Steely Dan's body listening to [Bob] Dylan and the Beach Boys while fasting for Lent." The music is profoundly nostalgic, harkening back to a time of beautiful, simple melodies. McAloon mixes a poetic wordiness with an eccentric compositional style. *Melody Maker* deemed the songs a blend of "sculpted, elaborate melodies and achingly beautiful chord changes." *Creem* called it "melodic, high-gloss pop," noting "colorful impressionistic lyrics sung in Paddy's naive, soulful voice."

Critical blather notwithstanding, *Swoon* caught the ear of several influential pop artists, including Thomas Dolby, who offered to produce the band's next album. The result was 1985's *Steve McQueen (Two Wheels Good* in the U.S.), with drummer Neil Conti newly on board. Hailed by many critics as the best album of the year—even the decade—several felt it stood alongside eclectic gems like the Beatles' *Revolver,* the Byrds' *Notorious Byrd Brothers,* and the Beach Boys' *Pet Sounds. Melody Maker's* Pye called it "an incredible achievement; its melodic and textural qualities are stunning enough, but the vision behind it all has produced a work that is not just consistently excellent but positively inspirational." Rob Tannenbaum, on the other hand, wrote in *Rolling Stone* that "while the rich, fresh writing tempts you back to *Two Wheels Good,* the music often makes listening a chore—like sifting through mud to uncover a few specks of gold."

Commercial Success Elusive

Although beloved by many a critic, Prefab Sprout has never been much of a commercial success. Their biggest hit was a throwaway tune off their fourth album, 1988's *From Langley Park to Memphis.* Ironically, "King of Rock 'n' Roll" was a song about a one-hit wonder that McAloon whipped off in 20 minutes.

Langley countered the critical cries of "fey," "wimpy," and "precious" that had held the band back, though McAloon had dismissed such name-calling all along. "I'm not a wimp," he told *Creem's* Simmons, "I'm physically frail. I'm also guilty of being poor, so the songs I've recorded in the past haven't had a brilliant sound because I couldn't afford the right guitar. But that's not wimpy. I'm not eccentric; in fact I'm probably coldbloodedly straight-ahead in what I do. I'm not a clever bastard genius."

Indeed, McAloon is a product of his environment and thus can't help that he always sounds "so bloody academic," as he put it to Simmons. Educated in a Catholic seminary from the ages of 11 to 19, McAloon holds a degree in English literature and can hardly help writing intelligently. "And I relish my reputation as this introspective, precious brooder, because I know that's not me," he told David Wild in *Rolling Stone,* "I know I'm not the guy in the moody picture." In fact, the inward-looking songs he writes are most often a product of his imagination. "A song's just a point of view," he explained to David Stubbs in *Melody Maker.* "I just try and be consistent to the law of that particular song, even if it isn't how I necessarily feel."

Some of the critical hubbub surrounding the band can be attributed to writers who just didn't get it—they missed the jokes and McAloon's wry sense of humor, taking him much too seriously. Though expressing some misgivings about the record, *Melody Maker's* Chris Roberts, for one, did locate the humor in *Langley.* "Prefab Sprout get away with things which should normally be stomped on from a great height. Quite why the melodic and crafted *Langley Park* is a truly *delicious* record is making me scratch my [head].... It's something to do with a poignancy which is too happily coloured with good-natured tricks to be maudlin.... I am baffled as to why this, like its noble predecessor *Steve McQueen,* hangs my guts from the lampshade every time."

No Road Warriors

With each record, critics and a cult of fans in the U.K. and U.S. continued to rave, but the band was unable to achieve mainstream popularity. This could be attributed to their disinclination to tour in support of their albums. Prefab Sprout toured very early in their career and again in the early 1990s, but never in the U.S. McAloon told the *Independent on Sunday,* "I can do it, and I will do it, and it doesn't break my heart to do it. But it's possible that it destroys the mystery which surrounds the records and I'd rather be at home trying to write the big one." Many hinted that the band could not recreate their complex sound in a live setting. But McAloon told Robert Sandall in the London *Sunday Times* of his concern that "you see what certain songs do to your audience every night, and you start writing to please them." To *Rolling Stone's* Wild he admitted, "I'm burnt by every day that I don't [write]. It reduces me."

McAloon spent years working on *Langley's* follow-up, *Jordan: The Comeback,* which was almost universally lauded as his masterpiece. "Exquisite, sumptuous, marvelously intricate, angelically forceful," wrote taste-maker Simon Reynolds in *Melody Maker.* In the same magazine, Paul Lester enthused, "Prefab Sprout have, alongside their knowingness and intelligence and post-modern deliberation, a certain incidental beauty that could never be contrived." Lester went on to sum up

McAloon's gift: "[His] genius is his ability to take those few breathtaking seconds from your favorite record—the thrilling intro or swoonsome chorus that you play over and over—and construct whole songs of them.... In [*Jordan*] there are numerous instances of Paddy's ability to sustain freak moments over three or four sublime minutes."

Jordan was an ambitious record, lengthy and ranging in themes from God to Elvis Presley. Where most reviewers gushed shamelessly, some found the disc a little too perfect. In the *Guardian,* Adam Sweeting opined that "nothing [Prefab Sprout] ever do appears to spring from impulse. It's always a pastiche, an echo or a gesture, as if McAloon has studied music from books and old movies and set about turning his discoveries into a crossword.... It's skillful, but it's a little like sitting in an examination." Nonetheless, *Sounds* contributor George Berger represented the majority when he noted McAloon's simple "knowledge of beauty, in itself rare," calling the songwriter "a Shakespeare in a world of cheap novels."

After a brief U.K. tour for *Jordan,* McAloon again sat down to a mammoth project: *Earth: The Story So Far.* In the meanwhile, the rise of a new radio format in the U.S. called Adult Album Alternative boded well for the band's commercial prospects; this type of radio station, which plays a softer, singer-songwriter-oriented form of "alternative" rock, including older songs befitting such tastes, had already taken a liking to Prefab Sprout. For the first time, radio listeners in America could hear Prefab Sprout on commercial airwaves.

Selected discography

On Kitchenware Records/Sony in the U.K., Epic Records in the U.S.

Swoon, 1984.
Steve McQueen (*Two Wheels Good* in the U.S.), 1985.
Protest Songs, 1989.
From Langley Park to Memphis (includes "King of Rock 'n' Roll"), 1988.
Jordan: The Comeback, 1990.
A Life of Surprises, The Best of Prefab Sprout, 1992.

Sources

Billboard, September 20, 1988.
Consumer's Research Magazine, March 1993.
Creem, February 1986; October 1988.
Guardian, August 23, 1990.

Independent on Sunday (London), June 28, 1992.

Melody Maker, March 10, 1984; June 1, 1985; June 8, 1985; February 6, 1988; March 12, 1988; March 26, 1988; June 24, 1989; August 4, 1990; August 18, 1990; January 5, 1991; June 20, 1992.

New Musical Express, August 18, 1990; June 20, 1992.

Q, September 1990.

R/M, August 22, 1990.

Rolling Stone, October 24, 1985; June 16, 1988; March 7, 1991.

Sounds, August 22, 1990.

Spin, January 1991.

Sunday Times (London), September 9, 1990.

Time Out, August 22, 1990.

Today, August 31, 1990.

Vox, August 1990; July 1992.

Additional information for this profile was obtained from Kitchenware Records publicity materials, 1994 and 1995.

—*Joanna Rubiner*

André Previn

Composer, pianist, conductor

AP/Wide World Photos

Jack Priwin was an energetic, successful criminal lawyer who lived and worked in pre-World War II Berlin, Germany, along with his wife, Charlotte, their son, Stefan, and daughter, Leonore. He was also an avid classical music enthusiast who often dreamed of siring the next Mozart. With the birth of Ludwig Andreus Priwin on April 6, 1929, the elder Priwin's wishes, it seemed, were granted: A short five years later, at the boy's first piano lesson, it was clear that he was destined for musical greatness. Although he has yet to achieve the same rank as famed composer Wolfgang Amadeus Mozart—or his namesake, Ludwig von Beethoven— André Previn, as the precocious child came to be known, has left an indelible stamp upon the world of music as conductor, composer, arranger, orchestrator, and virtuoso pianist in both the classical and jazz arenas. "All it took was one beat," he explained in *André Previn: A Biography,* "and I knew I would spend the rest of my life chasing after music."

Starting at age five, each child in the Priwin family was required to begin musical instruction on the piano. Although Stefan and Leonore both did well, it was André who shone. His father immediately recognized the boy's gift and undertook to train his son in the classics. Jack collected countless phonograph records of Beethoven, Brahms, Haydn, and Mozart, and played these for André at every occasion. He also escorted the boy to innumerable classical concerts and performances. When his son reached age six, Jack arranged to have André admitted to the venerable Berlin Conservatory.

Difficult Times

The young André's career was nearly cut short, however, when the fascist Nazi party, who upheld a policy of exterminating Jews, rose to power in Germany. Being of Jewish descent, the family was forced to flee their native land when André was nine. Having waited too long to leave, they were unable to bring any of their material possessions. Thus it was that the Previns, who changed their name during their trans-Atlantic voyage, arrived nearly penniless in Hollywood, California, in 1939.

The whole family worked together in order to survive. Jack, like the rest of his family, could not speak a word of English, and the family lacked the money for him to study American law. Instead, Jack Previn became the neighborhood piano teacher. Stefan—now Steve— worked as a messenger at Universal Studios. André continued to study the piano and also took odd, short-term musical employment. It wasn't long, however, before André, with the help of his American-born film composer uncle, Charlie Previn, landed a job at MGM

Born Ludwig Andreus Priwin, April 6, 1929, in Berlin, Germany. As a child, emigrated with family to U.S.; married Betty Bennett (a singer), 1952 (divorced, 1957); married Dory Langdon (a lyricist), 1958 (divorced, 1969); married Mia Farrow (an actress), 1969 (divorced, 1978); married Heather Hales, 1982; has several children.

Composer, conductor, and pianist. While in high school, worked as arranger and orchestrator for MGM Studios, Hollywood, CA; became film composer for MGM; began recording career as a jazz artist; conductor with Houston Symphony Orchestra, beginning in 1966; London Symphony Orchestra, 1968-75; Pittsburgh Symphony Orchestra, 1975-84; and Los Angeles Philharmonic Orchestra, 1985-88; recorded a series of jazz albums on the Telarc label. Composer of numerous film scores. Author of memoir *No Minor Chords: My Days in Hollywood*, Doubleday, 1991. *Military service:* Served in the National Guard in Korean War.

Awards: Academy awards for film scores *Gigi*, 1958, *Porgy and Bess*, 1959, *Irma La Douce*, 1963, and *My Fair Lady*, 1964; Academy Award nominations for film scores *Three Little Words*, 1950, *Kiss Me Kate*, 1953, *It's Always Fair Weather*, 1955, *Bells Are Ringing*, 1960, *Elmer Gantry*, 1960, *Two for the Seesaw*, 1962, *Thoroughly Modern Millie*, 1967, and *Jesus Christ Superstar*, 1973; Grammy Award for jazz album *Plays Songs by Harold Arlen*, 1960; Grammy Award nomination for jazz album *After Hours*, 1989.

Addresses: *Home*—Surrey, England. *Record company*—Telarc, 23307 Commerce Park Rd., Cleveland, OH 44122.

Studio's music department. The boy's prodigious talent quickly elevated him from part-time arranger to full-fledged composer and orchestrator. By 1948, not yet 20, he had scored his first film.

After graduating from Beverly Hills High School, Previn continued to study music and work at MGM. At that time there was still a possibility in the United States that any young man in his early twenties could be called upon to serve in the armed forces. Like many others, Previn thought the best legal way to avoid being drafted into the army was to join the National Guard—that is, until his unit was mobilized in 1950 at the start of the Korean War.

Previn was anything but a typical soldier—he was called away from latrine-digging duty one day to be informed of his nomination for an Academy Award. In addition, his musical experience earned him a place as composer and arranger for the 6th Army band rather than as an infantry soldier in Korea. He was stationed in San Francisco and, already enamored with jazz piano legend Art Tatum, would often accompany his fellows to local bebop jazz clubs. Previn soon became fascinated with what to him was a completely new world of music. He would use his passes to sit in with jazz bands all over the city in an attempt to master this fresh art form. As always, André was quick to make friends, and when discharged from the army, he remained in San Francisco to study the classics with the prestigious conductor Pierre Monteux, and also to play jazz with his newly formed combo.

Troubled Personal Life

In 1952, with his impulsive marriage to jazz singer Betty Bennett, Previn began a tumultuous and public romantic life that would eventually overshadow, at times, his extraordinary musical career. During this period he returned to Hollywood to resume scoring films for MGM. He found that he had become more valuable than ever before as a classical composer capable of understanding jazz, and his talents were much in demand. Previn also found time to form a new combo and a long-lasting friendship with noted jazz percussionist Shelly Manne. As if that were not enough, in the mid-1950s the composer became a best-selling recording artist for the jazz label Contemporary Records. His album *My Fair Lady* earned the status of the biggest-selling jazz record to date. However, Previn was at the same time nursing a deep-seated dissatisfaction with where his life was heading. He ended his marriage with Bennett in 1957, only a few months before the birth of their second child.

Not satisfied being chained to MGM, Previn continued to score films as an independent agent and also to play and record jazz. In 1958 he married Dory Langdon, a lyricist who had been invited by studio management to collaborate with Previn on songs for several of his movie soundtracks. They worked together successfully for some years and saw a number of their songs receive Academy Award nominations. Previn, however, was becoming increasingly displeased with his film work. He had always desired to conduct, and when his father died in 1962, Previn decided it was time to leave Hollywood—and the jazz life—firmly behind him.

As with nearly all of his endeavors, Previn threw himself into his new occupation with astonishing single-mindedness and energy. He accepted every guest-conducting invitation he received, and to improve his image as a "serious" musician, he also accepted invitations to perform at the piano in classical concerts. He often conducted directly from the piano stool. Previn made his first recording as a conductor in 1962 with the St. Louis Symphony, which was released to critical plaudits. By 1966 he had made such a name for himself that he was offered the position of conductor of the Houston Symphony.

"I'm frightened by the glory of the music I have to work with, and plagued by personal inadequacies."

Unfortunately, at the same time his career was soaring, Previn's marriage to Dory Langdon began to disintegrate. Langdon had a history of mental illness and had begun a series of extended visits to various sanitariums. Previn's constant absence only served to worsen the situation, since his wife was deathly afraid of air travel and could not join him.

Meanwhile, Previn's work with the Houston Symphony brought him glowing reviews and worldwide acclaim, and in 1968 he accepted the position of conductor of the renowned London Symphony Orchestra (LSO). Around this time, gossip columnists began to notice him frequently in the company of actress Mia Farrow, who was previously married to popular singer Frank Sinatra. Farrow became pregnant with Previn's twin sons, and the scandal that ensued resulted in his leaving the Houston Symphony.

Previn divorced Langdon—at the time residing in a California mental hospital—and married Farrow in the fall of 1969. The couple settled with their children in the English countryside. Previn also redoubled his efforts with the LSO, touring with them around the world and using his pop-star image to tirelessly promote the orchestra on television and in the news media. His diligence was to earn him the longest tenure with the LSO of any single conductor.

The 1970s were once again tumultuous for Previn. In 1975 internal squabbling led him to leave the LSO to become the full-time musical director of the Pittsburgh Symphony, a post he retained until 1984. His marriage to Mia Farrow, with whom he had three children and three adopted orphans, finally broke up in 1978 due

largely to their conflicting careers. Previn seemed always to be off in some corner of the world conducting, while Farrow was busy furthering her acting career. In 1984 Previn left the Pittsburgh Symphony over a clash with management about his casual attire and too-modern musical choices and was almost immediately snatched up by the Los Angeles Philharmonic for the 1985 to 1986 season. He remained as conductor for the Los Angeles Philharmonic until 1988, departing, as he had with other orchestras in the past, due to conflicts with management.

Since then, Previn has led a life of comparative stability. In 1982 he married Englishwoman Heather Hales and settled into his home—dubbed the Haven—in the wooded hills of Surrey. Despite the fact that he eventually came to look upon the years he spent in jazz as time squandered (he feels his true destiny has always been in conducting), Previn made something of a comeback in that arena, gathering his old friends to record a series of albums for the Telarc label. The first of these, *After Hours,* received a Grammy nomination in 1989. Previn also continues to accept guest conducting positions with various orchestras throughout the world.

A Sense of Peace

In 1991 Previn published a memoir of his days as a film composer. It is titled *No Minor Chords: My Days in Hollywood,* in reference to a proclamation against minor chords issued by a studio magnate who heard a passage he disliked in a score for one of Previn's films. Notwithstanding the fact that Previn spent many years trying to shake his "Tinsel Town" image, and has on occasion expressed nothing but contempt for the movie industry and nearly all those involved in it, he wrote, "I have to say that I can't consider my ... years in Hollywood as any kind of waste. They were entertaining and educational and highly paid, and I am thankful for all that."

Previn has, though, finally and fully embraced his chosen profession of orchestral conductor. As he explained in *No Minor Chords,* conducting provides the "healthy and sobering experience of constantly working with music that is invariably better than any performance of it can be. It keeps final goals out of reach and it means that boredom is a very rare occurrence. I have always found it necessary for my work to scare me. It doesn't do any good to be totally secure in the knowledge that tomorrow's efforts will not be too difficult, and [that] they will, with rare exception, be accepted with praise. Nowadays, worry and self-doubt are roommates of mine. I'm frightened by the glory of the music I have to work with, and plagued by personal inadequacies. In my profession, triumphs and failures are allowed to be more private, and mass opinions neither make nor break a lifetime career."

Selected scores

The Sun Comes Up, 1949.
Challenge to Lassie, 1949.
Scene of the Crime, 1949.
Border Incident, 1949.
Tension, 1949.
Kim, 1950.
The Outriders, 1950.
Three Little Words, 1950.
Violent Hour, 1950.
Shadow on the Wall, 1950.
Cause for Alarm, 1951.
Small Town Girl, 1953.
The Girl Who Had Everything, 1953.
Kiss Me Kate, 1953.
Give a Girl a Break, 1953.
Bad Day at Black Rock, 1954.
Kismet, 1955.
It's Always Fair Weather, 1955.
The Fastest Gun Alive, 1956.
The Catered Affair, 1956.
Invitation to the Dance, 1956.
House of Numbers, 1957.
Designing Woman, 1957.
Silk Stockings, 1957.
Hot Summer Night, 1957.
Gigi, 1958.
Porgy and Bess, 1959.
Who Was That Lady?, 1960.
The Subterraneans, 1960.
Bells Are Ringing, 1960.
Elmer Gantry, 1960.
The Four Horsemen of the Apocalypse, 1961.
All in a Night's Work, 1961.
One, Two, Three, 1961.
Two for the Seesaw, 1962.
Long Day's Journey into Night, 1962.
Irma La Douce, 1963.
Dead Ringer, 1964.
Goodbye Charlie, 1964.
My Fair Lady, 1964.
Kiss Me Stupid, 1964.

Inside Daisy Clover, 1965.
The Fortune Cookie, 1966.
Thoroughly Modern Millie, 1967.
Jesus Christ Superstar, 1973.

Selected discography

Double Play, Contemporary, 1957.
My Fair Lady, Contemporary, 1957.
Pal Joey, Contemporary, 1957.
Gigi, Contemporary, 1958.
Plays Songs by Vernon Duke, Contemporary, 1958.
Plays Songs by Jerome Kern, Contemporary, 1959.
Secret Songs for Young Lovers, 1959.
West Side Story, Contemporary, 1959.
André Previn's Trio Jazz: King Size!, Contemporary, 1960.
Give My Regards to Broadway, Columbia, 1960.
Plays Songs by Harold Arlen, Contemporary, 1960.
Like Love, 1960.
After Hours, Telarc, 1989.
Uptown, Telarc, 1990.
Old Friends, Telarc, 1992.
What Headphones?, Angel, 1993.
A Touch of Elegance, Legacy, 1994.
The Essence of André Previn, Legacy, 1994.
Previn at Sunset, Black Lion/da music, 1994.

Sources

Books

Bookspan, Martin, and Ross Yockey, *André Previn: A Biography*, Doubleday, 1981.
Previn, André, *No Minor Chords: My Days in Hollywood*, Doubleday, 1991.
Ruttencutter, Helen, *Previn*, St. Martin's, 1985.

Periodicals

Down Beat, January 1990.
Esquire, September 1984.
Keyboard, January 1991.
Time, May 8, 1989.

—*Alan Glenn*

Jimmy Reed

Singer, guitarist, harmonica player

MICHAEL OCHS ARCHIVES/Venice, CA

Jimmy Reed was one of the most popular blues artists of the mid- to late 1950s. He had a "real gift for hooks," and a "very personal groove—a dense electric rumble pierced by keening harp leads" that "helped transform Chicago rhythm and blues into rock and roll," according to *Rolling Stone.* During his heyday from 1954 until 1963, Reed's songs ascended the rhythm and blues charts dozens of times. "Ain't That Lovin' You Baby," "Baby What You Want Me to Do," "Big Boss Man," and "Bright Lights, Big City," for example, have become blues and rock and roll standards. An alcoholic, Reed had many drunken misadventures for which he became notorious. He was also epileptic, and his addiction to alcohol worsened his epilepsy. In 1976, at the age of 51, he died after a gig in Oakland, California. Fifteen years later, he was inducted into the Rock and Roll Hall of Fame.

Mathis James Reed was born on a plantation in Mississippi on September 6, 1925. At the age of ten he began learning to play the guitar. After working in the fields, he would meet with his friend Eddie Taylor. "When we'd come out' the field from work," he recalled in *Living Blues* magazine, "we'd practically just meet and both us get a box, and we'd decide to go out an set under a shade tree and just see who could find what on a box.... We wasn't nothin' but little old kids."

Reed also displayed an early talent for singing. He and two other boys formed a gospel singing group that became popular in the Pilgrim Rest Baptist Church in Meltonia, Mississippi. But gospel turned out to be an inappropriate genre of music for someone as footloose as Reed. At age 14 he moved to Duncan, Mississippi, to farm with his brother; there, he continued his guitar playing. "I used to slip out of the cotton patch," he told *Living Blues,* "and go up on to the house, and get me a cold drink of water and steal my brother's old piece of guitar, you know and sit 'round there and hide and fool around."

After a year in Duncan, Reed traveled to Chicago to live with his brother Tommy. He worked for the downtown Young Men's Christian Association (YMCA) and then for the Hefter Coal Company. In 1943, when he was 18, he was drafted into the U.S. Navy. He spent much of World War II working in a base kitchen in Riverside, California. Though he started drinking heavily while in the service, his stint in the navy also gave him the chance to learn to read.

After his discharge, Reed visited home and got married. In 1946 he returned to Chicago and started working in the steel industry. While on a job at the Valley Mould Iron Works, he met a washtub bass player named Willie Joe "Jody" Duncan. He and Duncan began playing togeth-

For the Record . . .

Born Mathis James Reed, September 6, 1925, in Leland (one source says Dunleith), MS; died of respiratory failure, August 29, 1976, in Oakland, CA; son of Joseph Reed (a sharecropper) and Virginia Ross (a sharecropper); married Mary Lee "Mama" Reed, 1945; children: Loretta, Jimmy, Jr., Arlene, Michael, Malinda, Roslyn, Rosemary, Avery.

Singer, guitarist, and harmonica player, 1948-76. Worked variously for Young Men's Christian Association (YMCA), Hefter Coal Company, and in the steel industry, Chicago, IL. Played in streets and clubs for tips, often with Willie Joe "Jody" Duncan, 1948; played with Eddie Taylor, 1949 to early 1960s; recording artist, 1953-76; recorded for Vee-Jay label, 1953-65; toured extensively, 1953-76; toured England, 1963-64, and Europe, 1968; recorded for ABC/BluesWay label, 1966-68. *Military service:* U.S. Navy, 1944-45.

Awards: Inducted into Rock and Roll Hall of Fame, 1991.

er, first in each other's houses and then in beer joints, stores, and on street corners. They played for tips, which were often substantial. "I'm tellin' you," Reed remembered in *Living Blues,* "them folks would load that old hat of Jody's up with nickels, dimes, quarters and halves, and dollars and things."

Duncan eventually left town but Reed continued playing and joined a combo with drummer Kansas City Red and pianist Blind John Davis. He also sat in regularly with the blues duo of John and Grace Brim. He was eventually reunited with his childhood pal, guitarist Eddie Taylor. Reed and Taylor became a regular duo, playing on the South Side of Chicago or in nearby Gary, Indiana. When the jobs were big enough, they added other musicians.

Around this time, Reed added harmonica to his guitar playing and singing. Though he had been playing harmonica since childhood, he had never been able to achieve the bending sound he wanted. It was not until he came up to Chicago and started playing "Marine Band" harmonicas that he developed his simple yet distinctive style. "I got hold of me one of [those harmonicas]," he explained in *Living Blues,* "and then I started trying that thing and therefore I don't know exactly just what happened that I started playing that devilish harmonica, 'cause couldn't nobody teach me to play it."

By the early 1950s, Reed began to get ambitious about recording. He made several albums in "do-it-yourself" booths and auditioned for Leonard Chess, owner of the famous Chess Records blues label, which was busy with famed blues artists Muddy Waters, Little Walter, and Howlin' Wolf. Reed, however, was soon approached by Vivian Carter, a disc jockey from Gary who was starting a new label called Vee-Jay.

Reed began recording for Vee-Jay in 1953, and within a year he hit the charts with "You Don't Have to Go." Other singles followed: "Ain't That Lovin' You Baby," "You've Got Me Dizzy," "Bright Lights Big City," "I'm Gonna Get My Baby," and "Honest I Do." Through the remainder of the 1950s and the early 1960s, Reed was among the biggest-selling blues artists in the United States.

Reed's wife, Mary Lee "Mama" Reed, whom he had married in 1945, was usually present during his recording sessions. She wrote several of his songs and would whisper the words into Reed's ear just before he sang. If one listens closely to his records, her voice is often audible.

Reed toured constantly during this time—usually with Taylor backing him up. Outside of Chicago, Reed proved particularly popular among white audiences. His songs were consistently covered by white rhythm and blues groups, while his classic tune "Big Boss Man" was adopted by blues and country artists alike.

On the road, Reed became infamous for his drinking problem. "I used to get so lit up," he admitted in *Living Blues,* "and so tore down off that Scotch and junk, man, till where all I could practically picture out was just my instrument and think about just what I was going to do." To help him with the demands of the touring life, Reed hired Al Smith as his road manager. Smith proved to be a significant influence on Reed's career, eventually becoming his agent and writing some of his songs.

In the early 1960s, sales of Reed's records flagged. Vee-Jay tried various gimmicks to revive his career, but the changing times, along with Reed's alcoholism and worsening epilepsy, undermined his ability to make a comeback. When Vee-Jay went bankrupt in 1966, Reed cut a few unsuccessful sides for the ABC/BluesWay label. In the mid-1960s his epileptic seizures grew worse, and in 1969 he entered a Veteran's Administration hospital in an effort to give up drinking. He stayed under a doctor's care until 1973. Toward the end of his life, Reed became something of a recluse, embittered by the music industry and his failure to keep the money he had made. He died of respiratory failure on August 29, 1976, in Oakland, California.

Selected discography

Jimmy Reed at Carnegie Hall/The Best of Jimmy Reed,
   Mobile Fidelity, 1992.
(With Johnny Winter) *Live at Liberty Hall, Houston, Texas,
   1972*, reissued 1993.
Best Of, GNP Crescendo.
Greatest Hits, Hollywood.
Speak the Lyrics to Me, Mama Reed, Vee-Jay.

Sources

Billboard, September 12, 1953.
Blues Unlimited, August 1974.
Living Blues, May/June 1975.
Rolling Stone, February 7, 1991.

—*Jordan Wankoff*

Arturo Sandoval

Trumpeter, flugelhornist

The 1994 release *Arturo Sandoval Plays Trumpet Concertos* may have marked contemporary jazz label GRP's first foray into classical music, as Paul Verna commented in *Billboard,* but for trumpeter Arturo Sandoval it is a revisiting of the repertoire he studied as a youth in Cuba. There, according to Sandoval, "I never had a chance to perform with the symphony orchestra because it was always busy playing with Russian violinists and pianists. So I had to wait until I was free to be able to do it."

Born in 1949 in Artemis, a small village in the province of Havana, Cuba, Sandoval started playing at age 13 in the village band, where he learned the basics of music theory and percussion. After playing many instruments, he settled on the trumpet and the flugelhorn; with both he would eventually to dazzle listeners throughout the world.

As a child Sandoval had little exposure to jazz. In a 1993 interview with *Down Beat* he commented, "The only thing I used to hear was traditional Cuban music, what we call *son,* which was played by a septet with a trumpet and bongos." But one day, a trumpeter in Artemis played Sandoval a Dizzy Gillespie and Charlie Parker record from 1946. Sandoval recalled that, upon hearing the album, he exclaimed, "'Oh, man! This is so weird. I don't understand nothing about what they're trying to play.' But that changed my mind completely. And I'm still trying to find out what they were doing." In 1964 Sandoval entered the Cuban National School of Arts, where he studied classical trumpet for three years.

Played with Dizzy in Cuba and Beyond

Drafted into the military in 1971, Sandoval was able to play with the Orquesta Cubana de Musica Moderna. During that time he affirmed his ability daily. After his discharge he continued playing in the well-known group Irakere, which he cofounded in 1973 with fellow Cuban greats Paquito D'Rivera and Churcho Valdes. The group continues to play in Havana under Valdes's leadership. Irakere toured North and South America, Europe, and Africa, and Sandoval appeared at festivals in Berlin, Germany; Newport, Rhode Island; Montreux, Switzerland; and Warsaw, Poland, throughout the 1970s. In 1981 Sandoval started his own orchestra and continued touring worldwide.

Sandoval's talent has led him to associations with many great musicians, but perhaps the most important was with the great bebop trumpeter Dizzy Gillespie, a long-time proponent of Afro-Cuban music, whom Sandoval calls his "spiritual father," according to Juan Carlos

Coto in *Down Beat.* As Sandoval noted, the two musicians met in Cuba in 1977 when Gillespie was playing impromptu gigs throughout the Caribbean with saxophonist Stan Getz: "I went to the boat to find him. I've never had a complex about meeting famous people. If I respect somebody, I go there and try to meet them."

As Coto reported, Gillespie wanted to visit the black neighborhoods where musicians play *guaguanco* and *rumba* in the street. Sandoval offered to take Gillespie around in his car, and only later that night when he took the stage with Gillespie did Sandoval reveal himself as a musician. Their friendship remained strong as they continued to play and record together. It was while touring with Gillespie's Grammy Award-winning United Nation Orchestra in Rome that Sandoval requested political asylum.

Gillespie's greatest tribute to Sandoval was also perhaps the most embarrassing for Sandoval. Gillespie often asked Sandoval for trumpet lessons, Sandoval remembered in *Down Beat.* "I'd say, 'Oh, Diz, please,' and he'd say, 'Come on, man.' So I would give him some exercises and advice about embouchure and things, and he would come back and say, 'You know, man, that worked.' Nobody [could] give Dizzy advice about mu-

sic, but he asked me about technique, because he didn't have any classical training."

According to Kazimierz Czyz in *Jazz Forum,* "Latin American jazz has a decidedly dance character," and some of Sandoval's recordings provide an extreme example of this assessment. Czyz further pointed out, "The jazz element (architectonics, sound, phrasing) here occurs only as decoration to a well crafted kind of 'easy listening music.'" This can perhaps be explained for Sandoval by his early influences and the Cuban government's labeling of jazz as imperialist music.

"No Signs"

Characteristically, Sandoval revels in the diversity of his music. After moving to Havana as a teen, he was introduced to the playing of Luis Escalante, the first trumpeter in the National Symphony Orchestra. As Sandoval told *Down Beat,* Escalante played classical, jazz, and Cuban music. "I never forgot that, and it has been my goal all my life to play as many things as I can. I don't want any sign on me that says 'jazz' or 'salsa' or 'blues.' I'm a musician, man."

Sandoval, by his own admission, is no innovator. *Down Beat's* Larry Birnbaum termed him "a mainstream stylist whose forte is a mind-boggling technique that eclipses even Maynard Ferguson's for triple-tongued flash and high register razzle-dazzle." Indeed, according to Coto in *Down Beat,* Sandoval's music seems that of an ever-open émigré, resurrecting the ghosts of Cuba's great trumpeters while embracing U.S. jazz harmonies. And the influence goes both ways. Sandoval has observed that American musicians are learning to discard traditional 1-2-3-4 jazz lines and are beginning to play around the *clave,* Cuban music's rhythmic heartbeat of 1-2-3, 1-2, sometimes known as the "Bo Diddley beat." The trumpeter asserts that the Cuban influence has also been felt in late-twentieth-century pop music, which, with the ever-increasing trend toward world sounds, has appropriated Cuban percussion.

Sandoval's own performances, in the opinion of *Jazz Forum's* Czyz, exhibit "faultless technique, beautiful, clear trumpet tone, an uncanny precision and good chops." In addition, *Down Beat's* Birnbaum, reviewing a 1983 performance, pointed out the trumpeter's "machine-gun flurries, squawks, smears, growls and flutters." At the same performance, Birnbaum recounted, Sandoval explained in Spanish that the piano had been his first love and then proceeded to play a long, polished, piano solo. Later, Sandoval played timbales, scat-sang, and twanged the jaw harp, before picking up a *shekere,* an African calabash rattle, for a percussion interlude that almost stopped the show.

A New Life

Since his defection from Cuba in 1990, Sandoval has lived with his family in Miami, Florida, where he prizes, above all, his creative freedom. He is not altogether dismissive of his old country, noting in *Down Beat* that "there are good, bad, and regular human beings everywhere, in all social classes and all professions. In every country, too." Miami serves as a vital connection for Sandoval to his past, a place where he can be near his culture and food, what Cubans call *El Cubaneo.* "I can't live far from my people," Sandoval explained. "I couldn't live in Alaska or Switzerland."

Sandoval's desire to keep close ties with his Cuban heritage is reflected in his career moves as well. Though he has played with musicians all over the world, including jazz stars Billy Cobham, Woody Herman, Woody Shaw, Herbie Hancock, John McLaughlin, Jon Faddis, and Stan Getz, as well as symphony orchestras and military bands, one of the first things he did after moving to Florida was to form a band. "I like to work with the same people and have a repertoire," he told *Down Beat.* "I don't like to play with them now and then, inventing things randomly. I like to work with musicians who can create a wide range of sounds and who like to play a lot of different things." Since his arrival in the United States, Sandoval has performed on the soundtrack for Robert Redford's film *Havana* with fellow exile and former associate, saxophonist Paquito D'Rivera, and on pop singer Gloria Estefan's *Into the Light.* Whether playing with percussionist Tito Puente at the Village Gate in New York City or in the concert halls of Europe, Sandoval has proven himself a foremost a musician of the world.

Selected discography

To a Finland Station, Pablo, 1983.
Tumbaito, Messidor, 1986.
A.S. Plays for the Pandas, 1987.
No Problem, 1987.
Straight Ahead, Jazz House, 1988.
(Contributor) *Havana* (soundtrack), GRP, 1990.
(With others) *Flight to Freedom,* GRP, 1991.
(Contributor) Gloria Estefan, *Into the Light,* Epic, 1991.
(With others) *I Remember Clifford,* GRP, 1992.
Dream Come True, GRP, 1993.
Arturo Sandoval Plays Trumpet Concertos, GRP, 1994.
(With others) *Danzón,* GRP, 1994.
The Latin Train, GRP, 1995.
Breaking the Sound Barrier, Chicago Caribbean Arts.
Just Music, Jazz House.
Live at the Royal Festival Hall, Enja.
Reunion, Messidor.

Sources

Billboard, March 19, 1994; June 10, 1995.
Brass Bulletin, number 65, 1989; number 71, 1990.
Crescendo International, August 1989.
Down Beat, November 1983; July 1991; June 1992; June 1993; June 1995.
Jazz, May 1984; December 1985.
Jazz Forum, number 92, 1985.
Jazz Journal International, February 1990.
Jazz Podium, November 1990.
Jazz Times, December 1983.
Metro Times (Detroit), August 1, 1993.

—John Morrow

Bob Seger

Singer, songwriter

Bob Seger's unadorned, working-class songs and wistful, raspy vocal style reflect his Michigan roots and affection for rock and roll. Seger received national acclaim in 1976 with the album *Night Moves,* which was a sentimental journey back to his adolescent dating experiences. He had been touring and recording since 1963 and was already popular in his native Michigan when he met with long-awaited recognition. Between 1976 and 1984, Seger had 14 Top 40 singles in the United States and was dubbed the "Godfather" of no-frills rock music.

Seger has been credited with blazing a path for musicians like the Eagles, John Cougar Mellencamp, Bruce Springsteen, Jackson Browne, and Tom Petty, all of whom possessed a similar, straightforward style of rock music. *People* magazine's Carl Arrington described his music as "hard ... with grit, not glitter," and Seger told *Newsweek* in 1986: "Gritty guys like us will always be around, because we're the guys who work hardest and really care about what we do."

Seger was born in Ann Arbor, Michigan, on May 6, 1945, one of two sons of Stewart and Charlotte Seger. Stewart Seger, an in-house medic for the Ford Motor Company, led a 13-piece orchestra on weekends in the 1940s. He encouraged a preschool-aged Bob to learn to play the ukulele. By the time Seger had reached high school, he was playing the electric guitar and keyboards. He honed his musical skills in high school by performing at local parties in Ann Arbor in a three-piece band called the Decibels. Later, he was a member of bands called the Town Criers and the Omens. Seger's early influences included country musicians, whose songs were played on WLAC out of Nashville, and rhythm and blues artists, especially Wilson Pickett, Solomon Burke, Van Morrison, Otis Redding, James Brown, and Detroit's Mitch Ryder.

"Heavy Music"

Seger's father deserted his wife and sons when Seger was ten years old, leaving Seger's mother with little in the way of financial prospects. As a result, Seger's music often reflects hard-life experiences—this is particularly evident on "The Ring," "The Lonely One," "Against the Wind," and "Turn the Page"—and is fueled by an empathy for human loss, a compassion for societal problems, and a love of simple pleasures. After watching his father struggle with alcoholism, Seger vowed to avoid drug use and to impart something significant through music with honest emotion.

In 1964, at the age of nineteen, Seger formed the band Last Heard with the organ player from Del Shannon's

Born Robert Clark Seger, May 6, 1945, in Ann Arbor, MI; son of Stewart (an in-house medic for the Ford Motor Company and former orchestra leader) and Charlotte (a domestic) Seger; married, 1967 (divorced, 1967); married Annette (Nita) Sinclair (an actress), November 8, 1987; children: Cole, Samantha Char.

Learned to play the ukulele at the age of five; played electric guitar and keyboards in high school; performed at local parties in Ann Arbor, MI, in a three-piece band called the Decibels; later played in the Town Criers and the Omens; formed the band Last Heard, 1964, and recorded the singles "The Lonely One" and "East Side Story"; recorded single "Heavy Music" on the national Cameo-Parkway label, 1966; assembled the Bob Seger System, 1968, and released debut album *Ramblin' Gamblin' Man* on Capitol Records; *Live Bullet* double album released, 1976; Seger's bandmates—Chris Campbell (bass), Drew Abbott (guitar), Charlie Allen Martin (drums), Alto Reed (saxophone), and Rick Manasa (keyboards)—came to be known as the Silver Bullet Band.

Contributed to *Urban Cowboy* film soundtrack, 1980; soundtrack to *Risky Business* included Seger's "Old Time Rock and Roll"; soundtrack to *Forrest Gump* included "Against the Wind"; single "Like a Rock" used as the themesong for Chevy truck commercials, 1989-94.

Awards: (With the Silver Bullet Band) Lifetime Achievement Award, Motor City Music Awards, 1995.

Addresses: *Record company*—Capitol Records, 1750 Vine St., Hollywood, CA 90028; or 1290 Avenue of the Americas, 35th floor, New York, NY 10104.

band; they recorded the singles "The Lonely One" and "East Side Story." "East Side Story" caught the ear of a Detroit clubowner named Ed (Punch) Andrews, who owned Hideout Records. By 1965 Andrews and Seger had raised enough money to release "East Side Story," which sold 50,000 copies in the Detroit area. The pair became partners and shared a solid business relationship that has endured for over three decades.

A year later, in 1966, Seger recorded the single "Heavy Music" on the national Cameo-Parkway label, selling 66,000 copies. "Heavy Music" nearly reached the Top 100 charts in 1967, just as the Cameo-Parkway label

folded. The label's demise stunted the single's burgeoning popularity, but the pulsating tune illuminated Seger as a forceful vocalist.

In 1968 Seger assembled the Bob Seger System and released his debut album, *Ramblin' Gamblin' Man* on Capitol Records. It made the Top 20 list and included one of the first anti-Vietnam songs of the era—a powerful, hard-rock single titled "2 Plus 2=?." Capitol Records was skittish about releasing the song as a single at the time due to the nation's charged political atmosphere. Consequently, Seger and Andrews were skeptical about the label's commitment to Seger's career.

The next year, Seger released *Noah,* which did not fare as well as *Ramblin' Gamblin' Man.* In 1971 he quit playing music to go to college; he attended classes for only three weeks, then decided to leave school to pursue his musical aspirations. Later that same year, Seger teamed up with the duo Teegarden and Van Winkle—comprised of Dave Van Winkle and Skip Knape—to create the all-acoustic *Brand New Morning* and *On Our Way,* both of which met with limited acclaim. In 1972 Seger released *Smokin' O.P.s* on Ed Andrews's Palladium label (distributed nationally by Reprise). A strong album, it included the hit singles "If I Were a Carpenter," "Bo Diddley," and "Turn On Your Love Light." Seger released *Back in '72* on Reprise Records in 1973, featuring the soulful single "Turn the Page." J. J. Cale and the Muscle Shoals Rhythm Section joined forces with Seger the next year for a few tracks on *Seven.* Traveling by car, Seger sometimes played as many as 265 one-nighters a year, often earning less than $7,000 in a good year.

Basked in Blue-Collar Rock's Success

When *Beautiful Loser* was released in 1975, Seger began to cement a formidable following. *Beautiful Loser* featured the rock and roll classic "Katmandu," as well as the winning title track, "Travelin' Man," and a searing rendition of "Nutbush City Limits," by R&B singer-songwriter Tina Turner. When Seger's two-disc *Live Bullet* album was released in 1976, the musicians who had played with Seger on *Seven* and *Live Bullet*—Chris Campbell, Drew Abbott, Charlie Allen Martin, Alto Reed, and Rick Manasa—came to be known as the Silver Bullet Band. *Live Bullet* was recorded in Detroit's Cobo Hall, and the album broke through into the Top 40 album category. It remained on the charts for two years and five months and sold over a million copies.

Live Bullet was followed in 1976 by *Night Moves,* which reached the Top 10 album mark and included the singles "Rock and Roll Never Forgets," "The Fire Down

Below," "Mary Lou," "Come to Poppa," "Main Street," and the title track. Bruce Springsteen's burgeoning popularity at this time—as well as the popularity of other rock and roll balladeers—was linked favorably to Seger, as these musicians extolled youthful yearnings and the virtues of the working class through rock.

Stranger in Town was released in 1978, with the wistful single "Still the Same" reaching the Top Five on the music charts, the up-tempo "Hollywood Nights" reaching the Number 12 slot, and the ballad "We've Got Tonight" reaching Number 13. The album was recorded with Eagles members Glenn Frey and Don Felder. Other notable singles on *Stranger in Town* include "Feel Like a Number" and "Old Time Rock and Roll," the latter immortalized by jockey-shorted rock wanna-be Tom Cruise in the motion picture *Risky Business*.

Set on His Course

Seger's *Against the Wind* was released in 1980 with the Eagles on background vocals. It went to the top of the music album charts, with the title cut ranking Number Five. Seger contributed to the soundtrack of the film *Urban Cowboy* in 1980 with the singles "Nine Tonight" and "Tryin' to Live My Life without You." A second live, two-disc album, *Nine Tonight,* was released a year later.

Seger's 1982 release *The Distance* examines relationships, alienation, and isolation. Dave Marsh, in his book *Fortunate Son,* commented: "What's most amazing about *The Distance* is its ambition. This is Seger's first focused set of songs." Seger didn't release *Like a Rock* until four years later, in 1986, and the album reflects his maturity; he sings about hard-won wisdom and the lessons life had taught him over the course of 40 years. The Weather Girls provided back-up vocals for *Like a Rock,* and Seger shared the writing credits for the first time in his career—with former Grand Funk keyboardist Craig Frost. The single "Like a Rock" was used as the themesong for Chevy commercials from 1989 through 1994.

Seger released *The Fire Inside* in 1991, but the uneven album met with lukewarm response. The singer failed to tour because his mother's death coincided with the release of the album. Around the same time, Seger's wife, Nita, discovered she was pregnant. Their first child, a son, was born in 1991, and Seger felt a renewed sense of purpose as a result. His *Greatest Hits* album was released in 1994, featuring fourteen songs, and the album *Lock and Load* was slated for a 1995 release. In addition, the acclaimed 1994 film *Forrest Gump* included Seger's single "Against the Wind" in its soundtrack.

When Detroit *Metro Times* contributor Stewart Francke asked Seger what had sustained him during the long years before his breakthrough to a large audience, Seger answered: "Enough people kept saying we were good.... We knew we had something. When I got the right group of guys ... everybody saw the light at the end of the tunnel and they worked real hard."

Selected discography

Ramblin' Gamblin' Man, Capitol, 1968.
Noah, Capitol, 1969.
Mongrel, Capitol, 1970.
Brand New Morning, Capitol, 1971.
Smokin' O.P.s, Reprise, 1972.
Back in '72, Reprise, 1973.
Seven, Reprise, 1974.
Beautiful Loser, Capitol, 1975.
Live Bullet, Capitol, 1976.
Night Moves, Capitol, 1976.
Stranger in Town, Capitol, 1978.
Against the Wind, Capitol, 1980.
Nine Tonight, Capitol, 1981.
The Distance, Capitol, 1982.
Like a Rock, Capitol, 1986.
The Fire Inside, Capitol, 1991.
Greatest Hits, Capitol, 1994.
Lock and Load, 1995.

Sources

Books

Marsh, Dave, *Fortunate Son,* Random House, 1985.

Periodicals

Billboard, October 1, 1994.
Detroit Free Press, July 8, 1994.
Esquire, October 1980.
Metro Times (Detroit), October 26, 1994.
Newsweek, February 14, 1977; June 9, 1986.
People, July 24, 1978; May 30, 1983.
Pulse!, September 1992.
Rolling Stone, June 15, 1978; May 1, 1980; July 10, 1980; November 26, 1981; February 3, 1983.
Stereo Review, June 1983.
Teen, September 1980.
Time, June 12, 1978.

—B. Kimberly Taylor

Sonny Sharrock

Guitarist

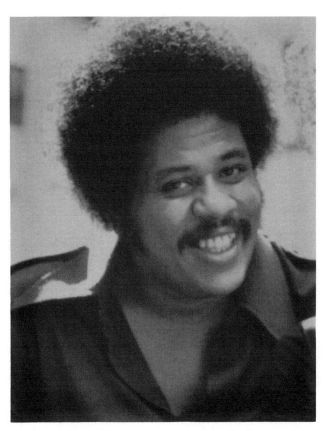

MICHAEL OCHS ARCHIVES/Venice, CA

Hailed as the father of free-jazz guitar, Sonny Sharrock carved his own unique niche in the world of jazz by adapting the free-form improvisational style pioneered by 1960s jazz horn players to the guitar. One of the first jazz guitarists to incorporate dissonance, distortion, feedback, and chord clusters into his playing style, he revolutionized jazz guitar concepts by developing an abstract, passionate, and truly original instrumental voice. His string-breaking, rule-shattering, free-for-all improvising influenced two generations of guitarists from jazz master Nicky Skopelitis to rock players Vernon Reid and Pearl Jam's Mike McCready. "My view of improvisation is very personal," Sharrock wrote in *Guitar Player*. "It's full of love, anger, truth, lies, and, in the end (I hope), sense."

Sharrock began his musical career in the late 1950s singing in local, street-corner doo-wop groups. He became intrigued by jazz in 1959 after hearing Miles Davis's *Kind of Blue* album. He began voraciously listening to jazz, particularly Davis, drummer Art Blakey, and saxophonists Cannonball Adderly, John Coltrane, and Ornette Coleman. By 1960 Sharrock was converted. "I was a total jazz head, and I wanted to be part of the music," he told Gary Parker Chapin in *Option*. "I was going through that period in my life that everyone goes through—you know, when you're 18 years old, you're out of high school, and you're looking for truth and meaning ... you go through all the arts. I tried to write, to sculpt, I tried to paint, and I was horrible at all of those things. But all this time I loved the music. So I decided to try to play."

The guitar was not Sharrock's first instrument of choice. Originally, he wanted to play saxophone, but asthma prevented this. So he bought a $12 guitar and started experimenting with jazz in 1960. From the beginning, Sharrock's approach to the guitar was unique; rather than basing his style on other jazz guitarists, he looked to his idols, horn players Davis, Coleman, and especially Coltrane, for inspiration.

Primarily self-taught and unable to read music, Sharrock credited his lack of formal music training as his biggest asset in developing his singular "shards of splintered glass" sound. "I just started playing," he explained to Mike Bourne in *Down Beat*. "I didn't have enough technique to copy anybody. So I just didn't bother. I used to just make up my own little things and eventually I just started playing like I do, and I never did play anybody's licks." Sharrock did, however, attend the Berklee School of Music from September of 1961 to February of 1962, studying composition.

Sharrock moved to New York City in 1965 to study with keyboardist and bandleader Sun Ra and play with

For the Record . . .

Born Warren Harding Sharrock, August 27, 1940, in Ossining, NY; died of a heart attack, May 25, 1994, in Ossining.

Sang in street corner doo-wop groups, 1954-59; took up guitar, 1960; played with various jazz musicians including Olatunji, Byard Lancaster, Pharaoh Sanders, Frank Wright, and Dave Burr, New York City, beginning in 1965; made first recorded appearance on Sanders's *Tauhid*, 1966; played, toured, and recorded with Herbie Mann, 1967-73; released first album as a leader, *Black Woman*, Vortex, 1970; led own band with wife Linda, 1973-75; worked with Bill Laswell's Material and Last Exit projects, 1985-90; released duet album with Nicky Skopelitis, *Faith Moves*, CMP, 1990; reunited with Sanders to record *Ask the Ages*, 1991.

Nigerian drummer Olatunji. He quickly became an integral part of the avant-garde New York jazz scene called the "New Thing." Between 1965 and 1967 he played with saxophonists Byard Lancaster, Pharaoh Sanders, and Frank Wright, and pianist Dave Burr. He made his first recorded appearance in 1966 on Sanders's album *Tauhid.*

Sharrock began collaborating with jazz flutist Herbie Mann in 1967 and played with him on and off for the next five years. He toured internationally with Mann, including appearances at both the Newport and Montreux jazz festivals. His work with Mann brought Sharrock to the attention of a number of other prominent jazz musicians who were eager to work with him. In 1969 he played on Mann's *Memphis Underground* and saxophonist Wayne Shorter's *Super Nova,* then made an uncredited appearance on Miles Davis's *Jack Johnson* the following year.

Sharrock gained critical acclaim for his work with Mann, but he felt constrained by the highly defined structure of Mann's bossa nova-based jazz. He broke out on his own with his first album as a leader, *Black Woman,* in 1970. In an interview in *Down Beat* shortly after the release of the album, he said, "I've got my own music and my own way of playing, and I have to do it. And, I can't do it with Herbie."

In 1973 Sharrock left Mann to form his own band along with his wife, jazz vocalist Linda Sharrock, bassist Sirone, drummer Milford Graves, and trumpeter Ted Daniel. The group released two albums between 1973 and 1975 and toured both the U.S. and Europe. Al-

though the projects brought Sharrock some renown and a wealth of playing experience, the band never really achieved widespread popularity. They disbanded in 1975. With the exception of an occasional club appearance, Sharrock was absent from the jazz scene for the remainder of the 1970s.

Sharrock returned to the experimental spotlight in 1985 with the critically acclaimed album *Guitar.* That year bassist/producer Bill Laswell asked him to sit in on the recording of his band Material's album *Memory Serves.* In addition to releasing the solo effort *Seize the Rainbow* in 1987, Sharrock continued his association with Laswell throughout the late 1980s, appearing on albums with both Laswell's Material and Last Exit projects, including *Headfirst into the Flames* and *Iron Path.*

Sharrock joined with guitar protégé Nicky Skopelitis in 1990 to record an album of free-style duets entitled *Faith Moves.* Also in 1990 he made a successful bid for more commercial recognition with the rock-oriented album *Highlife.* He returned to his uncompromising style of jazz in 1991 with *Ask the Ages.* That album, a ferocious, free-flowing session that reunited Sharrock with his mentor, Pharaoh Sanders, is considered by many to be Sharrock's best.

In 1994, Sharrock signed a big-budget deal with RCA Records to record a rock-oriented album that would identify him as "the godfather of grunge"—grunge being a popular rock style notable for noisy guitar—and feature guest performances by younger guitarists he had inspired. But, the album would never be made. Warren Harding "Sonny" Sharrock died of a heart attack in his home in Ossining, New York, on May 25, 1994.

America's leading exponent of free-jazz guitar for nearly 30 years, Sharrock secured his place in the annals of the great jazz innovators by refusing to follow in anyone's footsteps. "Imitating someone else's sound is unforgivable," he wrote in *Guitar Player.* "No one remembers the imitators. Miles is Miles, Coltrane is Coltrane, and Sonny Sharrock is Sonny Sharrock. For better or worse you are your own truth. Your improvisation must have feeling. It must swing, and it must have beauty, be it the fragile beauty of a snowflake or the terrible beauty of an erupting volcano. Beauty—no matter how disturbing or how still—is always true. Don't be afraid to let go of the things you know. Defy your weaker, safer self. Create. Make music."

Selected discography

Black Woman, Vortex, 1969.
Paradise, Atco, 1975.
Guitar, Enemy, 1986.

Last Exit, Enemy, 1986.
Seize the Rainbow, Enemy, 1987
Live in New York, Enemy, 1989.
Faith Moves, CMP, 1990.
Highlife, Enemy, 1990.
Ask the Ages, Axiom, 1991.

Sources

Books

Feather, Leonard G., *Encyclopedia of Jazz in the Seventies,*
    Horizon Press, 1976.
Jazz: The Essential Companion, Prentice Hall Press, 1988.

Periodicals

Down Beat, June 11, 1970; June 1992; July 1993; August
    1994.
Guitar Player, February 1989; January 1992; September
    1994.
Musician, February 1993.
Option, January 1, 1990.
Rolling Stone, July 14, 1994.

Additional information for this profile was obtained from the
All-Music Guide, Matrix Software, 1994.

—*Thaddeus Wawro*

Hank Shocklee

Producer, lyricist

In the early 1980s, hip-hop music experienced a revolution. The creative hub of the genre moved from the inner-city streets of Harlem and the Bronx to the suburbs of New York City. Out of Long Island came a new, angry sound—a rebellious noise that would change hip-hop music forever. Hank Shocklee was one of the key architects of that noise. As a founding member and producer of the incendiary rap group Public Enemy, he helped develop the distinctive, multilayered sound that became the group's trademark and influenced an entire generation of rappers. In addition to his work with Public Enemy, Shocklee added his unique production approach to recordings by acts ranging from Dr. Dre, 3rd Bass, and Bell Biv DeVoe to such pop and rock artists as Ziggy Marley, Paula Abdul, and Anthrax.

Shocklee's early involvement in music was as a student at New York City's Adelphi University. In the early 1980s, he worked as a promoter and deejay, setting up shows and parties in and around Long Island. At Adelphi, he met Carlton Ridenour, who would later take the name Chuck D and become lead rapper for Public Enemy. Ridenour shared Shocklee's interest in hip-hop, and it wasn't long before he was emceeing Shocklee's parties. Shocklee and Ridenour went on to form a deejay collective they called Spectrum. This collaboration—which would grow to include rappers Flavor Flav (William Drayton), Keith Shocklee (Hank's brother), Carl

Ryder, Eric Sadler, and DJ Terminator X (Norman Rogers)—laid the groundwork for Public Enemy.

Created Unique Production Style on Live Radio

In 1983 Shocklee and Ridenour attracted the attention of Bill Stephney, program director for WBAU, Adelphi's campus radio station. Stephney asked them to host a hip-hop show on Saturday nights. The duo agreed and the Super Spectrum Mixx Show—one of the first programs to feature rap and hip-hop music—hit the airwaves. The show was so far ahead of its time that Shocklee and Ridenour had difficulty filling a three-hour time slot because of the relatively few rap and hip-hop albums commercially available at the time. To solve this problem, they began recording their own rhythm tracks, rapping and mixing live on the air.

"The original Public Enemy sound was created on-air," Shocklee explained in *Option* magazine. "We were sampling stuff, taking a beat, pausing it up and doing a rap over it. This was still at a time when most of the other rap records were using a lot of live instruments. We were doing stuff without any live [instruments]. When we got the choruses, there would be nothing but scratching ... absolutely no instruments ... none! It's the only way we could do our music on the radio.... Even for sampling effects, we'd just have Chuck repeating his vocals. He would go something like 'Public Enemy Number One... One-One-One... One...' because we didn't have any sampling machines at the time."

"Public Enemy Number One"

The multilayered "noise" of those homemade recordings was something entirely new to rap and hip-hop. Over the next three years, Shocklee and Ridenour recorded hundreds of songs and gained a large cult following. But in 1986, one particular song put them over the top and set the stage for the birth of Public Enemy. As Shocklee recounted in *Option,* "Chuck had brought in Flavor Flav, and there was this one particular thing we did where at the beginning Flavor goes: 'Yo Chuck, man, brothers think you can't rhyme...,' and then, 'Yo, why don't you show these suckers how to do it.' It was just another one of those battle raps called 'Public Enemy Number One.' That record was the number-one smash hit on WBAU for *three* months or so. Out of all the stuff we were playing—even the new records that were coming out—that was the number-one song."

The success of "Public Enemy Number One" did not go unnoticed by record companies. Rick Rubin offered Shocklee and Ridenour a recording contract with his

Attended Adelphi University, Long Island, NY, c. 1980-86.

Began as a mobile DJ and concert promoter, early 1980s; formed DJ collective Spectrum with Carl Ryder, Eric Sadler, and brother Keith Shocklee, and future Public Enemy members Chuck D (Carlton Ridenour), Flavor Flav (William Drayton), and DJ Terminator X (Norman Rogers); with Chuck D, hosted rap/hip-hop radio program on WBAU, Adelphi University, 1983-86.

Public Enemy signed with Def Jam, and Shocklee formed the Bomb Squad with Ryder, Sadler, and brother Keith; Bomb Squad produced Public Enemy's first album, *Yo! Bum Rush the Show,* 1987; with Bill Stephney, formed S.O.U.L. (Sound of Urban Listeners) Records, 1990; produced Public Enemy's *Apocalypse '91: The Enemy Strikes Black,* 1991; signed and produced two albums on S.O.U.L. for rap group Young Black Teenagers, 1991-93; left S.O.U.L. and formed Shocklee Entertainment with Keith Shocklee, 1993; helped produce Public Enemy's *Muse Sick N Hour Mess Age,* 1994.

Addresses: *Record company*—Def Jam/Columbia, 550 Madison Ave., New York, NY 10022-3211.

newly formed rap label, Def Jam Records. They refused, believing that rap artists were targets for victimization by record companies. Rubin continued to pursue them, until finally, in 1987—after Bill Stephney joined Def Jam—Ridenour (now Chuck D), Flavor Flav, and DJ Terminator X signed with Def Jam and officially became Public Enemy. To produce the album, Shocklee put together a production team he called the Bomb Squad, which included former Spectrum members Carl Ryder, Eric Sadler, and Shocklee's brother Keith.

From the beginning, Shocklee wanted Public Enemy's sound to be distinct. But he also wanted it to grab the listener's attention in a way that would play off Chuck D's raw, pointed raps and immediately identify it as a Public Enemy song. "We wanted to make something obnoxious," Shocklee told Lewis Cole in *Rolling Stone.* "When people are asleep, you have to take drastic means to wake them up." He elaborated further in *Spin,* "We wanted to put certain hooks in the sound so that when you heard it coming out of a car, you knew what record it was on. It was Noise [with a] capital N.... We wanted to submerge you in sound, a thunderstorm of sound.

And Chuck's voice would come out of it like the voice of God."

The result was Public Enemy's first album, 1987's *Yo! Bum Rush the Show.* Shocklee's chaotic rhythm tracks and mixes, which *Detroit Free Press* music critic Gary Graff described as "an aural assault of buzzes, sirens, knife-edged guitar riffs, turntable scratches, and a bass-drum attack that pummels like uppercuts to the chin," were the perfect foil for the aggressive, often militant, political raps he wrote with Chuck D. The album was an instant hit, selling more than 400,000 copies without the benefit of radio airplay. Almost single-handedly, Shocklee and Chuck D created a new form of rap. Unlike the "party-music" rap that preceded it, this new genre was loud, angry, and provided a forum for serious social and political commentary. It gave people something to think about as well as listen to, and it would inspire both late 1980s rappers like Run-D.M.C. and L.L. Cool J. and the "gangsta" rappers of the 1990s.

Star Producer to the Birth of S.O.U.L.

Between 1987 and 1990, Shocklee and the Bomb Squad produced two more albums for Public Enemy, *It Takes a Nation of Millions to Hold Us Back* (1988), and *Fear of a Black Planet* (1990). Credited with masterminding Public Enemy's distinctive sound, Shocklee became a much sought after star producer. Between producing and helping write lyrics for Public Enemy albums, he produced and mixed singles for a wide variety of other artists ranging from Ice Cube and 3rd Bass to Sinead O'Connor and Paula Abdul.

In 1990 Shocklee struck out on his own and formed S.O.U.L. (Sound of Urban Listeners) Records with Bill Stephney. Their goal was to help promote rap and hip-hop by signing smart young acts. The partnership didn't last long: Stephney left S.O.U.L. in 1991 over business differences with Shocklee. Undeterred, Shocklee went on to sign and produce records for a number of artists, including Son of Bazerk and Raheem. Shocklee's only real success, though, came with the Young Black Teenagers, an ironically named, all-white New York City rap ensemble. He produced two top-selling albums with the group, *Young Black Teenagers* (1991) and *Dead Enz Kids Doin' Lifetime Bidz* (1993).

Shocklee remained with S.O.U.L. until late 1993. During his time with the label, he regularly did production and remix work for groups both inside and outside of the rap/hip-hop realm. He produced albums for Public Enemy (*Apocalypse 91: The Enemy Strikes Black*) and Another Bad Creation, and he remixed previously released tracks by Peter Gabriel, alternative metal band Helmet, and heavy metal group Anthrax.

In November of 1993 Shocklee left S.O.U.L. to form Shocklee Entertainment, a production firm and record label, with his brother Keith. The following year the two brothers served as producers on Public Enemy's release *Muse Sick N Hour Mess Age.*

An innovator with a purpose, Shocklee remains a driving force in the world of rap. As Public Enemy's producer and co-lyricist, he helped transform rap from party music into a medium for serious political and social commentary. Shocklee summed up his philosophy of rap in *Option:* "When we started Public Enemy, I had a vision of what I thought music should sound like in the future. We started Public Enemy because we wanted to project this vision and the messages we had in as strong a way as possible. We worked hard on our sound ... because we felt there was a crucial need for that kind of power in rap. We made a decision to go straight to the people, to be our own media, to reach them on our own terms and let them understand that we don't believe things are correct on this planet. And we wanted to be noisy about it."

Selected discography

As producer and co-lyricist; albums by Public Enemy; on Def Jam

Yo! Bum Rush the Show, 1987.
It Takes a Nation of Millions to Hold Us Back, 1988.
Fear of a Black Planet, 1990.
Apocalypse '91: The Enemy Strikes Black, 1991.
Muse Sick N Hour Mess Age, 1994.

As producer

Terminator X, *Terminator X and The Valley of the Jeep Beets,* Division/RAL/Columbia, 1991.
Young Black Teenagers, *Young Black Teenagers,* S.O.U.L., 1991.
Young Black Teenagers, *Dead Enz Kids Doin' Lifetime Bidz,* S.O.U.L./MCA, 1993.

Sources

Books

Rees, Dafydd, and Luke Crampton, *Rock Movers & Shakers,* Billboard Books, 1991.

Periodicals

Details, March 1993.
Detroit Free Press, October 2, 1991.
Musician, October 1991.
Option, May 1, 1991.
Playboy, September 1994.
Rolling Stone, August 10, 1989; October 19, 1989; November 16, 1989; May 17, 1990; January 23, 1991; October 3, 1991; November 23, 1993.
Schwann Spectrum, spring 1994.
Spin, January 1991; September 1991; October 1991; March 1993.
Time, November 11, 1991; September 19, 1994.

Additional information for this profile was obtained from the *All-Music Guide,* Matrix Software, 1994.

—*Thaddeus Wawro*

Percy Sledge

Rhythm and blues singer, songwriter

Courtesy of Artists International Management

Percy Sledge's best-known hit, "When a Man Loves a Woman," was first released in 1966 but continued to keep the soul performer in the headlines a quarter of a century later. The classic single, which was the first soul recording to reach Number One on the pop charts, became his most successful release. In 1987 its appearance on the soundtrack of *Platoon,* a film about the Vietnam War, revived both the song and Sledge's career for a new generation of listeners. Four years later its impassioned lyrics were sung by Top 40 singer Michael Bolton, and "When a Man Loves a Woman" again soared to the top of the charts. Bolton earned a Grammy Award for his version but failed to mention Sledge in his acceptance speech at the cermony; Bolton took heat for his oversight from those who considered recognition for Sledge as a passionate soul vocalist long overdue.

Another recording by Sledge became mired in controversy in 1992 when the teen singing group New Kids on the Block appeared in court to answer charges that a 1990 Number One single they co-wrote for Tommy Page, "I'll Be Your Everything," was remarkably similar in parts to Sledge's 1974 hit of the same name. Sledge, however, did not allow all of the negative press surrounding his early work to stop him from releasing *Blue Night,* a comeback album on a French record label, in 1994. The album was noted for its contributions from a host of guest musicians, including rhythm and blues singer Bobby Womack and former Rolling Stone guitarist Mick Taylor.

Achieved Local Popularity Early

Sledge was born on November 25, 1940, in the rural farming area of Leighton, Alabama. As a child he helped his family with farming chores, and the backbreaking work convinced Sledge to dream of a less arduous way of earning a living. He began singing in local bands when still a teenager, and at the age of 20 joined a group called the Esquires Combo. The act—known in the area for its covers of songs by the Beatles and Smokey Robinson—became enormously popular in both Alabama and Mississippi and could often be found playing on college campuses in the early 1960s. Yet Sledge was still holding down a day job as a hospital orderly at Colbert County Hospital near Leighton and was barely making ends meet. He also performed with the choir at the local Gallillee Baptist Church.

In 1965 Sledge's former music teacher invited him to perform at a Christmas party. The $50 fee helped Sledge entice his friends, bass player Cameron Lewis and organist Andrew Wright, to join him. At the time, Sledge was depressed about a woman with whom he

For the Record...

Born November 25, 1940, in Leighton, AL; married; wife's name, Rosie.

Worked as an orderly at Colbert County Hospital, near Leighton, AL, in the early 1960s; began singing career with the Esquires Combo, Muscle Shoals, AL; launched solo career with single "When a Man Loves a Woman," 1966; signed with Capricorn Records, 1974; released comeback album, *Blue Night,* Sky Ranch Records, 1994.

Awards: "When a Man Loves a Woman" named one of the "best 100 singles of the last 25 years" by *Rolling Stone* magazine, 1988; first recipient of Career Achievement Award, R&B Foundation, 1989; five gold records and two platinum records.

Addresses: *Home*—Baton Rouge, LA. *Management*—Artists International Management Inc., 9850 Sandalfoot Blvd., Suite 458, Boca Raton, FL 33428. *Record company*—Virgin, 550 Madison Ave., New York, NY 10022-3211.

had been romantically involved, thinking she was dating someone else. "I had a couple of Jack Daniels, and my eyes were as big as hen eggs. I was feeling light as a feather, and I just wanted to speak my mind," Sledge recounted in *Rolling Stone* in 1988. As he sang, he began pouring out the heart-wrenching lyrics to a track he called "Why Did You Leave Me." Later, in a better mood, he polished the song into "When a Man Loves a Woman."

A friend convinced Sledge to contact Quin Ivy, a record-store owner and producer in Sheffield, Alabama. Ivy had been a disc jockey in Memphis, knew his way around the music business, and owned a recording studio. Inside Ivy's Tune Town record store, Ivy asked Sledge to sing for him on the spot, and Sledge obliged. Shortly thereafter, Sledge found himself in a recording studio for the first time in his life.

"When a Man Loves a Woman" was cut early in 1966 in Ivy's Quinvy Recording Studio with the help of musicians borrowed from another Alabama recording enterprise, Rick Hall's Fame Studio in Muscle Shoals. Ivy and Marlin Greene produced the cut, with Greene doubling as the session's guitar player. Other local musicians helping out in the studio were Junior Lowe on bass, Spooner Oldham on organ, Roger Hawkins on drums,

and Jimmy Johnson on lead guitar. Reportedly, Hall called Atlantic Records President Jerry Wexler and told him about the session and its electrifying result; Wexler was sent a tape and soon Atlantic had signed Sledge to a contract. Sledge also needed a manager, and a professional by the name of Phil Walden, who had worked with Otis Redding, stepped into the picture. Unfortunately, Sledge's new manager could not rectify the singer's regrettable decision to give songwriting credit to Lewis and Wright.

"When a Man Loves a Woman" made its first appearance on the charts on April 9, 1966, and by the end of May was the Number One song in the United States. Sledge's single was also a hit overseas. A full-length album of the same name was released, and within a few years Sledge had become an enormously popular soul singer.

Although none of his subsequent records achieved the success of his first, Sledge's songs were nonetheless modest hits. Atlantic released "Warm and Tender Love" in July of 1966, and the song reached Number 17; "It Tears Me Up" debuted in October of the same year. "Baby, Help Me" and "Out of Left Field" were both released in early 1967, followed by four more throughout the year. "Take Time to Know Her" became Sledge's best-selling single after "When a Man Loves a Woman," reaching Number 11 after its release in March of 1968. The decade closed with three more efforts by Sledge—"Sudden Stop," "My Special Prayer," and "Any Day Now"—that made respectable showings on the soul charts.

Songs Reached Across Barriers

Sledge's success catapulted him onto a world stage. Major concert tours helped spark record sales and bring new audiences to Sledge's tunes and no-holds-barred vocal delivery. In the summer of 1970 the singer traveled to South Africa to give performances and make a concert film entitled *Soul Africa.* Many black performers had been officially boycotting the country since 1965 because of its racist policies of apartheid, and at the time Sledge was criticized for traveling and performing there. Controversy marked his stay.

He had been booked to perform only for black crowds at the specific directive of the South African government, but during his first shows, white teenagers in fez hats and black makeup attempted to gain entry. Finally, the authorities allowed Sledge and his management to schedule some performances for white audiences during his tour. In a 1971 interview with Orde Coombs for the *New York Times,* the singer defended his tour against critics: "I went to entertain all those people who buy my records, the people who keep me in bread."

In the early 1970s Sledge's career lost some of its early momentum. His last recorded single for Atlantic was "Sunshine," released in 1973. The next year Sledge signed with Capricorn Records, a label headed by his manager, Phil Walden. In November of 1974 Sledge released "I'll Be Your Everything," a song that reached Number 15 on the soul charts but was also his last to place in the Top 100 for over a decade. In 1992 the single would became the centerpiece of a legal battle in U.S. District Court in New York. It had been written for Sledge by George Soule, and the company that had purchased its copyright charged that pop performer Tommy Page, along with two members of the pop group New Kids on the Block, had lifted parts of the melody of the original Sledge hit. All three composers claimed never to have heard either the Sledge song or subsequent remakes by other performers. A jury acquitted the defendants based on insufficient evidence.

A Song and a Career Reborn

The revival of Sledge's performing career began in 1987 when director Oliver Stone selected "When a Man Loves a Woman" for the soundtrack of his Vietnam War-era film, *Platoon*. The song was also re-released as a single overseas and reached Number Two on *Billboard* magazine's Hits of the World chart. Sledge received further recognition in 1987 by performing on the NBC television program *Saturday Night Live*.

In 1989 Sledge became the first recipient of the R&B Foundation's Career Achievement Award. The singer was also in the news in early 1992 when popular ballad crooner Michael Bolton, often criticized for straining to emulate the vocal styles of African American singers, won a Grammy Award for his cover of "When a Man Loves a Woman." Bolton, in his elation over the award, never once mentioned the man who originally made the song famous. Bolton was pilloried in the press for the oversight and made a point to express gratitude to Sledge in subsequent interviews as well as in a letter to him. Bolton wrote, "I have always felt that your performance was the element that made a great song a truly classic record and a standard."

In the early 1990s Sledge signed a three-record deal with a new label, and his first full-length album since the early 1970s was released in 1994. Entitled *Blue Night,* the album earned praise from the man who helped propel Sledge to his early success, Jerry Wexler. Wexler wrote the liner notes to the comeback album, which appeared on France's Sky Ranch Records. The label is devoted to releasing recordings by American rhythm and blues artists; it entered into a distribution deal with Virgin Records for *Blue Night.*

Sledge recorded *Blue Night* in a Los Angeles studio, a first for him, and was joined by a host of other performers for the session. Contemporary rhythm-and-blues singer Bobby Womack and former Rolling Stone Mick Taylor were guest musicians, and Bee Gees Barry and Robin Gibb and Swedish singer Mikael Rickfors—former Hollies vocalist—also contributed tracks. In addition, *Blue Night* contains Sledge and Rickfors's duet on a cover of "I Wish It Would Rain," originally recorded by the Temptations.

A major concert tour throughout Europe was scheduled to coincide with *Blue Night's* release, but plans were changed when Sledge pleaded guilty to charges of tax evasion that summer. He failed to report $260,000 in income earned between 1987 and 1989 and was sentenced to serve six months in a halfway house. Acknowledging that he could have faced 15 years in prison, Sledge commented at his sentencing, "Thank you, Jesus. I appreciate what the court has done for me." Sledge's fans around the world were also grateful.

Selected discography

Singles; on Atlantic, except where noted

"When a Man Loves a Woman," 1966.
"Warm and Tender Love," 1966.
"It Tears Me Up," 1966.
"Baby, Help Me," 1967.
"Out of Left Field," 1967.
"Love Me Tender," 1967.
"What Am I Living For," 1967.
"Just out of Reach," 1967.
"Cover Me," 1967.
"Take Time to Know Her," 1968.
"Sudden Stop," 1968.
"My Special Prayer," 1969.
"Any Day Now," 1969.
"Sunshine," 1973.
"I'll Be Your Everything," Capricorn, 1974.

Albums

When a Man Loves a Woman, Atlantic, 1966.
When a Man Loves a Woman (The Ultimate Collection), Atlantic, 1987.
It Tears Me Up: The Best of Percy Sledge, Rhino, 1992.
Blue Night, Sky Ranch/Virgin, 1994.
Best of Percy Sledge, Atlantic.

Sources

Books

Bronson, Fred, *Billboard Book of Number One Hits,* Billboard
    Publications, 1985.
Murrells, Joseph, compiler, *The Book of Golden Discs: The
    Records That Sold a Million,* Barrie and Jenkins Ltd., 1978.
Stambler, Irwin, *The Encyclopedia of Pop, Rock & Soul,* St.
    Martin's, 1974.

Periodicals

Billboard, April 11, 1987; April 18, 1987; June 13, 1992; June
    27, 1992; August 27, 1994; April 22, 1995.
Detroit Free Press, July 2, 1994.
Entertainment Weekly, June 2, 1995.
New York Times, June 27, 1971.
People, April 25, 1994.
Rolling Stone, September 8, 1988.
USA Today, August 18, 1988.

Additional information for this profile was provided by Artists
International Management Inc., 1995.

—Carol Brennan

Suicidal Tendencies

Rock band

Photograph by Michael Llewellyn, courtesy of Epic Records

Music generally acts as a reflection of its time and surroundings. Suicidal Tendencies took this to heart and became the chameleons of aggressive rock 'n' roll. Starting with their debut album in 1983, the band progressed from the punk rock genre into heavy metal and then alternative rock. Throughout this development, singer, founder, and leader Mike Muir broadcast his own message with wit and wisdom to anyone who would listen.

In 1982 Suicidal Tendencies emerged from Venice, California, with a dedicated audience among area skaters and surfers. As they established themselves on the Los Angeles punk scene, the group released their self-titled debut on Frontier Records with songs like "Institutionalized," "Fascist Pig," and "Suicide's an Alternative." *Suicidal Tendencies* became the bestselling American punk album of all time and launched the band into their long-lasting career.

After the video for "Institutionalized" broke through the MTV airwaves as the first hardcore video for the channel, the song gained further notoriety on the soundtrack for the cult film *Repo Man* in 1984. Three years later, Suicidal Tendencies released *Join the Army* on Caroline Records. It became the first independent hardcore rock release to break *Billboard*'s Hot 100 sales chart. The album's success led to a contract with Epic Records, and the band began to gradually change their musical shade.

Censorship Controversy

In 1988 Mike Muir started over with a whole new band lineup that included lead guitarist Rocky George and rhythm guitarist Mike Clark. Their first release on Epic, *How Will I Laugh Tomorrow ... When I Can't Even Smile Today,* set Suicidal Tendencies on the road into the heavy metal genre. The album sold more than the band's self-titled debut and featured the popular single "Trip at the Brain." Suicidal Tendencies toured throughout the United States and Europe. The success of the tour and the obvious number of imitators cemented the band's influence in rock 'n' roll.

"Forerunners of the skate/metal punk hybrid sound and style that's so prevalent," one reviewer wrote in *Seconds,* as quoted in an Epic press kit, "Mike Muir and his numerous musical cohorts are simply one of the most imitated and/or interpreted acts around."

Suicidal Tendencies released *Controlled by Hatred / Feel Like Shit ... Deja Vu*—nine songs packaged by Epic as an EP—in 1989. However, the Recording Industry Association of America never classified it as an EP. The title of the release grabbed the attention of the Parents Music Resource Center (PMRC), who attempted to force Epic and the band to pull the record from retail chains. The record company supported Suicidal Tendencies in their resistance.

In the band's record company biography, Muir commented on PMRC founder Tipper Gore's attempt to "save" young music fans from the influence of "unacceptable" music. "Let's be honest," Muir said. "If you took 20 people off the streets of D.C., put them in a room, and took 20 people who listen to music that she deems unacceptable, put them in another room, and asked Tipper who she'd rather stay with for two weeks, she'd stay with the people listening to 'wrong' music. Not because she's trying to save them ... because she'd be scared out of her ass to stay with those other people!"

Their next and highly acclaimed album, *Lights ... Camera ... Revolution*, was released on Epic in 1990. Joe Gore described the album in *Guitar Player* as "a breath of fresh fire from a classic hardcore band that sounds more metallic with each record. Relentlessly intense fret-flaying courtesy of Rocky George, a blues-metal screamer. Warning, pacemaker wearers: some tempos exceed 300 beats per minute."

Muir called the album's single, "You Can't Bring Me Down," Suicidal Tendencies' "signature." "It's about believing in yourself," he said in the band's biography, "knowing *what* you're doing, *why* you're doing it, and then *doing* it." After the release of *Lights ... Camera ... Revolution*, Suicidal Tendencies toured the world with

fellow metal bands Slayer, Megadeth, and Testament. In 1991 the band received a Grammy nomination for best metal performance.

Returned to Hometown

Despite their worldwide expansion and success, Suicidal Tendencies was banned from playing their hometown for nearly six years. Los Angeles city authorities had restricted the band from performing within the city limits. Because of the ban, Suicidal Tendencies was unable to schedule a show within a 400-mile radius of L.A., since the restriction frightened most area concert promoters. Finally, in April of 1991, Queensryche invited Suicidal Tendencies to open for them on their national arena tour, and the ban in L.A. was lifted.

Along with their work in Suicidal Tendencies, Muir and bassist Robert Trujillo formed a side project called Infectious Grooves before the release of *The Art of Rebellion* in 1992. When ST's previous drummer, R. J. Herrera, left the band to start a family, Infectious Grooves drummer Josh Freese stepped in to record the album.

The Art of Rebellion signified yet another progression for Suicidal Tendencies. The single "Asleep at the Wheel" transported the band's music onto the alternative rock radio stations and into yet another genre of music. Muir insisted the continuous expansion of the group's style and audience was never planned. "Instead of playing it safe, we always kind of turned our backs on [our last record] and just made a great new-sounding record," Muir told Bruce Buckley in *Billboard*. This time, Suicidal Tendencies toured the world with Ozzy Osbourne.

A Decade Celebration

Ten years after the release of their debut, Suicidal Tendencies revisited their early years with *Still Cyco After All These Years*. The album featured new recordings of selected songs from their first two albums, including "Institutionalized" and "I Saw Your Mommy." The band followed the release with a U.S. tour that included Muir and Trujillo's side project Infectious Grooves.

In 1994 Suicidal Tendencies put out yet another dose of new material with *Suicidal for Life*. "If you want ST's usual aggro, it's here, but the album's more poignant songs are the ones that will leave you drained emotionally," Kira L. Billik wrote in *RIP*. "'What Else Could I Do?' and particularly 'Love vs. Loneliness' will no doubt move anyone who ever felt worthless or ostracized."

Musically and lyrically Suicidal Tendencies continued to reflect the world around them in spite of the many misinformed judgments thrown their way. According to a *Los Angeles Times* clip included in the Epic press kit, "Suicidal is everything a great rock 'n' roll band is supposed to be: loud, exciting, awesome on stage, and deeply threatening to authority." Suicidal Tendencies' "Cyco" Mike Muir, like a chameleon, doesn't strategize where the band will go next. He simply recounts the world as he sees it.

Selected discography

Suicidal Tendencies, Frontier Records, 1983.
(Contributors) *Repo Man* (soundtrack), 1984.
Join the Army, Caroline Records, 1987.
How Will I Laugh Tomorrow ... When I Can't Even Smile Today, Epic, 1988.
Controlled by Hatred / Feel Like Shit ... Deja Vu, Epic, 1989.
Lights ... Camera ... Revolution, Epic, 1990.
The Art of Rebellion, Epic, 1992.
Still Cyco After All These Years, Epic, 1993.
Suicidal for Life, Epic, 1994.

Sources

Books

The Trouser Press Record Guide, edited by Ira A. Robbins, Collier, 1991.

Periodicals

Billboard, October 6, 1990; August 8, 1992; April 24, 1993.
Entertainment Weekly, May 28, 1993.
Guitar Player, September 1990; December 1990; September 1992.
Metro Times (Detroit), June 29, 1994.
New York Times, November 13, 1992.
RIP, October 1994.
Rolling Stone, August 11, 1994.
Stereo Review, October 1984.

Additional information for this profile was obtained from the on-line *All-Music Guide,* 1994, and Epic Records publicity materials, 1992 and 1993.

—*Thaddeus Wawro*

Al
Teller

Record company executive

Courtesy of Lester Cohen

Al Teller, chairman and chief executive officer (CEO) of the MCA Music Entertainment Group, is at the helm of two of the music industry's major companies. While climbing his way up to such a venerable spot, he has guided the careers of innumerable artists, ranging from contemporary rhythm and blues singer Bobby Brown to rock star Bruce Springsteen, from country's Lyle Lovett to pop's Billy Joel, and from the alternative sounds of Fine Young Cannibals to the twangs of Wynonna. The *Los Angeles Times* once called Teller a technology junkie, and the six computers in his home will attest to that. His attraction to the machines stems from a particular interest in the possibilities of meshing music creativity with emerging technologies. Since early in his career, Teller has shown a strong and often vocal commitment to the future of the music industry and to the future of music itself.

Although Teller originally studied engineering—he has two degrees in the field from Columbia University—his pure love of music led him to pursue a career in the music business. During a summer break from Harvard Business School, Teller worked at CBS Records for consultant McKinney & Co. In 1969, having just graduated, Teller landed a job at CBS as the assistant to the president. He soon left to become director of corporate development for Playboy Enterprises, but returned to CBS in 1971 as vice-president of merchandising. Three years later Teller again left CBS, this time to become president of United Artists Records, and then president of Windsong Records in 1978. He returned once more to CBS, leading Columbia Records from 1981 until 1985, when he was named president of CBS Records.

Teller established early in his career a strong commitment to the future of the industry. Through speeches and trade paper editorials he constantly encouraged his peers to seek out new technologies and to anticipate their creative uses. At the same time that he attempted to grapple with the new compact discs (CD) and digital audiotapes (DAT), Teller also showed concern for the industry's history. In his keynote address at the 1988 National Association of Record Merchandisers (NARM) convention, Teller expressed kind words for the "senior citizen of the music business," the LP. "There's still plenty of demand out there for it," *Billboard* quoted him as saying. "Let's treat it with the respect every senior citizen deserves. Let's not let it be mugged and left for dead, as was the case for the 8-track cartridge." Teller's keen awareness of the marketplace and sixth sense for the future anticipated the debate regarding the merits of analog over digital sound and the resurgence of the vinyl LP.

In the same speech, Teller also prognosticated the elevation of alternative rock to the mainstream in the

1990s. He chided album-oriented rock stations for beating the classic rock format to death and for no longer seeking out the newest music of interest to the active music buyer. He praised alternative and college stations for their courage and creativity. "I urge you to pay close attention to and strongly support the college and alternative formats. They are the cutting edge of rock radio today and could well be the rock-radio mainstream of tomorrow."

With the reorganization of his label after its purchase by Sony in 1988, and due to a strained relationship with the company's then-music chief, Walter Yetnikoff, Teller stepped down as CBS Records president. Just a few months later he was scooped up by MCA Records, becoming its president and chief operating officer. MCA had enjoyed major successes with their contemporary R&B/hip-hop and country music acts, but had not done as well in the rock sector. Noting that Teller's tenure at CBS had been marked by such commercial breakthrough artists as George Michael and Terence Trent D'Arby, the label hoped to tap Teller's talent for discovering hot young stars. As Teller forecasted in

Billboard, "We're going to be very aggressive out on the streets looking for great young talent; it's as simple as that."

Within a year Teller was appointed chairman of the MCA Music Entertainment group, while still retaining the responsibilities of MCA Record's head. He went on to oversee MCA's acquisition of GRP and Geffen Records, as well as new ventures in Germany, Japan, and other international markets. Adding Geffen to the group helped boost MCA's share of the alternative audience Teller deemed so important. DGC Records, an imprint of Geffen Records and one for which MCA handled distribution, was responsible for launching Nirvana, the grunge band that heralded the mainstream success of a drove of alternative rock bands, many of whom sprang from the Geffen roster.

Once again touting the merits of underground rock, Teller told *Musician's* Thom Duffy, "Alternative music really reflects the good old-fashioned way of developing an artist—a band gets together, builds a following in clubs, builds a local buzz—all independent of the record company." He was also quick to deny that he was focusing on any one kind of new music, stressing that it wasn't the genre, but an artist's ability, that mattered. "I've always believed that any definition of superstar has to include the ability to affect thousands of people who see you do it live, to transport people as a performer."

With the explosion of easy home access to the information superhighway in the 1990s, Teller continued to be a leader in bringing the record industry into the twenty-first century. In a commentary for *Billboard* Teller wrote, "The biggest barrier we face now is not technological but human. It's inertia.... Success has become a habit. And no one resists change more stubbornly than the successful." He sent out a call to retailers and music companies to join together in envisioning a future in which the record store is not obsolete but "a store that will turn technology into a motivating experience in retail theater.... One of the most potent marketing tools we have," he continued, "is our capacity to build demand for our products through the selling power of the retail environment. If we sacrifice this to technology, we not only lose a vital arena in which to expose and promote new products, the consumer loses too—loses the freedom to browse, to sample, to discover, and to buy on a whim."

In 1994, in line with his philosophy of keeping the music business up to date with technology, Teller established the position of vice-president of interactive media, whose mandate is to identify, implement, and help market interactive media projects from the MCA Music Group family of artists. Teller's own mandate for the future became that of his company's; as he told the *Los Angeles Times'* James Bates, "The core vision of (MCA) will be music itself, but as technology provides all sorts of new vehicles to hear music with, we will follow that path. Who's to say what form it will take?"

Sources

Billboard, March 26, 1988; September 3, 1988; September 16, 1989; September 28, 1991; October 5, 1991; April 10, 1993; March 5, 1994; March 8, 1994; May 14, 1994; April 22, 1995.

Cash Box, October 6, 1990; September 7, 1991; September 21, 1991.

Entertainment Weekly, October 30, 1992.

Los Angeles Times, December 28, 1993; January 7, 1994; March 25, 1994.

Musician, April 1992.

New York Times, March 13, 1994.

Variety, April 20, 1988; April 27, 1988; August 31, 1988; September 13, 1989; March 29, 1993.

Wall Street Journal, March 24, 1994.

Additional information for this profile was obtained from MCA Records, Inc., publicity materials, 1994.

—Joanna Rubiner

Tesla

Rock band

As Tesla bassist Brian Wheat told *Billboard's* Terry Wood in 1989, "We're the epitome of a no-makeup band. We just wear our jeans and T-shirts and go out and play. We're a good live band, and people like that. People notice we don't use sequencers or drum machines. We're just an honest rock band." Thus assured in their identity, Tesla have resolutely taken their career down an unusual path. Foremost in this approach has been their refusal to release a quick succession of formulaic albums to capitalize on their early success. Instead, the group records every two to three years, with each release taking a chance by featuring tracks that explore a new direction for the band.

Perhaps most unexpectedly, the Northern California-based members of Tesla eschew the rock-star image or fast-lane Los Angeles lifestyle, remaining close to where they were raised and keeping out of trouble. Nevertheless, the hard-rock quintet enjoys touring, even submitting to grueling nine-month treks that take them through North America, Europe, and the Far East. Seasoned road warriors that they are, though, Tesla refuse to play

Photograph by Ross Halfin, © 1994 Geffen Records, Inc.

the encore game with audiences in which performers run offstage until enough applause brings them back out; lead singer Jeff Keith simply tells the audience: "We're not going to hide behind the amplifiers," and asks, "Do you want to hear another?"

Breaking the mold has brought Tesla longevity in a genre in which bands either rise rapidly then fade away with similar speed, or become such icons that expectations for them are impossible to meet. "Falling prey to neither the glam image of the early '80s, nor the angst-driven grunge trend of the '90s, Tesla carved out a niche for themselves as 'everyperson's' band," declared *RIP* magazine. "Performing equally well on their aggressive, power-rock tunes as on their emotionally resonant acoustic ones, the band pleased a growing following who stood by them no matter what was in vogue musically."

Not Your Average Bar Band

Tesla came together in the Sacramento, California, area as City Kidd in 1984. They were a cover band hired to play music originally made popular by groups like ZZ Top. When they began including their own songs in their set, bar patrons didn't seem to notice the difference and even appeared to be enjoying the tunes. The owner of the Oasis, a frequent venue for the band, liked these originals so much that he booked them one night to play only their own material. This developed into a series of performances, which, combined with a demonstration tape, attracted the attention of Geffen Records scouts. The band soon signed a recording contract. But rather than quickly rush out an album, they rehearsed and

sharpened their songwriting abilities for the next 18 months.

It was also during this period that they renamed themselves Tesla. The name was an homage to inventor Nikola Tesla, a forgotten genius who died in 1943. The eccentric scientist made crucial discoveries in alternating current that paved the way for modern applications of electricity, radio chief among them. His dedication inspired the band. "He did it for the love of his work, not for the hype or anything," bass player Wheat explained to *Detroit Free Press* writer Gary Graff. "We write songs straight from the heart.... We believe in what we do." The band's first release, *Mechanical Resonance,* appeared in record stores in 1986. Tesla was described by *Rolling Stone* contributor J. D. Considine as "fast and flashy" in a review of *Mechanical Resonance,* and "offering little content but plenty of excitement." The reviewer also speculated on the band's future, predicting it "unlikely to offer more than a brief spark of excitement before fading away entirely."

Early sales of *Mechanical Resonance* were in fact dismal, but this was dramatically altered when the band went on tour with Van Halen, then at the height of their popularity. "Up to that point, [*Mechanical Resonance*] had only sold about 25,000 copies. During just those eight weeks on the road, we sold 200,000 more," Wheat told *Billboard* writer Terry Wood. Tesla's next big break came later that year when when they toured Europe with British heavy-metal giants Def Leppard. Radio airplay on album-oriented rock stations helped boost U.S. sales further over the next few months, and *Mechanical Resonance* eventually went platinum, selling over one million copies.

Radio Controversy Praised for Diversity

The group released its sophomore effort, *The Great Radio Controversy,* in 1989. The first single, a ballad called "Love Song," quickly became a hit. Kim Neely reviewed the album for *Rolling Stone* and found its diversity—from the aforementioned "Love Song" to louder cuts like "Be a Man"—especially commendable, noting, "Oddly, nothing seems contrived or out of place." Neely praised Tesla's second release as "a shining example of what can happen when a talented band puts on blinders, ignores what everybody else is selling and forges ahead on instinct." This instinct earned Tesla another platinum record for *The Great Radio Controversy.*

As they had become known for their heavy sound, Tesla took something of a risk in releasing a slow, love song as the first single from *Radio Controversy;* their third album represented an even bigger leap of faith. While touring with Motley Crue after the release of *Radio Controversy,* Tesla would show up at local clubs on the East Coast to play acoustic sets of their repertoire. This diversion so excited the bandmembers that they soon brought in a mobile facility to record some of these sets. They thought they might use some of the material as B-sides on forthcoming releases. Next, Tesla enlisted a video crew to tape the gigs.

The band's enthusiasm for these stripped-down performances was contagious, and Geffen decided to release the cuts as a live album and the footage as a companion video, which resulted in 1990's *Five Man Acoustical Jam* and the video *Five Man Video Band.* Tesla's first single from *Five Man Acoustical Jam,* the extremely popular "Signs," was a cover of a 1971 tune written by Les Emmerson, the lead vocalist of a long-forgotten act called The Five Man Electrical Band. In effect, Tesla can be credited with helping spawn the "unplugged" phenomenon of the 1990s, in which artists demonstrate to fans that they can shine without amplification, production assistance, or mechanical tricks.

Helped Unleash *Unplugged* Craze with Live Recording

Tesla objected when record company executives hinted at overdubbing (augmenting or correcting) some of the tracks on *Five Man Acoustical Jam* and insisted that the album be released just as they had played it. Since then, a plethora of rock acts—most notably Eric Clapton and Nirvana—have released acoustic albums, many taped on a popular, live-before-a-studio-audience feature on MTV called *Unplugged.* A *Rolling Stone* review of *Five Man Acoustical Jam* remarked that when heavy-metal bands go acoustic, they often demonstrate just how talentless they are, but, asserted the magazine, Tesla possesses "better chops and tunes than most of the competition," which helped make the album "a lot more fun than it might have been."

With the 1991 release of *Psychotic Supper,* Tesla aroused a bit of controversy when they slammed guitarist/hunting advocate Ted Nugent in the album's liner notes. Lead singer Keith is active in the animal-rights movement and had been offended by Nugent's constant broadsides about the joys of bow-and-arrow hunting. Later, after a tart reply from Nugent, the self-effacing Tesla appeared embarrassed about the flap and tried to play it down. While touring for *Psychotic Supper,* the group demonstrated their altruistic side by staging a contest in which they awarded backstage passes to fans. Entrants donated canned goods to earn a chance

at the passes; the food was donated to local shelters. *Psychotic Supper* marked the band's fourth platinum platter.

In 1994 the group released *Bust a Nut,* sending "Mama's Fool" to radio as the lead single. *RIP* called the record "a complicated piece of business. Boasting grand shadings of majestic guitars ('Shine Away'), bluesy soul ... and intense, thought-provoking lyrics ('Wonderful World,' 'Solution'), *Bust a Nut* could well be the album that boosts Tesla from 'facelessness' to mainstream status." To charges that the band is just another identity-deficient heavy-metal ensemble, lead singer Keith responded in *RIP,* "As soon as the music starts, our 'face' comes out. We're here to play music." Keith also pointed out in the group's Geffen publicity material: "What you're seeing and hearing is real. We're proud of that and people pick up on it. It's a bond with our audience we don't want to break. They know we're not going to shock everybody and start wearing mascara and they appreciate that. The loyalty of our fans is really something. We work off each other and have a good time together. Maybe it's because we're fans of Tesla too, and play what we really like to hear." By the summer of 1995, *Bust a Nut* had been certified a gold record, with platinum projections abounding.

Selected discography

On Geffen Records

Mechanical Resonance, 1986.
The Great Radio Controversy, 1989.
Five Man Acoustical Jam, 1990.
Psychotic Supper, 1991.
Bust a Nut, 1994.

Sources

Billboard, March 25, 1989; June 1, 1991; September 3, 1994.
Detroit Free Press, May 11, 1989.
Entertainment Weekly, October 7, 1994.
RIP, December 1994.
Rolling Stone, May 21, 1987; May 4, 1989; December 13, 1990.
Spin, August 1992.

Additional information for this profile was obtained from Geffen Records publicity materials, 1994.

—*Carol Brennan*

The The

Rock entity

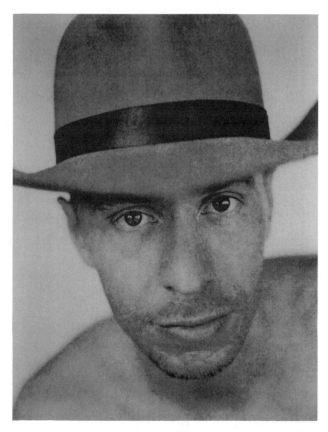

The post-punk rock movement of the early 1980s was a battlefield strewn with the corpses of one-hit wonders. One of the few survivors was Matt Johnson, founder and frontman of The The, who succeeded by adopting the flag of angst that his new wave peers had left behind. While other bands succumbed to the perky sounds of prevalent chart hits, Johnson clung fiercely to his own agenda. His songwriting focuses on self-degradation, obsessive-compulsive behavior, and general anxiety about being alive. The appeal of Johnson's music largely stems from the self-revealing language he uses throughout his lyrics. Whether the theme is political and social commentary or sexual love, he bares his soul in an achingly authentic manner.

Johnson, born in 1961 in the East End of London, is one of four sons of a pub owner. His father's Two Puddings pub employed as musical acts the likes of David Essex, Rod Stewart, and the Small Faces, while Johnson's uncle—who owned several London dance halls and nightclubs—promoted artists like Muddy Waters and the Kinks. This early exposure to the excitement of live rock performance led to the 11-year-old Johnson's formation of a band with several school friends.

After leaving school at age 15, Johnson was determined to pursue a career in music. He contacted just about every British record company before De Wolfe, a small publishing house in London, employed him as their tea boy and eventually assistant engineer. Absorbing every aspect of the music business he could, Johnson used his spare time to record his own demos and later placed an advertisement in *New Music Express* that led to an early incarnation of The The.

The The initially consisted of core member Johnson and part-time musicians such as Keith Laws (keyboards), Tom Johnston (bass), and Peter Ashworth (drums). The hiring of supplemental performers to augment Johnson's vocals and guitar would become the pattern for future The The recordings. In 1980 the band released their first independent U.K. single, "Controversial Subject," while Johnson worked on a solo album, *Burning Blue Soul*. These releases made a small impact on the British alternative scene, but it was the synthesizer-based 1983 LP *Soul Mining* that catapulted the band into the British Top 30 and ultimately became a gold record.

Showcasing session musicians like ex-Squeeze keyboardist Jools Holland, Johnson fully realized the potential of his open-band policy. Meanwhile, the lyrics on *Soul Mining* only hinted at the lonely despair Johnson would express on later releases: "All my childhood dreams are bursting at the seams/ And the cancer of love has eaten out my heart."

For the Record . . .

Band consists of Matt Johnson, born in 1961 in England.

Singer, songwriter, and guitarist. The The has at various times featured keyboardists Jools Holland and Keith Laws, guitarist Johnny Marr, bassist Tom Johnston, and drummers David Palmer and Peter Ashworth; released first album, *Burning Blue Soul,* 4AD, 1981.

Addresses: *Home*—London, England. *Record company*—Sony Music Entertainment Inc., 550 Madison Avenue, New York, NY 10022-3211.

Soul Mining included a broad mix of themes, but musically, The The had yet to find a voice until the 1986 release of the harder-edged *Infected.* The album focused on heady political issues, exemplified in songs like "Heartland," a harsh commentary on the influence the United States has had on Great Britain: "Well it ain't written in the papers/ But it's written on the walls/ The way this country is dividing to fall/ The ammunition's been passed/ But the wars on the televisions will never be explained." The first single, "Sweet Bird of Truth," finds a dying American pilot over the Gulf of Arabia filled with self-doubt. It was quickly banned in Great Britain after the controversial U.S. air attack on Libya. Johnson himself perhaps best summed up his songs when he observed in *Melody Maker,* "They're like crystallized feelings. When people put the stylus on the record and hear it, the song bursts and it melts. The songs come to life in people's hearts."

Minor commercial and global success finally came in 1989 with the release of *Mind Bomb* and the Top 20 U.K. single "The Beat(en) Generation." Special guest Johnny Marr (former guitarist for the Smiths) lent his expertise to *Mind Bomb* and shared co-writing credits with Johnson on "Gravitate to Me," a powerful incantation to attract a destined love. Johnson's songs had now evolved into more melodic statements, and he continued to utilize acoustic and electric guitars to drive the beat.

It was *Mind Bomb*'s "The Beat(en) Generation," though, that became the vehicle for Johnson's acerbic intellect to reach a new audience. In the song, he describes a new generation of youth "Reared on a diet/ Of prejudice and misinformation/ Hypnotised by the satellites/ Into believing what is good and what is right." In *Melody Maker,* Johnson described his feelings after writing the song: "I've noticed a change. There's a tragic degree of ignorance but people I talk to are wondering what it's about; they're starting to question their lives and their environment."

The more introspective *Dusk,* released in 1993, continued Johnson's partnership with Marr and many of the musicians from *Mind Bomb. Dusk* featured a newly stripped-down instrumentation comprised of acoustic and electric guitars, piano, and harmonica. The hit "Slow Emotion Replay" helped push the album into the Number Two position on the British charts. Although The The still did not achieve widespread commercial success, Johnson's insightful lyrics received critical acknowledgment. *Rolling Stone's* Thom Jurek called The The "a band in full command of its gifts at the very beginning of collective musical discovery." Johnson's writing, according to Jurek, is "in the language of raw need" as he admits in the track "Slow Emotion Replay" that "Everybody knows what's going wrong with the world/ I don't even know what's going on in myself."

Johnson took an unpredictable musical turn when, in 1995, he released *Hanky Panky,* a cover album of the songs of country music legend Hank Williams, Sr., whose lyrics typify the melancholic edge for which The The strives. With a new lineup, Johnson mixed obscure and popular Williams songs with The The's raw sound. Johnson's discovery of Williams's talent and subsequent research into the country legend's psyche led to strong emotional feelings that translated into The The's reworkings of the songs. As Johnson commented in *New York,* "Country didn't like [Williams]. They thought of him as an oaf, an unsophisticated, unreliable drunk. They threw him off the Grand Ole Opry, and the moment he died, they reclaimed him and rewrote history." The combination of the two artists seemed logical. A *USA Today* reviewer stated, "There is something both dark and sweet about Johnson's sound that's akin to that of the youthful Williams," while *People* magazine called *Hanky Panky* "a compelling experiment."

Each evolution of The The adds a new set of variations to the twisted psychological profile of Johnson. His inner struggles are laid bare while he searches for meaning in the violent and seemingly godless world in which he lives. The The's songs seem to grab the listener by the throat and never let go until he or she has swallowed whatever fresh pain and suffering Johnson has to offer. Johnson's philosophy is one of dissatisfaction, and he will no doubt continue to express it until he achieves a sense of control and evenness in his life. As Johnson revealed in *Details,* "I had therapy, but I got bored. I've tried drugs and promiscuity, but that's like drinking salt water: The more you do, the emptier you get. I suppose I just want to feel more alive, and I'm trying anything I can get my hands on. But nothing seems to satisfy." Until Matt Johnson is satiated, he is making sure through his unique brand of music that the world feels his loneliness and heartache.

Selected discography

Burning Blue Soul, 4AD, 1981.
Soul Mining, Epic, 1983.
Infected, Epic, 1986.
Mind Bomb, Epic, 1989.
Dusk, Epic, 1993.
Solitude (consists of EPs *Shades of Blue* and *Dis-Infected*), Epic, 1994.
Hanky Panky, Sony/550 Music, 1995.

Sources

Details, April 1993.
Melody Maker, May 13, 1989.
Musician, April 1987.
New York, March 1995.
People, March 6, 1995.
Raygun, March 1995.
Rolling Stone, February 4, 1993.
USA Today, March 17, 1995.

—Debra Power

Throwing Muses

Rock band

Since she first picked up a guitar at the age of nine, Kristin Hersh has never fit easily into a typical music-marketing mold. "What most fans don't realize is that Throwing Muses has always been Kristin's band," Randee Dawn Cohen wrote in *Alternative Press* about the group that was considered "alternative" before alternative rock came into vogue and which paved the way in the mid-1980s for bands like the Pixies and the Breeders.

Hersh began writing songs in junior high with her stepsister, Tanya Donelly. "I've spent my life looking for the perfect chord, the perfect combination of notes, and it was fascinating for me to build those chords with hundreds of melodies flying in and out," Hersh told *Guitar Player*. This experimentation led Hersh and Donelly to develop a distinct sound: intricate cross rhythms and disparate melodies that often sounded like two separate songs played simultaneously. With these riffs, Hersh's haunting lyrics, high school buddy Dave Narcizo on drums, and the addition of Elaine Adamedes, the first of many bassists, Throwing Muses was born. The

Photograph by Steve Gullick, © 1994 Sire Records Company

For the Record . . .

Members include **Bernard Georges,** bass; **Kristin Hersh** (born c. 1965, in Atlanta, GA), vocals, guitar; and **David Narcizo** (born c. 1965), drums. Former members include **Elaine Adamendes** and **Leslie Langston,** both on bass, and **Tanya Donelly** (born c. 1965) keyboards, guitar, vocals.

Band formed in Providence, RI, late 1970s; originally called the Muses; signed with 4AD label, mid-1980s, and released self-titled debut album; signed with Sire Records, 1987, and released *House Tornado,* 1988; disbanded, 1991; reformed as trio, 1993, and released *University,* 1995; Hersh released solo album, *Hips and Makers,* Sire, 1994.

Addresses: *Record company*—Sire Records, 3300 Warner Blvd., Burbank, CA 91505-4694.

band quickly garnered a devoted cult following in the Boston area.

Work Distinguished by Unsettling Lyrics

Though they have released numerous albums on the 4AD and Sire labels, the Muses have never attained widespread commercial success. Indeed, Hersh's lyrics and unsettling stage presence are anything but mainstream. Known to begin songs with lines like: "Get your black hands/ out of my mouth," Hersh early on developed a reputation for emotional imbalance. On one song, "Delicate Cutters," she sang: "And the walls began to scream.... I throw my hands through the window. Crash. Like poetry ... a room full of delicate cutters," lyrics that Neil Strauss of *Rolling Stone* called "as chilling an account of a mind that has lost its balance as [poet] Sylvia Plath's *The Bell Jar* or [writer] Charlotte Perkins Gilman's *The Yellow Wallpaper.*"

CMJ called Hersh's detailed dialogues about her hallucinations "frightening and downright eerie." In fact, Hersh has waged and is winning a battle with mental illness. Her troubling experiences, nonetheless, have inspired some of her greatest work. And her dedication to presenting her creative vision in its purest form—commercial rewards be damned—has taken its toll on Throwing Muses; it wasn't until early 1994 and the success of the band's seventh album, *University,* that bandmates Nacizo and bassist Bernard Georges were finally able to support themselves through music alone.

Hersh told *CMJ,* "I've been poor, but that didn't push me to write a bunch of cute catchy songs that put food on the table. I'd rather be a waitress."

Friends Became Sisters, Formed Band

Born in Atlanta, Georgia, Hersh was raised by free-thinking parents and influenced by the allegorical landscape of bible stories read to her by Southern Baptist grandparents. Her parents moved to Newport, Rhode Island, when she was six and divorced when she was 11. Hersh credits her introduction to music to her father, a professor who taught yoga, Zen Buddhism, and courses on Native American mythology at Salve Regina College. Her father taught her all the guitar chords he knew, but he soon could not keep up with the demands of his nine-year-old musical prodigy. "I got frustrated with his limited knowledge," Hersh admitted in *Alternative Press,* "because I'd be writing songs and asking him what the chords would be, and he'd just hand me the guitar and say 'You make it up.'" For several years Hersh played around with the guitar, coming up with her own chords, but at the age of 14, her method changed. Hersh began hearing voices in her head; she would write what she heard and these transcriptions became songs. The voices became so regular that the line between reality and songs began to blur.

Hersh's life during this period was also filled with domestic upheaval: her mother, a teacher of the learning disabled, married the father of Tanya Donelly, Hersh's best friend at school. After about a year of prodding, Donelly finally agreed to start a band with Hersh; she played keyboards and sang backup, later picking up the guitar as well. With bassist Elaine Adamedes, the band known then simply as the Muses was asked to play at a high school party at the house of Dave Narcizo, whom Hersh and Donelly had known since the first grade. After the party, Hersh asked Narcizo to join as the Muses' drummer, and the band was complete. However, since the only drums that Narcizo had ever played were marching drums, he failed to notice that the drum set he borrowed to practice with his new band lacked cymbals. Narcizo taught himself to play without cymbals, and this has become his signature.

Early Muses songs were quirky, the band producing a new wave sound with bass, keyboard, guitar, and random percussion played on hubcaps and pieces of hardware. "People said that the main problem with our music was that you couldn't ignore it," Hersh told *CMJ.* "I hope this doesn't sound egotistical, but our music is music you have to sleep with, you have to go all the way with it. I know it's hard to follow and hard to take. I have a lot of respect for people sitting through our shows." These shows took place in clubs that the bandmembers wouldn't have been permitted to enter under normal circumstances as they were underage. Just out of high school, Throwing Muses led a wild lifestyle, playing nightly for little money in dives in the Boston and Providence area. Hersh had guns pulled on her, was groped by drunks, and was dragged into cars and vans. "It amazes me that I survived all those years in clubs as a very young girl," she reflected in *Melody Maker*.

But if Hersh had any misgivings during those days, she didn't show it; Throwing Muses were gaining great respect on the British punk scene, and music fans were starting to take notice of the band at home. In *Melody Maker*, Hersh described the intense emotional feelings she was experiencing at that time as "a heat." In 1978 she walked through a a raging blizzard for 24 hours hoping to cool this inner fire. "I was burning up so much inside that there was no room for fear," she revealed. "I was so angry with myself for turning into a crazy person that there was no fear.... All I was, was the music."

Although Hersh's bizarre psychic state made for arresting Throwing Muses material, her behavior from 1986 to 1990 revealed a deeply young troubled woman. Many events during that period served to disrupt an already frenetic life: In 1987, after one album and an EP on the British label 4AD, Throwing Muses were signed to the larger Sire Records; Donelly and Hersh's parents divorced; Hersh, majoring in archetypal psychology and philosophy at Salve Regina by day and going to art school at night, dropped out with only one semester left because she was pregnant with her first child, son Dylan; and the band relocated to Boston with new bassist Leslie Langston, continuing to play shows nearly every night.

Hersh Diagnosed with Bipolar Disorder

In the meanwhile, Throwing Muses produced what some consider their best music, albums like *House Tornado*, *The Fat Skier*, and *Hunkpapa*. But Hersh's inner life remained in turmoil. She broke up with Dylan's father, and a court determined that she was an unfit mother and relieved her of her custody rights. She began to have frequent seizures. In 1990 she finally checked herself into a mental institution. There she was diagnosed as having bipolar disorder, a condition similar to schizophrenia. "I tried really hard to keep my band and my family out of it ... because it felt so dangerous," she told *Melody Maker*. "I didn't want it to spill over onto them."

Also that year, Hersh married Sire executive Billy O'Connell and tried to focus her attention on being a wife and mother. Throwing Muses began to unravel. Langston left the band and moved to California. Donelly began recording with a side project, the Breeders. She usually only contributed one or two songs per Throwing Muses album, but she came up with about seven for the band's fifth album, 1991's *The Real Ramona*. This caused tension between Donelly and Hersh, especially since Donelly's songs were more pop-oriented and thus more appealing to a mainstream audience. "I had tunnel vision when it came to the band," Hersh told *Alternative Press*. "It was my child and my life. And it was probably rude not to take her stuff seriously, but it was only because it was my band." So Donelly left the fold and started her own band, Belly. Soon thereafter Hersh disbanded Throwing Muses due to legal battles with their former manager and problems with income taxes.

> *"I've spent my life looking for the perfect chord, the perfect combination of notes."*
> —Kristin Hersh

Though she had vowed to stay out of the music business after giving birth to her second son, Ryder, Hersh began rehearsing and collaborating with Narcizo again. In 1992 they released a new Muses album, *Red Heaven*. Hersh told *Alternative Press*, "In the Muses I always felt that Dave and I were (the real) partners." Former roadie Bernard Georges joined up on bass and Throwing Muses, now a trio, recorded their next album, *University*.

University was completed in 1993, but Georges and Narcizo agreed to sit on the recording for a year to allow Hersh to release her first solo LP, *Hips and Makers*. This turned out to be a good decision both for Hersh and the band; in 1994 *Hips and Makers* sold over 52,000 copies, securing Hersh's place as a songwriting force on the burgeoning alternative rock scene made popular by formerly underground bands like Nirvana and Pearl Jam.

Hersh wrote most of the songs for *Hips and Makers* while on tour with Throwing Muses, though "The Letter" dates back to the early Muses days, and "Houdini Blues" was the first song her father ever wrote, a find upon which she stumbled while rummaging through an old filing cabinet. The eerily stark "Your Ghost," was written while Hersh was in Glasgow, Scotland, and was initially recorded in a horse stable back in the States. On the final version, Hersh decided to keep the sounds of horses moving in the background and added the voice of her close friend, lead singer of R.E.M. Michael Stipe. "I didn't expect anyone to listen to it. It was almost the soundtrack to my photo album at home," Hersh said of the solo release in an interview with *Billboard*. "I just wanted to get it out of my head and out of the band's way." Hersh also released an album called *Strings,* which featured songs from *Hips and Makers* with a distinct string background.

Hips and Makers paved the way for *University*. "Bright Yellow Gun," the propulsive first single from the record, exploded in 1995 at the top of the alternative rock singles charts. *Rolling Stone* called the album "one of [the band's] best," describing the songs as "among the Muse's brightest and most energetic." In the spring of 1995, Throwing Muses embarked on a national club tour to promote *University*. The band was finally poised to achieve national recognition. "You take this ride, or it takes you," Hersh concluded in *Alternative Press,* "and in the end, you're just the clay you started out with, you're just a body, and you can't get higher than that, and you can't get lower than that, and what a great reason to take the ride."

Selected discography

Throwing Muses, 4AD, 1986.
The Fat Skier (EP), 4AD, 1987.
House Tornado, Sire, 1988.
Hunkpapa, Sire, 1989.
The Real Ramona, Sire, 1991.
Red Heaven, Sire, 1992.
Hips and Makers (solo album by Kristin Hersh), Sire, 1994.
Strings (solo album by Hersh), Sire, 1994.
University, Sire, 1995.

Sources

Alternative Press, April 1994.
Billboard, January 22, 1994; December 10, 1994; January 21, 1995.
CMJ, January 1995.
Guitar Player, January 1993; May 1994.
Melody Maker, January 15, 1994.
Musician, January 1995; March 1995.
Rolling Stone, April 7, 1994; February 23, 1995; March 9, 1995; May 4, 1995.
Spin, April 1994; June 1995.

—*Sarah Messer*

TLC

R&B/hip-hop trio

Many celebrities with teenage followings welcome the support of those fans, but simultaneously insist that they shouldn't have to act as role models. This is not the case, however, with the three young women in TLC, a trio known for its hip-hop spin on the R&B revival known as "New Jill Swing." Tionne "T-Boz" Watkins, Lisa "Left Eye" Lopes, and Rozonda "Chilli" Thomas embrace the opportunity to influence the lives of the young women who buy their records. Their music has a message, but TLC longs to do more; "We want to go to middle schools and high schools," Thomas told J. R. Reynolds of *Billboard,* "and let people know about life from someone their age. Sometimes we're all that kids have—they might not have that sister or auntie to talk to." The threesome have even stuck to this path through a fair amount of scandal—most notably Lopes's arrest for burning down the home she shared with her boyfriend, Andre Rison of the Atlanta Falcons.

When newspapers reported the fire on June 9, 1994, Lopes was already a media celebrity as the rapper for TLC. The group was much in the public eye, not just

Photograph by Dah Len, courtesy of LaFace Records

because their 1992 debut album, *Oooooooohhh ... On the TLC Tip,* sold nearly three million copies, but also because they achieved that success while radically redefining the R&B "girl group." While past trios, exemplified by the legendary Supremes and contemporary incarnations including Jade and SWV, presented themselves as sultry and sophisticated, TLC burst onto the music scene with baggy, boyish clothes and a hip-hop attitude borrowed from male ensembles. They approached the usual musical topics, love and sex, from an unusual angle, opting to talk directly to young women about self-assertiveness and self-protection. Left Eye earned her nickname for the habit of wearing a condom over the left lens of her glasses, while all three used the colorful packages to accessorize. Young black women were watching them; Joan Morgan declared in *Vibe,* "The trio damn near led a grassroots womanist revolution, banji-girl style."

Difficult Backgrounds

Self-confidence is something all three singers say they had to learn themselves before they could begin to communicate with others. Each also attributes that struggle to her father's limitations as a parent. While Lopes's relationship with her father, who died in 1991, was characterized by violence, Thomas and Watkins essentially lacked fathers: Thomas's was absent altogether and Watkins's may as well have been. "It's better just not to have one at all," Watkins commented to Tonya Pendleton when encouraged to talk about her father in *YSB.* "Let the family replace the love that the father couldn't give." Consequently, Watkins's mother—who

bore her daughter in Des Moines, Iowa, in 1970—provided the groundwork for Tionne's self-esteem. Watkins's earliest experience as a singer was nurtured by her mother, with whom she would sing in church. In the ensuing years, she saw music as a route away from the drudgery of a regular job, which she pursued for a while in the beauty trade, working as a hair model, a shampoo girl, and a manicurist.

Thomas was able to move away from the projects through the support of her mother, who was 17 at her daughter's birth, and her great-grandmother. The native Atlantan first set her sights on the fashion industry, spending two years at Georgia Southern University. She was faced with a choice between fashion and entertainment when an offer to manage a store and one to dance for a hip-hop artist came at the same time. She went with the dancing—which brought her to the attention of R&B singer and producer Pebbles.

Lopes's story has received the most attention. Born in Philadelphia in 1971, she was reared by an abusive man who, paradoxically, also helped her to see her own talent and strength. "My dad was real strict," she recalled for *Vibe*'s Morgan. "He was in the military, and he treated me, my sister, my brother, and my mother like we were in boot camp. He looked at me like I was the brightest, and expected more from me. I always got beaten before they did." She also informed Morgan that her father bonded with her through alcohol, explaining that "my father is responsible for my drinking. He gave me my first drink, and my hundredth drink."

Her father was a more positive force in recognizing the girl's gifts. She taught herself to play piano by age five. In her teen years, she demonstrated ability as a composer, writer, visual artist, designer, and rapper. She honed her performance skills in talent shows and offered her expertise behind the scenes at various venues. But she was also having trouble at home, as the many times she ran away as a teenager illustrate. She left permanently at 17, ending up in Atlanta with a boyfriend. Before she joined TLC three years later, she had been forced to support herself "by any means necessary," as she told Morgan.

TLC was formed in 1991 by a *C*—Crystal—who faded from sight when Watkins and Lopes discovered that they worked better together without her. The duo also met Pebbles that year; she became their manager. Pebbles had a good deal of sway with L.A. Reid, her husband and one of the founders of Atlanta-based LaFace Records. A recording contract followed. Rozonda Thomas came on board soon after, discovered by Pebbles while rehearsing a dance routine for a Damian Dane music video. Thomas added a different kind of vocal skill and dance experience; she choreographs TLC videos and live performances. Her "look" also complemented the territory already mapped by Watkins and Lopes; where "Tionne is almost like a guy," songwriter and producer Dallas Austin told Morgan, "Chilli is a girl.... And Lisa has always been pretty much rebellious."

"We all have our parts," Chilli told *BRE,* "our own areas and we respect them. I don't try to rap and Left Eye doesn't try to sing, but we all dance." Jeff Lorez commented in *Blues and Soul* that they "had the perfect blend—Left Eye's rebellious, outrageous rhymes, T-Boz's cooled out, nonchalant vocals and Rozonda 'Chilli' Thomas' sweet, soulful cooing." Morgan went into greater detail, trying to capture the distinct quality that each woman provided. "T-Boz's raspy harmonies are the funk," she wrote, "the voice of the blue-collar sister who works hard during the week, parties her ass off on Friday, saves the lovin' for Saturday, and makes it to church every Sunday morning. Lisa's rap is the grit, the sound of the urban street that grounds the group." Morgan pegged Thomas's voice as the one that "personifies the magic of falling in—and making—love."

Shook Up the New Jill Swing

When *Ooooooohhh ... On the TLC Tip* hit the market in 1992, listeners welcomed it enthusiastically, both for how it rode the New Jill Swing trend and for how it disrupted it. The instant excitement over TLC's look and sound prompted Morgan to argue that the album "put LaFace Records on the map." Looking back at the debut, *Los Angeles Times* writer Dennis Hunt recalled that when "the trio ... burst on the hip-hop scene, it was a breath of fresh air, bringing a cocky, macho sensibility to the prissy girl-group genre.... A wacky, cartoonish quality coupled with a reckless inhibition made that debut something special." Watkins pointed out in *BRE* that they had "proven that you don't have to wear tight slinky outfits to make it. We stand up for the [girl groups] who always wanted to dress like this, but couldn't. We didn't show a stitch of our skin and we made it."

The album became, as Alan Light wrote in *Rolling Stone,* "a New Jill Swing gem." It did so, at least in part, on the basis of its run of chart-topping singles. "Ain't 2 Proud 2 Beg" and "What About Your Friends" each reached the Number Two spot on *Billboard's* R&B singles chart, becoming, respectively, platinum and gold. "Baby Baby Baby" also went platinum and took the Number One spot. These songs traded the usual girl-group fare of broken hearts and tortuous seduction for "a determination to have women free themselves from the labels

given to those who dare to assert themselves sexually," according to *Word Up!* magazine. Light lavished praise on the group's "independent, street-level feminism," while *YSB's* Pendleton noted that although "the seriousness of their safe-sex message could have distanced potential fans, their openness and sense of humor about the necessity of condoms made them even more popular."

> *I want them to be larger than just hip-hop. I want them to be thought of as true creative forces."*
> —L. A. Reid

An unexpectedly long hiatus intervened between *Tip* and the group's second full-length production. Some of the distraction was work-related: they appeared in the film *House Party 3* and contributed a song to the soundtrack for the Janet Jackson film *Poetic Justice;* they exposed audiences to their hyperactive live act while on tour with Hammer in 1992 and Bobby Brown in 1993. Furthermore, despite the success of the first album, the trio decided that they needed a different management direction, consequently ending their professional relationship with Pebbles. They stayed with LaFace Records, but began working instead with manager Hiriam Hicks. Lopes also moved into management herself, dedicating a portion of her time to Left Eye Management, which sponsored young hip-hop performers.

Unfortunately, however, much of the two-year period was lost to personal problems—and most of these were Lopes's. After Lopes met Andre Rison in the spring of 1993, the two began an intense, tumultuous relationship, Lopes moving into Rison's mansion in the suburbs outside of Atlanta. On June 9, 1994, one of their fights led to news stories across the country. Rison's version of the incident appeared in *People* a few weeks later: after a night out with friends, Rison returned home at 6 a.m. to find Lopes in the driveway, furious with him. "I started taking blows to the face," he said. "Finally, I grabbed her and asked her what was wrong. But she kept coming at me." Unable to stop the assault, he slapped her, Rison claimed, "not to hurt her, but to calm her. Didn't work. We were inside the house now, and I picked her up and slammed her on the bed and sat on her. I still couldn't control her. So I left. I went on a 20-mile walk." Lopes then started a fire with cardboard in a bathtub; the ensuing conflagration destroyed the mansion. As the house burned, she vandalized three of the cars in the driveway and drove away in another.

Lopes turned herself in to police the next day to face arson and criminal damage charges. Soon after, she entered a rehab clinic to seek treatment for alcohol abuse, suggesting that her drinking had played a role in what had happened.

"There is no damn way in the world," Lopes argued in Morgan's interview, "I would have intentionally started that fire. I lived in that house for a whole year. I had a year's worth of time invested in that house, that relationship. Anybody with common sense should know that there were stories behind what happened." Lopes attempted to fill out the picture a few days after the fire, giving police photographs of herself with bruises on her face. Similarly, several observers have argued that the fire was Lopes's effort to fight back in an abusive relationship. Morgan, for example, noted an incident reported in September 1993, when Lopes and Rison were seen fighting in a grocery store parking lot. "According to two passersby," recorded Morgan, "Rison hit Lopes and then fired a 9mm handgun when they tried to intervene." Such actions, many commentators surmised, probably characterized their relationship.

Demonstrated Growth on *Crazysexycool*

Label head L. A. Reid has concurred with this view, telling Morgan that "Lisa is a victim more than anything. People have got to ask themselves how there can be a 'fight' between an All-Pro athlete and a little girl. It's hard, because in Lisa's head, her relationship is not an abusive relationship but a relationship where something bad happened." Later that year, it appeared that any major conflict had been resolved; in December, Watkins explained to *Blues and Soul* contributor Lorez that "Andre and Lisa are still together.... Her court case hasn't come up yet ... but we've forgotten about it." (On December 29, 1994, Lopes pleaded guilty to destroying Rison's million-dollar home. According to *People,* she "was sentenced to several months in a halfway house and five years' probation. She was also ordered to pay a $10,000 fine, undergo treatment for alcohol abuse, and receive battered-woman counseling. [Rison admitted in court to hitting Lopes]. Rison has said he has forgiven Lopes for the blaze and plans to marry her.")

When production did get under way for a second album, TLC and their producers found themselves struggling with trying to top the success of the first. Since the debut album had displayed a particularly "young" character, the three had to demonstrate growth in order not to appear stagnant beside their maturing fans, but they couldn't change so drastically that they abandoned that audience. Ultimately, changes made for the album included more than just growth in musical style. "The hardest part about coming out this time was thinking about our clothes, because our image was as big as our music," Thomas told Sonia Murray of the *Atlanta Constitution.* "My challenge," said Reid, who acted as creative director for *Crazysexycool,* according to *Vibe's* Morgan, "was to give their fans good music but allow TLC to grow in a way that would keep them around. I want them to be larger than just hip-hop. I want them to be thought of as true creative forces."

One decision found the three showing more skin—on the album cover and in videos—than they had before. They generally pursued a more mature approach to sexuality, expressing this in the album's title. "*Crazysexycool* is a word we created to describe what's in every woman," Lopes told Morgan. *Crazysexycool* also found the artists more involved in their own recording; Lopes, who had always written her own raps, contributed the songs "Waterfalls" and "Kick Your Game" and joined in the actual production of the record. ("Waterfalls" would become a hit single during the summer of 1995).

When *Crazysexycool* hit the market late in 1994, it immediately took the Number Two spot on the R&B chart. Critics waxed poetic over the group's growth. Writing for *People,* Jeremy Helligar declared that the "sharp funk and libidinous R&B of *Crazysexycool* easily outgrooves its predecessor's sloganeering bubblegum hip-hop." *Billboard's* Reynolds reported that the "musical evolution of TLC is marked by stronger voices, closer harmonies, and tighter raps" and *Time's* Christopher John Farley found "the vocals ... stronger and the melodies more piquant than ... on the first album." David Sprague, covering the release for *Fanfare,* argued that "TLC's second album reaffirms that the three members aren't cut from the same designer-showroom cloth as most contemporary dance acts. Every note of *Crazysexycool* ... is invested with plainspoken approachability that makes TLC sound like libido-conscious girls next door, rather than genetically engineered fantasy objects." *Crazysexycool* also spawned the hits "Creep" and "Red Light Special" and spent numerous weeks in the pop Top Ten.

The trio seemed bent on shaping its growth with an eye toward the message they send to young women; while remaining uncompromisingly frank about sexuality— insisting that women can make the moves and draw the lines—TLC still maintained that the most important thing was a young woman's self-esteem and self-determination. Talking with Pendleton, Watkins reiterated her commitment to female autonomy: "Even if I married a rich man, I would never quit and just let him take care of me. We have all met [men], whether they were selling drugs or whatever, with *hell-a-money,* and we could have been set up a long time ago. But everybody don't want to do it like that. I don't care how many kids I have, my husband could be the richest man in the world, I will still work. I ain't never gonna be no housewife."

Selected discography

Oooooooohhh ... On the TLC Tip (includes "Baby Baby Baby," "What About Your Friends," and "Ain't 2 Proud 2 Beg"), LaFace/Arista, 1992.

Crazysexycool (includes "Creep," "Waterfalls," "Kick Your Game" and "Red Light Special"), LaFace/Arista, 1994.

Sources

Atlanta Constitution, November 14, 1994.
Billboard, October 1, 1994.
Black Beat, February 1995.
Blues and Soul, December 13-26, 1994.
BRE, December 9, 1994.
Details, March 1995.
Entertainment Weekly, November 18, 1994; December 9, 1994.
Fanfare, November 27, 1994.
Gavin, December 2, 1994.
Jet, June 27, 1994.
Los Angeles Times, November 13, 1994.
Mademoiselle, January 1995.
Network Forty (Burbank, CA), November 4, 1994; January 16, 1995.
People, June 27, 1994; December 5, 1994.
Rolling Stone, May 28, 1992.
Time, December 19, 1994.
Vibe, November 1994.
Word Up!, January 1, 1995.
YSB, June/July 1994.

—*Ondine E. Le Blanc*

Crystal Waters

Singer, songwriter

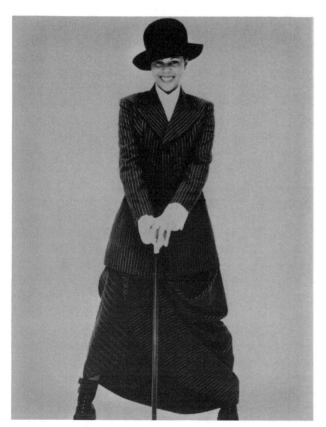

Courtesy of Mercury Records

House music songwriter and vocalist Crystal Waters has the odd distinction of making a comeback with the release of her second album. After she topped the *Billboard* singles charts in 1991 with a dance hit called "Gypsy Woman (She's Homeless)," her ensuing debut album failed to impress critics. She was consequently filed away under "one-hit wonder." Nonetheless, a few years of hard work and careful repackaging saw Waters back in the market, garnering praise and sales with her second album, *Storyteller,* and another slew of dance hits. This time, critics declared that the quality of her work *didn't* surprise them—they had always known she had something special to offer house music: an uncompromising house beat that also managed to carry substantial intelligence.

Waters arrived as a music celebrity in adulthood, after a full stint of education and nine-to-five employment necessary to support two children. Since she remains very private about her personal life, the curious can only speculate about the date of her birth, which appears to have been sometime in the early 1960s in Camden, New Jersey. Talking with *New American*'s Karu Daniels, Waters described "south Jersey" as a place where "there is really nothing to do except open fire hydrants and go out and play." She would eventually try to capture that atmosphere in a song, "Ghetto Day," for her second album.

Unexpected Music Celebrity

Music made its way into the Waters home on the strength of family history: Crystal's father, Junior Waters, was a jazz musician; her great aunt, Ethel Waters, was one of the first African-American vocalists to appear in mainstream Hollywood musicals. Waters's mother, Betty, described her daughter's childhood activities for *Interview*'s Jeremy Helligar, telling him, "At eleven or twelve [Crystal] was writing poetry about the soul and other deep things. And I would ask, `How do you know about this stuff?'" She took her writing seriously enough to be inducted into the American Poetry Society when she was 14, the youngest person ever to receive that honor.

The shape of Waters's life as a young adult seemed to be directing her towards a practical, middle-class self-sufficiency—nothing glamorous, but highly respectable. She studied business at Howard University; not surprisingly, her creative work dropped off during this period, since she found less time for it. After earning her college degree in 1985, Waters secured a job with the Washington, D.C., parole board, making a living from her business and computer skills that would support her two children. Consistent with her business experience,

Waters first approached the music world in 1987 as a behind-the-scenes worker, writing demos for a production team known as the Basement Boys. She secured a writing contract with Mercury Records in 1989.

Given the character and progress of her life to that point, Waters's emergence into the show business spotlight was wholly unexpected. While many performers ply their trade for years before being declared an "overnight sensation" by the music press, in 1991 Waters actually did burst into celebrity on the basis of what appeared to be a fluke. In one of her assignments as a demo writer, Waters penned a song called "Gypsy Woman" for dance diva Ultra Naté and recorded a demo cut of the song. The producers were so taken by her rendition that they drew up a contract with her for that one song, never passing it on to Ultra Naté. The recording had the production nurturance of the Basement Boys, who were known for their hit-making skills.

"Gypsy Woman" topped both the dance and pop charts; on the former, it stayed at Number One for six weeks, and on the latter, it maintained a respectable spot in the Top Ten. Daniels summarized the single's reputation when she recalled that the "song and it's unforgettable, infectious, catchy hook la-da-dee, la-da-da became a little legend in itself." In fact, almost every critic who even briefly mentioned the single immortalized that hook on paper. Helligar called it "the hook heard round the world" and *Rolling Stone's* reviewer declared that the song's "deliciously nagging chorus `La-da-dee-la-da-da' was indisputably the Hook of the Year." The critic also christened it "a rare bright spot of originality and blessed simplicity amid a '91-long plague of Identikit house records and overwrought remixes." Amy Linden recalled the song's rise for *People* in 1994, writing that in the "club-music world, dominated as it is by big-mama belters, Waters was a postmodern minimalist, her weirdness a breath of fresh air."

Album Built around Single

On the strength of the single, Mercury decided to market Waters full strength. She was sent around the country to perform, to talk to the press, and to basically promote herself and her music. In a rush to make the most of her popularity, the record company also asked Waters to cut an album. She produced *Surprise* in a matter of weeks, penning and recording songs at a pace that deprived her of the opportunity for careful crafting. Her lack of time showed in the results: critics found the album disappointing. A *Rolling Stone* reviewer argued, "Waters and her production team ... hammer the 'Gypsy Woman' formula into the ground on *Surprise,* an album made up largely of not-so-subtle variations on the original." Even Waters criticized the recording, telling *Billboard* in March of 1994 that she "wasn't too happy with the sound of the ... album."

In the *New American,* Daniels blamed the failure of Waters's debut album on Mercury's marketing tactics, which the reviewer described as "the over saturation of the song and overexposure of the artist." The effects of too much publicity soon became evident in the media's turn against Waters, the most vicious example of which, perhaps, was a parody on the Fox television network's show *In Living Color.* "I felt like I was in the middle of this crazy whirlwind," Waters revealed in *Billboard* in March of 1994. "Try to imagine being a really shy person who is suddenly being looked at and pursued by everyone in the world. At times, it was very scary." Bad publicity followed on bad production. Waters was dragged through a lawsuit with a woman performer from another country who claimed that "Gypsy Woman" was her material. Nonetheless, the album produced more dance hits—"Makin' Happy" and "Surprise"—and did reach gold status.

Storyteller Received with Enthusiasm

Waters approached her second album with the lessons of the first in mind. She told the *New American's* Daniels that she "got off the road in December '92 and started writing the new album." Ultimately, the work took her two years. She determined that she would carefully control the quality of her product this time—and that the quality would be high. "With this album," she told *Billboard,* "I had to make sure that I could feel good about every word and note. That was—and is—much more important to me than having one gigantic single." She was, at least in part, motivated by the response to her first album; "I tried my best," she recalled for Daniels, "because they are not going to say that I'm a one hit wonder. I can write and I'm gonna write some hit songs."

The first single not only repeated the story of "Gypsy Woman," it also set the tone for what would follow. In its first weeks, "100% Pure Love" escalated through the *Billboard* charts and saturated radio station playlists. By late October of 1994, Larry Flick was tracing the song's success in a *Billboard* article, in which he declared, "There is a reason for citizens of clubland to rejoice this week." The single had gone gold, and, explained Flick, "Though gold records are a common occurrence in the pop and urban mainstream, it has been more than a hot second since a house-rooted release ... earned such a high sales profile." In the *New American* Daniels described *Storyteller*'s second single, "Ghetto Day," as a "splash of mid-tempo, cool retro-funk," an assessment that captured the tune's change in gears. "What I Need" also found favor, breaking the Top Ten on two more *Billboard* charts.

On the strength of its first two singles, *Storyteller* found the favor *Surprise* had missed. Jonathan Bernstein wrote in *Spin* that Waters "flies in the face of the received wisdom that there are no second acts in American dance music by delivering a full-flavored sequel album." Ernest Hardy wrote in *Request,* "Waters dazzles by delivering an absolutely flawless collection of state-of-the-club dance music." He concluded with a description of "Daddy Do," noting, "Waters not only turns in her best vocal performance (on her best lyrics), but the controlled frenzy of the production brilliantly, if surprisingly, complements the subject matter." Hardy also pushed the album in a *Los Angeles Times* article, in which he went into more detail about the substance of Waters's appeal. "Blending hip-hop textures and sensibilities, swinging jazz inflections and sizzling funk with state of the art dance grooves," he wrote, "Waters comes across as a serious talent. At the core of that talent is her lyrical style ..., which fuses many elements—sexy playfulness with compassion, a keen eye for detail with social consciousness."

Recognition for Waters's *Storyteller* proved that she had come a long way from her initial job with the Washington, D.C. parole board. Late in 1994 the artist augmented her public reputation as a musician with a contract with Ford Models followed by her first struts down the catwalk in European fashion shows. The former computer analyst and "one-hit wonder" found her creativity and talent more than confirmed.

Selected discography

Surprise (includes "Gypsy Woman [She's Homeless]," "Makin' Happy," and title track), Mercury/PolyGram, 1991.
Storyteller (includes "100% Pure Love," "Ghetto Day," and "Daddy Do"), Mercury/PolyGram, 1994.

Sources

Billboard, March 5, 1994; October 22, 1994.
Fab Magazine (Toronto), July 22, 1994.
Interview, June 1994.
Los Angeles Times, May 22, 1994.
New American, June 23, 1994.
New York Amsterdam News, September 3, 1994.
People, July 25, 1994.
Pulse!, June 1994.
Request, June 1994.
Rolling Stone, December 12, 1991; August 25, 1994.
Spin, June 1994.
Vibe, December 1994/January 1995.

Additional information for this profile was obtained from Mercury Records publicity materials, 1995.

—*Ondine E. Le Blanc*

Randy Weston

Pianist, composer

Photograph by Cheung Ming, courtesy of Antilles Records

Jazz and world-music pianist/composer Randy Weston boasts a range of musical influences. Born and raised in Brooklyn, New York, he later lived in Africa for many years, both playing and studying African music. The result of his lifelong work and his far-reaching adventures is a beautiful and balanced hybrid of classic American jazz and ancient African rhythms and tonalities.

Weston grew up in the Bedford-Stuyvesant section of Brooklyn, where his father, the owner of a soul food diner, emphasized to his son, "You are an African born in America." The elder Weston laid down a strict rule for Randy: Practice the piano at home each day or feel the edge of a ruler on your knuckles. When the now six-foot-eight Weston was in his early teens he was already six-feet-two-inches tall and eager to play basketball, but his father ensured that he did not stray too far from his piano. Passing along his vast knowledge of calypso, jazz, and blues on to his son, Weston's father frequently took him to see bandleader Duke Ellington at the Sonia Ballroom or Brooklyn Palace, as well as to Harlem to hear calypso. In addition, Weston's mother, who was from Virginia, exposed her young son to spirituals.

While Weston was a youngster in Brooklyn in the 1930s and 1940s, musicians Miles Davis, Max Roach, and George Russell all lived in the borough at one time or another, and each had stopped into the elder Weston's luncheonette for soul food. Weston felt steeped in the African American music community as a teenager; he especially made a point of seeing Coleman Hawkins perform whenever possible, and through Hawkins, was able to meet pianist Thelonious Monk. Weston spent many hours at home listening to Monk's recordings.

At the age of 14, Weston was taught by drummer Al Harewood how to play a tune on the piano by ear; Weston was then able to imitate current releases by Ellington, Hawkins, and Count Basie. Weston used to go to the Atlantic Avenue section of Brooklyn to hear Arabic musicians play the *oud,* a type of lute. He told *Down Beat's* Fred Bouchard, "We were searching for new sounds. We'd get into quarter and eighth tones. But here was Monk doing it, with spirit power, with magic!... For me it was pure African piano." Besides Monk, Basie, Hawkins, and Ellington, jazz greats Nat King Cole and Art Tatum were also early influences for Weston.

Voted "new star pianist" in a 1955 *Down Beat* critics' poll, Weston spent most of the 1950s playing in clubs around New York City with Cecil Payne and Kenny Dorham. He also toured colleges with historian Marshall Stearns, who lectured while Weston and a few other musicians performed African, calypso, Dixieland, and bebop music. Weston wrote a string of popular songs,

For the Record . . .

Born Randolph Edward Weston, April 6, 1926, in Brooklyn, NY; son of Frank Edward Weston (a restaurant owner); married; two children, including a son, Azzedin (formerly named Niles).

Pianist and composer. Released first album, *Cole Porter in a Modern Mood*, Riverside, 1954; has toured Africa and lived in Tangiers and Paris; appeared in television special *Randy Weston: A Legend in His Own Time*, WGBH-TV, Boston, MA, 1982; subject of jazz documentary films *Jazz Entre Amigos, Randy in Tangiers,* and *African Rhythms.*

Awards: Voted "new star pianist" in a *Down Beat* critic's poll, 1955; voted "pianist most deserving wider recognition," *Down Beat,* 1972; Grammy Award nomination for best jazz performance, 1971, for *Tanjah;* first prize from Academie du Jazz, France, 1976; Randy Weston Week established by Brooklyn Borough President's Office and the Brooklyn Academy of Music, 1986; named "world's best jazz pianist," International Roots Festival, Lagos, Nigeria, 1988.

Addresses: *Management*—The Brad Simon Organization, Inc., 122 East 57th St., New York, NY 10022. *Record company*—Antilles, 400 Lafayette St., 5th Floor, New York, NY 11050.

including "Saucer Eyes," "Pam's Waltz," "Little Niles," and his best-known tune, "Hi-Fly," which is about being six-foot-eight and looking at the ground. Among the 11 albums he released during the fifties were *Cole Porter in a Modern Mood* (1954), *Randy Weston Trio* (1955), *Piano a La Mode* (1957), and *Little Niles* (1958).

In 1960 Weston recorded *Uhuru Africa* with composer, arranger, and trombonist Melba Liston. *Uhuru Africa* featured narration by writer Langston Hughes and featured African traditional styles with a jazz orchestra. Weston told Bouchard in *Down Beat,* "I developed a lot playing with African drummers: Candido, Chief Bey, Big Black, Olatunji."

Weston's first encounter with African musicians was in Lagos, Nigeria. The rhythms impressed themselves on Weston's psyche, and he eventually traveled and played in 18 African nations. In 1966 he visited 14 African countries while on a U.S. State Department tour. Finally deciding to settle in Tangiers, Morocco, he owned a nightclub there from 1968 until 1972. He then lived in Paris during the mid- to late 1970s, and his recordings—frequently licensed from European labels—appeared sporadically throughout the decade. He continued to perform in Africa, including at the 1977 Nigerian Festival, which attracted musicians from 60 different culture. The pianist told *Down Beat's* Bouchard, "Africa is like a huge tree with branches to Brazil, to Cuba, and America. The approach to music is identical: rhythm, polyrhythm, call and response."

The 1980s saw Weston receive recognition for his unique style of blending various cultures in his music. In 1982 the televsion special *Randy Weston: A Legend in His Own Time* was filmed for WGBH-TV in Boston. Randy Weston Week was declared in 1986 by the Brooklyn Borough President's Office and the Brooklyn Academy of Music in 1986, and two years later Weston won an award the World's Best Jazz Pianist category at the International Roots Festival in Lagos, Nigeria. And, between 1987 and 1989, Weston was the subject of three documentary films: *Jazz Entre Amigos,* for Spanish television, *Randy in Tangiers,* for Spanish and French television, and *African Rhythms,* for WGBH-TV.

At the close of the 1980s Weston released a trilogy of compact discs (CDs) for the Antilles/Polygram label. Presenting the music of Ellington, Monk, and himself, *Portraits* was designed to boost Weston's exposure and popularity in the United States. Weston's sparse playing on the *Portraits* series is a departure from his earliest work, and *Portraits* can best be described as a Moroccan-Arabic-jazz fusion that features a tone ranging from ancient to futuristic.

The early to mid-1990s were busy years for Weston, whose appearances included a tour with a Moroccan Gnawa group, a troupe of dancers and musicians traveling from Morocco to the Niger region. In 1992 the pianist released another album, *Spirits of Our Ancestors,* underscoring the African link between forms of modern-day American music and featuring musicians Melba Liston, Pharoah Sanders, Dizzy Gillespie, and Dewey Redman. *Volcano Blues* was released a year later and was followed by Weston's *Monterey '66* in 1994. Two albums were cut in 1995, *The Splendid Master Musicians of Morocco* and *Marrakesh: In the Cool of the Evening.*

Weston's music reflects his diverse paths in life and his desire to interweave the past with the future, and traditional with new sounds. Like Morocco and Africa itself, his music sounds both mysterious and beautifully simple. In an *Earshot Jazz* article, Gary Bannister gave Weston a well-deserved compliment when he referred to the multifaceted pianist as "Monk's greatest heir."

Selected discography

Cole Porter in a Modern Mood, Riverside, 1954.
Randy Weston Trio, Riverside, 1955.
Piano a la Mode, Jubilee, 1957.
Little Niles, United Artists, 1958.
Uhuru Africa, Roulette, 1960.
Music of the New African Nations, Colpix, 1963.
Randy, Bakton, 1964.
African Rhythms, Polydor, 1969.
Blue Moses, CTI, 1972.
Big Band Tanjah, Polydor, 1973.
Bantu, Roulette, 1976.
Randy Weston Live at the Five Spot, Blue Note, 1976.
Berkshire Blues, Arista, 1977.
The Healers, Cora, 1980.
Blue, Arch, 1984.
The Healers, with Saxophonist David Murray, Black Saint, 1987.
Portraits of Ellington, Polygram, 1990.
Portraits of Monk, Polygram, 1990.
Self Portraits, Polygram, 1990.
Spirits of Our Ancestors, Antilles, 1992.
Volcano Blues, Antilles, 1993.
Monterey '66, Antilles, 1994.

The Splendid Master Musicians of Morocco, Antilles, 1995.
Marrakesh: In the Cool of the Evening, Antilles, 1995.

Weston also wrote film scores for *The Africans* and *The African Queens,* both 1981, and *Portrait of Billie Holiday* and *African Sunrise,* both 1985.

Sources

Billboard, March 28, 1992.
CMJ (College Music Journal), January 8, 1993.
Down Beat, May 1992, November 1990.
Earshot Jazz, October 1992.
JazzTimes, December 1992.
Montreal Gazette, July 10, 1993.
News & Observer (Raleigh, NC), November 22, 1993.
New York Times, September 16, 1991.
Pulse!, November 1993.
Rolling Stone, May 14, 1992.
Washington Post, January 29, 1993.

Additional information for this profile was provided by The Brad Simon Organization, Inc., 1995.

—*B. Kimberly Taylor*

Jerry Wexler

Producer, record company executive

AP/Wide World Photos

At the age of 12, Jerry Wexler was a New York City brat, hanging out at Artie's poolroom on 181st Street in Washington Heights and learning to talk fast and act tough. These traits would serve him well in the recording industry. In 1952 Wexler became a producer at fledgling Atlantic Records, an independent label dedicated to the genre that Wexler himself rechristened "rhythm and blues" in a 1941 *Billboard* article.

With an intense passion for jazz and soul, Wexler became an expert at distinguishing talent, and during his years at Atlantic, he launched many artists who became world-famous: Ray Charles, Aretha Franklin, Otis Redding, the Clovers, and the Drifters. He also discovered country legend Willie Nelson before the singer moved to CBS Records and stardom. Wexler's enthusiasm and intellectual edge, in fact, provided the support necessary for many artists' best work. Among the plethora of musicians he has promoted are Joe Turner, Wilson Pickett, Patti LaBelle, Cher, Sam and Dave, Dr. John, Doug Sahm, and Etta James.

The Washington Heights area where Jerry Wexler grew up was a hodgepodge of poor immigrants—many of whom had just arrived in the United States. Wexler's mother, Elsa, who married Wexler's Polish immigrant father, Harry, in 1916, had aspirations about a literary life for her unmotivated son. Elsa scrimped and saved tuition for preparatory schools, and Jerry promptly flunked out of all of them. Ultimately, he took a job with his father, washing windows. Throughout his youth, however, Wexler managed to make frequent visits to Manhattan nightclubs, featuring swing and the big bands—Fletcher Henderson at the Savoy, Jimmy Lunceford, Count Basie, and Benny Goodman. Wexler read books about jazz and blues, and collected the latest 78 rpm records.

Learned Discipline in the Army

After a stint in 1936 at Kansas State College, where he studied journalism—and haunted the wild Kansas City clubs—Wexler returned to New York. He fell in love with a teenager named Shirley Kampf, and as a sign of his adoration, he took her to see Ella Fitzgerald and Chick Webb at the Apollo Theater. Shirley became his confidant and co-worker for the next two decades. After marrying in 1941, the couple moved in with Wexler's father, who was temporarily estranged from Elsa. Wexler finally landed a job, as a customs officer, but was drafted into the U.S. Army in 1942.

As noted in his 1993 autobiography, *Rhythm and the Blues: A Life in American Music,* Wexler credits the army for instilling discipline into his character. He received a

Born Gerald Wexler in 1917 in New York, NY; son of Harry (a window washer) and Elsa (Spitz) Wexler; married Shirley Kampf, 1941 (divorced 1973); married Renee Pappas, 1973 (divorced 1982); married Jean Arnold, 1985; children: Anita (died 1989), Lisa, Paul. *Education:* Received journalism degree from Kansas State College.

Producer and record company executive. Worked for Broadcast Music, Inc. (BMI); reporter, *Billboard* magazine, until 1951; promotions director, MGM Studios; became partner with Ahmet Ertegun of Atlantic Records, 1952; produced releases by numerous artists, including LaVern Baker, the Drifters, Ray Charles, Aretha Franklin, Betty Carter, Bob Dylan, Willie Nelson, and Etta James; left Atlantic and produced releases for Warner Bros. and wrote film scores. Author, with David Ritz, of autobiography *Rhythm and the Blues: A Life in American Music,* Knopf, 1993. *Military service:* Served in U.S. Army.

Addresses: *Record company*—Elektra Entertainment, 75 Rockefeller Plaza, New York, NY 10019.

stateside assignment as a military police officer, presumably because of his customs experience. In Miami Beach, Florida, then in Wichita Falls, Texas, he was responsible for administering behavioral tests. After his discharge, he went back to Kansas State to finish his degree, began to write, and had a few articles published. He then headed to New York City to look for a newspaper job. Unsuccessful in his search, he found work at the newly formed Broadcast Music, Inc. (BMI), a radio group challenging the American Society of Composers, Authors and Publishers' (ASCAP) domination of the music publishing industry. A bout with pneumonia forced Wexler to give up that position, but *Billboard* magazine soon hired him. Now 30, he was able to move with his wife into his first apartment.

Two lifelong preoccupations surfaced in Wexler at this time: bebop—the music of Charlie Parker, Miles Davis and Dizzy Gillespie—and the food of the great Broadway delis like Lindy's on 51st Street. The song peddlers who frequented the restaurants, especially a man named Juggy Gayles, introduced Wexler to the world of record production. In his position of reporter for *Billboard,* Wexler chose from the thousand of demos that crossed his desk, the "Tennessee Waltz," and gave it to singer Patti Page's agent, Jack Ruel. She recorded it as the B-side of "Boogie Woogie Santa Claus," and it became her signature song. Wexler can also take credit for alerting Mitch Miller of Columbia Records to two songs that became Number One hits: "Cry" performed by Johnny Ray, and a Hank Williams tune, "Cold, Cold Heart," sung by Tony Bennett.

Put Atlantic Records on the Map

Eventually, a rift developed between Wexler and *Billboard's* editors. According to Wexler, during the McCarthy era—when many Americans entertainers were being blacklisted for their alleged communist leanings—he had refused to work up a blacklist dossier on the folk group the Weavers. He left the magazine in 1951 to become promotions director for MGM Studios' music publishing division, the Big Three. His reputation earned him a job offer from Atlantic Records, but he turned it down; he had insisted upon being made a partner. A year later, the owner of Atlantic, Ahmet Ertegun, acquiesced to Wexler's demand when Ertegun's partner, Herb Abrahamson, left to join the army. Wexler raised $2,063.25 to claim a 13 percent share of the company. Ertegun in turn used the money to buy Wexler a green Cadillac with fins.

Ertegun and Wexler were well matched: Ertegun was cool while Wexler was frenetic. Both men had an extensive knowledge of literature and art, as well as of rhythm and blues. Their office over Patsy's Restaurant at 234 West 57th Street became a beehive of sessions that put Atlantic Records on the map.

The Atlantic Records business was run like a mom-and-pop grocery. Wexler worked intimately with the performers, helping Clyde McPhatter of the Drifters, for example, write "Honey Love" and playing tambourine for Ray Charles. Atlantic succeeded in changing the negligent attitude that record labels traditionally had taken toward black music. Wexler treated the performers with respect, rehearsing and developing clear, precise harmonies. He produced recordings for LaVern Baker, then Joe Turner, and, most notably, Ray Charles. Wexler claimed that he merely stood back and let the great pianist invent, but Charles' work at Atlantic—combining bebop, gospel, and blues—proved to be his finest.

By 1956 Wexler was producing a dozen recording acts. He bid $30,000—an amount he did not have—for Elvis Presley, but lost out to RCA's $40,000 offer. He soon hooked up with Jerry Lieber and Mike Stoller, a songwriting team that created a steady output of pop music masterpieces, including "Stand By Me," "Charlie Brown," "Poison Ivy," and "There Goes My Baby." Wexler's hustle kept the then-independent Atlantic Records label competitive with the deep-pocket major studios. In the 1960s Atlantic brought guitarist Jimmy Page to the United States from England, and Page's band, Led Zeppelin, became Atlantic's biggest seller.

Architect of Franklin's "Respect"

Ertegun and Wexler became estranged during the 1970s, as Ertegun's taste switched to the more lucrative pop acts, and Wexler became notorious for backing purist failures in the R&B realm. As Ahmet gravitated toward Los Angeles and London, Jerry headed south to Tennessee, Alabama, and Florida. He was a pioneer in the southern renaissance that merged R&B and country sounds. One of Wexler's best-known projects was Aretha Franklin, a gospel singer who blossomed under the producer's auspices. She reworked blues performer Otis Redding's "Respect" on her first album, and the song became a feminist anthem.

Wexler's personal life, however, suffered from his workaholic nature. His wife, Shirley divorced him in 1973 when she discovered that he was seeing another woman, Renee Pappas, whom Wexler promptly married. He would later cope with the death of his daughter Anita of AIDS in 1989. A professional association ended as well when he sold his share in Atlantic to smooth over friction with Ertegun.

In 1985 Wexler moved to Sarasota, Florida, and married playwright and novelist Jean Arnold. He continued to pursue independent projects, working on film director Francis Ford Coppola's *The Cotton Club* and *Jelly's Last Jam* on Broadway. He joined forces with folk troubadour Bob Dylan for the singer's Christian albums *Slow Train Coming* and *Saved*. In the 1990s, having reached his seventies, he was still producing, making an album called *The Right Time* with his old friend Etta James.

Selected discography

As producer

1950-60

Lavern Baker, *Soul on Fire: The Best of Lavern Baker*.
Ruth Brown, *Miss Rhythm: Greatest Hits and More*.
The Clovers, *Down the Alley: The Best of the Clovers*.
The Drifters, *Let the Boogie-Woogie Roll, 1953-1958*.
Ray Charles, *The Birth of Soul: The Complete Atlantic Rhythm and Blues Recordings, 1952-1959*.
Ray Charles and Milt Jackson, *Brothers*.
Joe Turner, *His Greatest Hits*.

1960-70

The Drifters, *1959-1965: All-Time Greatest Hits and More*.
Solomon Burke, *Home in Your Heart: The Best of Solomon Burke*.
Wilson Pickett, *A Man and a Half: The Best of Wilson Pickett*.
Betty Carter, *'Round Midnight*.
Aretha Franklin, *I Never Loved a Man (The Way I Love You)*.
King Curtis, *Plays the Memphis Greatest Hits*.
Dusty Springfield, *Dusty in Memphis*.
Cher, *3614 Jackson Highway*.

1970-80

Aretha Franklin, *Amazing Grace*.
Ronnie Hawkins, *Ronnie Hawkins*.
Dr. John, *Gumbo*.
Doug Sahm, *Doug Sahm and Friends: The Best of Doug Sahm's Atlantic Sessions*.
The Wiz (soundtrack).
Willie Nelson, *Shotgun Willie*.
Willie Nelson, *Phases and Stages*.
Dire Straits, *Communiqué*.

1980-95

McGuinn-Hillman, *McGuinn-Hillman*, EMI.
Bob Dylan, *Saved*, Columbia.
One More Time (original cast recording).
Lou Ann Barton, *Old Enough*, Asylum.
Carlos Santana, *Havana Moon*, Columbia.
Jo Jo Starbuck, Your Life Is Calling (soundtrack), Warner.
Kenny Drew, Jr., *Kenny Drew, Jr.*, Antilles.
Etta James, *The Right Time*, Elektra.

Sources

Books

Wexler, Jerry, and David Ritz, *Rhythm and the Blues: A Life in American Music*, Knopf, 1993.

Periodicals

Baltimore Sun, July 7, 1993.
Billboard, April 17, 1993.
Boston Herald, June 11, 1993.
Chicago Sun-Times, June 20, 1993.
Daily News (New York), May 30, 1993.
Entertainment Weekly, June 4, 1993.
Rolling Stone, February 18, 1993.
San Jose Mercury News, July 11, 1993.
Sarasota Magazine, May 1, 1993.

—Paul E. Anderson

Lari White

Singer, songwriter, guitarist

Courtesy of RCA Records

An attractive, energetic woman with a big, soulful voice, Lari White—her first name is pronounced "*Lau*-rie"—burst onto the country music scene in 1993. With songs that reflect both a nineties feminine savvy and independence and the romance reminiscent of torch ballads of the 1940s and 1950s, she has amassed a popularity that shows no signs of dimming. Praised equally for her abilities as a vocalist and her sensitivity as a songwriter, White has been hailed as one of the more talented of the performers to stand beneath Nashville's "young country" banner.

Born on May 13, 1965, in Dunedin, Florida, White grew up in a household where music was an integral part of family life. "Mom and Dad always had all kinds of music in the house," she recalled to Jennifer Fusco-Giacobbe in *Country Song Roundup.* "We sang as a family ... close gospel harmonies and rock 'n' roll. We had classical records, and atonal modern music, right next to Ray Charles and John Denver albums. So I have a really varied musical background." White and her family travelled to regional churches, festivals, and community gatherings as a trio. Calling themselves the White Family Singers, the group featured Lari as an integral member from the time she was four. In addition to serving as singer, she soon became the band's guitarist and part-time pianist.

When she hit her teen years, White struck out on her own musical path, entering talent competitions and singing in a rock band while still in high school. Her academic achievements earned her a full scholarship to the University of Miami, where she majored in music engineering and minored in voice—and spent her free time in recording studios performing background vocals and jingles as a part-time job. With one eye constantly fixed on the spotlight, White began composing her own songs during her senior year in college. Her efforts toward capturing a recording contract at a major label brought her a step closer to her goal in 1988, when she became an overall winner in the Nashville Network's (TNN) *You Can Be a Star* cable television show. The prize money was enough to support a stint in Nashville.

White credits her experience with *You Can Be a Star*—the auditioning, stage performances, and time spent in Music City among people in the country music industry—with giving her music a focus. After several years spent singing in a variety of vocal styles, including rock, pop, and jazz, White found herself won over by the pop-based "young country" sounds coming out of Nashville. She spent a year hard at work along Music Row, trying to find her niche in the country music industry. A gig at Nashville's Bluebird Cafe sparked the interest of a publishing company owned by veteran country artist

For the Record...

Born May 13, 1965, in Dunedin, FL; married Chuck Cannon (a songwriter), 1994. *Education:* Graduated from University of Miami.

Began performing with White Family Singers, c. 1969; overall winner, *You Can Be a Star* talent search television show, the Nashville Network (TNN), 1988; staff writer for Ronnie Milsap's publishing company, Nashville, TN, 1989-90; backup vocalist on Rodney Crowell's concert tour, 1991; signed with RCA Records and released debut EP, *Lead Me Not,* 1993; made acting debut in television pilot *XXX's and OOO's,* 1994.

Awards: Nominated for best new female vocalist award, Academy of Country Music, 1994.

Addresses: *Record company*—RCA Records, One Music Circle North, Nashville, TN 37203. *Management*—Carter Career Management, 1028-B 18th Avenue South, Nashville, TN 37212.

Ronnie Milsap. White was brought on board as a staff writer and her songs would be cut by artists like Tammy Wynette. But it was White's performance of her own music at a songwriter's showcase sponsored by the American Society of Composers, Authors and Publishers (ASCAP) that led her out from behind the scenes to stand behind a microphone onstage.

In addition to catching the interest of several other labels, White found that veteran country performer Rodney Crowell liked what he heard from her. The two hit it off, and White quickly began to rely on Crowell as a mentor. In addition to engaging her as a backup singer in his band, the Cherry Bombs, during his 1991 tour, Crowell got White a spot on the artist's showcase that led to an offer by RCA Records. White signed with the label, with the understanding that Crowell would continue to be active in her career. Her first album for RCA, the EP *Lead Me Not,* was coproduced by Crowell, Cherry Bombs guitarist Steuart Smith, and White.

White wrote or co-wrote eight of the ten songs on *Lead Me Not,* which was released in 1993. While accurately reflecting her strong vocal talent and the diversity of her musical influences—from blues and Latin rhythms to gospel and country pop—*Lead Me Not* encompassed too broad a chunk of the musical spectrum to please mainstream country radio programmers. While critics were wowed by White's stylistic range—*Country Amer-*

ica's Neil Pond called it "a sensory pleasure, like a road trip with unexpectedly wonderful scenic turns"—the singles released from *Lead Me Not* "confused country radio, where [they] never got a strong foothold," according to *Billboard.*

While similar to her *Lead Me Not* in both its thematic diversity and the fact that White had a hand in writing most of the material, 1994's *Wishes* proved to be a more focused project. And that focus was strong enough to provide the breakthrough that White needed. "That's My Baby," an up-beat, rollicking ode to her husband, songwriter Chuck Cannon, was just what country radio was looking for; as the album's lead single, it started up the charts soon after its spring release. In addition, "That's How You Know," a ballad that features White's powerful vocals saluting true love, was quick to follow.

In an effort to overcome her shyness onstage, White had taken several acting lessons soon after her arrival in Nashville. Her talent was soon obvious to her teacher, who encouraged her to audition for roles in and around the city. In addition to leading to a television sitcom pilot called *XXX's and OOO's,* White found that the experience of acting fueled her songwriting. "It's amazing the effect it had on my songwriting, in terms of developing believable characters and getting a feel for voice," she noted in an RCA Records press release. White's theatrical training has enabled her to interact more effectively with her audience in between numbers and has given her the ability to handle whatever comes up with an easy sense of humor.

White credits her producers—Crowell, Smith, and Garth Fundis, the architect of *Wishes*—with allowing her to contribute to the production of her albums, a state of affairs that has not always existed, especially for female country artists. "We've definitely come a long way in the amount of input female artists have in the songs we sing and the sound of the records and the way our careers are run," she commented to *Country Song Roundup*'s Deborah Price Evans. "There were a lot of women who fought to pave the way for us and we're benefiting from their hard work."

Throughout her career of songwriting and performing, White has felt it important to share who she is with her audience, expressing her unique personality and view of the world to her fans. "Performing is the best part of the whole deal," noted the artist in her press release. "There's a relationship between you and the audience. It's like they communicate with you to give you permission to be extravagant and emotional and extreme, things maybe they don't have the luxury of doing because they're trying to put food on the table and raise kids. And that's where I feel the most at home."

Selected discography

Lead Me Not, RCA, 1993.
Wishes (includes "That's My Baby," "Now I Know," and "That's How You Know"), RCA, 1994.

Sources

Books

Comprehensive Country Music Encyclopedia, Random House, 1994.

Periodicals

Billboard, May 14, 1994.
Country America, October 1992.
Country Music, June 1993; July/August 1994.
Country Music City News, June 1994.
Country Song Roundup, February 1994; August 1994.

Additional information for this profile was obtained from RCA Records publicity materials, 1994.

—Pamela L. Shelton

Marion Williams

Gospel singer

Marion Williams was a popular and highly regarded gospel singer whose musical influence can be felt in the realms of rhythm and blues and rock and roll. Williams performed for more than 45 years, singing only gospel music, and in the last year of her life she received a prestigious "genius" grant from the MacArthur Foundation. Reflecting on Williams's legacy to rock and pop music, *Vogue* magazine contributor Margo Jefferson called the singer "the lady who gave [soul singer] Little Richard his *whooo*." Jefferson added that Williams's voice was "uncanny, encompassing a lusty preacher's shout and a plangent soprano." Throughout her life, Williams performed not for mere personal recognition but for a higher calling—the glorification of God through song.

Marion Williams was born in 1927 in Miami, Florida. Her father was an immigrant from the West Indies who worked as a barber; her mother was employed in a laundry. Williams's father died when she was nine, and her formal schooling was cut short so she could help to support the family. She followed her mother into the laundry, where she labored from sunup until sundown through her teen years. She had no formal voice training but was inspired by such gospel greats as Sister Rosetta Tharpe and Mary Johnson Davis. A more worldly older brother who owned a jukebox introduced her to the blues and jazz music that was popular during World War II.

"For Williams ... gospel wasn't just great music—it was life and belief," wrote Susan Richardson in *Rolling Stone*. The singer began her own performing career as a child in Sanctified churches in the Miami area. As her reputation grew she began traveling throughout the South as a soloist. Her break came in 1947, when she auditioned for a position with the nationally known Ward Singers, a gospel group headed by Madame Ward and her daughters Clara and Willa. Hired as a backup vocalist for the Ward Singers, Williams soon became the lead. She worked with the group for 11 years and with them recorded some of her best-known songs, including "Surely God Is Able," "I'm Climbing Higher and Higher," and "Packin' Up."

The 1950s saw much experimentation in popular music and many unconventional blends of style and influence. Early rock and roll pioneers found much to admire in Williams's spirited gospel work, from her octave-skipping falsetto "whoops" to her sheer backwoods energy and emotional delivery. Little Richard has cited her as an influence, and the Isley Brothers' "Shout" was an intentional homage. Nor was Williams's considerable talent ignored by other gospel singers. Aretha Franklin—whose father was Williams's close friend—has recorded some of Williams's songs and considers her an

AP/Wide World Photos

For the Record . . .

Born August 29, 1927, in Miami, FL; died of vascular disease July 2, 1994, in Philadelphia, PA; daughter of a barber and a laundress; married; children: Robin (son).

Gospel singer, 1947-94. Member of groups the Ward Singers, 1947-58, and the Stars of Faith, 1958-65; solo performer, 1965-94; has recorded albums for labels including Savoy, Vee Jay, Columbia, Atlantic, and Spirit Feel.

Selected awards: Grand Prix du Disque, 1976, for *Prayer Changes Things;* Kennedy Center Honors and MacArthur Foundation "genius" grant, both 1993.

important mentor. Richardson noted that Williams was "in a sense, the woman behind the men behind rock & roll."

Williams left the Ward Singers in 1958 and formed another ensemble, the Stars of Faith. In 1961 the group appeared on Broadway in a gospel musical by Langston Hughes called *Black Nativity.* Williams stayed with the Stars of Faith until 1965, then embarked on a solo career. She was one of the first gospel singers to perform in Africa on a major tour sponsored by the U.S. State Department. She also recorded a number of albums, both with groups and as a soloist, for labels as diverse as Savoy, Vee Jay, Columbia, Atlantic, and Spirit Feel.

Perhaps Williams's most memorable performances were her a cappella hymns, which recall the emotional song stylings of overworked field and factory hands. According to Anthony Heilbut in *Black Women in America,* her a cappella work recalls a previous era, "but her stylistic authority is such that one doubts whether these traditional hymns have ever been so compellingly sung." Two of Williams's a cappella performances were featured in the film *Fried Green Tomatoes,* which was also dedicated to her, and another solo was added to the soundtrack of the 1992 movie *Mississippi Masala.* Her rendition of "Amazing Grace" was chosen by the Public Broadcasting Service (PBS) to highlight a documentary about that hymn.

Remarkably, Williams performed for almost half a century without ever singing or recording a secular number. She was completely dedicated to gospel music, seeing it as her particular ministry for troubled souls. She also refused for many years to sing in venues that served alcohol, effectively curtailing any nightclub or supper club appearances. She eased that restriction in the 1980s with a long engagement at the Cookery in Greenwich Village, New York, and gradually took her act to other similar supper clubs.

Williams's most important national honors came late in her life. In 1993 she was chosen as a Kennedy Center Honors recipient. That same year she also received a grant from the MacArthur Foundation in recognition of her life's work. Williams continued to record albums and to tour until kidney disease forced her into semiretirement in 1992. Even then she continued to sing at her local church in Philadelphia and to do an occasional concert. She died of vascular disease on July 2, 1994, at the Albert Einstein Medical Institute in Philadelphia.

Vogue's Margo Jefferson called Williams one of "the finest singers America has produced," a virtuoso at home "where spiritual force meets technical artistry." Explaining her particular gifts in the *New York Times,* Williams said: "When I'm singing, I get inspired by God. I call it 'the anointing.' It's an extra-special thing." Laughing, she added: "When the inspiration of God is missing, I just rely on talent."

Selected discography

I've Come So Far, Spirit Feel, 1987.
Born To Sing the Gospel, Spirit Feel, 1988.
(Contributor) *Gospel Warriors,* Spirit Feel, 1988.
Surely God Is Able, Spirit Feel, 1990.
(Contributor) *The Gospel Sound,* Spirit Feel, 1991.
Strong Again, Spirit Feel, 1991.
(Contributor) *The Great Gospel Women,* Spirit Feel, 1992.
My Soul Looks Back: The Genius of Marion Williams 1962-1992, Spirit Feel, 1994.

Sources

Books

Black Women in America, Volume 2, Carlson, 1993.
Heilbut, Anthony, *The Gospel Sound: Good News and Bad Times,* Limelight Editions, 1985.

Periodicals

New York Times, July 4, 1994.
Rolling Stone, August 25, 1994.
Vogue, October 1987.

—Anne Janette Johnson

Angela Winbush

Singer, songwriter, producer, arranger

Photograph by George Holz, courtesy of Elektra Entertainment

Drawing on her gospel roots and her professional experience dating back to Stevie Wonder's group Wonderlove in the late 1970s, Angela Winbush has established herself as a gifted rhythm and blues singer and songwriter and as one of the few successful women producers and arrangers in the industry. On her 1994 album, *Angela Winbush,* she combined the best of new production technology and the old-fashioned bottom line—musical talent. "It's fun to create new things, and I'm not against that," she told J. D. Considine of *Musician* in 1994. "But I am against losing a sense of how to pass on a certain type of creativity and musicianship.... I look for the feel, so I find myself trying to mix the two so I don't lose either one."

In addition to her solo work, Winbush has made her mark as a producer, mixing 1990s beat-heavy "New Jack" sound with impressive vocals and instrumentation. She has earned production credits on albums by such artists as Janet Jackson, the Isley Brothers, Sheena Easton, Stephanie Mills, and Lalah Hathaway. After doing some recording, in 1990 she started her own production company, Angela Winbush Productions, which she manages with her husband, Ronald Isley. Commenting on Winbush's musical talent, Jeryl Barginear of the *Michigan Citizen* wrote, she is "a musician's musician with a savvy approach, sassy delivery and effortless sensuality."

Gospel Roots

Born in St. Louis, Missouri, Winbush grew up grounded in gospel. In a feature in the *Philadelphia Tribune* on the impact of the Black Church on African-American music, Judson Alexia wrote, "From gospel to jazz, rap to rock, the tentacles of the Black Church's influence stretches the musical gamut." Winbush herself attested to the importance of the church to music and cited her own involvement in the church and in other musical circles. "I grew up in the church," she recalled in the *Philadelphia Tribune.* "I'm still in the church. I also grew up on jazz and I love it."

A music teacher in St. Louis recognized Winbush's talent early on and encouraged her to develop her gifts. Winbush listened. She enrolled at Howard University in Washington, D.C., and took lessons from the same vocal coach who had instructed Roberta Flack and Donny Hathaway. Winbush was soon singing with Stevie Wonder.

In the late 1970s, Winbush began her career singing live and in the studio with Wonder and a number of other artists, including Lenny Williams, Jean Carn, and Dolly Parton. Wonder's group, Wonderlove, and the album

Born in St. Louis, MO; married Ronald Isley (a recording artist), 1993. *Education:* Attended Howard University.

Singer with Stevie Wonder's Wonderlove, late 1970s; singer with René & Angela, 1980; embarked on solo recording career and released *Sharp,* Mercury, 1987; coproducer for the Isley Brothers, beginning in 1987; toured U.S., England, and Japan with the Isley Brothers, beginning in 1990; writer, arranger, and producer for such artists as Janet Jackson, Sheena Easton, Stephanie Mills, and Lalah Hathaway, beginning in 1980s; founded production company Angela Winbush Productions, 1990; released solo LPs *The Real Thing,* Mercury, 1989, and *Angela Winbush,* Elektra, 1994.

Addresses: *Record company*—Elektra Entertainment, 75 Rockefeller Plaza, New York, NY 10019.

Songs in the Key of Life provided Winbush with her start. From the positive notices she received from that work, Winbush began singing in the duo René & Angela and launched a career as a producer in mainstream pop and R&B. By the mid-1980s, she was enjoying broad success.

Scored Hits as Half of René & Angela

In 1985 René & Angela gained notoriety with their *Street Called Desire* LP. The Top Ten R&B album included Winbush's song "I'll Be Good"—a hit on the dance chart—and the popular rap-tinged single featuring Kurtis Blow, "Save Your Love (For #1)." Five singles in all made it to the Top Ten of the R&B chart. *Rolling Stone's* Davitt Sigerson offered a positive yet qualified review: "René and Angela are like lovers who drive you crazy for just long enough to convince you they know what they're doing but stop before they finish you off." While some of the tracks were superb, noted some critics, the album as a whole was uneven. Winbush explained *Street Called Desire's* eclectic mix as a refection of the character of the duo René & Angela itself. "I think what we've done is blended two different flavors and chemistries together, and then we try to show those in all capacities," she observed in *Musician.*

Street Called Desire was René & Angela's fourth album. Winbush and René Moore had begun recording together on the Capitol label in 1980, with guidance from bassist Bobby Watson of the R&B group Rufus. For *Street Called Desire,* the pair switched to the Polygram label Mercury and hired engineer Bruce Swedien to finish up their studio work. While working as one half of René & Angela, Winbush also did some solo work, writing the Number One R&B hit "Your Smile" and the Number Two single "You Don't Have to Cry."

In 1987 Winbush's producing career flourished, and she also went solo as a singer. She provided a sharp boost to the Isley Brothers by coproducing their *Smooth Sailin'* album, which achieved gold sales. Although they had split into two bands in 1984, with the older O'Kelly, Ronald, and Rudolf remaining the Isley Brothers and the younger Ernie and Marvin Isley breaking off into Isley Jasper Isley, the Isley Brothers have been creating lasting hits since the late 1950s. Early Isley Brothers originals include 1959's "Shout" and 1962's "Twist and Shout." The group also wrote and produced the Grammy Award-winning Sly and the Family Stone classic "It's Your Thing" and helped develop the harder funk of the mid-1970s with "Fight the Power (Part I)." Winbush has remained with the Isley Brothers as coproducer and married Ronald Isley in 1993, the year after the group was inducted into the Rock and Roll Hall of Fame.

Also in 1987, Winbush saw the release of her solo debut, *Sharp,* which included the Number One R&B single "Angel" and the Number Two cut "Run to Me." *Essence* reviewer Eric Copage lauded her singing: "On *Sharp,* the LP Winbush coproduced, cowrote and arranged, her voice cuts through a wide range and variety of textures, from a piercing purity to a husking whisper, bringing a unique intensity to the lyrics." According to Copage, the album combines dance music, "reggae rhythms," "earnest bedroom vocals," and a slower, "jazzy" sound, as in the song "Angel." Copage suggested that the tune "Sensual Lover" could stand beside R&B legend Marvin Gaye's "Sexual Healing."

Phenomenal Solo Success

Since the mid-1980s, Winbush has gained increasing prominence in her career as both a producer and singer. In 1989 she followed *Smooth Sailin'* with a second production success, the Isley Brothers' *Spend the Night.* Although the album did not receive universal acclaim—Andrew Smith of *Melody Maker,* for example, complained, "*Spend the Night* is stuffed with downbeat smoochers addressed to one 'gurl' or another.... It's all so bloody comfortable"—it achieved gold sales and sponsored another Number One single. One of the few women producers in mainstream pop and R&B, Winbush has also written, arranged, and produced for

Stephanie Mills and Janet Jackson. Finally, Winbush set up Angela Winbush Productions, a production company and "rigorous training ground for still more Black talent, much like Motown or Stax [labels] in their heyday," according to Carol Cooper of *Essence*.

Winbush's really phenomenal success, though, has been in her own solo work. In 1989 she released *The Real Thing* on Mercury to acclaim. "In addition to superbly entertaining you with her four-octave soprano, Winbush demonstrates—on all nine tunes—that she is a talented producer and writer as well," declared Lynn Norment of *Ebony*. Following that release, Winbush took four years off from her solo work and switched to the Elektra label before cutting her next LP. She emerged in 1994 with *Angela Winbush*, on which she sings with her husband, Ronald Isley, on the duet "Baby Hold On" and with Ernie and Marvin Isley, George Duke, Chuckii Booker, and Gerald Albright. The single "Treat U Rite" made *Jet*'s Top 20 singles list while the LP reached Number Six on the magazine's Top 20 albums chart.

On *Angela Winbush* the singer concentrated on capturing her characteristic mix of new production technology and traditional musical talent. On her cover of Marvin Gaye's "Inner City Blues," for example, Winbush's band strove for that balance. "We tried to keep a natural groove and bring the new drums to it," Winbush told *Musician*'s Considine. For the duet "Baby Hold On," Winbush and Isley handed over the orchestration to Philadelphia soul star Thom Bell. "Certain chord changes just lend themselves to ... I don't want to say a 'Philly sound,' but there's a certain sound he had. I don't know if it's relevant for today—I just knew I wanted that," Winbush confided to Considine.

After touring with the Isleys across the United States as well as in England and Japan and the release of her successful self-titled Elektra debut, in the mid-1990s Winbush hoped for more success on her new career path. "I feel I have more freedom now, on Elektra," she was quoted as saying in the label's publicity materials. "That's been very important in the transition I'm making. I'm looking forward to good things and new horizons."

Selected discography

Singles

"Treat U Rite," Elektra, 1994.

Albums

(With René & Angela) *Street Called Desire* (includes "I'll Be Good" and "Save Your Love [For #1]), Mercury, 1985.
Sharp (includes "Angel" and "Run to Me"), Mercury, 1987.
(As producer) the Isley Brothers, *Smooth Sailin',* Warner Bros., 1987.
The Real Thing, Mercury, 1989.
(As producer) the Isley Brothers, *Spend the Night,* Warner Bros., 1989.
Angela Winbush (includes "Treat U Rite," "Inner City Blues," and "Baby Hold On"), Elektra, 1994.

Sources

Billboard, November 4, 1989; February 12, 1994.
Ebony, April 1990.
Essence, January 1988; February 1990.
Jet, May 23, 1994.
Los Angeles Sentinel, July 28, 1994.
Michigan Citizen, April 16, 1994.
Musician, January 1986; September 1987; March 1994.
New Pittsburgh Courier, March 23, 1994.
Philadelphia Tribune, June 3, 1994.
Rolling Stone, March 27, 1986; February 6, 1992.

Additional information for this profile was obtained from Elektra Entertainment publicity materials.

—*Nicholas Patti*

Andrew York

Guitarist, composer

Courtesy of GSP Recordings

With their strong folk-rock influence, Andrew York's classical guitar compositions and performances have attracted a number of listeners with their accessibility. Although this quality—along with York's inclusion on the 1988 *Windham Hill Guitar Sampler*—led some to label him a New Age guitarist, he has since made a name for himself in the United States' classical guitar world. His compositions have been recorded by several well-known guitarists, including John Williams and Christopher Parkening. The respected Los Angeles Guitar Quartet, which York joined in the early 1990s, has also recorded some of York's work.

York's musical training began in his childhood, during which he was surrounded by the sounds of his father's folk guitar playing and his mother's singing. "My father and uncle would get together and play and sing all night long," York related in his GSP Records press biography. "My mother sings and her voice is in my mind and heart from my earliest memories.... My father has an extremely good ear, and though his harmonic language was simple (diatonic folk harmony), he was quite aware of the beauty and power represented by even the simplest harmonic change, and this understanding was instilled within me."

York learned to play folk and classical guitar at an early age and considered writing music a natural part of that process. In fact, his compositions are as acclaimed as his guitar playing. In high school his discovery of rock and roll led him to buy an electric guitar. Although at that time he focused on rock and roll, and then later on jazz playing, he never allowed his classical skills to deteriorate. Every few months he would return to his acoustic guitar to practice his way back to what he called "acceptable levels." York rounded out this eclectic background by spending some time mastering bluegrass guitar playing, having had ample exposure to flatpickers while growing up in Virginia.

Returned to Classical after Jazz Experiments

York studied music at James Madison University in Virginia, where he earned a bachelor of music degree in 1980. He then attended the University of Southern California, adding a master of music degree to his accomplishments in 1986. Upon receiving both degrees, he graduated magna cum laude. Although York focused on classical guitar during his undergraduate years, much of his study on the graduate level had been devoted to jazz technique, and he looked forward to a career as a professional jazz player. Near the end of his formal schooling, however, he decided to return to classical music, devoting himself to playing and composing in that genre.

For the Record . . .

Born in 1958 in Atlanta, GA. *Education:* James Madison University, bachelor of music, 1980; University of Southern California, master of music, 1986.

Classical guitarist and composer. Compositions "Lullaby" and "Sunburst" recorded by John Williams; released first album, *Perfect Sky,* Timeless Records, 1989; joined Los Angeles Guitar Quartet, early 1990s.

Addresses: *Home*—California. *Record company*—GSP Recordings, 514 Bryant St., San Francisco, CA 94107-1217.

York's first big break came in 1986 during study in Spain. In a concert at the end of the course, he played one of his original compositions, "Sunburst." Guitarist John Williams, who happened to be in the audience, was impressed with the piece. He asked York to transcribe it and send it to him in England. Williams's interest in the piece was not a momentary thing: not only did Williams add it to his performances, but he also recorded it. A few years later Williams began performing another York composition, "Lullaby," eventually recording it on his *Spirit of the Guitar—Music of the Americas* album.

First Recording

Having two compositions as part of Williams's repertoire gave York credibility and recognition. Guitar Solo Publications agreed to publish both pieces, and subsequently added several other compositions of York's to their catalog, including "Chilean Dance," "Sunday Morning Overcast," and "Perfect Sky." All of these pieces received favorable reviews and underscored York's versatility. Chris Kilvington wrote in a 1990 issue of *Classical Guitar,* "I've seen quite a number of York scores and he really does write expertly in his style, cool sometimes, occasionally poignant, and elsewhere creating chic flash which is irresistible to the ear. 'Sunburst' falls into this latter category." Of "Lullaby," Kilvington praised, "There are no tricks, just a serene and open piece of well written guitar music."

"Chilean Dance," with its folk-rock influence and the flashy opening figure that repeats throughout the work, drew comparisons to "Sunburst." Although *Classical Guitar* critic Paul Fowles termed it a "charming miniature," he also warned York against overexploiting a formula. Although probably not as a result of this advice,

York soon published "Perfect Sky," which departed from his popular folky style. Lorraine Eastwood described the piece in *Classical Guitar* as a "beautifully constructed composition," and as having "a sustained, fragile, almost trance-like melody."

York's first recording, *Perfect Sky,* was released in 1989, but was originally cut in 1986 as a demo tape. The recording shows off York's eclectic background, with the musician playing both electric and acoustic guitar; drawing on classical, folk, rock, and jazz traditions; and sampling works by famous composers and his own compositions. The most praised portions of the recording were his performances of his original works, including the steel-string version of "Sunburst."

York's easily accessible music and its folk and jazz influences have led some to label him a New Age guitarist, a tag he has vehemently repudiated. In a 1990 interview in *Classical Guitar,* he explained, "My problem with [New Age music] is that it has—I'm going to get in trouble here, but so be it—New Age to me has a non-intellectual base.... If you totally disregard the intellectual portion of music and just go with textures, although that may be fine in certain contexts, that personally doesn't feed me. I need a bit of both." Describing himself as a contemporary classical guitarist, York explained that "most of my pieces are very well thought-out, but they do draw from elements of the Renaissance and Medieval folk traditions. Also ethnic music and American folk styles.... I take in all sorts of influences." The classical composers York cites as having an early impact on him include Ludwig van Beethoven and Johann Sebastian Bach. He cites Russian-born Stravinsky as his favorite twentieth-century composer, admiring in particular his way of using and developing themes.

Ensemble Compositions

York composed in slightly new directions in the early 1990s. His "Evening Dance," recorded by Christopher Parkening and David Brandon, was written for two guitars. He followed with other ensemble pieces: "Rosetta," composed specifically for the Pro Arte Trio, was written for requinto, standard guitar, and 8-string guitar. "Virtu," another guitar duet, was penned for the Eastwood-Kilvington Duo. Chris Kilvington described these last two pieces in *Classical Guitar* as "very different, rhythmically complex, fascinating but by no means like [York's] former works." York also began arranging pieces for the Los Angeles Quartet, which he had joined in 1990.

Denouement, York's second recording, was released in 1994 to favorable reviews. Diane Gordon's assessment in *Acoustic Guitar* was typical: "York's pieces are re-freshingly composed, with a beginning, middle and end. Added to the winning combination of York's impeccable technique and finely crafted compositions is the music's potential to join the workhorse etudes for the guitar." Jim Ferguson in *Guitar Player* declared that the five original suites that make up the recording "demonstrate [York's] exceptional compositional breadth, commanding instrumental abilities, and rich tone. Rife with folk, jazz, and ancient influences, the material ranges from challenging to simple yet highly musical."

Selected compositions

Published by Guitar Solo Publications

Sunburst, 1990.
Lullaby, 1990.
Chilean Dance, 1991.
Sunday Morning Overcast, 1991.
Perfect Sky, 1992.
Faire, 1993.

Emergence, 1993.
Evening Dance, 1993.

Selected discography

Perfect Sky, Timeless Records, 1989.
Denouement, GSP, 1994.

Sources

Acoustic Guitar, November/December 1994.
Classical Guitar, January 1990; June 1990; December 1991; January 1992; June 1992; April 1993; December 1993.
Guitar Player, December 1989; July 1994.

Additional information for this profile was provided by GSP Recordings publicity materials, 1995.

—Susan Windisch Brown

Neil Young

Singer, songwriter, guitarist

Photograph by Edward Siegel, © 1991 Reprise Records

In the 1991 *Trouser Press Record Guide,* writer Jon Young chose a host of adjectives to describe Neil Young: "Dirty rock 'n' roller and hippie narcissist. Rockabilly hepcat and techno-troubadour. Folkie romantic and bluesy bad boy." To that list could be added "godfather of grunge," since by the early 1990s Young's iconoclastic music and personal style had been discovered by a new generation of music aficionados desperately in search of a credible hero. His longevity in the sometimes fatal world of rock and roll, exploration of radically different musical styles, and the consistency of his own distinct sound over time all combined to bring Young renewed popularity as he turned 50 in 1995.

Born in Toronto in 1945, Young is the son of a sports reporter and local television personality. Bouts with diabetes, polio, and epilepsy marred his childhood, and after his parents divorced Young and his mother relocated to the city of Winnipeg in Manitoba. While his first musical endeavors involved a ukulele, Young later switched to guitar, and by the early 1960s he had performed with a number of local bands. His first steady success came with a folk-rock ensemble called the Squires, a group that made regular appearances in both Manitoba and Ontario. In 1965, at a bar in a small Ontario town, Young first encountered Stephen Stills, an American musician who would become an occasional collaborator of Young's over the next few decades.

Slowly establishing a base in his birthplace of Toronto, by 1966 Young was playing with a group called Rickey James and the Mynah Birds. James later became famous in the 1980s for his hit "Super Freak" and some well-publicized legal troubles. With the Mynah Birds Young achieved some minor successes, including a jaunt to Detroit for recording sessions at the legendary Motown studios. Yet the tracks were never released, and the Mynah Birds disbanded when James clashed with authorities in 1966. At that point Young and another band member, Bruce Palmer, decided to leave for greener pastures.

The Rise and Fall of Buffalo Springfield

Young and Palmer bought a hearse, filled it with everything they owned, and drove out to California. In a Los Angeles traffic jam, Stephen Stills spotted the vehicle and recognized the Canadians. With Stills's friend Richie Furay and a fifth member, Dewey Martin, the Buffalo Springfield was formed. The group was an almost immediate success and released three albums, but the quick money and fame was difficult for the still-youthful musicians. Buffalo Springfield was often plagued by

Born November 12, 1945, in Toronto, Ontario, Canada; son of Scott (a sports reporter) and Edna (a television celebrity) Young; first wife's name, Susan (divorced, 1970); second wife's name, Pegi; children: Zeke (with actor Carrie Snodgrass), Ben, Amber (with Pegi Young).

Guitarist, singer, and songwriter. Member of rock bands the Squires, 1962-64, Rickey James and the Mynah Birds, c. 1965, Buffalo Springfield, 1966-68, Crosby, Stills, Nash & Young, 1969-71, and the Stills-Young Band, 1976; solo artist (and with accompaniment from bands Crazy Horse, the Bluenotes, the Shocking Pinks, and Pearl Jam), 1969—; composer of soundtracks for films, including *Where the Buffalo Roam,* 1980, and *Dead Man,* 1995; director of films (under pseudonym Bernard Shakey), including *Journey through the Past,* 1972, *Rust Never Sleeps,* 1979, and *Human Highway* (co-directed with Dean Stockwell), 1982.

Awards: Winner of *Rolling Stone* Music Award for album of the year, 1975, for *Tonight's the Night;* citations in *Rolling Stone* critics' poll for best rock artist, best male vocalist, and best album, 1979, all for *Rust Never Sleeps,* Reprise.

Addresses: *Home*—La Honda, CA. *Office*—c/o Lookout Management, 9120 Sunset Blvd., Los Angeles, CA 90069; *Record company*—Reprise, 3300 Warner Blvd., Burbank, CA 91510.

temporary defections, including Young's own just before the pivotal Monterey (California) Pop Festival in June of 1967.

By 1968 Buffalo Springfield had disbanded permanently, leaving Young free to record his first solo album. The self-titled work was released in January of 1969, and Young has sometimes referred to the record as "overdub city" for its rather overproduced sound. Later that year, Young formed a band with some former members of a local L.A. group called the Rockets. With Danny Whitten on guitar, Ralph Molina playing drums, and Billy Talbot on bass, the ensemble took shape as Crazy Horse, and within a short time they recorded their first release together, *Everybody Knows This Is Nowhere.* The 1969 work "marked the first of many radical shifts, turning to the raw, driving rock many feel still suits him best," wrote Jon Young in the *Trouser Press*

Record Guide. The writer also noted that Young's backing band "display the ratty fervor of punk years before the fact."

As the 1960s drew to a close, Young was fast becoming a pivotal figure in music. He reunited with Stills in the latter's new band, Crosby, Stills & Nash, in the summer of 1969, and together the act played at the Woodstock Festival in August of that year. Their first studio effort together was *Deja Vu,* released in 1970, followed by *4-Way Street* a year later. Meanwhile, Young continued to work with Crazy Horse and recorded a number of well-received albums during the seventies, including *After the Gold Rush* and *Harvest,* a 1972 work remembered for Young's only Number One single, "Heart of Gold." The musician later wrote in the liner notes to 1977's *Decade* of the mixed demons this country-rock ballad brought out in him. "This song put me in the middle of the road," he said of "Heart of Gold." "Travelling there soon became a bore so I headed for the ditch. A rougher ride but I saw more interesting people there."

Work Became More Autobiographical

The success of the *Harvest* album was marred by tragedy when Young's guitarist, Whitten, succumbed to the rock lifestyle and died of a drug overdose shortly before a scheduled tour. The resultant turmoil in Young's life was evident on the 1973 release *Time Fades Away,* and on *Tonight's the Night,* written and recorded during this period but not released until 1975. In a 1978 *Newsweek* article, Tony Schwartz called *Tonight's the Night* "a depressing tribute—out of tune and repetitive, but hauntingly memorable." Young told Schwartz that it was his personal favorite. "When I handed it in to Warner [Bros. Records], they hated it. We played it ten times as loud as they usually play things and it was awful," he recalled in the interview. "*Tonight's the Night* was a story of death and dope. It was about a sleazy, burned-out rock star just about to go, about what fame and crowds do to you. I had to exorcise those feelings. I felt like it was the only chance I had to stay alive."

Young rejoined Crosby, Stills & Nash briefly in 1974 for some unreleased recordings and a tour and continued to put out albums with Crazy Horse. He also reunited with Stills for the 1976 release *Long May You Run.* Young's 1977 work *American Stars 'n Bars* was memorable for its hit "Like a Hurricane." The following year he released *Comes a Time,* another switch back to a less rock-influenced, more country sound, toward which Young often veered during this time. The softer sound prompted Young to tell Schwartz in *Newsweek* that "folk music can be as authentic as rock 'n' roll. It's the in-between that bothers me. Soul and depth matter most."

Forty musicians appeared as guests on *Comes a Time,* while ten engineers added their production skills. The too-many-cooks maxim seemed to work against the LP. Young was dissatisfied with the final product at its first pressing. His label re-did it, and offered to mix in with the first pressing the shipments of the better records at a later date. Young purchased all copies of this first pressing himself for a dollar apiece, setting him back $200,000.

Young's status in the pantheon of living rock legends had achieved epic proportions by the late 1970s. He released his acclaimed *Rust Never Sleeps* album in 1979 and toured the same year in support of the LP, selling out shows across North America. Sailing with his wife, Pegi, and young son across the Pacific, Young came up with the scenario for the *Rust* tour: he would awaken atop oversized amplifiers, role-playing a youngster seduced by rock 'n' roll and then dwarfed by the industry and hype of it. Evil-looking "road-eyes" with glowing eyes and hooded heads moved the giant "equipment" around. Young played an acoustic set the first half, replayed announcements recorded at Woodstock during the intermission, then returned with Crazy Horse for a full-blown electric set. *Live Rust,* a chronicle of this tour, was released later in 1979.

Building "the Bridge"

As the 1980s progressed, Young was sometimes accused of having lost his cutting edge. Yet his musical efforts had taken second place in his life to some other, more personal, issues. His first son, Zeke, with actor Carrie Snodgrass, was born with a mild form of cerebral palsy. A second child, with his wife, Pegi, was also born with the condition, but in a more severe form. In a 1988 *Rolling Stone* interview, Young spoke of the then-nine-year-old Ben with writer James Henke. Explaining that Ben was quadriplegic and unable to speak, Young described his attempts to develop his son's communication skills through games and computer technology. "A lot of the things that we take for granted, that we can do, he can't do. But his soul is there, and I'm sure that he has an outlook on the world that we don't have, because of the disabilities."

Having two children afflicted with cerebral palsy from different mothers prompted Young to be tested, and doctors told him that it was literally a one-in-a-million coincidence. A third child, daughter Amber, was not affected. "Often in my life, I've felt that I was singled out for one reason or another for extreme things to happen," Young told Henke. "This was hard to deal with ... and we've learned to turn it around into a positive thing

and to keep on going." Pegi became involved in setting up a Bay Area school for disabled children called the Bridge School, while Young put together an annual fundraising benefit noted for its celebrity roster.

Trouser Press's Jon Young termed Young's releases both with and without Crazy Horse during the eighties "particularly erratic." 1980's *Hawks & Doves* contained "a few incisive tunes amidst the throwaways," the writer noted, and was followed by "a series of genre exercise that seem more arbitrary than heartfelt." Two years later, *Trans* ventured into a heavily synthesized sound, while *Everybody's Rockin'* of 1983 experimented with rockabilly. A 1987 work, *Life,* was made with Crazy Horse and occasionally exhibited "a tough edge not glimpsed in years," according to Jon Young. The work was Neil Young's last for Geffen Records, who initiated a lawsuit against the artist. *Rolling Stone's* Alan Light explained that the court action was taken by the label against the iconoclastic musician "for making what the company called 'unrepresentative' albums—for making albums that didn't sound like Neil Young albums, whatever that could possibly mean."

A bluesy, big-band sound on *This Note's for You,* released in 1988 with a backing band called the Bluenotes, brought Young back into the limelight. The title song was a biting indictment of the selling-out of rock— the use of classic tunes in advertisements hawking everything from beer to sneakers, and the near-necessity of winning large corporate sponsorship contracts with beverage giants in order to underwrite the increasingly overblown costs of putting on large-scale tours. Young's video for the title song was banned for a time on MTV, but the network relented and eventually it was voted best video of 1988 in its annual video awards. The year also saw the reunion of Young with former bandmates for a well-received but unimpressive Crosby, Stills, Nash & Young album entitled *American Dream.*

Young ventured back into the world of amplified, guitar-driven rock with 1989's *Freedom.* Like some of his other releases, the work contained some softer, acoustic numbers as well. It opened and closed with two versions of the same song, "Rockin' in the Free World," "a sing-along ball spinning on an axis of deadly irony, its superficial cheerleading charm soured by Young's parade of victims," declared David Fricke in *Rolling Stone.*

In the same review, Fricke also spoke of an apparent pattern in Young's career: As each decade neared to a close, he released a seminal, biting record that tore apart what rock music, and the promise of the decade, had really devolved into in the preceding years. In the lyrics of this album, Young seemed to indict the hollow patriotic slogans of U.S. President George Bush's administration, and pay homage to the underclass of destitute people government policies of the decade created. "*Freedom* is the sound of Neil Young, another decade on, looking back again in anger and dread," Fricke noted. The album, he wrote, "leaves you feeling both exhausted and invigorated, dismayed at what we've wrought yet determined to set it right."

Entered Cult-Hero Pantheon

It was also in 1989 that *The Bridge: A Tribute to Neil Young* was released, marking the beginning of the aging rocker's entry into the status of cultural icon for a new generation. Several alternative rock acts, at the time heard little outside the college-radio circuit, covered Young's songs for *The Bridge*. Artsy New York noise band Sonic Youth took one of his early 1980s forays into electronic music, "Computer Age," while Minneapolis rockers Soul Asylum submitted a version of "Barstool Blues." The project was the idea of a dedicated Young fan, Terry Tolkin, who coordinated the bands and arranged for part of the tribute album's proceeds to go to the Bridge School, the institution set up with the help of Pegi Young. *Rolling Stone's* Fricke lauded *The Bridge* for saluting "not only Young's enduring songwriting but the iconoclastic spirit and anarchic glee with which he continually challenges rock myth and defies rock convention."

Ragged Glory was Young's first 1990 release and was recorded with Crazy Horse in a few weeks at Young's northern California ranch in a session memorable for the series of local earthquakes on its final day. By this point Young and Crazy Horse had been working together for almost two decades, a relationship marked by members' periodic artistic differences. After one particularly grueling European tour, Young had declared that he was through working with them, but they regrouped for *Ragged Glory* and another tour. "It's just cycles," Young commented in a *Rolling Stone* interview of the bond between himself and the band. "You wear something out, and you can beat it into the ground, or you can leave it and let the rain fall on it and the sun shine on it and see if it comes back. We've always done that. We've had musical low points and musical high points throughout the last twenty years. I think this is one of the high points."

Ragged Glory was marked by longer, solo-laden tracks—some stretching on toward ten minutes—and a mood Henke compared to Young's first release with Crazy Horse, 1969's *Everybody Knows This Is Nowhere.* The writer termed it "a classic Crazy Horse

album, with lots of rough edges, screeching guitar and feedback." Another *Rolling Stone* writer, Kurt Loder, praised the collaboration between Young and his backing band, whom he termed "maybe the last great garage band of our time and definitely Neil's greatest group." Loder called the record "a monument to the spirit of the garage—to the pursuit of passion over precision, to raw power and unvarnished soul."

"Folk music can be as authentic as rock 'n' roll. It's the in-between that bothers me. Soul and depth matter most."

Young and Crazy Horse also announced plans for a tour—to be designated the "Don't Spook the Horse" tour, named after a seven-minute bonus track on *Ragged Glory.* Young invited several alternative acts, such as Sonic Youth, Dinosaur Jr., and Social Distortion, to open dates. The tour was held in smaller arenas left behind in the wake of the predominance of the mammoth sports stadiums. "I'm tired of the sheds," the veteran performer told *Rolling Stone's* Henke in 1990. "It's like you go into this big box that's got a brand name on it and play for all these people who are paying exorbitant prices. And everybody's got these big shows, because they got all this money from the sponsor."

The aural result of the successful 1991 tour in the smaller venues could be heard on the double compact disc *Weld,* released later that year. The tour began during the Persian Gulf crisis, and Young rearranged the set list to include a cover of Bob Dylan's antiwar protest song "Blowin' in the Wind." A companion release to *Weld* called *Arc,* 30 minutes of feedback-drenched live guitar, also appeared in 1991. The brainchild of Sonic Youth guitarist Thurston Moore, *Arc* took introductions and endings to Young classics, as well as some solo moments, and distorted them into what *Rolling Stone's* Fricke called "utter melodic holocaust" and perhaps "the most extreme record he's ever released."

Young's next move was the release of a follow-up of sorts to his acclaimed folk-rock album of 20 years earlier, *Harvest.* The 1992 offering, entitled *Harvest Moon,* was an introspective look back. Deaths of friends, the disabilities of his sons, and his legal battle with Geffen seemed to have taken their toll. *Rolling Stone's* Light called the record "a chronicle of survival, focusing on loss and compromise and the ultimate triumphs of being a married father approaching fifty." Performers who had guest spots on the 1972 work—such as Linda Ronstadt, Nicolette Larson, and James Taylor—made reappearances on *Harvest Moon*. Young also performed on MTV's popular acoustic show, *Unplugged,* in support of the record. The year was also marked by Young's performances in separate concert tours with such disparate veterans and sixties legends as Bob Dylan and Booker T. and the M.G.s.

Words Come Back to Haunt

In the spring of 1994 Young's seminal title track from *Rust Never Sleeps* release became tragically infamous when a line from it—"it's better to burn out than to fade away"—was quoted in the suicide note left by Kurt Cobain, frontman of Seattle, Washington's breakthrough alternative act Nirvana. Young had heard about Cobain's drug-related problems and, shortly before Cobain's death, had unsuccessfully tried to contact him through Nirvana's manager. The title track of Young's 1994 *Sleeps with Angels* is a response to the death of the young musician.

Sleeps with Angels' other songs seemed to condemn the increasingly violent and consumerist nature of American culture, and the 14-minute "Change Your Mind" was characterized by *Newsweek's* Jay Cocks as "equal parts rhapsody and guitar dementia that describes the full course of a difficult love affair." *Stereo Review* writer Steve Simels lauded the LP's plethora of instrumentation and unusual production techniques, a "kind of studied primitivism [that] disguises a canny sophistication" comparable to Young's earlier works with Crazy Horse. Simels found *Sleeps with Angels* rife with "extremely interesting songs and a consistently vivid atmosphere."

In a *Rolling Stone* review, Fricke termed *Sleeps with Angels* "as charged with fighting spirit and romantic optimism as it is fraught with warzone shell shock and deathbed fear." The critic also reflected that the work "is not the first album Young has made about the widening cracks in the American dream or what's left of it for the teen-age refugees after the broken promises of the '60s and the worthless covenants of the [Ronald Reagan-George Bush] era [of conservative politics]. But it is among his best, a dramatic wrestling of song and conscience that suggests—no, *insists*—that walking through fire doesn't necessarily mean you have to go up in flames."

As Young's prolific career chugged well into its third decade, his legions of dedicated fans were awaiting a

definitive multi-CD release. "That's a giant," he told Rolling Stone's Kurt Loder in 1990. "I'm still working on it. It's ridiculous." Young supposedly possessed hundreds of hours of unreleased material, and a retrospective record would incorporate many of those as-yet-unheard songs. Young's own creativity continued to hinder the release—he had began working on it in the late 1980s, and was continually interrupted by the need to write more songs while digging up the older ones from his archives. The artist had also considered headlining the annual alternative music-industry festival, Lollapalooza, in what would have been the ultimate act of 1990s career reincarnation.

In 1995 Young released the well-received album *Mirror Ball,* a collaboration with the highly acclaimed and popular alternative act, Pearl Jam. Although Pearl Jam's name does not appear on the LP's cover—reportedly for legal reasons—the group serves as Young's backup band on every song. Commenting on the generational gap between himself and the young grunge band, Young told *Time's* Christopher John Farley, "Actually, in many ways, I feel like Pearl Jam is older than me.... There's an ageless thing to the way they play." The result of the two acts' winter 1995 recording session in Seattle is, according to Farley, "one of the most consistently rewarding works of [Young's] long, winding career." Further accolades for *Mirror Ball* came from *Rolling Stone's* J. D. Considine, who gave the album a four-star rating, and *Entertainment Weekly* critic David Browne, who gave it an A-.

At the age of 50, Young continued to provide inspiration for a younger breed of colleagues wary of the artifice and mainstream hype that periodically corrupts even the most groundbreaking of rock trends. As *Rolling Stone's* Alan Light explained, "Young's primitive guitar screech and yowling voice have served as lasting inspiration for wandering souls and f—— ups of several generations now. In the 1990s, Neil Young is simply so anachronistic that he's cutting edge." Young perhaps best summed up the philosophy behind creating the music that has earned him such a devoted cross-generational following when he told *Time's* Farley, "I just play what I feel like playing ... and every once in a while I'll wake up and feel like playing something else."

Selected discography

Solo and with Crazy Horse (unless otherwise noted)

Neil Young, Reprise, 1969.
Everybody Knows This Is Nowhere, Reprise, 1969.

After the Gold Rush, Reprise, 1970.
Harvest, Warner Bros., 1972.
Journey through the Past, Reprise, 1973.
Time Fades Away, Reprise, 1973.
On the Beach, Reprise, 1974.
Tonight's the Night, Reprise, 1975.
Zuma, Reprise, 1975.
American Stars 'n Bars, Reprise, 1977.
Decade, Reprise, 1977.
Comes a Time, Reprise, 1978.
Rust Never Sleeps, Reprise, 1979.
Live Rust, Reprise, 1979.
Hawks and Doves, Reprise, 1980.
Reactor, Reprise, 1981.
Trans, Geffen, 1982.
(With the Shocking Pinks) *Everybody's Rockin',* Geffen, 1983
Old Ways, Geffen, 1985.
Landing on Water, Geffen, 1986.
Life, Geffen, 1987.
(With the Bluenotes) *This Note's for You,* Reprise, 1988.
Freedom, Reprise, 1989.
Ragged Glory, Reprise, 1990.
Weld, Reprise, 1991.
Arc, Reprise, 1991.
Harvest Moon, Reprise, 1992.
Sleeps with Angels, Reprise, 1994.
(With Pearl Jam) *Mirror Ball,* Reprise, 1995.

With Buffalo Springfield

Buffalo Springfield, Atco, 1967
Buffalo Springfield Again, Atco, 1967.
Last Time Around, Atco, 1968.
Retrospective, Atco, 1969.

With Crosby, Stills, Nash & Young; on Atlantic

Deja Vu, 1970.
4-Way Street, 1971.
So Far, 1974.
American Dream, 1988.

With the Stills-Young Band

Long May You Run, Reprise, 1976.

Sources

Books

Contemporary Musicians, volume 2, Gale, 1990.
Trouser Press Record Guide, fourth edition, Collier Books, 1991.

Periodicals

Billboard, August 19, 1995.
Entertainment Weekly, October 14, 1994; June 30-July 7, 1995.
Newsweek, November 13, 1978.
Rolling Stone, June 4, 1987; November 2, 1989; September 20, 1990; October 4, 1990; November 14, 1991; November 28, 1991; October 15, 1992; January 21, 1993; August 25, 1994; July 13-27, 1995.
Spin, May 1995.
Stereo Review, October 1994.
Time, October 17, 1994; July 3, 1995.

—Carol Brennan

John Zorn

Saxophonist, composer

Saxophonist John Zorn's everything-but-the-kitchen-sink music jumps from style to style the way a television picture does when a deranged channel surfer has the remote control. Zorn views all musical styles as equal, and he thinks nothing of segueing from a quick-paced workout of an Ornette Coleman jazz tune to a pastiche of country and western riffs. "I'm making music by including everything that I've listened to," he explained in *Rolling Stone.* He further commented in the Detroit *Metro Times,* "All this music is on equal grounds and there's no high art and low art. Pop music has musicians creating lasting works of art and also schlock ... and the same thing in the classical world."

What unifies Zorn's work—his compositions range from evocative sound collages, to game pieces with rules for improvisation, to forays into bebop—is his interest in creating transitory situations that convey his various moods and philosophies. He combines, for example, the cerebral cool of modern jazz with the punk attitude of heavy metal. According to the *Metro Times,* Zorn tests his listeners to find out which people "like to run away" from his wide-open improvisatory situations, and "which are very docile," and "who tries very hard to get more control and power."

Early Life

As a youngster Zorn was exposed to a diverse catalog of music. His mother, a professor of education, liked classical music and world ethnic recordings; his father, a hairdresser, listened to jazz, country and French chansons. Zorn's older brother was responsible for bringing doo wop and 1950s rock and roll into the house. Zorn grew up playing the piano. As a teenager, he developed a taste for modern composers. Fascinated by Stravinsky, Webern, Ives, Varese—as well as experimenters like Stockhausen and Mauricio Kagel—he also took an interest in rock and, according to the *Atlantic,* "was listening to the Doors and playing bass in a surf band."

Zorn also became an avid fan of film music, especially of scores by Carl Stalling, who composed for Warner Bros. cartoons. Zorn points to film composition as the model for his own work. "A film composer has to know ... many styles ... in order to complement the images," he remarked in the *Atlantic* in 1991 "In that sense ... I think the great film composers are the precursors of what my generation is doing today."

In the early 1970s Zorn attended Webster College in St. Louis, Missouri, where he encountered the avant-garde jazz of musicians associated with the Chicago-based Association for the Advancement of Creative Musicians and St. Louis's Black Artists Group. Oliver Lake of the Black Artists Group taught at Webster and introduced Zorn to the music of Anthony Braxton, Roscoe Mitchell, Leo Smith, and others.

Spillane and Beyond

Influenced by Mitchell and Braxton, Zorn began to play the saxophone and introduce improvisation into his own works. By the mid- to late 1970s he was writing pieces in which improvisation was guided by a set of rules rather than a conventional score. His aim, he pointed out in the *Nation,* was to encourage musicians to make "the most possible decisions in the smallest amount of time, so that everything is jam-packed together and the music changes incredibly fast."

Zorn sought out new relationships among musicians and searched for fresh sounds. He practiced saxophone eight or more hours a day and experimented with duck calls, which he sometimes played under water. Many audiences were less than enchanted. In 1980 he complained to *Down Beat* that he was "tired of reading reviews where all they talk about is how I sound like a herd of elephants or whatever."

In the mid-1980s Zorn embarked on a series of sound collages that he made in the studio with a group of improvisatory musicians from New York City. These pieces "codified his quick cut improvisational approach,"

according to the *New York Times,* and in them Zorn introduced a programmatic element: telling stories through music. In the 1985 piece *Godard,* for example, Zorn clearly imitates the quick, cutting style of the celebrated French film director of the same name. The following year he rearranged the music of Italian film composer Ennio Morricone for *The Big Gundown* and was lauded by the *Atlantic* for creating a "perfect salute to [Morricone]." Perhaps the most successful of Zorn's sound collages, though, was 1987's *Spillane,* in which he "successfully evoked the testosterone-and-bile ethos" of pulp novelist Mickey Spillane, according to the *Atlantic.*

Collaborators

In each of Zorn's collage pieces, he was able to orchestrate remarkably abrupt shifts; his band would often stop on a dime then continue in a completely different style. "That's my whole trip in a nutshell, those really fast changes," he summed up in *Down Beat* in 1984. On Zorn's recordings, these changes sound as if they were created with the help of studio technology. But the artist is able to replicate his stops and starts in concert, accomplishing his musical feats via what *Down Beat* described as his "meticulous systems for organizing blocks of sound."

Two other factors are also important in executing Zorn's improvisatory changes. The first is the quality of the musicians with whom he works—the list of his collaborators reads like a Hall of Fame for the avant-garde. The second factor is the type of open communication Zorn encourages among his musicians. He observed in *Down Beat,* "There's a lot of eye contact and talking and direct communications among musicians in my pieces."

Zorn has always recognized the importance of his collaborators. He himself first came to public attention in the late 1970s playing with experimental rockabilly guitarist Eugene Chadbourne. Since the mid-1980s Zorn has been making music with keyboardist Wayne Horvitz and guitarists Bill Frisell and Fred Frith. In the late 1980s this group, along with drummer Joey Baron and singer Yamtatsuke Eye, eventually coalesced into the band Naked City. The Detroit *Metro Times* praised Naked City's music as "wild and adventuresome," while *Rolling Stone* found the group's self-titled debut album "Zorn's most user-friendly recording to date."

A man as hyperkinetic as Zorn could not be limited to one project, however. In 1987 he recorded a trio session with guitarist Frisell and trombonist George Lewis. The resulting album, *News for Lulu,* took an unconventional approach to bebop and caused some critics to question Zorn's musicianship. In 1989 he formed the band

Spy vs. Spy and played the compositions of Ornette Coleman at what *Down Beat* called "insane" tempos. Critic Francis Davis of *Atlantic* complained that Spy vs. Spy ground "Coleman's music down into a feelingless, monochromatic din."

By the early 1990s, Zorn, who has revealed a fascination with Japan, was developing an audience in the country. In 1992 the Japanese Jazz label DIW released several of his solo albums and gave him his own label, Avant. He released *More News For Lulu,* another collection of bebop covers and in 1993 curated the Radical New Jewish Culture Festival at New York City's avant-garde Knitting Factory. That same year, the Knitting Factory presented a month-long celebration of Zorn's work.

Two more Naked City albums were released in 1994: *Absinthe,* which *Down Beat* called "not-quite-ambient nervous moon music," and *Radio,* whose "catalog of sounds and styles," was, according to *Down Beat,* a brilliant "mishmash of Mahavishnu mixes with imploding surf music, strained and strait cartoonish ditties, bent country and western riffs, and (of course) vocal and saxophonic screams." Showing no signs of settling on a particular musical genre, in 1995 Zorn released *Masada,* which, as a *Rolling Stone* reviewer noted, "finds the unlikely common ground between Jewish folk melodies and the open-ended improvisational ploys of Ornette Coleman."

Selected discography

With others

The Big Gundown (John Zorn Plays the Music of Ennio Morricone), Elektra/Nonesuch, 1987.

Spillane, Elektra/Nonesuch, 1987.
Cobra, Hat Hut, 1987.
News for Lulu, Hat Hut, 1988.
Spy vs. Spy, Elektra/Musician, 1989.
Naked City, Elektra/Nonesuch, 1990.
More News for Lulu: Live in Paris and Basil, 1989, Hat Hut, 1992.
Filmworks: 1986-90, Electra/Nonesuch, 1992.
Masada, DIW, 1995.
(With Derek Bailey and George Lewis) *Yankees,* Celluloid.

With Naked City; on Avant Records

Heretic, 1992.
Radio, 1994.
Absinthe, 1994.
Grand Guignol.

Sources

Atlantic, January 1991.
Down Beat, February 1984; December 1985; April 1988; September 1990; May 1992; May 1994.
Metro Times (Detroit), November 25, 1992; December 7, 1992; February 23, 1994.
Musician, January/February 1995.
Nation, January 30, 1988.
New York Times, September 3, 1993; September 16, 1993.
Pulse!, September 1992.
Rolling Stone, May 17, 1990; June 29, 1995.
Spin, July 1994.

—*Jordan Wankoff*

Cumulative Indexes

Cumulative Subject Index

Volume numbers appear in **bold**.

Schuman, William **10**
Segovia, Andres **6**
Shankar, Ravi **9**
Solti, Georg **13**
Stern, Isaac **7**
Sutherland, Joan **13**
Takemitsu, Toru **6**
Toscanini, Arturo **14**
Upshaw, Dawn **9**
von Karajan, Herbert **1**
Weill, Kurt **12**
Wilson, Ransom **5**
Yamashita, Kazuhito **4**
York, Andrew **15**
Zukerman, Pinchas **4**

Composers
Adams, John **8**
Allen, Geri **10**
Alpert, Herb **11**
Anka, Paul **2**
Atkins, Chet **5**
Bacharach, Burt **1**
Benson, George **9**
Berlin, Irving **8**
Bernstein, Leonard **2**
Blackman, Cindy **15**
Bley, Carla **8**
Bley, Paul **14**
Braxton, Anthony **12**
Britten, Benjamin **15**
Brubeck, Dave **8**
Burrell, Kenny **11**
Byrne, David **8**
    Also see Talking Heads
Cage, John **8**
Cale, John **9**
Casals, Pablo **9**
Clarke, Stanley **3**
Coleman, Ornette **5**
Cooder, Ry **2**
Cooney, Rory **6**
Copeland, Stewart **14**
Copland, Aaron **2**
Crouch, Andraé **9**
Davis, Chip **4**
Davis, Miles **1**
de Grassi, Alex **6**
Dorsey, Thomas A. **11**
Elfman, Danny **9**
Ellington, Duke **2**
Eno, Brian **8**
Enya **6**
Foster, David **13**
Frisell, Bill **15**
Gillespie, Dizzy **6**
Glass, Philip **1**
Gould, Glenn **9**
Grusin, Dave **7**
Guaraldi, Vince **3**
Hamlisch, Marvin **1**
Hancock, Herbie **8**
Handy, W. C. **7**
Hargrove, Roy **15**
Harris, Eddie **15**

Hartke, Stephen **5**
Herrmann, Bernard **14**
Hunter, Alberta **7**
Isham, Mark **14**
Jarre, Jean-Michel **2**
Jarrett, Keith **1**
Jones, Hank **15**
Jones, Quincy **2**
Joplin, Scott **10**
Jordan, Stanley **1**
Kenny G **14**
Kern, Jerome **13**
Kitaro **1**
Kottke, Leo **13**
Lee, Peggy **8**
Lewis, Ramsey **14**
Lincoln, Abbey **9**
Lloyd Webber, Andrew **6**
Loewe, Frederick
    See Lerner and Loewe
Mancini, Henry **1**
Marsalis, Branford **10**
Marsalis, Ellis **13**
Masekela, Hugh **7**
McPartland, Marian **15**
Menken, Alan **10**
Metheny, Pat **2**
Mingus, Charles **9**
Monk, Meredith **1**
Monk, Thelonious **6**
Morricone, Ennio **15**
Morton, Jelly Roll **7**
Nascimento, Milton **6**
Newman, Randy **4**
Nyman, Michael **15**
Ott, David **2**
Palmieri, Eddie **15**
Parker, Charlie **5**
Peterson, Oscar **11**
Ponty, Jean-Luc **8**
Porter, Cole **10**
Previn, André **15**
Puente, Tito **14**
Reich, Steve **8**
Reinhardt, Django **7**
Ritenour, Lee **7**
Roach, Max **12**
Rollins, Sonny **7**
Rota, Nino **13**
Satriani, Joe **4**
Schickele, Peter **5**
Schuman, William **10**
Shankar, Ravi **9**
Shaw, Artie **8**
Shorter, Wayne **5**
Solal, Martial **4**
Sondheim, Stephen **8**
Sousa, John Philip **10**
Story, Liz **2**
Strayhorn, Billy **13**
Summers, Andy **3**
Sun Ra **5**
Takemitsu, Toru **6**
Talbot, John Michael **6**
Taylor, Billy **13**

Taylor, Cecil **9**
Thielemans, Toots **13**
Threadgill, Henry **9**
Tyner, McCoy **7**
Washington, Grover, Jr. **5**
Weill, Kurt **12**
Weston, Randy **15**
Williams, John **9**
Wilson, Cassandra **12**
Winston, George
Winter, Paul **10**
Worrell, Bernie **11**
Yanni **11**
York, Andrew **15**
Zimmerman, Udo **5**
Zorn, John **15**

Conductors
Bacharach, Burt **1**
Bernstein, Leonard **2**
Britten, Benjamin **15**
Casals, Pablo **9**
Copland, Aaron **2**
Domingo, Placido **1**
Fiedler, Arthur **6**
Herrmann, Bernard **14**
Jarrett, Keith **1**
Jones, Hank **15**
Levine, James **8**
Mancini, Henry **1**
Marriner, Neville **7**
Masur, Kurt **11**
Mehta, Zubin **11**
Menuhin, Yehudi **11**
Previn, André **15**
Rampal, Jean-Pierre **6**
Schickele, Peter **5**
Solti, Georg **13**
Toscanini, Arturo **14**
von Karajan, Herbert **1**
Welk, Lawrence **13**
Williams, John **9**
Zukerman, Pinchas **4**

Contemporary Dance Music
Abdul, Paula **3**
Aphex Twin **14**
Bee Gees, The **3**
B-52's, The **4**
Brown, Bobby **4**
Brown, James **2**
Cherry, Neneh **4**
Clinton, George **7**
Deee-lite **9**
De La Soul **7**
Depeche Mode **5**
Earth, Wind and Fire **12**
English Beat, The **9**
En Vogue **10**
Erasure **11**
Eurythmics **6**
Exposé **4**
Fox, Samantha **3**
Gang of Four **8**
Hammer, M.C. **5**

Tucker, Tanya **3**
Twitty, Conway **6**
Van Shelton, Ricky **5**
Van Zandt, Townes **13**
Wagoner, Porter **13**
Walker, Jerry Jeff **13**
Watson, Doc **2**
Wells, Kitty **6**
West, Dottie **8**
White, Lari **15**
Whitley, Keith **7**
Williams, Don **4**
Williams, Hank, Jr. **1**
Williams, Hank, Sr. **4**
Willis, Kelly **12**
Wills, Bob **6**
Wynette, Tammy **2**
Wynonna **11**
   Also see Judds, The
Yearwood, Trisha **10**
Yoakam, Dwight **1**
Young, Faron **7**

Dobro
Auldridge, Mike **4**
   Also see Country Gentlemen, The
   Also see Seldom Scene, The
Burch, Curtis
   See New Grass Revival, The
Knopfler, Mark **3**

Drums
See **Percussion**

Dulcimer
Ritchie, Jean **4**

Fiddle
See **Violin**

Film Scores
Anka, Paul **2**
Bacharach, Burt **1**
Berlin, Irving **8**
Bernstein, Leonard **2**
Blanchard, Terence **13**
Britten, Benjamin **15**
Byrne, David **8**
   Also see Talking Heads
Cafferty, John
   See Beaver Brown Band, The
Cahn, Sammy **11**
Cliff, Jimmy **8**
Copeland, Stewart **14**
Copland, Aaron **2**
Crouch, Andraé **9**
Dibango, Manu **14**
Dolby, Thomas **10**
Donovan **9**
Eddy, Duane **9**
Elfman, Danny **9**
Ellington, Duke **2**
Ferguson, Maynard **7**
Froom, Mitchell **15**
Gershwin, George and Ira **11**

Gould, Glenn **9**
Grusin, Dave **7**
Guaraldi, Vince **3**
Hamlisch, Marvin **1**
Hancock, Herbie **8**
Harrison, George **2**
Hayes, Isaac **10**
Hedges, Michael **3**
Herrmann, Bernard **14**
Isham, Mark **14**
Jones, Quincy **2**
Knopfler, Mark **3**
Lennon, John **9**
   Also see Beatles, The
Lerner and Loewe **13**
Mancini, Henry **1**
Marsalis, Branford **10**
Mayfield, Curtis **8**
McCartney, Paul **4**
   Also see Beatles, The
Menken, Alan **10**
Mercer, Johnny **13**
Metheny, Pat **2**
Morricone, Ennio **15**
Nascimento, Milton **6**
Nilsson **10**
Nyman, Michael **15**
Peterson, Oscar **11**
Porter, Cole **10**
Previn, André **15**
Reznor, Trent **13**
Richie, Lionel **2**
Robertson, Robbie **2**
Rollins, Sonny **7**
Rota, Nino **13**
Sager, Carole Bayer **5**
Schickele, Peter **5**
Shankar, Ravi **9**
Taj Mahal **6**
Waits, Tom **12**
   Earlier sketch in CM **1**
Weill, Kurt **12**
Williams, John **9**
Williams, Paul **5**
Willner, Hal **10**
Young, Neil **15**
   Earlier sketch in CM **2**

Flugelhorn
Sandoval, Arturo **15**

Flute
Anderson, Ian
   See Jethro Tull
Galway, James **3**
Rampal, Jean-Pierre **6**
Ulmer, James Blood **13**
Wilson, Ransom **5**

Folk/Traditional
Arnaz, Desi **8**
Baez, Joan **1**
Belafonte, Harry **8**
Black, Mary **15**
Blades, Ruben **2**

Bloom, Luka **14**
Brady, Paul **8**
Bragg, Billy **7**
Buckley, Tim **14**
Bulgarian State Female Vocal Choir,
   The **10**
Byrds, The **8**
Carter Family, The **3**
Chapin, Harry **6**
Chapman, Tracy **4**
Cherry, Don **10**
Chieftains, The **7**
Childs, Toni **2**
Clegg, Johnny **8**
Cockburn, Bruce **8**
Cohen, Leonard **3**
Collins, Judy **4**
Colvin, Shawn **11**
Crosby, David **3**
   Also see Byrds, The
Cruz, Celia **10**
de Lucia, Paco **1**
DeMent, Iris **13**
Donovan **9**
Dr. John **7**
Dylan, Bob **3**
Elliot, Cass **5**
Enya **6**
Estefan, Gloria **15**
   Earlier sketch in CM **2**
Feliciano, José **10**
Galway, James **3**
Gilmore, Jimmie Dale **11**
Gipsy Kings, The **8**
Griffith, Nanci **3**
Guthrie, Arlo **6**
Guthrie, Woody **2**
Hakmoun, Hassan **15**
Harding, John Wesley **6**
Hartford, John **1**
Havens, Richie **11**
Hinojosa, Tish **13**
Iglesias, Julio **2**
Indigo Girls **3**
Ives, Burl **12**
Khan, Nusrat Fateh Ali **13**
Kingston Trio, The **9**
Kottke, Leo **13**
Kuti, Fela **7**
Ladysmith Black Mambazo **1**
Larkin, Patty **9**
Lavin, Christine **6**
Leadbelly **6**
Lightfoot, Gordon **3**
Los Lobos **2**
Makeba, Miriam **8**
Masekela, Hugh **7**
McLean, Don **7**
Melanie **12**
Mitchell, Joni **2**
Morrison, Van **3**
Morrissey, Bill **12**
Nascimento, Milton **6**
N'Dour, Youssou **6**
Near, Holly **1**

Haley, Bill **6**
Harrison, George **2**
Hatfield, Juliana **12**
    Also see Lemonheads, The
Havens, Richie **11**
Healey, Jeff **4**
Hedges, Michael **3**
Hendrix, Jimi **2**
Hillman, Chris
    See Byrds, The
    Also see Desert Rose Band, The
Hitchcock, Robyn **9**
Holly, Buddy **1**
Hooker, John Lee **1**
Hopkins, Lightnin' **13**
Howlin' Wolf **6**
Iommi, Tony
    See Black Sabbath
Ives, Burl **12**
James, Elmore **8**
Jardine, Al
    See Beach Boys, The
Johnson, Robert **6**
Jones, Brian
    See Rolling Stones, The
Jordan, Stanley **1**
Kantner, Paul
    See Jefferson Airplane
King, Albert **2**
King, B. B. **1**
Klugh, Earl **10**
Knopfler, Mark **3**
Kottke, Leo **13**
Larkin, Patty **9**
Leadbelly **6**
Lennon, John **9**
    Also see Beatles, The
Lindley, David **2**
Lockwood, Robert, Jr. **10**
Marr, Johnny
    See Smiths, The
    Also see The The
May, Brian
    See Queen
Mayfield, Curtis **8**
McClinton, Delbert **14**
McCoury, Del **15**
McGuinn, Roger
    See Byrds, The
McLachlan, Sarah **12**
McLaughlin, John **12**
McReynolds, Jim
    See McReynolds, Jim and Jesse
Metheny, Pat **2**
Mitchell, Joni **2**
Montgomery, Wes **3**
Morrissey, Bill **12**
Nugent, Ted **2**
Owens, Buck **2**
Page, Jimmy **4**
    Also see Led Zeppelin
    Also see Yardbirds, The
Parkening, Christopher **7**
Parnell, Lee Roy **15**
Pass, Joe **15**

Patton, Charley **11**
Perkins, Carl **9**
Perry, Joe
    See Aerosmith
Petty, Tom **9**
Phair, Liz **14**
Phillips, Sam **12**
Prince **14**
    Earlier sketch in CM **1**
Raitt, Bonnie **3**
Ray, Amy
    See Indigo Girls
Reed, Jimmy **15**
Reid, Vernon **2**
    Also see Living Colour
Reinhardt, Django **7**
Richards, Keith **11**
    Also see Rolling Stones, The
Richman, Jonathan **12**
Ritenour, Lee **7**
Robbins, Marty **9**
Robertson, Robbie **2**
Robillard, Duke **2**
Rodgers, Nile **8**
Rush, Otis **12**
Saliers, Emily
    See Indigo Girls
Santana, Carlos **1**
Satriani, Joe **4**
Scofield, John **7**
Segovia, Andres **6**
Sharrock, Sonny **15**
Shines, Johnny **14**
Skaggs, Ricky **5**
Slash
    See Guns n' Roses
Springsteen, Bruce **6**
Stewart, Dave
    See Eurythmics
Stills, Stephen **5**
Stuart, Marty **9**
Summers, Andy **3**
Taylor, Mick
    See Rolling Stones, The
Thielemans, Toots **13**
Thompson, Richard **7**
Tippin, Aaron **12**
Townshend, Pete **1**
Travis, Merle **14**
Tubb, Ernest **4**
Ulmer, James Blood **13**
Vai, Steve **5**
Van Halen, Edward
    See Van Halen
Van Ronk, Dave **12**
Vaughan, Jimmie
    See Fabulous Thunderbirds, The
Vaughan, Stevie Ray **1**
Wagoner, Porter **13**
Waits, Tom **12**
    Earlier sketch in CM **1**
Walker, Jerry Jeff **13**
Walker, T-Bone **5**
Walsh, Joe **5**
    Also see Eagles, The

Watson, Doc **2**
Weir, Bob
    See Grateful Dead, The
Weller, Paul **14**
White, Lari **15**
Wilson, Nancy
    See Heart
Winston, George **9**
Winter, Johnny **5**
Yamashita, Kazuhito **4**
Yarrow, Peter
    See Peter, Paul & Mary
York, Andrew **15**
Young, Angus
    See AC/DC
Young, Malcolm
    See AC/DC
Young, Neil **15**
    Earlier sketch in CM **2**
Zappa, Frank **1**

Harmonica
Dylan, Bob **3**
Guthrie, Woody **2**
Lewis, Huey **9**
Little Walter **14**
McClinton, Delbert **14**
Musselwhite, Charlie **13**
Reed, Jimmy **15**
Thielemans, Toots **13**
Waters, Muddy **4**
Williamson, Sonny Boy **9**
Wilson, Kim
    See Fabulous Thunderbirds, The
Young, Neil **15**
    Earlier sketch in CM **2**

Heavy Metal
AC/DC **4**
Aerosmith **3**
Alice in Chains **10**
Anthrax **11**
Black Sabbath **9**
Danzig **7**
Deep Purple **11**
Def Leppard **3**
Faith No More **7**
Fishbone **7**
Ford, Lita **9**
Guns n' Roses **2**
Iron Maiden **10**
Judas Priest **10**
King's X **7**
Led Zeppelin **1**
L7 **12**
Megadeth **9**
Metallica **7**
Mötley Crüe **1**
Motörhead **10**
Nugent, Ted **2**
Osbourne, Ozzy **3**
Pantera **13**
Petra **3**
Queensrÿche **8**
Reid, Vernon **2**
    Also see Living Colour

Reznor, Trent 13
Roth, David Lee 1
    Also see Van Halen
Sepultura 12
Slayer 10
Soundgarden 6
Spinal Tap 8
Stryper 2
Suicidal Tendencies 15
Whitesnake 5

Humor
Coasters, The 5
Jones, Spike 5
Lehrer, Tom 7
Pearl, Minnie 3
Russell, Mark 6
Schickele, Peter 5
Shaffer, Paul 13
Spinal Tap 8
Stevens, Ray 7
Yankovic, "Weird Al" 7

Inventors
Fender, Leo 10
Harris, Eddie 15
Paul, Les 2
Scholz, Tom
    See Boston
Teagarden, Jack 10

Jazz
Adderly, Cannonball 15
Allen, Geri 10
Anderson, Ray 7
Armstrong, Louis 4
Bailey, Mildred 13
Bailey, Pearl 5
Baker, Anita 9
Baker, Chet 13
Basie, Count 2
Belle, Regina 6
Benson, George 9
Berigan, Bunny 2
Blackman, Cindy 15
Blakey, Art 11
Blanchard, Terence 13
Bley, Carla 8
Bley, Paul 14
Blood, Sweat and Tears 7
Brand New Heavies, The 14
Braxton, Anthony 12
Brown, Ruth 13
Brubeck, Dave 8
Burrell, Kenny 11
Burton, Gary 10
Calloway, Cab 6
Canadian Brass, The 4
Carter, Benny 3
Carter, Betty 6
Carter, Ron 14
Charles, Ray 1
Cherry, Don 10
Christian, Charlie 11
Clarke, Stanley 3

Clooney, Rosemary 9
Cole, Nat King 3
Coleman, Ornette 5
Coltrane, John 4
Connick, Harry, Jr. 4
Corea, Chick 6
Davis, Miles 1
DeJohnette, Jack 7
Di Meola, Al 12
Eckstine, Billy 1
Eldridge, Roy 9
Ellington, Duke 2
Ferguson, Maynard 7
Fitzgerald, Ella 1
Fleck, Bela 8
    Also see New Grass Revival, The
Fountain, Pete 7
Frisell, Bill 15
Galway, James 3
Getz, Stan 12
Gillespie, Dizzy 6
Goodman, Benny 4
Gordon, Dexter 10
Grappelli, Stephane 10
Green, Grant 14
Guaraldi, Vince 3
Haden, Charlie 12
Hampton, Lionel 6
Hancock, Herbie 8
Hargrove, Roy 15
Harris, Eddie 15
Hawkins, Coleman 11
Hedges, Michael 3
Henderson, Joe 14
Herman, Woody 12
Hines, Earl "Fatha" 12
Hirt, Al 5
Holiday, Billie 6
Horn, Shirley 7
Horne, Lena 11
Hunter, Alberta 7
Isham, Mark 14
Jackson, Milt 15
James, Harry 11
Jarreau, Al 1
Jarrett, Keith 1
Jones, Elvin 9
Jones, Hank 15
Jones, Quincy 2
Jordan, Stanley 1
Kennedy, Nigel 8
Kenny G 14
Kirk, Rahsaan Roland 6
Kitt, Eartha 9
Klugh, Earl 10
Kronos Quartet 5
Krupa, Gene 13
Laine, Cleo 10
Lee, Peggy 8
Lewis, Ramsey 14
Lincoln, Abbey 9
Lopez, Israel "Cachao" 14
Lovano, Joe 13
Mancini, Henry 1
Manhattan Transfer, The 8

Marsalis, Branford 10
Marsalis, Ellis 13
Marsalis, Wynton 6
Masekela, Hugh 7
McFerrin, Bobby 3
McLaughlin, John 12
McPartland, Marian 15
McRae, Carmen 9
Metheny, Pat 2
Mingus, Charles 9
Monk, Thelonious 6
Montgomery, Wes 3
Morgan, Frank 9
Morton, Jelly Roll 7
Nascimento, Milton 6
Norvo, Red 12
Oliver, King 15
Palmieri, Eddie 15
Parker, Charlie 5
Parker, Maceo 7
Pass, Joe 15
Paul, Les 2
Peterson, Oscar 11
Ponty, Jean-Luc 8
Powell, Bud 15
Previn, André 15
Professor Longhair 6
Puente, Tito 14
Rampal, Jean-Pierre 6
Redman, Joshua 12
Reid, Vernon 2
    Also see Living Colour
Reinhardt, Django 7
Rich, Buddy 13
Roach, Max 12
Roberts, Marcus 6
Robillard, Duke 2
Rodney, Red 14
Rollins, Sonny 7
Sanborn, David 1
Sandoval, Arturo 15
Santana, Carlos 1
Schuur, Diane 6
Scofield, John 7
Scott, Jimmy 14
Scott-Heron, Gil 13
Severinsen, Doc 1
Sharrock, Sonny 15
Shaw, Artie 8
Shorter, Wayne 5
Simone, Nina 11
Solal, Martial 4
Strayhorn, Billy 13
Summers, Andy 3
Sun Ra 5
Take 6 6
Taylor, Billy 13
Taylor, Cecil 9
Teagarden, Jack 10
Thielemans, Toots 13
Threadgill, Henry 9
Torme, Mel 4
Tucker, Sophie 12
Turner, Big Joe 13
Turtle Island String Quartet 9

Tyner, McCoy **7**
Ulmer, James Blood **13**
Vaughan, Sarah **2**
Walker, T-Bone **5**
Washington, Dinah **5**
Washington, Grover, Jr. **5**
Webb, Chick **14**
Weston, Randy **15**
Williams, Joe **11**
Wilson, Cassandra **12**
Wilson, Nancy **14**
Winter, Paul **10**
Young, Lester **14**
Zorn, John **15**

Keyboards, Electric
Aphex Twin **14**
Bley, Paul **14**
Brown, Tony **14**
Corea, Chick **6**
Davis, Chip **4**
Dolby, Thomas **10**
Emerson, Keith
    See Emerson, Lake & Palmer/Powell
Eno, Brian **8**
Foster, David **13**
Froom, Mitchell **15**
Hancock, Herbie **8**
Jackson, Joe **4**
Jarre, Jean-Michel **2**
Jones, Booker T. **8**
Kitaro **1**
Manzarek, Ray
    See Doors, The
McDonald, Michael
    See Doobie Brothers, The
McVie, Christine
    See Fleetwood Mac
Pierson, Kate
    See B-52's, The
Shaffer, Paul **13**
Sun Ra **5**
Waller, Fats **7**
Wilson, Brian
    See Beach Boys, The
Winwood, Steve **2**
Wonder, Stevie **2**
Worrell, Bernie **11**
Yanni **11**

Liturgical Music
Cooney, Rory **6**
Talbot, John Michael **6**

Mandolin
Bush, Sam
    See New Grass Revival, The
Duffey, John
    See Seldom Scene, The
Hartford, John **1**
Lindley, David **2**
McReynolds, Jesse
    See McReynolds, Jim and Jesse
Monroe, Bill **1**

Rosas, Cesar
    See Los Lobos
Skaggs, Ricky **5**
Stuart, Marty **9**
Musicals
Allen, Debbie **8**
Allen, Peter **11**
Andrews, Julie **4**
Andrews Sisters, The **9**
Bacharach, Burt **1**
Bailey, Pearl **5**
Baker, Josephine **10**
Berlin, Irving **8**
Brown, Ruth **13**
Buckley, Betty **1**
Burnett, Carol **6**
Carter, Nell **7**
Channing, Carol **6**
Chevalier, Maurice **6**
Crawford, Michael **4**
Crosby, Bing **6**
Curry, Tim **3**
Davis, Sammy, Jr. **4**
Garland, Judy **6**
Gershwin, George and Ira **11**
Hamlisch, Marvin **1**
Horne, Lena **11**
Jolson, Al **10**
Kern, Jerome **13**
Laine, Cleo **10**
Lerner and Loewe **13**
Lloyd Webber, Andrew **6**
LuPone, Patti **8**
Masekela, Hugh **7**
Menken, Alan **10**
Mercer, Johnny **13**
Moore, Melba **7**
Patinkin, Mandy **3**
Peters, Bernadette **7**
Porter, Cole **10**
Robeson, Paul **8**
Rodgers, Richard **9**
Sager, Carole Bayer **5**
Shaffer, Paul **13**
Sondheim, Stephen **8**
Waters, Ethel **11**
Weill, Kurt **12**

Opera
Adams, John **8**
Anderson, Marian **8**
Baker, Janet **14**
Bartoli, Cecilia **12**
Battle, Kathleen **6**
Bumbry, Grace **13**
Callas, Maria **11**
Carreras, José **8**
Caruso, Enrico **10**
Copeland, Stewart **14**
Cotrubas, Ileana **1**
Domingo, Placido **1**
Freni, Mirella **14**
Gershwin, George and Ira **11**
Hampson, Thomas **12**
Hendricks, Barbara **10**

Herrmann, Bernard **14**
Horne, Marilyn **9**
McNair, Sylvia **15**
Norman, Jessye **7**
Pavarotti, Luciano **1**
Price, Leontyne **6**
Sills, Beverly **5**
Solti, Georg **13**
Sutherland, Joan **13**
Te Kanawa, Kiri **2**
Toscanini, Arturo **14**
Upshaw, Dawn **9**
von Karajan, Herbert **1**
Weill, Kurt **12**
Zimmerman, Udo **5**

Percussion
Baker, Ginger
    See Cream
Blackman, Cindy **15**
Blakey, Art **11**
Bonham, John
    See Led Zeppelin
Burton, Gary **10**
Collins, Phil **2**
    Also see Genesis
Copeland, Stewart **14**
DeJohnette, Jack **7**
Densmore, John
    See Doors, The
Dunbar, Aynsley
    See Jefferson Starship
    Also see Whitesnake
Dunbar, Sly
    See Sly and Robbie
Fleetwood, Mick
    See Fleetwood Mac
Hampton, Lionel **6**
Hart, Mickey
    See Grateful Dead, The
Henley, Don **3**
Jones, Elvin **9**
Jones, Kenny
    See Who, The
Jones, Spike **5**
Kreutzman, Bill
    See Grateful Dead, The
Krupa, Gene **13**
Mason, Nick
    See Pink Floyd
Moon, Keith
    See Who, The
N'Dour, Youssou **6**
Palmer, Carl
    See Emerson, Lake & Palmer/Powell
Palmieri, Eddie **15**
Peart, Neil
    See Rush
Powell, Cozy
    See Emerson, Lake & Palmer/Powell
Puente, Tito **14**
Rich, Buddy **13**
Roach, Max **12**
Sheila E. **3**
Starr, Ringo **10**
    Also see Beatles, The

Crosby, David **3**
     Also see Byrds, The
Crowded House **12**
Daltrey, Roger **3**
     Also see Who, The
D'Arby, Terence Trent **3**
Darin, Bobby **4**
Dave Clark Five, The **12**
Davies, Ray **5**
Davis, Sammy, Jr. **4**
Davis, Skeeter **15**
Dayne, Taylor **4**
DeBarge, El **14**
Denver, John **1**
Depeche Mode **5**
Des'ree **15**
Devo **13**
Diamond, Neil **1**
Dion **4**
Dion, Céline **12**
Doc Pomus **14**
Donovan **9**
Doobie Brothers, The **3**
Doors, The **4**
Duran Duran **4**
Dylan, Bob **3**
Eagles, The **3**
Earth, Wind and Fire **12**
Easton, Sheena **2**
Edmonds, Kenneth "Babyface" **12**
Electric Light Orchestra **7**
Elfman, Danny **9**
Elliot, Cass **5**
Enigma **14**
En Vogue **10**
Estefan, Gloria **15**
     Earlier sketch in CM **2**
Eurythmics **6**
Everly Brothers, The **2**
Everything But The Girl **15**
Exposé **4**
Fabian **5**
Feliciano, José **10**
Ferguson, Maynard **7**
Ferry, Bryan **1**
Fiedler, Arthur **6**
Fisher, Eddie **12**
Fitzgerald, Ella **1**
Flack, Roberta **5**
Fleetwood Mac **5**
Fogelberg, Dan **4**
Fordham, Julia **15**
Foster, David **13**
Four Tops, The **11**
Fox, Samantha **3**
Frampton, Peter **3**
Francis, Connie **10**
Franklin, Aretha **2**
Frey, Glenn **3**
     Also see Eagles, The
Garfunkel, Art **4**
Gaye, Marvin **4**
Gayle, Crystal **1**
Geldof, Bob **9**
Genesis **4**

Gershwin, George and Ira **11**
Gibson, Debbie **1**
Gift, Roland **3**
Goodman, Benny **4**
Gordy, Berry, Jr. **6**
Grant, Amy **7**
Grebenshikov, Boris **3**
Green, Al **9**
Guthrie, Arlo **6**
Hall & Oates **6**
Hammer, M.C. **5**
Hancock, Herbie **8**
Harding, John Wesley **6**
Harrison, George **2**
     Also see Beatles, The
Harry, Deborah **4**
     Also see Blondie
Healey, Jeff **4**
Henley, Don **3**
     Also see Eagles, The
Herman's Hermits **5**
Hitchcock, Robyn **9**
Holland-Dozier-Holland **5**
Horne, Lena **11**
Hornsby, Bruce **3**
Houston, Whitney **8**
Ian, Janis **5**
Idol, Billy **3**
Iglesias, Julio **2**
Indigo Girls **3**
Ingram, James **11**
Isaak, Chris **6**
Isley Brothers, The **8**
Jackson, Janet **3**
Jackson, Joe **4**
Jackson, Michael **1**
     Also see Jacksons, The
Jacksons, The **7**
Jam, Jimmy, and Terry Lewis **11**
James **12**
James, Harry **11**
James, Rick **2**
Jarreau, Al **1**
Jayhawks, The **15**
Jefferson Airplane **5**
Jodeci **13**
Joel, Billy **12**
     Earlier sketch in CM **2**
Johansen, David **7**
John, Elton **3**
Jolson, Al **10**
Jones, Quincy **2**
Jones, Rickie Lee **4**
Jones, Tom **11**
Joplin, Janis **3**
Khan, Chaka **9**
King, Ben E. **7**
King, Carole **6**
Kiss **5**
Kitt, Eartha **9**
Knight, Gladys **1**
Knopfler, Mark **3**
Kool & the Gang **13**
Kraftwerk **9**
Kristofferson, Kris **4**

LaBelle, Patti **8**
Lauper, Cyndi **11**
Lee, Brenda **5**
Leiber and Stoller **14**
Lemper, Ute **14**
Lennon, John **9**
     Also see Beatles, The
Lennon, Julian **2**
Lewis, Huey **9**
Liberace **9**
Lightfoot, Gordon **3**
Loggins, Kenny **3**
Lovett, Lyle **5**
Lowe, Nick **6**
Lush **13**
Lynne, Jeff **5**
MacColl, Kirsty **12**
Madonna **4**
Mancini, Henry **1**
Manhattan Transfer, The **8**
Manilow, Barry **2**
Marley, Bob **3**
Marley, Ziggy **3**
Marsalis, Branford **10**
Martin, Dean **1**
Martin, George **6**
Marx, Richard **3**
Mathis, Johnny **2**
McCartney, Paul **4**
     Also see Beatles, The
McFerrin, Bobby **3**
McLachlan, Sarah **12**
McLean, Don **7**
Medley, Bill **3**
Melanie **12**
Michael, George **9**
Midler, Bette **8**
Miller, Mitch **11**
Miller, Roger **4**
Milli Vanilli **4**
Mills Brothers, The **14**
Mitchell, Joni **2**
Monkees, The **7**
Montand, Yves **12**
Morrison, Jim **3**
Morrison, Van **3**
Morrissey **10**
Mouskouri, Nana **12**
Moyet, Alison **12**
Murray, Anne **4**
Myles, Alannah **4**
Neville, Aaron **5**
     Also see Neville Brothers, The
Neville Brothers, The **4**
New Kids on the Block **3**
Newman, Randy **4**
Newton, Wayne **2**
Newton-John, Olivia **8**
Nicks, Stevie **2**
Nilsson **10**
Nitty Gritty Dirt Band **6**
Nyro, Laura **12**
Oak Ridge Boys, The **7**
Ocasek, Ric **5**
Ocean, Billy **4**
O'Connor, Sinead **3**

Spector, Phil **4**
Sure!, Al B. **13**
Sweat, Keith **13**
Swing, DeVante
   See Jodeci
Toussaint, Allen **11**
Vandross, Luther **2**
Walden, Narada Michael **14**
Wexler, Jerry **15**
Willner, Hal **10**
Wilson, Brian
   See Beach Boys, The
Winbush, Angela **15**

Promoters
Clark, Dick **2**
Geldof, Bob **9**
Graham, Bill **10**
Hay, George D. **3**
Simmons, Russell **7**

Ragtime
Joplin, Scott **10**

Rap
Arrested Development **14**
Bambaataa, Afrika **13**
Basehead **11**
Beastie Boys, The **8**
Biz Markie **10**
Black Sheep **15**
Campbell, Luther **10**
Cherry, Neneh **4**
Cypress Hill **11**
Das EFX **14**
De La Soul **7**
Digable Planets **15**
Digital Underground **9**
DJ Jazzy Jeff and the Fresh Prince **5**
Dr. Dre **15**
   Also see N.W.A.
Eazy-E **13**
   Also see N.W.A.
EPMD **10**
Eric B. and Rakim **9**
Gang Starr **13**
Geto Boys, The **11**
Grandmaster Flash **14**
Hammer, M.C. **5**
Heavy D **10**
House of Pain **14**
Ice Cube **10**
Ice-T **7**
Jackson, Millie **14**
Kane, Big Daddy **7**
Kid 'n Play **5**
Knight, Suge **15**
Kool Moe Dee **9**
Kris Kross **11**
KRS-One **8**
L.L. Cool J. **5**
MC Lyte **8**
MC Serch **10**
Naughty by Nature **11**
N.W.A. **6**

P.M. Dawn **11**
Public Enemy **4**
Queen Latifah **6**
Riley, Teddy **14**
Rubin, Rick **9**
Run-D.M.C. **4**
Salt-N-Pepa **6**
Scott-Heron, Gil **13**
Shanté **10**
Shocklee, Hank **15**
Simmons, Russell **7**
Sir Mix-A-Lot **14**
Sure!, Al B. **13**
TLC **15**
Tone-Loc **3**
Tribe Called Quest, A **8**
Vanilla Ice **6**
Young M.C. **4**
Yo Yo **9**

Record Company Executives
Ackerman, Will **3**
Alpert, Herb **11**
Brown, Tony **14**
Busby, Jheryl **9**
Davis, Chip **4**
Davis, Clive **14**
Ertegun, Ahmet **10**
Foster, David **13**
Geffen, David **8**
Gordy, Berry, Jr. **6**
Hammond, John **6**
Harley, Bill **7**
Jam, Jimmy, and Terry Lewis **11**
Knight, Suge **15**
Koppelman, Charles **14**
Krasnow, Bob **15**
Marley, Rita **10**
Martin, George **6**
Mayfield, Curtis **8**
Mercer, Johnny **13**
Miller, Mitch **11**
Mingus, Charles **9**
Near, Holly **1**
Penner, Fred **10**
Phillips, Sam **5**
Reznor, Trent **13**
Rhone, Sylvia **13**
Robinson, Smokey **1**
Rubin, Rick **9**
Simmons, Russell **7**
Spector, Phil **4**
Teller, Al **15**
Wexler, Jerry **15**

Reggae
Black Uhuru **12**
Burning Spear **15**
Cliff, Jimmy **8**
Inner Circle **15**
Marley, Bob **3**
Marley, Rita **10**
Marley, Ziggy **3**
Sly and Robbie **13**
Steel Pulse **14**

Third World **13**
Tosh, Peter **3**
UB40 **4**
Wailer, Bunny **11**

Rhythm and Blues/Soul
Abdul, Paula **3**
Alexander, Arthur **14**
Baker, Anita **9**
Ball, Marcia **15**
Basehead **11**
Belle, Regina **6**
Berry, Chuck **1**
Bland, Bobby "Blue" **12**
Blige, Mary J. **15**
Blues Brothers, The **3**
Bolton, Michael **4**
Boyz II Men **15**
Brown, James **2**
Brown, Ruth **13**
Bryson, Peabo **11**
Burdon, Eric **14**
   Also see War
Busby, Jheryl **9**
Campbell, Tevin **13**
Carey, Mariah **6**
Charles, Ray **1**
Cole, Natalie **1**
Cooke, Sam **1**
   Also see Soul Stirrers, The
Cropper, Steve **12**
D'Arby, Terence Trent **3**
DeBarge, El **14**
Des'ree **15**
Dibango, Manu **14**
Diddley, Bo **3**
Domino, Fats **2**
Dr. John **7**
Earth, Wind and Fire **12**
Edmonds, Kenneth "Babyface" **12**
En Vogue **10**
Fabulous Thunderbirds, The **1**
Four Tops, The **11**
Fox, Samantha **3**
Franklin, Aretha **2**
Gaye, Marvin **4**
Gordy, Berry, Jr. **6**
Green, Al **9**
Hall & Oates **6**
Hayes, Isaac **10**
Holland-Dozier-Holland **5**
Ingram, James **11**
Isley Brothers, The **8**
Jackson, Freddie **3**
Jackson, Janet **3**
Jackson, Michael **1**
   Also see Jacksons, The
Jackson, Millie **14**
Jacksons, The **7**
Jam, Jimmy, and Terry Lewis **11**
James, Etta **6**
Jodeci **13**
Jones, Booker T. **8**
Jones, Grace **9**
Jones, Quincy **2**

Chapin, Harry **6**
Chapman, Steven Curtis **15**
Chapman, Tracy **4**
Charles, Ray **1**
Chenier, C. J. **15**
Childs, Toni **2**
Chilton, Alex **10**
Clapton, Eric **11**
  Earlier sketch in CM **1**
    Also see Cream
    Also see Yardbirds, The
Cleveland, James **1**
Clinton, George **7**
Cockburn, Bruce **8**
Cohen, Leonard **3**
Cole, Lloyd **9**
Cole, Nat King **3**
Collins, Albert **4**
Collins, Judy **4**
Collins, Phil **2**
Cooder, Ry **2**
Cooke, Sam **1**
  Also see Soul Stirrers, The
Collie, Mark **15**
Cooper, Alice **8**
Corgan, Billy
  See Smashing Pumpkins
Costello, Elvis **12**
  Earlier sketch in CM **2**
Crenshaw, Marshall **5**
Croce, Jim **3**
Crofts, Dash
  See Seals & Crofts
Cropper, Steve **12**
Crosby, David **3**
  Also see Byrds, The
Crowe, J. D. **5**
Crowell, Rodney **8**
Daniels, Charlie **6**
Davies, Ray **5**
  Also see Kinks, the
DeBarge, El **14**
DeMent, Iris **13**
Denver, John **1**
Des'ree **15**
Diamond, Neil **1**
Diddley, Bo **3**
Difford, Chris
  See Squeeze
Dion **4**
Dixon, Willie **10**
Doc Pomus **14**
Domino, Fats **2**
Donovan **9**
Dorsey, Thomas A. **11**
Doucet, Michael **8**
Dozier, Lamont
  See Holland-Dozier-Holland
Dylan, Bob **3**
Edge, The
  See U2
Edmonds, Kenneth "Babyface" **12**
Eitzel, Mark
  See American Music Club
Elfman, Danny **9**

Ellington, Duke **2**
Emerson, Keith
  See Emerson, Lake & Palmer/Powell
Enigma **14**
Ertegun, Ahmet **10**
Estefan, Gloria **15**
  Earlier sketch in CM **2**
Etheridge, Melissa **4**
Everly, Don
  See Everly Brothers, The
Everly, Phil
  See Everly Brothers, The
Fagen, Don
  See Steely Dan
Faithfull, Marianne **14**
Ferry, Bryan **1**
Flack, Roberta **5**
Flatt, Lester **3**
Fogelberg, Dan **4**
Fogerty, John **2**
Fordham, Julia **15**
Foster, David **13**
Frampton, Peter **3**
Frey, Glenn **3**
  Also see Eagles, The
Fripp, Robert **9**
Frizzell, Lefty **10**
Gabriel, Peter **2**
Garcia, Jerry **4**
Gaye, Marvin **4**
Geldof, Bob **9**
George, Lowell
  See Little Feat
Gershwin, George and Ira **11**
Gibb, Barry
  See Bee Gees, The
Gibb, Maurice
  See Bee Gees, The
Gibb, Robin
  See Bee Gees, The
Gibbons, Billy
  See ZZ Top
Gibson, Debbie **1**
Gift, Roland **3**
Gill, Vince **7**
Gilley, Mickey **7**
Gilmour, David
  See Pink Floyd
Goodman, Benny **4**
Gordy, Berry, Jr. **6**
Grant, Amy **7**
Green, Al **9**
Greenwood, Lee **12**
Griffith, Nanci **3**
Guthrie, Arlo **6**
Guthrie, Woodie **2**
Guy, Buddy **4**
Haggard, Merle **2**
Hall, Daryl
  See Hall & Oates
Hall, Tom T. **4**
Hamlisch, Marvin **1**
Hammer, M.C. **5**
Hammerstein, Oscar
  See Rodgers, Richard

Harding, John Wesley **6**
Harley, Bill **7**
Harris, Emmylou **4**
Harrison, George **2**
  Also see Beatles, The
Harry, Deborah **4**
  Also see Blondie
Hart, Lorenz
  See Rodgers, Richard
Hartford, John **1**
Hatfield, Juliana **12**
  Also see Lemonheads, The
Hawkins, Screamin' Jay **8**
Hayes, Isaac **10**
Healey, Jeff **4**
Hedges, Michael **3**
Hendrix, Jimi **2**
Henley, Don **3**
  Also see Eagles, The
Hiatt, John **8**
Hidalgo, David
  See Los Lobos
Hillman, Chris
  See Byrds, The
  Also see Desert Rose Band, The
Hinojosa, Tish **13**
Hitchcock, Robyn **9**
Holland, Brian
  See Holland-Dozier-Holland
Holland, Eddie
  See Holland-Dozier-Holland
Holly, Buddy **1**
Hornsby, Bruce **3**
Howard, Harlan **15**
Hutchence, Michael
  See INXS
Hynde, Chrissie
  See Pretenders, The
Ian, Janis **5**
Ice Cube **10**
Ice-T **7**
Idol, Billy **3**
Isaak, Chris **6**
Jackson, Alan **7**
Jackson, Joe **4**
Jackson, Michael **1**
  Also see Jacksons, The
Jackson, Millie **14**
Jagger, Mick **7**
  Also see Rolling Stones, The
Jam, Jimmy, and Terry Lewis **11**
James, Rick **2**
Jarreau, Al **1**
Jennings, Waylon **4**
Jett, Joan **3**
Joel, Billy **12**
  Earlier sketch in CM **2**
Johansen, David **7**
John, Elton **3**
Johnson, Matt
  See The The
Jones, Brian
  See Rolling Stones, The
Jones, George **4**
Jones, Mick
  See Clash, The

Cumulative Musicians Index

Volume numbers appear in **bold**.

Binks, Les
  See Judas Priest
Birchfield, Benny
  See Osborne Brothers, The
Bird
  See Parker, Charlie
Birdsong, Cindy
  See Supremes, The
Biscuits, Chuck
  See Danzig
Bishop, Michael
  See Gwar
Biz Markie 10
Björk
  See Sugarcubes, The
Black, Clint 5
Black, Frank 14
Black, Mary 15
Black Crowes, The 7
Black Francis
  See Black, Frank
Blackman, Cindy 15
Blackmore, Ritchie
  See Deep Purple
Black Sabbath 9
Black Sheep 15
Black Uhuru 12
Blades, Ruben 2
Blake, Norman
  See Teenage Fanclub
Blakey, Art 11
Blanchard, Terence 13
Bland, Bobby "Blue" 12
Bley, Carla 8
Bley, Paul 14
Blige, Mary J. 15
Blondie 14
Blood, Sweat and Tears 7
Bloom, Luka 14
Blues, Elwood
  See Blues Brothers, The
Blues, "Joliet" Jake
  See Blues Brothers, The
Blues Brothers, The 3
Blues Traveler 15
Blunt, Martin
  See Charlatans, The
BoDeans, The 3
Bogaert, Jo
  See Technotronic
Bogdan, Henry
  See Helmet
Bogguss, Suzy 11
Bolade, Nitanju
  See Sweet Honey in the Rock
Bolan, Marc
  See T. Rex
Bolton, Michael 4
Bonebrake, D. J.
  See X
Bonham, John
  See Led Zeppelin
Bon Jovi 10
Bon Jovi, Jon
  See Bon Jovi

Bono
  See U2
Bonsall, Joe
  See Oak Ridge Boys, The
Books
  See Das EFX
Boone, Pat 13
Booth, Tim
  See James
Bordin, Mike
  See Faith No More
Bostaph, Paul
  See Slayer
Boston 11
Bostrom, Derrick
  See Meat Puppets, The
Bottum, Roddy
  See Faith No More
Bouchikhi, Chico
  See Gipsy Kings, The
Bowen, Jimmy
  See Country Gentlemen, The
Bowens, Sir Harry
  See Was (Not Was)
Bowie, David 1
Boyd, Liona 7
Boyz II Men 15
Brady, Paul 8
Bragg, Billy 7
Bramah, Martin
  See Fall, The
Brand New Heavies, The 14
Branigan, Laura 2
Brantley, Junior
  See Roomful of Blues
Braxton, Anthony 12
B-Real
  See Cypress Hill
Bream, Julian 9
Brickell, Edie 3
Bright, Ronnie
  See Coasters, The
Briley, Alex
  See Village People, The
Britten, Benjamin 15
Brix
  See Fall, The
Brockie, Dave
  See Gwar
Bronfman, Yefim 6
Brooke, Jonatha
  See Story, The
Brookes, Jon
  See Charlatans, The
Brooks, Garth 8
Brooks, Leon Eric "Kix"
  See Brooks & Dunn
Brooks & Dunn 12
Broonzy, Big Bill 13
Brown, Bobby 4
Brown, Clarence "Gatemouth" 11
Brown, George
  See Kool & the Gang
Brown, Harold
  See War

Brown, James 2
Brown, Jimmy
  See UB40
Brown, Junior 15
Brown, Marty 14
Brown, Norman
  See Mills Brothers, The
Brown, Ruth 13
Brown, Selwyn "Bumbo"
  See Steel Pulse
Brown, Tony 14
Browne, Jackson 3
  Also see Nitty Gritty Dirt Band, The
Brubeck, Dave 8
Bruce, Jack
  See Cream
Bruford, Bill
  See Yes
Bruster, Thomas
  See Soul Stirrers, The
Bryan, David
  See Bon Jovi
Bryant, Elbridge
  See Temptations, The
Bryson, Bill
  See Desert Rose Band, The
Bryson, Peabo 11
Buchholz, Francis
  See Scorpions, The
Buck, Mike
  See Fabulous Thunderbirds, The
Buck, Peter
  See R.E.M.
Buck, Robert
  See 10,000 Maniacs
Buckingham, Lindsey 8
  Also see Fleetwood Mac
Buckley, Betty 1
Buckley, Tim 14
Buckwheat Zydeco 6
Budgie
  See Siouxsie and the Banshees
Buffett, Jimmy 4
Bulgarian State Female Vocal Choir,
  The 10
Bulgarian State Radio and Television
  Female Vocal Choir, The
  See Bulgarian State Female Vocal
  Choir, The
Bumbry, Grace 13
Bumpus, Cornelius
  See Doobie Brothers, The
Bunker, Clive
  See Jethro Tull
Burch, Curtis
  See New Grass Revival, The
Burdon, Eric 14
  Also see War
Burgess, Tim
  See Charlatans, The
Burke, Clem
  See Blondie
Burnett, Carol 6
Burnett, T Bone 13
Burnette, Billy
  See Fleetwood Mac

Chuck D
　See Public Enemy
Chung, Mark
　See Einstürzende Neubauten
Church, Kevin
　See Country Gentlemen, The
Church, The **14**
Clapton, Eric **11**
　Earlier sketch in CM **1**
　　Also see Cream
　　Also see Yardbirds, The
Clark, Dave
　See Dave Clark Five, The
Clark, Dick **2**
Clark, Gene
　See Byrds, The
Clark, Mike
　See Suicidal Tendencies
Clark, Roy **1**
Clark, Steve
　See Def Leppard
Clarke, "Fast" Eddie
　See Motörhead
Clarke, Michael
　See Byrds, The
Clarke, Stanley **3**
Clarke, Vince
　See Depeche Mode
　　Also see Erasure
Clarke, William
　See Third World
Clash, The **4**
Clayderman, Richard **1**
Claypool, Les
　See Primus
Clayton, Adam
　See U2
Clayton, Sam
　See Little Feat
Clayton-Thomas, David
　See Blood, Sweat and Tears
Cleaves, Jessica
　See Earth, Wind and Fire
Clegg, Johnny **8**
Clemons, Clarence **7**
Cleveland, James **1**
Cliburn, Van **13**
Cliff, Jimmy **8**
Cline, Patsy **5**
Clinton, George **7**
Clooney, Rosemary **9**
Coasters, The **5**
Cobain, Kurt
　See Nirvana
Cockburn, Bruce **8**
Cocker, Joe **4**
Cocteau Twins, The **12**
Coe, David Allan **4**
Coffie, Calton
　See Inner Circle
Cohen, Jeremy
　See Turtle Island String Quartet
Cohen, Leonard **3**
Cohen, Porky
　See Roomful of Blues

Cole, Lloyd **9**
Cole, Natalie **1**
Cole, Nat King **3**
Coleman, Ornette **5**
Collie, Mark **15**
Collin, Phil
　See Def Leppard
Collins, Albert **4**
Collins, Allen
　See Lynyrd Skynyrd
Collins, Bootsy **8**
Collins, Judy **4**
Collins, Mark
　See Charlatans, The
Collins, Phil **2**
　　Also see Genesis
Collins, Rob
　See Charlatans, The
Collins, William
　See Collins, Bootsy
Colomby, Bobby
　See Blood, Sweat and Tears
Colt, Johnny
　See Black Crowes, The
Coltrane, John **4**
Colvin, Shawn **11**
Comess, Aaron
　See Spin Doctors
Como, Perry **14**
Conneff, Kevin
　See Chieftains, The
Connick, Harry, Jr. **4**
Conti, Neil
　See Prefab Sprout
Cooder, Ry **2**
Cook, Jeff
　See Alabama
Cook, Paul
　See Sex Pistols, The
Cooke, Sam **1**
　　Also see Soul Stirrers, The
Cooney, Rory **6**
Cooper, Alice **8**
Cooper, Michael
　See Third World
Coore, Stephen
　See Third World
Copeland, Stewart **14**
Copland, Aaron **2**
Copley, Al
　See Roomful of Blues
Corea, Chick **6**
Corgan, Billy
　See Smashing Pumpkins
Corina, Sarah
　See Mekons, The
Cornell, Chris
　See Soundgarden
Cornick, Glenn
　See Jethro Tull
Costello, Elvis **12**
　Earlier sketch in CM **2**
Cotoia, Robert
　See Beaver Brown Band, The
Cotrubas, Ileana **1**

Cotton, Caré
　See Sounds of Blackness
Cougar, John(ny)
　See Mellencamp, John "Cougar"
Country Gentlemen, The **7**
Coverdale, David
　See Whitesnake **5**
Cowan, John
　See New Grass Revival, The
Cowboy Junkies, The **4**
Cox, Andy
　See English Beat, The
Cracker **12**
Crain, S. R.
　See Soul Stirrers, The
Cranberries, The **14**
Crash Test Dummies **14**
Crawford, Ed
　See fIREHOSE
Crawford, Michael **4**
Cray, Robert **8**
Creach, Papa John
　See Jefferson Starship
Cream **9**
Crenshaw, Marshall **5**
Cretu, Michael
　See Enigma
Criss, Peter
　See Kiss
Croce, Jim **3**
Crofts, Dash
　See Seals & Crofts
Cropper, Steve **12**
Crosby, Bing **6**
Crosby, David **3**
　　Also see Byrds, The
Crouch, Andraé **9**
Crowded House **12**
Crowe, J. D. **5**
Crowell, Rodney **8**
Cruz, Celia **10**
Cure, The **3**
Curless, Ann
　See Exposé
Currie, Steve
　See T. Rex
Curry, Tim **3**
Curve **13**
Cypress Hill **11**
Cyrus, Billy Ray **11**
Dacus, Donnie
　See Chicago
Dacus, Johnny
　See Osborne Brothers, The
Daddy Mack
　See Kris Kross
Daellenbach, Charles
　See Canadian Brass, The
Dahlheimer, Patrick
　See Live
Daisley, Bob
　See Black Sabbath
Dale, Dick **13**
Daley, Richard
　See Third World

Dorsey Brothers, The **8**
Doucet, Michael **8**
Douglas, Jerry
  See Country Gentlemen, The
Dowd, Christopher
  See Fishbone
Downes, Geoff
  See Yes
Downey, Brian
  See Thin Lizzy
Downing, K. K.
  See Judas Priest
Dozier, Lamont
  See Holland-Dozier-Holland
Drayton, Leslie
  See Earth, Wind and Fire
Dreja, Chris
  See Yardbirds, The
Drew, Dennis
  See 10,000 Maniacs
Dryden, Spencer
  See Jefferson Airplane
Duffey, John
  See Country Gentlemen, The
    Also see Seldom Scene, The
Duffy, Martin
  See Primal Scream
Dunbar, Aynsley
  See Jefferson Starship
    Also see Whitesnake
Dunbar, Sly
  See Sly and Robbie
Duncan, Steve
  See Desert Rose Band, The
Duncan, Stuart
  See Nashville Bluegrass Band
Dunlap, Slim
  See Replacements, The
Dunn, Holly **7**
Dunn, Larry
  See Earth, Wind and Fire
Dunn, Ronnie
  See Brooks & Dunn
Dupree, Champion Jack **12**
Duran Duran **4**
Dutt, Hank
  See Kronos Quartet
Dylan, Bob **3**
E., Sheila
  See Sheila E.
Eagles, The **3**
Earl, Ronnie **5**
    Also see Roomful of Blues
Earth, Wind and Fire **12**
Easton, Sheena **2**
Eazy-E **13**
    Also see N.W.A.
Echeverria, Rob
  See Helmet
Eckstine, Billy **1**
Eddy, Duane **9**
Edge, The
  See U2
Edmonds, Kenneth "Babyface" **12**
Edwards, Dennis
  See Temptations, The

Edwards, Gordon
  See Kinks, The
Edwards, Mike
  See Electric Light Orchestra
Einheit
  See Einstürzende Neubauten
Einstürzende Neubauten **13**
Eitzel, Mark
  See American Music Club
Eldon, Thór
  See Sugarcubes, The
Eldridge, Ben
  See Seldom Scene, The
Eldridge, Roy **9**
Electric Light Orchestra **7**
Elfman, Danny **9**
Elias, Manny
  See Tears for Fears
Ellefson, Dave
  See Megadeth
Ellington, Duke **2**
Elliot, Cass **5**
Elliot, Joe
  See Def Leppard
Ellis, Terry
  See En Vogue
ELO
  See Electric Light Orchestra
Ely, John
  See Asleep at the Wheel
Emerson, Bill
  See Country Gentlemen, The
Emerson, Keith
  See Emerson, Lake & Palmer/Powell
Emerson, Lake & Palmer/Powell **5**
Emery, Jill
  See Hole
English Beat, The **9**
Enigma **14**
Eno, Brian **8**
Enos, Bob
  See Roomful of Blues
Enright, Pat
  See Nashville Bluegrass Band
Entwistle, John
  See Who, The
En Vogue **10**
Enya **6**
EPMD **10**
Erasure **11**
Eric B.
  See Eric B. and Rakim
Eric B. and Rakim **9**
Erlandson, Eric
  See Hole
Ertegun, Ahmet **10**
Eshe, Montsho
  See Arrested Development
Estefan, Gloria **15**
    Earlier sketch in CM **2**
Estrada, Roy
  See Little Feat
Etheridge, Melissa **4**
Eurythmics **6**
Evan, John
  See Jethro Tull

Evans, Dick
  See U2
Evans, Mark
  See AC/DC
Everlast
  See House of Pain
Everly, Don
  See Everly Brothers, The
Everly, Phil
  See Everly Brothers, The
Everly Brothers, The **2**
Everman, Jason
  See Soundgarden
Everything But The Girl **15**
Ewen, Alvin
  See Steel Pulse
Exkano, Paul
  See Five Blind Boys of Alabama
Exposé **4**
Extreme **10**
Fabian **5**
Fabulous Thunderbirds, The **1**
Fadden, Jimmie
  See Nitty Gritty Dirt Band, The
Fagan, Don
  See Steely Dan
Faithfull, Marianne **14**
Faith No More **7**
Fakir, Abdul "Duke"
  See Four Tops, The
Falconer, Earl
  See UB40
Fall, The **12**
Fallon, David
  See Chieftains, The
Fältskog, Agnetha
  See Abba
Farley, J. J.
  See Soul Stirrers, The
Farndon, Pete
  See Pretenders, The
Farrell, Perry
  See Jane's Addiction
Farris, Dionne
  See Arrested Development
Farriss, Andrew
  See INXS
Farriss, Jon
  See INXS
Farriss, Tim
  See INXS
Fay, Martin
  See Chieftains, The
Fearnley, James
  See Pogues, The
Feinstein, Michael **6**
Fela
  See Kuti, Fela
Felder, Don
  See Eagles, The
Feliciano, José **10**
Fender, Freddy
  See Texas Tornados, The
Fender, Leo **10**
Ferguson, Keith
  See Fabulous Thunderbirds, The

Gilbert, Ronnie
  See Weavers, The
Gilkyson, Tony
  See X
Gill, Andy
  See Gang of Four
Gill, Janis
  See Sweethearts of the Rodeo
Gill, Pete
  See Motörhead
Gill, Vince 7
Gillan, Ian
  See Deep Purple
Gillespie, Bobby
  See Primal Scream
Gillespie, Dizzy 6
Gilley, Mickey 7
Gillian, Ian
  See Black Sabbath
Gilmore, Jimmie Dale 11
Gilmour, David
  See Pink Floyd
Gingold, Josef 6
Gioia
  See Exposé
Gipsy Kings, The 8
Glass, Philip 1
Glasscock, John
  See Jethro Tull
Glennie, Jim
  See James
Glover, Corey
  See Living Colour
Glover, Roger
  See Deep Purple
Gobel, Robert
  See Kool & the Gang
Godchaux, Donna
  See Grateful Dead, The
Godchaux, Keith
  See Grateful Dead, The
Golden, William Lee
  See Oak Ridge Boys, The
Goldstein, Jerry
  See War
Gooden, Ramone PeeWee
  See Digital Underground
Goodman, Benny 4
Gordon, Dexter 10
Gordon, Kim
  See Sonic Youth
Gordon, Mike
  See Phish
Gordy, Berry, Jr. 6
Gore, Martin
  See Depeche Mode
Gorham, Scott
  See Thin Lizzy
Gorman, Steve
  See Black Crowes, The
Gosling, John
  See Kinks, The
Gossard, Stone
  See Pearl Jam
Gott, Larry
  See James

Goudreau, Barry
  See Boston
Gould, Billy
  See Faith No More
Gould, Glenn 9
Gracey, Chad
  See Live
Gradney, Ken
  See Little Feat
Graham, Bill 10
Graham, Johnny
  See Earth, Wind and Fire
Gramolini, Gary
  See Beaver Brown Band, The
Grandmaster Flash 14
Grant, Amy 7
Grant, Lloyd
  See Metallica
Grappelli, Stephane 10
Grateful Dead, The 5
Gray, Del
  See Little Texas
Gray, Ella
  See Kronos Quartet
Gray, Tom
  See Country Gentlemen, The
  Also see Seldom Scene, The
Gray, Walter
  See Kronos Quartet
Grebenshikov, Boris 3
Green, Al 9
Green, Charles
  See War
Green, Grant 14
Green, Karl Anthony
  See Herman's Hermits
Green, Peter
  See Fleetwood Mac
Green, Susaye
  See Supremes, The
Green, Willie
  See Neville Brothers, The
Greenhalgh, Tom
  See Mekons, The
Greenspoon, Jimmy
  See Three Dog Night
Greenwood, Lee 12
Gregg, Paul
  See Restless Heart
Gregory, Dave
  See XTC
Griffin, Bob
  See BoDeans, The
Griffith, Nanci 3
Grohl, Dave
  See Nirvana
Grotberg, Karen
  See Jayhawks, The
Groucutt, Kelly
  See Electric Light Orchestra
Grove, George
  See Kingston Trio, The
Grusin, Dave 7
Guaraldi, Vince 3
Guard, Dave
  See Kingston Trio, The

Gudmundsdottir, Björk
  See Sugarcubes, The
Guerin, John
  See Byrds, The
Guest, Christopher
  See Spinal Tap
Guns n' Roses 2
Gunther, Cornell
  See Coasters, The
Guru
  See Gang Starr
Guss, Randy
  See Toad the Wet Sprocket
Gustafson, Steve
  See 10,000 Maniacs
Gut, Grudrun
  See Einstürzende Neubauten
Guthrie, Arlo 6
Guthrie, Robin
  See Cocteau Twins, The
Guthrie, Woody 2
Guy, Billy
  See Coasters, The
Guy, Buddy 4
Gwar 13
Hacke, Alexander
  See Einstürzende Neubauten
Hackett, Steve
  See Genesis
Haden, Charlie 12
Hagar, Sammy
  See Van Halen
Haggard, Merle 2
Hakmoun, Hassan 15
Haley, Bill 6
Haley, Mark
  See Kinks, The
Halford, Rob
  See Judas Priest
Hall, Daryl
  See Hall & Oates
Hall, Lance
  See Inner Circle
Hall, Randall
  See Lynyrd Skynyrd
Hall, Tom T. 4
Hall, Tony
  See Neville Brothers, The
Hall & Oates 6
Halliday, Toni
  See Curve
Hamilton, Frank
  See Weavers, The
Hamilton, Milton
  See Third World
Hamilton, Page
  See Helmet
Hamilton, Tom
  See Aerosmith
Hamlisch, Marvin 1
Hammer, M.C. 5
Hammerstein, Oscar
  See Rodgers, Richard
Hammett, Kirk
  See Metallica

Hopkins, Lightnin' **13**
Hopwood, Keith
    See Herman's Hermits
Horn, Shirley **7**
Horn, Trevor
    See Yes
Horne, Lena **11**
Horne, Marilyn **9**
Hornsby, Bruce **3**
Horovitz, Adam
    See Beastie Boys, The
Horowitz, Vladimir **1**
Hossack, Michael
    See Doobie Brothers, The
House, Son **11**
House of Pain **14**
Houston, Cissy **6**
Houston, Whitney **8**
Howard, Harlan **15**
Howe, Steve
    See Yes
Howell, Porter
    See Little Texas
Howlin' Wolf **6**
Hubbard, Greg "Hobie"
    See Sawyer Brown
Hubbard, Preston
    See Fabulous Thunderbirds, The
    Also see Roomful of Blues
Hudson, Garth
    See Band, The
Huffman, Doug
    See Boston
Hughes, Bruce
    See Cracker
Hughes, Glenn
    See Black Sabbath
Hughes, Glenn
    See Village People, The
Hughes, Leon
    See Coasters, The
Hunt, Darryl
    See Pogues, The
Hunter, Alberta **7**
Hunter, Mark
    See James
Hunter, Shepherd "Ben"
    See Soundgarden
Hurley, George
    See fIREHOSE
Hutchence, Michael
    See INXS
Huth, Todd
    See Primus
Hütter, Ralf
    See Kraftwerk
Hutton, Danny
    See Three Dog Night
Huxley, Rick
    See Dave Clark Five, The
Hyman, Jerry
    See Blood, Sweat and Tears
Hynde, Chrissie
    See Pretenders, The
Ian, Janis **5**

Ian, Scott
    See Anthrax
Ibbotson, Jimmy
    See Nitty Gritty Dirt Band, The
Ibold, Mark
    See Pavement
Ice Cube **10**
    Also see N.W.A
Ice-T **7**
Idol, Billy **3**
Iglesias, Julio **2**
Iha, James
    See Smashing Pumpkins
Indigo Girls **3**
Inez, Mike
    See Alice in Chains
Infante, Frank
    See Blondie
Ingram, James **11**
Inner Circle **15**
Innes, Andrew
    See Primal Scream
Innis, Dave
    See Restless Heart
INXS **2**
Iommi, Tony
    See Black Sabbath
Iron Maiden **10**
Irons, Jack
    See Red Hot Chili Peppers, The
Isaak, Chris **6**
Isham, Mark **14**
Isles, Bill
    See O'Jays, The
Isley, Ernie
    See Isley Brothers, The
Isley, Marvin
    See Isley Brothers, The
Isley, O'Kelly, Jr.
    See Isley Brothers, The
Isley, Ronald
    See Isley Brothers, The
Isley, Rudolph
    See Isley Brothers, The
Isley Brothers, The **8**
Ives, Burl **12**
Ivey, Michael
    See Basehead
J, David
    See Love and Rockets
Jabs, Matthias
    See Scorpions, The
Jackson, Alan **7**
Jackson, Eddie
    See Queensrÿche
Jackson, Freddie **3**
Jackson, Jackie
    See Jacksons, The
Jackson, Janet **3**
Jackson, Jermaine
    See Jacksons, The
Jackson, Joe **4**
Jackson, Karen
    See Supremes, The
Jackson, Mahalia **8**

Jackson, Marlon
    See Jacksons, The
Jackson, Michael **1**
    Also see Jacksons, The
Jackson, Millie **14**
Jackson, Milt **15**
Jackson, Randy
    See Jacksons, The
Jackson, Tito
    See Jacksons, The
Jackson 5, The
    See Jacksons, The
Jacksons, The **7**
Jacobs, Walter
    See Little Walter
Jacox, Martin
    See Soul Stirrers, The
Jagger, Mick **7**
    Also see Rolling Stones, The
Jairo T.
    See Sepultura
Jam, Jimmy
    See Jam, Jimmy, and Terry Lewis
Jam, Jimmy, and Terry Lewis **11**
Jam Master Jay
    See Run-D.M.C.
James **12**
James, Andrew "Bear"
    See Midnight Oil
James, Cheryl
    See Salt-N-Pepa
James, Doug
    See Roomful of Blues
James, Elmore **8**
James, Etta **6**
James, Harry **11**
James, Richard
    See Aphex Twin
James, Rick **2**
Jane's Addiction **6**
Jardine, Al
    See Beach Boys, The
Jarobi
    See Tribe Called Quest, A
Jarre, Jean-Michel **2**
Jarreau, Al **1**
Jarrett, Irwin
    See Third World
Jarrett, Keith **1**
Jasper, Chris
    See Isley Brothers, The
Jay, Miles
    See Village People, The
Jayhawks, The **15**
Jeanrenaud, Joan Dutcher
    See Kronos Quartet
Jefferson Airplane **5**
Jefferson Starship
    See Jefferson Airplane
Jennings, Greg
    See Restless Heart
Jennings, Waylon **4**
Jessie, Young
    See Coasters, The
Jesus and Mary Chain, The **10**
Jethro Tull **8**

Kirwan, Danny
　See Fleetwood Mac
Kiss **5**
Kisser, Andreas
　See Sepultura
Kissin, Evgeny **6**
Kitaro **1**
Kitt, Eartha **9**
Klein, Jon
　See Siouxsie and the Banshees
Klugh, Earl **10**
Knight, Gladys **1**
Knight, Jon
　See New Kids on the Block
Knight, Jordan
　See New Kids on the Block
Knight, Suge **15**
Knopfler, Mark **3**
Knowledge
　See Digable Planets
Knudsen, Keith
　See Doobie Brothers, The
Konto, Skip
　See Three Dog Night
Kool & the Gang **13**
Kool Moe Dee **9**
Kooper, Al
　See Blood, Sweat and Tears
Koppelman, Charles **14**
Koppes, Peter
　See Church, The
Kottke, Leo **13**
Kotzen, Richie
　See Poison
Kowalczyk, Ed
　See Live
Kraftwerk **9**
Kramer, Joey
　See Aerosmith
Kramer, Wayne
　See MC5, The
Krasnow, Bob **15**
Krause, Bernie
　See Weavers, The
Krauss, Alison **10**
Kravitz, Lenny **5**
Krazy Drayz
　See Das EFX
Kretz, Eric
　See Stone Temple Pilots
Kreutzman, Bill
　See Grateful Dead, The
Krieger, Robert
　See Doors, The
Kris Kross **11**
Kristofferson, Kris **4**
Krizan, Anthony
　See Spin Doctors
Kronos Quartet **5**
KRS-One **8**
Krupa, Gene **13**
Krusen, Dave
　See Pearl Jam
Kulick, Bruce
　See Kiss

Kunkel, Bruce
　See Nitty Gritty Dirt Band, The
Kuti, Fela **7**
LaBelle, Patti **8**
Ladybug
　See Digable Planets
Lady Miss Kier
　See Deee-lite
Ladysmith Black Mambazo **1**
Lafalce, Mark
　See Mekons, The
Laine, Cleo **10**
Lake, Greg
　See Emerson, Lake & Palmer/Powell
LaLonde, Larry "Ler"
　See Primus
Lally, Joe
　See Fugazi
Lamm, Robert
　See Chicago
Lane, Jay
　See Primus
Lang, K. D. **4**
Langford, Jon
　See Mekons, The
Langley, John
　See Mekons, The
Langston, Leslie
　See Throwing Muses
Lanois, Daniel **8**
Larkin, Patty **9**
Laswell, Bill **14**
Lataille, Rich
　See Roomful of Blues
Lauper, Cyndi **11**
Laurence, Lynda
　See Supremes, The
Lavin, Christine **6**
Lavis, Gilson
　See Squeeze
Lawlor, Feargal
　See Cranberries, The
Lawrence, Tracy **11**
Lawry, John
　See Petra
Laws, Roland
　See Earth, Wind and Fire
Lawson, Doyle
　See Country Gentlemen, The
Leadbelly **6**
Leadon, Bernie
　See Eagles, The
　　Also see Nitty Gritty Dirt Band, The
Leavell, Chuck
　See Allman Brothers, The
LeBon, Simon
　See Duran Duran
Leckenby, Derek "Lek"
　See Herman's Hermits
Ledbetter, Huddie
　See Leadbelly
LeDoux, Chris **12**
Led Zeppelin **1**
Lee, Beverly
　See Shirelles, The
Lee, Brenda **5**

Lee, Geddy
　See Rush
Lee, Peggy **8**
Lee, Pete
　See Gwar
Lee, Sara
　See Gang of Four
Lee, Tommy
　See Mötley Crüe
Leese, Howard
　See Heart
Lehrer, Tom **7**
Leiber, Jerry
　See Leiber and Stoller
Leiber and Stoller **14**
Lemmy
　See Motörhead
Lemonheads, The **12**
Lemper, Ute **14**
Le Mystère des Voix Bulgares
　See Bulgarian State Female Vocal
　Choir, The
Lenners, Rudy
　See Scorpions, The
Lennon, John **9**
　Also see Beatles, The
Lennon, Julian **2**
Lennox, Annie
　See Eurythmics
Leonard, Glenn
　See Temptations, The
Lerner, Alan Jay
　See Lerner and Loewe
Lerner and Loewe **13**
Lesh, Phil
　See Grateful Dead, The
Levene, Keith
　See Clash, The
Levert, Eddie
　See O'Jays, The
Levine, James **8**
Levy, Andrew
　See Brand New Heavies, The
Levy, Ron
　See Roomful of Blues
Lewis, Huey **9**
Lewis, Ian
　See Inner Circle
Lewis, Jerry Lee **2**
Lewis, Otis
　See Fabulous Thunderbirds, The
Lewis, Peter
　See Moby Grape
Lewis, Ramsey **14**
Lewis, Roger
　See Inner Circle
Lewis, Roy
　See Kronos Quartet
Lewis, Samuel K.
　See Five Blind Boys of Alabama
Lewis, Terry
　See Jam, Jimmy, and Terry Lewis
Libbea, Gene
　See Nashville Bluegrass Band
Liberace **9**

McBride, Martina **14**
McCall, Renee
  See Sounds of Blackness
McCarrick, Martin
  See Siouxsie and the Banshees
McCartney, Paul **4**
  Also see Beatles, The
McCarty, Jim
  See Yardbirds, The
McCary, Michael S.
  See Boyz II Men
MC Clever
  See Digital Underground
McClinton, Delbert **14**
McConnell, Page
  See Phish
McCoury, Del **15**
McCoy, Neal **15**
McCracken, Chet
  See Doobie Brothers, The
McCready, Mike
  See Pearl Jam
McDaniels, Darryl "D"
  See Run-D.M.C.
McDonald, Barbara Kooyman
  See Timbuk 3
McDonald, Michael
  See Doobie Brothers, The
McDonald, Pat
  See Timbuk 3
McDorman, Joe
  See Statler Brothers, The
McDowell, Hugh
  See Electric Light Orchestra
McEntire, Reba **11**
MC Eric
  See Technotronic
McEuen, John
  See Nitty Gritty Dirt Band, The
McFee, John
  See Doobie Brothers, The
McFerrin, Bobby **3**
MC5, The **9**
McGeoch, John
  See Siouxsie and the Banshees
McGinley, Raymond
  See Teenage Fanclub
McGuinn, Jim
  See Byrds, The
McGuinn, Roger
  See Byrds, The
M.C. Hammer
  See Hammer, M.C.
McIntosh, Robbie
  See Pretenders, The
McIntyre, Joe
  See New Kids on the Block
McKagan, Duff
  See Guns n' Roses
McKay, Al
  See Earth, Wind and Fire
McKay, John
  See Siouxsie and the Banshees
McKean, Michael
  See Spinal Tap
McKee, Maria **11**

McKernen, Ron "Pigpen"
  See Grateful Dead, The
McKnight, Claude V. III
  See Take 6
McLachlan, Sarah **12**
McLaughlin, John **12**
McLean, Don **7**
McLeod, Rory
  See Roomful of Blues
MC Lyte **8**
McMeel, Mickey
  See Three Dog Night
McMurtry, James **10**
McNair, Sylvia **15**
McPartland, Marian **15**
McQuillar, Shawn
  See Kool & the Gang
McRae, Carmen **9**
M.C. Ren
  See N.W.A.
McReynolds, Jesse
  See McReynolds, Jim and Jesse
McReynolds, Jim
  See McReynolds, Jim and Jesse
McReynolds, Jim and Jesse **12**
MC Serch **10**
McShane, Ronnie
  See Chieftains, The
McVie, Christine
  See Fleetwood Mac
McVie, John
  See Fleetwood Mac
Mdletshe, Geophrey
  See Ladysmith Black Mambazo
Meat Loaf **12**
Meat Puppets, The **13**
Medley, Bill **3**
Medlock, James
  See Soul Stirrers, The
Megadeth **9**
Mehta, Zubin **11**
Meine, Klaus
  See Scorpions, The
Meisner, Randy
  See Eagles, The
Mekons, The **15**
Melanie **12**
Melax, Einar
  See Sugarcubes, The
Mellencamp, John "Cougar" **2**
Mengede, Peter
  See Helmet
Menken, Alan **10**
Menuhin, Yehudi **11**
Menza, Nick
  See Megadeth
Mercer, Johnny **13**
Merchant, Natalie
  See 10,000 Maniacs
Mercier, Peadar
  See Chieftains, The
Mercury, Freddie
  See Queen
Mesaros, Michael
  See Smithereens, The

Metallica **7**
Meters, The **14**
Methembu, Russel
  See Ladysmith Black Mambazo
Metheny, Pat **2**
Meyers, Augie
  See Texas Tornados, The
Michael, George **9**
Michaels, Bret
  See Poison
Midler, Bette **8**
Midnight Oil **11**
Midori **7**
Mike D
  See Beastie Boys, The
Mikens, Dennis
  See Smithereens, The
Mikens, Robert
  See Kool & the Gang
Miles, Richard
  See Soul Stirrers, The
Miller, Charles
  See War
Miller, Glenn **6**
Miller, Jacob "Killer" Miller
  See Inner Circle
Miller, Jerry
  See Moby Grape
Miller, Mark
  See Sawyer Brown
Miller, Mitch **11**
Miller, Rice
  See Williamson, Sonny Boy
Miller, Roger **4**
Miller, Steve **2**
Milli Vanilli **4**
Mills, Donald
  See Mills Brothers, The
Mills, Fred
  See Canadian Brass, The
Mills, Harry
  See Mills Brothers, The
Mills, Herbert
  See Mills Brothers, The
Mills, John, Jr.
  See Mills Brothers, The
Mills, John, Sr.
  See Mills Brothers, The
Mills, Sidney
  See Steel Pulse
Mills Brothers, The **14**
Milsap, Ronnie **2**
Mingus, Charles **9**
Ministry **10**
Miss Kier Kirby
  See Lady Miss Kier
Mr. Dalvin
  See Jodeci
Mitchell, Alex
  See Curve
Mitchell, John
  See Asleep at the Wheel
Mitchell, Joni **2**
Mizell, Jay
  See Run-D.M.C.
Moby Grape **12**

N.W.A. **6**
Nyman, Michael **15**
Nyolo, Sally
    See Zap Mama
Nyro, Laura **12**
Oakley, Berry
    See Allman Brothers, The
Oak Ridge Boys, The **7**
Oates, John
    See Hall & Oates
O'Brien, Dwayne
    See Little Texas
O'Bryant, Alan
    See Nashville Bluegrass Band
Ocasek, Ric **5**
Ocean, Billy **4**
Oceans, Lucky
    See Asleep at the Wheel
Ochs, Phil **7**
O'Connell, Chris
    See Asleep at the Wheel
O'Connor, Billy
    See Blondie
O'Connor, Daniel
    See House of Pain
O'Connor, Mark **1**
O'Connor, Sinead **3**
Odetta **7**
O'Donnell, Roger
    See Cure, The
Ohanian, David
    See Canadian Brass, The
O'Hare, Brendan
    See Teenage Fanclub
O'Jays, The **13**
Oje, Baba
    See Arrested Development
Olafsson, Bragi
    See Sugarcubes, The
Olander, Jimmy
    See Diamond Rio
Oliver, Joe
    See Oliver, King
Oliver, King **15**
Olson, Jeff
    See Village People, The
Olson, Mark
    See Jayhawks, The
Ono, Yoko **11**
Orbison, Roy **2**
O'Reagan, Tim
    See Jayhawks, The
O'Riordan, Cait
    See Pogues, The
O'Riordan, Dolores
    See Cranberries, The
Orlando, Tony **15**
Örn, Einar
    See Sugarcubes, The
Örnolfsdottir, Margret
    See Sugarcubes, The
Orr, Casey
    See Gwar
Orzabal, Roland
    See Tears for Fears

Osborne, Bob
    See Osborne Brothers, The
Osborne, Sonny
    See Osborne Brothers, The
Osborne Brothers, The **8**
Osbourne, Ozzy **3**
    Also see Black Sabbath
Oskar, Lee
    See War
Oslin, K. T. **3**
Osmond, Donny **3**
Ott, David **2**
Outler, Jimmy
    See Soul Stirrers, The
Owen, Randy
    See Alabama
Owens, Buck **2**
Owens, Ricky
    See Temptations, The
Page, Jimmy **4**
    Also see Led Zeppelin
    Also see Yardbirds, The
Page, Patti **11**
Paice, Ian
    See Deep Purple
Palmer, Carl
    See Emerson, Lake & Palmer/Powell
Palmer, David
    See Jethro Tull
Palmer, Robert **2**
Palmieri, Eddie **15**
Pankow, James
    See Chicago
Pantera **13**
Parazaider, Walter
    See Chicago
Parkening, Christopher **7**
Parker, Charlie **5**
Parker, Graham **10**
Parker, Kris
    See KRS-One
Parker, Maceo **7**
Parnell, Lee Roy **15**
Parsons, Alan **12**
Parsons, Gene
    See Byrds, The
Parsons, Gram **7**
    Also see Byrds, The
Parsons, Tony
    See Iron Maiden
Parton, Dolly **2**
Partridge, Andy
    See XTC
Pasemaster, Mase
    See De La Soul
Pass, Joe **15**
Patinkin, Mandy **3**
Patti, Sandi **7**
Patton, Charley **11**
Patton, Mike
    See Faith No More
Paul, Alan
    See Manhattan Transfer, The
Paul, Les **2**
Paul, Vinnie
    See Pantera

Paulo, Jr.
    See Sepultura
Pavarotti, Luciano **1**
Pavement **14**
Paxton, Tom **5**
Payne, Bill
    See Little Feat
Payne, Scherrie
    See Supremes, The
Payton, Denis
    See Dave Clark Five, The
Payton, Lawrence
    See Four Tops, The
Pearl, Minnie **3**
Pearl Jam **12**
Pearson, Dan
    See American Music Club
Peart, Neil
    See Rush
Pedersen, Herb
    See Desert Rose Band, The
Peduzzi, Larry
    See Roomful of Blues
Peeler, Ben
    See Mavericks, The
Pegg, Dave
    See Jethro Tull
Pendergrass, Teddy **3**
Pengilly, Kirk
    See INXS
Peniston, CeCe **15**
Penn, Michael **4**
Penner, Fred **10**
Perahia, Murray **10**
Peretz, Jesse
    See Lemonheads, The
Perez, Louie
    See Los Lobos
Perkins, Carl **9**
Perkins, John
    See XTC
Perkins, Percell
    See Five Blind Boys of Alabama
Perkins, Steve
    See Jane's Addiction
Perlman, Itzhak **2**
Perlman, Marc
    See Jayhawks, The
Perry, Doane
    See Jethro Tull
Perry, Joe
    See Aerosmith
Peter, Paul & Mary **4**
Peters, Bernadette **7**
Peterson, Oscar **11**
Petersson, Tom
    See Cheap Trick
Petra **3**
Pet Shop Boys **5**
Petty, Tom **9**
Pfaff, Kristen
    See Hole
Phair, Liz **14**
Phantom, Slim Jim
    See Stray Cats, The

Reid, Ellen Lorraine
   See Crash Test Dummies
Reid, Harold
   See Statler Brothers, The
Reid, Janet
   See Black Uhuru
Reid, Jim
   See Jesus and Mary Chain, The
Reid, Vernon 2
   Also see Living Colour
Reid, William
   See Jesus and Mary Chain, The
Reinhardt, Django 7
Relf, Keith
   See Yardbirds, The
R.E.M. 5
Reno, Ronnie
   See Osborne Brothers, The
Replacements, The 7
Residents, The 14
Restless Heart 12
Rex
   See Pantera
Reyes, Andre
   See Gipsy Kings, The
Reyes, Canut
   See Gipsy Kings, The
Reyes, Nicolas
   See Gipsy Kings, The
Reynolds, Nick
   See Kingston Trio, The
Reynolds, Robert
   See Mavericks, The
Reynolds, Sheldon
   See Earth, Wind and Fire
Reznor, Trent 13
Rhodes, Nick
   See Duran Duran
Rhone, Sylvia 13
Rich, Buddy 13
Rich, Charlie 3
Richard, Cliff 14
Richard, Keith
   See Richards, Keith
Richard, Zachary 9
Richards, Keith 11
   Also see Rolling Stones, The
Richie, Lionel 2
Richman, Jonathan 12
Rieckermann, Ralph
   See Scorpions, The
Rieflin, William
   See Ministry
Riley, Teddy 14
Riley, Timothy Christian
   See Tony! Toni! Toné!
Rippon, Steve
   See Lush
Ritchie, Brian
   See Violent Femmes
Ritchie, Jean 4
Ritenour, Lee 7
Roach, Max 12
Robbins, Marty 9
Roberts, Brad
   See Crash Test Dummies

Roberts, Brad
   See Gwar
Roberts, Dan
   See Crash Test Dummies
Roberts, Marcus 6
Robertson, Brian
   See Motörhead
   Also see Thin Lizzy
Robertson, Robbie 2
   Also see Band, The
Robeson, Paul 8
Robillard, Duke 2
   Also see Roomful of Blues
Robinson, Chris
   See Black Crowes, The
Robinson, Dawn
   See En Vogue
Robinson, R. B.
   See Soul Stirrers, The
Robinson, Rich
   See Black Crowes, The
Robinson, Smokey 1
Rockenfield, Scott
   See Queensrÿche
Rocker, Lee
   See Stray Cats, The
Rockett, Rikki
   See Poison
Rockin' Dopsie 10
Rodford, Jim
   See Kinks, The
Rodgers, Jimmie 3
Rodgers, Nile 8
Rodgers, Richard 9
Rodney, Red 14
Rodriguez, Sal
   See War
Roe, Marty
   See Diamond Rio
Roeder, Klaus
   See Kraftwerk
Rogers, Kenny 1
Rogers, Norm
   See Jayhawks, The
Rogers, Roy 9
Rogers, Willie
   See Soul Stirrers, The
Rolling Stones, The 3
Rollins, Henry 11
Rollins, Sonny 7
Romm, Ronald
   See Canadian Brass, The
Ronstadt, Linda 2
Roomful of Blues 7
Roper, De De
   See Salt-N-Pepa
Rosas, Cesar
   See Los Lobos
Rose, Axl
   See Guns n' Roses
Rose, Michael
   See Black Uhuru
Rosen, Gary
   See Rosenshontz
Rosen, Peter
   See War

Rosenshontz 9
Rosenthal, Jurgen
   See Scorpions, The
Rosenthal, Phil
   See Seldom Scene, The
Ross, Diana 1
   Also see Supremes, The
Rossi, John
   See Roomful of Blues
Rossington, Gary
   See Lynyrd Skynyrd
Rota, Nino 13
Roth, David Lee 1
   Also see Van Halen
Roth, Ulrich
   See Scorpions, The
Rotsey, Martin
   See Midnight Oil
Rotten, Johnny
   See Lydon, John
   Also see Sex Pistols, The
Rourke, Andy
   See Smiths, The
Rowe, Dwain
   See Restless Heart
Rubin, Rick 9
Rubinstein, Arthur 11
Rudd, Phillip
   See AC/DC
Rue, Caroline
   See Hole
Ruffin, David 6
   Also see Temptations, The
Rundgren, Todd 11
Run-D.M.C. 4
Rush 8
Rush, Otis 12
Rushlow, Tim
   See Little Texas
Russell, Alecia
   See Sounds of Blackness
Russell, Mark 6
Rutherford, Mike
   See Genesis
Rutsey, John
   See Rush
Ryan, David
   See Lemonheads, The
Ryan, Mick
   See Dave Clark Five, The
Ryder, Mitch 11
Ryland, Jack
   See Three Dog Night
Sabo, Dave
   See Bon Jovi
Sade 2
Sager, Carole Bayer 5
Sahm, Doug
   See Texas Tornados, The
Sainte-Marie, Buffy 11
St. Hubbins, David
   See Spinal Tap
St. John, Mark
   See Kiss
St. Marie, Buffy
   See Sainte-Marie, Buffy

Townes, Jeffery
  See DJ Jazzy Jeff and the Fresh
  Prince
Townshend, Pete 1
  Also see Who, The
Travers, Brian
  See UB40
Travers, Mary
  See Peter, Paul & Mary
Travis, Merle 14
Travis, Randy 9
Treach
  See Naughty by Nature
T. Rex 11
Tribe Called Quest, A 8
Tritt, Travis 7
Trucks, Butch
  See Allman Brothers, The
Trugoy the Dove
  See De La Soul
Trujillo, Robert
  See Suicidal Tendencies
Truman, Dan
  See Diamond Rio
Tubb, Ernest 4
Tubridy, Michael
  See Chieftans, The
Tucker, Moe
  See Velvet Underground, The
Tucker, Sophie 12
Tucker, Tanya 3
Tufnel, Nigel
  See Spinal Tap
Turbin, Neil
  See Anthrax
Turner, Big Joe 13
Turner, Joe Lynn
  See Deep Purple
Turner, Tina 1
Turtle Island String Quartet 9
Twitty, Conway 6
2Pac
  See Digital Underground
Tyler, Steve
  See Aerosmith
Tyner, McCoy 7
Tyner, Rob
  See MC5, The
Tyson, Ron
  See Temptations, The
UB40 4
Ulmer, James Blood 13
Ulrich, Lars
  See Metallica
Ulvaeus, Björn
  See Abba
Unruh, N. U.
  See Einstürzende Neubauten
Upshaw, Dawn 9
U2 12
  Earlier sketch in CM 2
Vachon, Chris
  See Roomful of Blues
Vai, Steve 5
  Also see Whitesnake

Valentine, Gary
  See Blondie
Valentine, Rae
  See War
Valli, Frankie 10
Vandenburg, Adrian
  See Whitesnake
Vandross, Luther 2
Van Halen 8
Van Halen, Alex
  See Van Halen
Van Halen, Edward
  See Van Halen
Vanilla Ice 6
Van Ronk, Dave 12
Van Shelton, Ricky 5
Van Vliet, Don
  See Captain Beefheart
Van Zandt, Townes 13
Van Zant, Johnny
  See Lynyrd Skynyrd
Van Zant, Ronnie
  See Lynyrd Skynyrd
Vaughan, Jimmie
  See Fabulous Thunderbirds, The
Vaughan, Sarah 2
Vaughan, Stevie Ray 1
Vedder, Eddie
  See Pearl Jam
Vega, Suzanne 3
Velvet Underground, The 7
Vettese, Peter-John
  See Jethro Tull
Vicious, Sid
  See Sex Pistols, The
    Also see Siouxsie and the Banshees
Village People, The 7
Vincent, Vinnie
  See Kiss
Vinnie
  See Naughty by Nature
Vinton, Bobby 12
Violent Femmes 12
Virtue, Michael
  See UB40
Vito, Rick
  See Fleetwood Mac
Volz, Greg
  See Petra
Von, Eerie
  See Danzig
von Karajan, Herbert 1
Vox, Bono
  See U2
Vudi
  See American Music Club
Wadenius, George
  See Blood, Sweat and Tears
Wadephal, Ralf
  See Tangerine Dream
Wagoner, Faidest
  See Soul Stirrers, The
Wagoner, Porter 13
Wahlberg, Donnie
  See New Kids on the Block

Wailer, Bunny 11
Wainwright, Loudon III 11
Waits, Tom 12
  Earlier sketch in CM 1
Wakeling, David
  See English Beat, The
Wakeman, Rick
  See Yes
Walden, Narada Michael 14
Walker, Colin
  See Electric Light Orchestra
Walker, Ebo
  See New Grass Revival, The
Walker, Jerry Jeff 13
Walker, T-Bone 5
Wallace, Sippie 6
Waller, Charlie
  See Country Gentlemen, The
Waller, Fats 7
Wallinger, Karl 11
Wallis, Larry
  See Motörhead
Walls, Chris
  See Dave Clark Five, The
Walls, Greg
  See Anthrax
Walsh, Joe 5
  Also see Eagles, The
War 14
Ward, Bill
  See Black Sabbath
Warnes, Jennifer 3
Warren, George W.
  See Five Blind Boys of Alabama
Warren, Mervyn
  See Take 6
Warwick, Dionne 2
Was, David
  See Was (Not Was)
Was, Don
  See Was (Not Was)
Washington, Chester
  See Earth, Wind and Fire
Washington, Dinah 5
Washington, Grover, Jr. 5
Was (Not Was) 6
Waters, Crystal 15
Waters, Ethel 11
Waters, Muddy 4
Waters, Roger
  See Pink Floyd
Watkins, Tionne "T-Boz"
  See TLC
Watley, Jody 9
Watson, Doc 2
Watt, Ben
  See Everything But The Girl
Watt, Mike
  See fIREHOSE
Watts, Charlie
  See Rolling Stones, The
Watts, Eugene
  See Canadian Brass, The
Weaver, Louie
  See Petra

Weavers, The **8**
Webb, Chick **14**
Webb, Jimmy **12**
Webber, Andrew Lloyd
    See Lloyd Webber, Andrew
Weiland, Scott "Weiland"
    See Stone Temple Pilots
Weill, Kurt **12**
Weir, Bob
    See Grateful Dead, The
Welch, Bob
    See Fleetwood Mac
Welk, Lawrence **13**
Weller, Paul **14**
Wells, Cory
    See Three Dog Night
Wells, Kitty **6**
Welnick, Vince
    See Grateful Dead, The
West, Dottie **8**
West, Steve
    See Pavement
Westerberg, Paul
    See Replacements, The
Weston, Randy **15**
Wexler, Jerry **15**
Weymouth, Tina
    See Talking Heads
Wheat, Brian
    See Tesla
Whelan, Gavan
    See James
White, Alan
    See Yes
White, Barry **6**
White, Clarence
    See Byrds, The
White, Freddie
    See Earth, Wind and Fire
White, Lari **15**
White, Mark
    See Mekons, The
White, Mark
    See Spin Doctors
White, Maurice
    See Earth, Wind and Fire
White, Roland
    See Nashville Bluegrass Band
White, Verdine
    See Earth, Wind and Fire
Whitehead, Donald
    See Earth, Wind and Fire
Whitesnake **5**
Whitford, Brad
    See Aerosmith
Whitley, Keith **7**
Whitwam, Barry
    See Herman's Hermits
Who, The **3**
Wiggins, Dwayne
    See Tony! Toni! Toné!
Wiggins, Raphael
    See Tony! Toni! Toné!
Wilder, Alan
    See Depeche Mode

Wilkeson, Leon
    See Lynyrd Skynyrd
Wilkinson, Keith
    See Squeeze
Williams, Andy **2**
Williams, Boris
    See Cure, The
Williams, Cliff
    See AC/DC
Williams, Dana
    See Diamond Rio
Williams, Deniece **1**
Williams, Don **4**
Williams, Hank, Jr. **1**
Williams, Hank, Sr. **4**
Williams, Joe **11**
Williams, John **9**
Williams, Lamar
    See Allman Brothers, The
Williams, Lucinda **10**
Williams, Marion **15**
Williams, Otis
    See Temptations, The
Williams, Paul **5**
Williams, Paul
    See Temptations, The
Williams, Phillard
    See Earth, Wind and Fire
Williams, Vanessa **10**
Williams, Walter
    See O'Jays, The
Williamson, Sonny Boy **9**
Willie D.
    See Geto Boys, The
Willis, Kelly **12**
Willis, Larry
    See Blood, Sweat and Tears
Willis, Pete
    See Def Leppard
Willis, Victor
    See Village People, The
Willner, Hal **10**
Wills, Bob **6**
Willson-Piper, Marty
    See Church, The
Wilson, Anne
    See Heart
Wilson, Brian
    See Beach Boys, The
Wilson, Carl
    See Beach Boys, The
Wilson, Carnie
    See Wilson Phillips
Wilson, Cassandra **12**
Wilson, Cindy
    See B-52's, The
Wilson, Dennis
    See Beach Boys, The
Wilson, Jackie **3**
Wilson, Kim
    See Fabulous Thunderbirds, The
Wilson, Mary
    See Supremes, The
Wilson, Nancy **14**
Wilson, Nancy
    See Heart

Wilson, Ransom **5**
Wilson, Ricky
    See B-52's, The
Wilson, Shanice
    See Shanice
Wilson, Wendy
    See Wilson Phillips
Wilson Phillips **5**
Wilton, Michael
    See Queensrÿche
Wimpfheimer, Jimmy
    See Roomful of Blues
Winans, Carvin
    See Winans, The
Winans, Marvin
    See Winans, The
Winans, Michael
    See Winans, The
Winans, Ronald
    See Winans, The
Winans, The **12**
Winbush, Angela **15**
Winfield, Chuck
    See Blood, Sweat and Tears
Winston, George **9**
Winter, Johnny **5**
Winter, Paul **10**
Winwood, Steve **2**
Wolstencraft, Simon
    See Fall, The
Womack, Bobby **5**
Wonder, Stevie **2**
Wood, Danny
    See New Kids on the Block
Wood, Ron
    See Rolling Stones, The
Wood, Roy
    See Electric Light Orchestra
Woods, Terry
    See Pogues, The
Woodson, Ollie
    See Temptations, The
Woody, Allen
    See Allman Brothers, The
Woolfolk, Andrew
    See Earth, Wind and Fire
Worrell, Bernie **11**
Wreede, Katrina
    See Turtle Island String Quartet
Wretzky, D'Arcy
    See Smashing Pumpkins
Wright, David "Blockhead"
    See English Beat, The
Wright, Jimmy
    See Sounds of Blackness
Wright, Norman
    See Country Gentlemen, The
Wright, Rick
    See Pink Floyd
Wright, Simon
    See AC/DC
Wurzel
    See Motörhead
Wyman, Bill
    See Rolling Stones, The
Wynette, Tammy **2**

Wynonna **11**
    Also see Judds, The
X **11**
XTC **10**
Ya Kid K
    See Technotronic
Yamamoto, Hiro
    See Soundgarden
Yamano, Atsuko
    See Shonen Knife
Yamano, Naoko
    See Shonen Knife
Yamashita, Kazuhito **4**
Yankovic, "Weird Al" **7**
Yanni **11**
Yardbirds, The **10**
Yarrow, Peter
    See Peter, Paul & Mary
Yates, Bill
    See Country Gentlemen, The
Yauch, Adam
    See Beastie Boys, The

Yearwood, Trisha **10**
Yella
    See N.W.A.
Yes **8**
Yoakam, Dwight **1**
York, Andrew **15**
York, John
    See Byrds, The
Young, Angus
    See AC/DC
Young, Faron **7**
Young, Fred
    See Kentucky Headhunters, The
Young, Gary
    See Pavement
Young, Grant
    See Soul Asylum
Young, Jeff
    See Megadeth
Young, Lester **14**
Young, Malcolm
    See AC/DC

Young, Neil **15**
    Earlier sketch in CM **2**
Young, Richard
    See Kentucky Headhunters, The
Young, Robert "Throbert"
    See Primal Scream
Young M.C. **4**
Yo Yo **9**
Yule, Doug
    See Velvet Underground, The
Zander, Robin
    See Cheap Trick
Zap Mama **14**
Zappa, Frank **1**
Zevon, Warren **9**
Zimmerman, Udo **5**
Zoom, Billy
    See X
Zorn, John **15**
Zukerman, Pinchas **4**
ZZ Top **2**